Soldiers,
Statesmen, and
Cold War Crises

Soldiers, Statesmen, and Cold War Crises

Richard K. Betts

Harvard University Press
Cambridge, Massachusetts
and London, England
1977

LIBRARY OF CONGRESS CATALOGING IN PUBLICATION DATA
Betts, Richard K   1947–
    Soldiers, statesmen, and cold war crises.
    Bibliography: p.
    Includes index.
    1. United States—Military policy.   2. United
States—Armed Forces.   3. United States—Foreign rela-
tions—1945–   I. Title.
UA23.B46   355.03′35′73   77–8068
ISBN 0–674–81741–9

In memory of John R. Betts
and Cecelia Fitzpatrick Betts

Preface

THIS book analyzes one element in American cold war decision making: military advice and influence on the use of force. In the early 1970s optimists would have thought that the emergence of détente and global economic interdependence should make the value of such a study strictly antiquarian. Unfortunately, however, the military dimension of foreign policy is no longer fading in relevance. The United States has emerged from the post-Vietnam period and the wave of sentiment against foreign interventions has crested; steady reductions of defense expenditures that occurred throughout the Nixon administration were reversed under Gerald Ford; and President Carter assumed office just as a new great debate took shape on the strategic balance with the Soviet Union. The use of force remains the most serious dimension of foreign policy, the last resort that poses the greatest risks in the nuclear age. The role of military advice in influencing presidential decisions, therefore, remains of crucial significance.

My study does not consider explicitly whether military influence on policy has been good or bad, which is ultimately a more important question, nor does it show whether professional soldiers have too much influence or too little, which can only be a judgment that depends on one's political preferences. This book does consider how the proportion of military influence, relative to that of civilian advisers, has varied since World War II. But since politics is the art of the possible, it is difficult to segregate empirical observations from normative conclusions, and it is appropriate to admit my own bias. Implicit in my analysis is the view that, with few exceptions, the military have had neither more nor less influence than they should have, and that they have erred—albeit in different ways—neither more nor less than their civilian colleagues.

The evidence underlying these possibly controversial conclusions was pieced together from executive documents, congressional hearings, memoirs, secondary studies of particular crises, journalistic investigations, and personal interviews with soldiers and civilians involved in decisions. None of these can be fully reliable and many of the most pertinent documentary sources—for example, the official history of the Joint Chiefs of Staff or the minutes of National Security Council meetings—remain beyond any hope of declassification. (Nothing in this book is based on any classified information to which I had access while I served on the staffs of the Senate Select Committee to Study Governmental Operations with Respect to Intelligence Activities or the National Security Council, and none of my views should be attributed to either organization.) A book that waits for a perfect evidential base, however, is never written. Although the evidence I have cited in a few places is uncomfortably thin, the overlapping agreement of several sources at most points provides a reasonable degree of confidence in the relevant data.

It would be difficult if not irresponsible to attempt a study of decision making without interviewing officials who were involved in the decisions. For many of these officials, however, confidentiality is the price for their frankness. I have tried to strike a balance between conflicting responsibilities to my sources and my readers. The notes indicate which of my assertions are based on interviews and whether the interviewee cited was a military official or a civilian. The list at the end of the book, which includes all those I interviewed except for a very few who demanded not to be acknowledged in any way, reveals the range of personal sources. Particular statements, however, are not attributed to specific individuals. This compromise arrangement is intellectually undesirable but practically unavoidable; at least it is an improvement over the unfortunate practice, now common even in academic studies of policy making, of refusing to cite or identify interviewees in any form.

Finally, this work is a comparative analysis of one aspect of a large number of decisions; it is not a definitive history of any one of them. General knowledge of cold war history is assumed. With the exception of chapter 2, which deals with the two wars fought since 1945, decisions are discussed topically at different points in the text rather than chronologically. This makes it especially important for the reader to scrutinize the distillation of the case studies that appears in Appendix A.

More people and institutions influenced this book than I can acknowledge. The intellectual godfather is Samuel Huntington. Although my conclusions diverge in some respects from his theory of civil-military relations and he is not responsible for any specific inaccuracies, I cannot absolve him of responsibility for the product, as authors normally do. His work inspired my research and his guidance improved it. Among the many who contributed to the development of my ideas or made helpful suggestions—some of which I obstinately rejected—were Graham Allison, Bernard Brodie, Maury Feld, Arthur Maass, Amos Perlmutter, Jerome Slater, John Steinbruner, and David Swickard. Their consciences can remain clear about the residual mistakes and inadequacies. Michael Handel was an invaluable friend, goad, and source of stimulation, pushing me toward greater confidence in my own ideas. The editorial expertise of Aida Donald and Beverly Miller was essential, forcing me to tighten the overlong original version and restrain my penchant for lurid prose. Yvonne Quinlan was instrumental in helping produce the manuscript, and Eric Richard performed above and beyond the call of friendship with some last minute editing.

For providing financial support and comfortable environments in which to think I am indebted to the Department of Government, the Program for Science and International Affairs, the Center for International Affairs, and the students and staff of Lowell House—all at Harvard University—as well as the International Studies Association and the Ford Foundation. The United States Army provided neither comfort nor remuneration, but my very brief experience in it provoked enough wry fascination with military institutions to make me consider writing a book on them. The most important causes behind this work, however, were not the proximate ones. My mother, whose imaginative vitality prodded my thinking from the beginning, and my father, from whom I inherited the scholarly vocation and temperament, should have lived to see this book. Their mark is there.

Arlington, Virginia   Richard K. Betts

Contents

Introduction

MILITARY confrontations were the most serious crises of the cold war. The United States used force many times in the quarter century after World War II and in most of the important regions of the world. Equally significant were instances where policy makers considered resorting to force but did not. For critics of American policy in this period civil-military relations in the decision-making process often figure prominently in explanations of who was at fault in critical mistakes in policy. Many on the Left who see United States inverventions abroad as mistaken or immoral have diagnosed the problem as too much military influence.[1] This view is especially tempting since the most extensive use of military power occurred under Democratic administrations; cryptofascist soldiers could be blamed for seducing or intimidating civilian leaders who were afraid of being considered weak. Some on the Right, however, who believe the United States backed down too often, think there was not enough military influence, and they blame United States defeats on a timorous or leftist State Department.

Both views reflect the prevalent assumption that military professionals are more aggressive than diplomats and politicians. But it is not clear that generals always advocate use of force in a crisis. Some scholars portray soldiers as cautious realists restraining civilian activists.[2] Either assumption about military inclinations can find justification in particular cases. Wrapped in intuition and the demonologies of the cold war, notions of military influence in crises have been premises of political debate more than conclusions of analysis. Despite a wealth of literature on military participation in decisions on defense budgets and weapons procurement, there has been no comprehensive survey of the postwar role of American military men

1

in decisions on their most essential function: the use of force in combat.

This book is such a study. It addresses four principal questions. First, when the use of force was an issue, what did military advisers recommend compared to civilian advisers? Second, what effect did the advice of the military have on presidential decisions, and how was their influence brought to bear? Third, since the evidence shows substantial variations in advice and different tendencies toward aggressiveness among different military officials, what factors account for these differences, and what determines military attitudes? What are the linkages between peacetime military organizational interests and perspectives and their advice in crises? Fourth, how should a President choose and organize his military advisers?[3]

The complex answers that emerge from the record of decisions since 1945 do not reinforce either of the common stereotypes of the military role in policy. The left-wing stereotype of military advisers as both fools and knaves—an implicitly inconsistent premise that ascribes to stupid people the power to convince or manipulate smarter ones—falters because military advisers taken as a whole have been less foolish and less powerful than assumed. But neither were they martyrs, shackled and reduced to impotence by appeasing civilian administrators, as the right-wing stereotype suggests. When the soldiers have not been complicit in civilian policy, they have been resourceful in finding ways to resist it. No one who seeks to fix responsibility for disasters in cold war crises by blaming only the military or only the civilians will find comfort in the evidence taken as a whole. There is enough blame to go around for both camps.

1 Military Advice and the Use of Force

The most grievous offense will be the academicians' effort to off-load the sins of this melancholy time on the military, who, skilled more with the sword than the pen, cannnot adequately defend themselves against egghead francs-tireurs blowing beanshooters from the sanctuary of their ivory towers.

George Ball, "In Defense of the Military"

One member of the Joint Chiefs of Staff, for example, argued that we could use nuclear weapons, on the basis that our adversaries would use theirs against us in an attack. I thought, as I listened, of the many times that I had heard the military take positions which, if wrong, had the advantage that no one would be around at the end to know.

Robert F. Kennedy, *Thirteen Days*

THE armed services are not a phalanx poised against civilian officials. A survey of incidents in which Presidents considered committing American forces to combat—beginning with the Berlin blockade of 1948 and ending with the 1972 Christmas bombing of Hanoi—reveals substantial diversity in the aggressiveness of military recommendations compared to those of principal civilian advisers.[1] There were often disagreements among the services and between personnel in the field and in Washington, and there was a pattern to them. (For the data on the relative aggressiveness of military advisers and the specific cases on which the following analysis is based, see the tabulations in Appendix A.) Since World War II the most bellicose recommendations have come from the chiefs of naval operations and field commanders, though army field commanders tend to be more cautious than air and naval commanders. The least aggressive recommendations have come from army chiefs of staff. In addition there is a distinct difference in the tendency to aggressiveness between recommendations about initiation of armed intervention and advice on escalation of the use of force once armed conflict has begun.

In decisions on whether to commit American armed forces, military advisers were usually divided, and their recommendations echoed civilian advice more often than they differed. With the exceptions of the chiefs of naval operations and field commanders, military leaders were less anxious than the majority of involved civilians to initiate United States commitment about as often as they were more aggressive. Joint Chiefs of Staff (JCS) members' views were virtually the same as the dominant civilian attitude more than half the time. The JCS chairman, who is closer to the administration than the service chiefs, had the highest rate of agreement. In contrast, commanders in the field who have more parochial spheres of responsibility than the JCS were more hawkish than civilian political leaders in more than a third of the cases. In no case did a fully united set of military advisers oppose united civilians. The only case in which the President was faced with a clear and nearly unanimous JCS recommendation for an armed attack was during the Cuban missile crisis; he rejected it, choosing a naval quarantine instead of the air strike pushed by the Chiefs. On this decision, though, the most severe critic of the President's judgment was not a soldier but a civilian hawk: Dean Acheson.

The stereotype of a belligerent chorus of generals and admirals intimidating a pacific civilian establishment is not supported by the evidence. In most of the cases where some soldiers were vocally ahead of the civilians in urging the use of force, there were other soldiers giving advice similar to or more cautious than that of principal civilians. This balanced the leverage that the aggressive officers could invoke on grounds of expertise. This picture changes, however, in decisions on the degree of force to use once a decision to commit conventional military units has been made. Generals prefer using force quickly, massively, and decisively to destroy enemy capabilities rather than rationing it gradually to coax the enemy to change his intentions. In escalation decisions, no military adviser was less aggressive than the major civilian officials, with one minor exception.[2] The diversity of military recommendations and the extent of consonance with civilian opinion indicate that military professionals rarely have dominated decisions on the use of force. Soldiers have exerted the greatest leverage on intervention decisions in those instances where they vetoed it. Disagreements with civilians were much greater on issues of the amount of force and the mode of implementation than on whether to commit American forces. In neither of the wars fought by the United States since 1945, however, nor in the 1962 Cuban crisis, which brought the nation closest to nuclear war, did civilian leadership cave in to military demands.

INFLUENCE, ALIENATION, AND AUTONOMY

Influence, defined here as causing decision makers to do something they probably would not have done otherwise,[3] is one of the most important and most elusive concepts in the study of politics. In decisions on use of force it is impossible to detect objectively whose influence is greatest; it can only be inferred because only the President—and maybe not even he—really knows what convinces him or changes his mind. There are two forms of military influence. Direct influence flows from formal and explicit recommendations, or control of operations. Indirect influence flows from ways in which the soldiers may control the premises of civilian decision through monopoly of information or control of options.

The indirect influence of the military establishment on foreign policy has increased since 1940. As in other bureaucracies, rapid growth in size and programs since the New Deal overtook the ability of elected political leaders to provide the same degree of direction they could exert over the modest executive branch establishment of earlier years. Major examples of indirect influence on use of force are the military intelligence and reporting systems that had a greater impact on Vietnam policy decisions than did direct military advice.

Direct military influence on policy, on the other hand, has declined since its apex in World War II. The Joint Chiefs fell from being the President's primary advisers on global policy during the war, when the State Department was weak and no authorities intervened between them and President Roosevelt, to a lesser role under Truman. Under Eisenhower their judgment was usually subordinated to a strong secretary of state and, at one remove, to the administration apostle of economy, Secretary of the Treasury George Humphrey. The soldiers' lowest estate was in the Kennedy administration when they had less influence on policy and strategy and even lost their traditional degree of control over operational tactics. Military influence rose slightly in the later years of the Johnson administration. The recommendations of the Joint Chiefs and commander in chief, Pacific (CINCPAC), for a quick, intensive, and comprehensive bombing campaign in Vietnam were not accepted by the secretary of defense or the President, but the target restrictions were slowly whittled down over time (although never completely) as each step in escalation failed to produce the response from Hanoi that the administration hoped for (and that the military, with the exception of Maxwell Taylor, never had believed would result). The military profile rebounded under President Nixon but remained lower than in the pre-Kennedy administrations.

Among many analysts of the national security bureaucracy, the view has persisted that military advisers, especially the Joint Chiefs, are more potent than their civilian colleagues in affecting presidential decisions.[4] This leverage was reduced, however, when Robert McNamara became an activist secretary of defense. Indeed, the curtailment had begun in 1958 when the reorganization of the Department of Defense brought unification of the services under a civilian secretariat in the Office of the Secretary of Defense (OSD) closer to reality. The Chiefs undeniably still had a large amount of influence, but in relative terms they had much less than they had previously. Although they were still influential in budget and procurement decisions, in decisions on use of force there were usually more powerful advisers, of the stature of the secretary of state or senior members of Congress, to counteract their prestige. The only cases in which military recommendations on use of force were considered irresistible were the instances in which they opposed intervention.

There is also a myth that high military figures have extraordinary influence and prevent their superiors from overruling them because of a unique tendency to resign and attack their administrations.[5] But the evidence does not support this theory. Generals Matthew Ridgway and Maxwell Taylor did not resign from the Eisenhower administration (the mistaken impression that they did is almost universal), nor did General Thomas Power quit under Kennedy, and there is no firm evidence that the Joint Chiefs threatened to resign in the Johnson administration.[6] This misconception arises because it is not widely known that the Chiefs, unlike any civilian officials except the heads of certain independent commissions, serve for fixed terms, which are specified in advance. Chiefs have been fired, not reappointed when it was expected they would be, or carried along with short reappointments, but none in the postwar period has ever resigned. Ridgway was not reappointed after his initial two-year term. Taylor, who opposed administration policy as vigorously as did his predecessor, served two consecutive two-year terms before retiring. While head of the Strategic Air Command, Power had quarreled with Secretary of Defense Neil McElroy in 1959 when he forbade publication of Power's book *Design for Survival,* but the general did not retire until five years later, under a different administration. William Westmoreland considered resigning as commander in Vietnam once in 1968 but not because of his disagreements with the administration. The issue was an interservice dispute with the marine corps concerning jurisdiction over tactical marine aircraft in the northern part of South Vietnam. Concerning his objections to administration strategy, he told one journalist in 1970 that he would have resigned if he had been in charge of the overall war effort in Vietnam.[7] Not only did he not resign, however, he was unwillingly replaced by the President. These departures testify more to the subservience of the generals than to their power.

In the 1960s a number of middle-level lieutenant colonels below the policy level did leave the service in frustration over Vietnam policy. John Paul Vann retired and later returned to Vietnam as a civilian official; William Corson and Edward King left their services to write muckraking books; Anthony Herbert retired after the avalanche of publicity about his war-crimes accusations, not in protest but because his superiors made it obvious that they wanted him out and that his career was finished; and Colonel David Hackworth dropped out to become a short-order cook in Australia. One simple legalistic-materialistic reason why disgruntled officers usually choose retirement (which is at the sufferance of the administration) rather than resignation is that resignation forfeits pension rights. In fact, the only publicized case of military protest resignation in recent years was a low-ranking navy lawyer, Lieutenant Commander Kirby Brant, who resigned in 1974 over oil companies' encroachment on government oil reserves.[8]

Military leaders became alienated from their administration superiors in direct proportion to the decline in their direct influence and their perception of the gap between their rightful and actual authority. Alienation is politically significant because there are constitutional methods at the disposal of the military to increase their influence. One is to exploit access to sympathetic public or congressional opinion. Another is to hope that the indirect influence of reports from the field will condition civilians to be more receptive to direct recommendations. Finally, military leaders can decide to bury their own disagreements and form a united front against the administration, presenting unanimous recommendations that make it more difficult for civilians to overrule their judgment. Except during the Vietnam War, however, the President has never been faced with completely united military advice more aggressive than that urged by his civilian lieutenants.

Even more than direct influence on policy decisions, the professional military value access to the President and autonomy over their internal organization and operations. They were most alienated under Presidents Kennedy and Johnson because they believed they had suffered losses in all of these areas. The Joint Chiefs had more harmonious relations with the Eisenhower and Nixon administrations, despite small budgets, which contrasted with higher defense expenditures under the Democrats, because they had more authority over their own activities. Military leaders prefer poverty with autonomy to wealth with dependency.

The Joint Chiefs also felt that they had more access to authoritative policy makers under the Republicans. President Kennedy kept in close touch with the Chiefs early in his administration—he met alone with them frequently and regularly sent his military assistant, Chester Clifton, to consult them so they would have an open conduit to the President around the secretary of defense—but he soon abandoned this practice as he developed absolute confidence in McNamara. During the Vietnam War until late 1967, President Johnson relied on McNamara as his primary channel for military advice and did not have anywhere near the amount of contact with the Chiefs common for Presidents in previous wars. In fact he rarely saw them. During the 1965–1968 escalation period he saw the chairman about once a week, and then almost never alone. When the Tuesday luncheon was established as the central forum for ongoing high-level discussion of Vietnam policy, no military representative was regularly included until mid-1967, when Senator John Stennis criticized the administration for ignoring military advice; after that JCS Chairman Earle Wheeler became a member of the group. After the Tet offensive decisions leading to deescalation, there were only two or three direct meetings per year between the Joint Chiefs and Presidents Johnson and Nixon.[9]

During the Nixon administration there was an infusion of military officers into Henry Kissinger's National Security Council staff. Kissinger's deputy was a colonel, Alexander Haig; within a few years the post was held by a three-star general, Brent Scowcroft (who succeeded to Kissinger's job in 1975). At the same time, Secretary of Defense Melvin Laird inaugurated "participatory management" in the Pentagon, which was a simultaneous slapping down of the civilian units in the Office of the Secretary of Defense, which had acquired power under McNamara—particularly the offices of International Security Affairs and Systems Analysis—and a reenfranchisement of the service chiefs in decision making. This increase of military autonomy in management was real, but the increase in access to the policy makers did not yield much more actual influence over the content of foreign policy. Kissinger's aggrandizement of authority and his secretive personal diplomacy excluded not only the State Department professionals and the military but much of his own staff as well and caused the bootlegging of National Security Council material to JCS Chairman Thomas Moorer.[10] The only true military insider was a middle-ranking officer outside the chain of command: Haig. Nevertheless, the outward good fortune of greater access, recovery of some lost autonomy, and greater confidence that their views were being heard at the top more regularly made the Nixon-Laird-Kissinger system a welcome relief to military leaders.

An even more hallowed value than access or autonomy in management of programs for the military is control over operational command and tactics, which also takes precedence over the importance of influence on the decision to intervene and is accentuated once force has been committed. Most of the field commanders in Korea resented their administration because they were denied the authority over tactics that they believed was commensurate with the responsibility of their mission. The ultimate tightening of operational discretion came under President Kennedy. On the night before the landing at the Bay of Pigs, the marine colonel detached to the Central Intelligence Agency who was in charge of coordinating the operation in Washington told his cohorts not to let the policy makers change any of the plans. Shortly thereafter, the President cancelled the scheduled second air strike, which some military leaders believed doomed the operation and which they considered an irresponsible decision that should have been made before the operation had begun. Later when it was decided in August 1961 to send the

First Battle Group down the autobahn from West Germany to Berlin after the wall had gone up, Kennedy paid elaborate personal attention to the preparations for the move, to the point of asking for the convoy commander's biography and becoming temporarily uneasy because the commander, Colonel Glover S. Johns, was not a West Pointer. He then violated the chain of command by establishing a direct telephone connection between the convoy en route and military assistant Chester Clifton at the White House. This tight control of tactics from the top was greater than in any previous crisis. A good contrasting example was the refusal by the President in the Spanish-American War not only to prescribe operational tactics but even to resolve disputes between autonomous field commanders.[11]

The most dramatic example of the resentment provoked by this usurpation of tactical command was the confrontation between McNamara and Chief of Naval Operations George Anderson during the Cuban missile crisis. McNamara had been spending time at the operational headquarters of the blockade, and the naval officers were irked at what they considered his interference. The secretary insisted on making detailed decisions about the operation of the blockade line, without regard to standard procedure or the chain of command. Friction mounted. McNamara then noticed that a single U.S. destroyer was standing outside the blockade line and asked Anderson what it was doing there. The secretary was anxious to make clear that the President did not want to harass any Soviet ships and wanted to allow the Russians to be able to stand off or retreat without humiliation. Anderson was reluctant to answer because some of the civilians in the secretary's party were not cleared for highly sensitive information, but he drew McNamara aside and explained that the ship was sitting on top of a Russian submarine.[12]

The final blowup came when McNamara demanded to know what the navy would do if a Soviet ship refused to divulge its cargo. Anderson brandished the *Manual of Navy Regulations* in McNamara's face and shouted, "It's all in there." The Secretary retorted, "I don't give a damn what John Paul Jones would have done. I want to know what you are going to do, now." Finally Anderson replied, "Now, Mr. Secretary, if you and your Deputy will go back to your offices, the Navy will run the blockade."[13] Within less than a year, Anderson was removed from his post.

In Vietnam, President Johnson's pithy warning, "I won't let those Air Force generals bomb the smallest outhouse north of the 17th parallel without checking with me," kept the soldiers on a taut leash. As a result, the military came to feel wasted and victimized.

Army leaders remained less alienated than those in the other services because they were less adamant than the navy and air force in their differences with administration strategy and because the President and the Office of the Secretary of Defense did not restrict or monitor ground tactics on anything approaching the scale on which they controlled the air war. But even JCS Chairman and ex-Army Chief Wheeler, who had gained McNamara's favor for his cooperation and vigor in implementing the administration's changes in the army and Pentagon, by late 1965 gave a speech complaining about "overcontrol and overmanagement" by civilians in the Pentagon and asking discretion for field commanders to "exercise command . . . on the spot," free of having "their hands tied by . . . theorists at higher headquarters."[14]

The soldiers believed that too many lives and excessive resources were needlessly squandered piecemeal, that they were denied the latitude necessary to win the war by civilian amateurs who did not know the requirements of tactical effectiveness, and that they were then left with the responsibility when they indeed failed to win. The obsession with lost autonomy became the prevalent military excuse for why the United States failed in Vietnam. They were all the more bitter because they believed they had predicted the outcome. In early 1965 Chief of Naval Operations David McDonald had returned from a White House meeting where, over the objections of the Joint Chiefs who favored heavy and decisive bombing, the civilian policy makers were planning the program of limited and graduated bombing. He reportedly told his aide that graduated response was militarily senseless and that when the war was over, the civilians responsible would no longer be in office and the only group left answerable for the war would be the military.[15] Just as the military became scapegoats for liberals and civilian veterans of McNamara's Pentagon, who were reluctant to admit the moral responsibility of a Democratic administration, the civilian analysts under McNamara (known as the "whiz kids") became scapegoats for the military and conservatives who would not admit that Vietnam was not a war that could be won.

While the Vietnam experience epitomizes the process of alienation, it represents only part of the spectrum of military advice and influence. When postwar decisions on intervention and escalation are examined together, four levels of military influence emerge. Influence was highest when it was direct and negative, that is, when military advisers recommended against use of force. Such instances were few but dramatic. The second level of impact is that of indirect and negative influence, when the military did not make explicit recommendations against force but presented a set of alternatives or conditions for endorsement of intervention that made the option of force seem impossible to the President. In some of these cases, the influence—that is, the effect it had on the policy makers—was unintended by the military. The third level is indirect and positive, when data or options supplied by the military encouraged decisions for force even though the military advice was not accepted. The fourth and lowest level of military influence is direct and positive, that is, when they explicitly recommended force. In most such instances the recommendations were either superfluous (complementing a civilian consensus) or rejected.

No matter what the level of influence, however, military alienation rarely resulted from the President's failure to accept advice on whether to use force. Instead, it arose much more from rejection of advice on escalation, or the form and pace of the application of force once the commitment was made. These were the instances in which the soldiers believed civilians overstepped their bounds, usurped their authority, and transformed civilian control into civilian command.

The Dichotomization of War and Peace: Justifying the Claim to Autonomy

With the exception of a few activists such as Arthur Radford, Maxwell Taylor, and Arleigh Burke, the Joint Chiefs of Staff since World War II have sought to maintain the formal division between policy decisions, which they participate in only as advisers, and pure military decisions in the subordinate area of administration and implementation over which they claim authority.[16] The postwar initiative for a radical increase in defense spending, the document known as NSC-68, came not from them but from the Department of State's Policy Planning Staff. General Collins's memoir of the Korean War frequently mentions the constant desire of the Chiefs for more policy guidance from the National Security Council and the occasional mutual demurrals over policy in conferences between the JCS and State Department personnel concerning goals in Korea.[17]

This combination of docility on most intervention decisions with indignation over civilian direction of tactical operations is not a paradox. The obverse of the internalized norm of civilian control, which establishes the realm of policy outside military responsibility, is that operations is the province of military expertise and is outside the competence of politicians. Soldiers readily accept that civilian leaders must make the decision to intervene but believe that the political content of decision is in the determination of policy—whether to use force, where and when to fight. Once that decision has been made, implementation, or how to fight, is a technical function that must be left to the technicians. Policy determination thus gives way to tactical determinism. The problem is not only that the boundaries between policy, strategy, and tactics are rarely clear but that civilian leaders may insist on the right to control operations because of their political implications.

The principle of tactical autonomy was shaken in Korea, where most of the field commanders resented limits on their authority to use tactics they considered necessary to defeat the North Korean and Chinese armies. General MacArthur especially believed in a separation between governmental decision and military implementation.[18] But the feud in this case was intramilitary, as well as between the armed forces and political superiors. The Joint Chiefs' preoccupation with the danger of war in Europe led them to support President Truman's restrictions on the effort in Asia. The gulf between policy and operations continued to develop as the military rationale for demanding tactical autonomy. It was fundamentally antithetical, however, to the theory of limited war promulgated by some civilian strategists in the 1960s.

The advent of sophisticated theories of limited conflict in the Kennedy defense program complicated the conceptual problem of differentiating war from peace. With the partial exception of the air force, the military agreed that it would be suicidal to fight a total war with the Soviet Union. A capability for limited war in Europe without resort to strategic nuclear exchange was welcomed by the ground forces. But most military men conceived *limited* as meaning nonthermonuclear, or local as opposed to global war. They did not immediately perceive the concept as a precursor of another semiconventional war, halfway between a "brush-fire" and a strategic confrontation, in which sanctuaries, targeting taboos, and restrictive rules of engagement would limit the effective application of force. This difference in how the defense intellectuals viewed the meaning of limited war and how most of the military saw it was typified in General Wheeler's objection to an interviewer's use of the term *escalation* to describe the widening combat commitment in Vietnam; Wheeler said that the military reserved the word for movement from the conventional level of warfare to the nuclear, not for variations in the extent of force used in a conventional conflict.[19]

What civilians called escalation soldiers called, more pejoratively, *piecemeal gradualism*. The increase in military pressure against

North Vietnam and the Vietcong between 1965 and 1968 was the application of the theories of graduated response in vogue with the civilian strategists of the early and middle 1960s. In direct contrast to the assumption of a chasm between preintervention political decision making on one hand and expert nonpolitical execution of decision on the other, McNamara's civilian theorists saw implementation as an extension of the policy-making process. War and peace were a continuum rather than a dichotomy. Orchestration of the use of force was a political tool, a signaling device. Whether the United States bombed a surface-to-air missile site or oil depot near Hanoi would communicate a message to the enemy and was hence a political decision that had to be made by political authority; it was not a purely military decision to be made by a subordinate commander. Affecting enemy intentions by discreet modulation of force was considered as important as or preferable to destroying his military capabilities.[20] It seemed especially impossible as well as undesirable to segregate policy, strategy, and tactics in an unconventional war. Where the enemy fought with irregular and phantom units and where revolutionary political organization was as much or more a source of his strength than the number of his battalions, it seemed obvious that policy and tactics were inextricable and constantly had to be adapted in tandem.

Few military leaders agreed. Retired leaders of the ground forces, such as Matthew Ridgway, James Gavin, and David Shoup, believed in limiting United States commitment on the ground once troops were dispatched in units to Vietnam. Of the active soldiers, only the one who was politically identified with the administration— Maxwell Taylor—favored gradual and incremental pressure rather than swift and massive action. Many professionals, especially airmen, did not see a compelling reason not to wage total war against North Vietnam, and they believed the administration gave them cause to believe serious limits would not be imposed. When Army Chief Harold Johnson asked for a policy determination about the extent of the United States commitment in March 1965, McNamara answered: "Policy is: Anything that will strengthen the position of the GVN will be sent." In this spirit, a month later when the first marine battalions had waded ashore at Danang, the Chiefs asked the secretary of defense to get rid of "all administrative impediments that hamper us in the prosecution of this war." They asked for increases in funding, changes in the organization of communications and the military assistance program, authority to extend military terms of service and consult with Congress on use of reserves, and relaxation of manpower ceilings. On most points they were turned down.[21]

Taylor's support of graduated response, along with his image as a political soldier and his activist domination of the JCS while he was chairman, helped make him unpopular with the Chiefs who served under him, and they came to distrust him. Taylor agreed with the civilian strategists through his service as ambassador to South Vietnam and into the early period of American combat involvement there. By the time the United States left the war, however, he had parted company and gone home to the military fold. He agreed that gradualism had been a mistake and that concentrated massive force should have been used immediately in 1965.[22] With the failure of administration strategy, the generals closed ranks and blamed it on armchair field marshals who never should have forced the soldiers to fight the war the wrong way. Where civilians tend to focus on the period up to 1965, lamenting the mistakes in the process that led to full military commitment, the military emphasize the period after 1965 and what they consider the mistakes in following through on the commitment.

2 Cases in Point

"But we are professionals; we have to go on fighting till the politicians tell us to stop. Probably they will get together and agree to the same peace that we could have had at the beginning, making nonsense of all these years." His ugly face, which had winked at me before the dive, wore a kind of professional brutality, like a Christmas mask from which a child's eyes peer through the holes in the paper. "You would not understand the nonsense, Fowler. You are not one of us."

Captain Trouin, in Graham Greene,
The Quiet American

"What do you do when they tell you to fly somewhere you can't get back from?"

"Me?" said Captain Wiley. "I wouldn't know. I'm here. They never sent me anywhere I couldn't get back from."

... This was one of the limits of human endeavor, one of those boundaries of the possible whose precise determining was, as General Nichols with his ascetic air of being rid of those youthful illusions, viewing with no nonsense the Here and the Now, always saw it, the problem. If you did not know where the limits were, how did you know that you weren't working outside them? If you were working outside them you must be working in vain. It was no good acting on a supposition that men would, for your purpose, be what they did not have it in them to be; just as it was unwise to beguile yourself, up there on top of the whirlwind, with the notion that the storm was going to have to do what you said.

James Gould Cozzens, *Guard of Honor*

THE most significant uses of American armed force in the postwar era were the two wars in Asia. Presidents were not lured into either conflict by the military. A professional soldier's advice, in fact, was crucial in forestalling United States entry into Indochina in 1954. When the United States did intervene, the action had the support of most civilians as well as soldiers. The soldiers could not credibly claim, however, that they were prevented from winning the wars. In the only case where the military united to protest restraints imposed by civilians—the second half of the Vietnam War—their rationalizations that the restrictions caused the failure sounded hollow because a large number of the limitations had been lifted before the war ended. Korea and Vietnam do not encompass the whole of the role of military advice on force in the cold war, but they highlight it and show the issues at their extremes.

CRUCIBLES OF THE COLD WAR:
KOREA AND THE INDOCHINA CRISIS, 1950–1954

In 1948 the Joint Chiefs recommended to Truman: "The United States should not become so irrevocably involved in the Korean situation that an action taken by any faction in Korea or by any other power in Korea could be considered a 'casus belli' for the United States." The JCS majority, assuming that conflict with the communists would take the form of general war, stated that Korea was not strategically important and could not be supported militarily because American forces would be needed in the more important theaters. Commander in Chief, Far East, Douglas MacArthur agreed and in 1949 supported the JCS reccommendation that United States troops be withdrawn from South Korea. Only Omar Bradley dissented, fearing United States withdrawal might provoke invasion. American troops (as well as Soviet forces in North Korea) were thus withdrawn.[1]

When North Korea struck across the thirty-eighth parallel in 1950, the recommendation to use American forces to repel the attack came from Secretary of State Dean Acheson, not Secretary of Defense Louis Johnson, who made no recommendation, or any of the military from the Pentagon. When the decision to use United States forces was transmitted to the commanders in the Far East, MacArthur and Vice-Admiral C. Turner Joy were surprised, having considered it an unlikely policy reversal. General of the Army George Marshall was not even consulted. What was striking about the intervention decision was the President's immediate certainty that the North Koreans had to be thrown back. Even before the first conference after the attack, President Truman declared that he would not let the communists succeed and that he was going to "hit them hard." "This is the Greece of the Far East," he said the day after the attack. "If we are tough enough now there won't be any next step." None of the President's advisers disagreed with him.[2]

Initially General Hoyt Vandenberg and Admiral Forrest Sherman believed air and naval forces might be enough to contain the invasion. On 29 June the Joint Chiefs of Staff recommended deploying troops to protect the evacuation of American civilians but did not propose committing them to action on the battlefield. From Korea, however, MacArthur concluded that only United States ground troops could stop the North Koreans; he said two divisions would be sufficient. The next day Truman approved Sherman's recommendation for a naval blockade of North Korea and authorized MacArthur to use United States troops in combat. The Joint Chiefs agreed to this step, although without enthusiasm. Civilian advisers were in consensus behind the decision, and congressional reaction was predominantly supportive.[3]

The first United States units into Korea were beaten back into the Pusan perimeter, but after the success of the autumn amphibious landings at Inchon, the issue arose whether to halt United Nations troops at the thirty-eighth parallel or pursue the North Korean Army and reunify the country. The President's civilian advisers were less inclined to cross the parallel than was MacArthur—though Acheson supported the move. Army Secretary Frank Pace was very reticent. The Joint Chiefs believed with MacArthur that military necessity required destruction of the enemy army and that operations could not be stabilized at the parallel. Truman and the Chiefs authorized the pursuit of the enemy into North Korea, although they instructed MacArthur that he could cross the boundary only to ensure the security of his command. MacArthur interpreted his orders liberally, marched to the Yalu River, retreated down the peninsula when the Chinese intervened, and was saved from disaster when Matthew Ridgway took over the Eighth Army and stabilized the United Nations line.[4] The issue for the next three years of the war was whether to push back to the Chinese border or settle for what United States forces had achieved before they crossed the parallel.

MacArthur chafed against restrictions on his command authority from the beginning. He was denied permission to pursue enemy aircraft into Chinese air space, bomb hydroelectric plants on the Yalu, and bomb Racin in North Korea on the Soviet border. On 30

December 1950 he recommended a blockade of China, destruction of China's industrial capacity by naval gunfire and air bombardment, reinforcement of the United Nations command with Nationalist Chinese troops, and unleashing Chiang Kai-shek for diversionary attacks against the mainland. His advice was rejected, limitations were placed on his freedom of action, and he complained bitterly that he was being shackled.[5] When he went too far in challenging administration instructions, ignoring directives to clear public statements with Washington, he was relieved.

Much of the military supported MacArthur's objections to Truman's limited goals. During the Senate hearings following his relief, a number of officers spoke out on restrictions on military action against China. Mark Clark, the commander who replaced Ridgway as commander in chief, Far East, and James Van Fleet, who commanded the Eighth Army under him, were as aggressive as MacArthur had been, although they were more obedient. According to Clark, "We could have obtained better truce terms quicker, shortened the war and saved lives, if we had gotten tougher faster . . . we should not have allowed the enemy a sanctuary north of the Yalu."[6]

The Joint Chiefs and Ridgway supported Truman in both public and secret congressional testimony. They feared provoking a Soviet attack on Europe and Japan, igniting another world war. In early 1951 Ridgway's and Van Fleet's tactical successes tempted the Chiefs to support a military solution in Korea, but, wary of draining United States resources, they supported negotiating a settlement instead. Bradley said as late as June 1951, "If Russia intervenes actively, we will have to get out."[7]

The Chiefs, Ridgway, and Marshall believed Russian intervention was a strong possibility and did not think escalation would cripple China in any case. Expanding the war to China, Bradley testified, "would probably delight the Kremlin" by sapping United States strength. And they saw an implicit quid pro quo: if they did not bomb Manchuria, the Soviets would not invade Europe and would not retaliate by destroying vulnerable United States supply lines in Korea and logistical bases in Japan. Pacific fleet commander Arthur Radford, along with MacArthur (who wanted to include the USSR's Port Arthur), favored a naval blockade of China, but Marshall and Chief of Naval Operations Sherman believed it would be both provocative and ineffective. The Chiefs, including Hoyt Vandenberg of the air force, opposed bombing Manchuria because they thought it would be counterproductive. Unless the trans-Siberian railway were bombed (which would lead to war with the Soviets), the

Chinese would be able to keep their supply lines functioning. Meanwhile attrition of United States aircraft over Manchuria would erode the capability for the air force's first priority: destruction of Soviet industrial potential in the event of general war. Major losses in Korea in 1951 would not have been replaceable until 1953. "The fact is that the United States is operating a shoestring air force," said Vandenberg, "in view of its global responsibilities." While MacArthur and Radford lamented the failure to use air power against Manchurian sanctuaries, neither advocated invasion of China. "No man in his proper senses would advocate throwing our troops in on the Chinese mainland," testified MacArthur. "I have never heard that advocated by ... any military man." But Bradley argued that air and naval action would not suffice; ground troops would have to invade the mainland to defeat China decisively. "Frankly, in the opinion of the Joint Chiefs of Staff," Bradley testified, "this strategy would involve us in the wrong war, at the wrong place, at the wrong time, and with the wrong enemy."

Mark Clark, commander in the Far East when Eisenhower came into office, hoped for approval to move for victory in Korea, but the new President decided to settle for an honorable truce. He did, however, authorize Clark in spring 1953 to escalate in the event the Chinese rejected the final offer in the truce talks.[8] (They did not.)

The wounds and divisions that three years of indecisive war had wrought within the miltary and between military and political leaders ran deep and led many to resolve not to be caught in another war of attrition. In the long term this frustration led to more acrimony between military and civilians from 1964 to 1968, as the United States slid into a limited war in Vietnam. In the shorter term, it led the soldiers to resist any ground combat commitment in Asia.

At the height of the Korean War in 1951, the Joint Chiefs of Staff had warned against any United States statement that might imply commitment of American forces to the Indochina war. By 1954, when United States intervention was being seriously considered, Mark Clark and others maintained that if the United States did enter, it would have to be without restrictions and to win. Vice-Admiral A. C. Davis, director of the office of foreign military affairs in the Office of the Secretary of Defense, wrote:

Involvement of United States forces in the Indochina war should be avoided at all costs. If, then, National Policy determines no other alternative, the United States should not be self-duped into believing the possibility of partial involvement

—such as "Naval and Air units only." One cannot go over Niagara Falls in a barrel only slightly.[9]

The disagreements among military leaders in the 1954 decisions had less to do with whether they considered intervention desirable in principle than with what they considered necessary for successful intervention. JCS Chairman Radford and Air Force Chief of Staff Nathan Twining considered air power sufficient. The ground forces and the chief of naval operations believed no decision could be reached without troops.

The first phase of decision in 1954 concerned the possibility of salvaging the French position at Dienbienphu. Eisenhower instructed Radford to do anything he could to help General Henri Navarre, the French commander in Indochina. What resulted was a highly secret plan (Operation Vulture) for air strikes designed to support the French garrison. Precautions against preserving any record of the plan were so extensive that even the *Pentagon Papers* researchers were unable to uncover any trace of it.[10] One result of the secrecy is that none of the published versions of the JCS disagreements on Vulture are accurate. Most writers have repeated journalist Chalmers Roberts's report (which he acknowledged years later was based on a leak from Congressman John McCormack) that all of the Chiefs but Radford opposed it. A number of others share Lieutenant General James Gavin's recollection that all of the Chiefs except Army Chief of Staff Ridgway supported the strike. According to the actual participants, Radford supported the plan strongly, and Air Force Chief Nathan Twining did also, but as a one-time action. Ridgway opposed it vigorously, Chief of Naval Operations Robert Carney and Marine Commandant Lemuel Shepherd leaned reluctantly toward this opposition. They did not believe that an air strike alone could relieve the French position.[11]

Political leadership was also divided, but the dominant officials leaned toward action. Most reports indicate that Secretary of State John Foster Dulles and President Eisenhower leaned toward limited intervention until Ridgway objected, warning forcefully that United States capabilities were inadequate. (Others suggest that Dulles's support was feigned, a ploy to influence the Russians, and that Dulles and Eisenhower attached so many conditions to the later plan for united action with allies to prevent it from being carried out).[12]

The second phase of the crisis was discussion of intervention on the ground in the delta area of northern Vietnam following the fall of Dienbienphu. In late 1953 the army had challenged assumptions that ground troops would not be needed for intervention in Indochina and therefore advised reassessment of the benefits as opposed to costs of commitment to holding Vietnam. In January 1954 General Walter Bedell Smith—taking a more equivocal position as civilian under secretary of state—said Indochina was so important that he would favor United States naval and air intervention but not use of ground troops.[13] Ridgway's opposition was even more strenuous after the fall of Dienbienphu than before. He briefed Eisenhower, at his own request, emphasizing the infeasibility and high cost of intervention on the ground. In summer 1954 the official report arrived from an army survey team Ridgway had dispatched to study the problems of intervention and reinforced the arguments (supported by British objections) that had led to cancellation of the intervention option.[14] In this first test of his domino theory Eisenhower decided to let half of the domino fall.

Following the decision to accept partition of Vietnam, the Joint Chiefs were reticent to become more heavily involved in South Vietnam. In September 1954, and again a month later, they opposed the State Department's desire to send a military assistance advisory group to Vietnam because of the unstable political situation there. They agreed to do so, as reluctant but obedient soldiers, only if "political considerations are overriding." They did not want responsibility for failure if they did not have the resources to ensure success. "The available record does not indicate any rebuttal of the JCS's appraisal of the situation," wrote the *Pentagon Papers* analysts. "What it does indicate is that the United States decided to gamble with very limited resources."[15] This inclination to gamble and parcel out chips gradually persisted for the next decade, and the more went into the pot, the less abstemious became the military. Given the commitments that grew in the 1950s and were reinforced in the early 1960s, decisions on intervention were not quite as clean or clear as in other cases. Though United States troop units were not involved, American advisers accompanied South Vietnamese units into combat and were being killed regularly by 1962. From 1955 to 1965 the issue for the military was not so much whether to make a commitment but whether to reinforce one that was already made.

VIETNAM, 1961–1975

Vietnam became one of the first issues on the Kennedy administration agenda. In January 1961 Brigadier General Edward Lansdale, an unconventional warfare specialist in the Office of the Secretary of

Defense, had just returned from a trip to Vietnam and forwarded to the White House an alarming, pessimistic, and critical analysis of Vietcong progress in 1960 and the prospects for Diem's government. White House aide Walt Rostow was so impressed by it that he forced it on the attention of the harried new President. In May the Joint Chiefs issued a memo emphasizing the strategic importance of Vietnam and recommending deployment of United States forces, "assuming that the political decision is to hold Southeast Asia outside the Communist sphere." (They did not advise using the American forces for combat against the Vietcong.) Shortly thereafter Lieutenant General Lionel McGarr, chief of the military assistance advisory group, requested 16,000 combat troops to bolster Vietnamese morale.[16] This request was rejected, but military assistance was increased.

The Joint Chiefs favored whatever commitment was necessary to keep South Vietnam independent, despite reluctance in the ground forces to become involved in a limited risky combat operation in Laos earlier in the year. This stance coincided with pressure from aggressive civilians such as Rostow. At the end of September Rostow recommended stationing 25,000 Southeast Asia Treaty Organization troops between the demilitarized zone and Cambodia to stop North Vietnamese infiltration. Rostow's proposal worried the military because it reflected an ignorance of the terrain and threatened to tie the troops down in an ineffective and dangerous deployment. They countered in early October with a proposal for 22,800 men (only 5,000 of whom would be United States ground troops), but to be located in the central highlands. "In hindsight," concluded the civilians writing the *Pentagon Papers*, "the JCS reasoning in rejecting the Rostow proposal looks unchallengeable." Assistant Secretary of Defense for International Security Affairs William Bundy shared Rostow's alarm and favored intervention as a 70 percent chance for success, which he thought worth the gamble. The day after Bundy's memo and two days after the Joint Chiefs' proposal, the President approved an augmentation of air force assistance under the military assistance advisory group and decided to send a special survey mission to Vietnam under his personal military representative, Maxwell Taylor.[17]

When Taylor reported back in November, his pessimism at the deterioration he had seen in the field led him to recommend dispatch of a military task force of 8,000 men to boost South Vietnamese morale, conduct logistical operations, and engage in combat only for purposes of base security, not to fight the Vietcong. He warned, "There is no limit to our possible commitment (unless we attack

the source in Hanoi)." The cover letter, written with Rostow, recommended consideration of an air offensive against North Vietnam
if Hanoi persisted in promoting the insurgency. The Joint Chiefs,
however, reasoned that 8,000 men would not resolve the problem
and that six divisions might be required to do the job; they advised
against implementing Taylor's proposals unless the United States
made a clear and firm policy commitment to prevent the fall of
South Vietnam. "We would be almost certain," wrote McNamara,
transmitting the JCS view to the President, "to get increasingly
mired down in an inconclusive struggle." Most of the President's
civilian advisers—with the exception of George Ball and Paul Nitze
—supported the report's recommendations. Before Taylor's trip,
however, Commander in Chief, Pacific, Harry Felt had opposed
combat troop deployment until other means were exhausted. And
because the Taylor-Rostow report had also advised assigning United
States military advisers down to batallion levels in the South Vietnamese army and extending helicopter support, air reconnaissance,
and naval patrolling, there were still other measures left to try.[18]

Early in 1962 chief McGarr of the military assistance advisory
group briefed a party from the Office of the Secretary of Defense
at a Honolulu conference on his plans to use the South Vietnamese
army to clean out Vietcong sanctuaries. Although the officials at
the meeting thought his proposal was perilous, they were scarcely
less aggressive than he was and replaced him with another militant
optimist. As the United States military assistance program grew, so
did divisions between military and civilians. The soldiers pushed the
administration to approve use of napalm, defoliants, free-fire zones,
and combat jets. The civilians held off but agreed on increasing the
advisory commitment. There were no severe disagreements between
civilians and military on commitment or strategy until late 1963.
"The central dilemma," say the *Pentagon Papers* of the two years
between this growth in doubt and the 1965 decisions to intervene
in force, "lay in the fact that while United States policy objectives
were stated in the most comprehensive terms the means employed
were both consciously limited and purposely indirect . . . Declaratory policy raced far ahead of resource allocations and use decisions." The government used limited measures for limitless aims.[19] A
civilian-military difference that came to complicate policy making
in 1964 was that for those in uniform, the articulated policy was the
independent variable that should drive tactics; to the civilians, policy
was a dependent variable subject to reevaluation in light of tactical
results.

Early in 1964 the JCS majority stated that National Security

Action Memorandum 273 "makes clear the resolve of the President to ensure victory." Later they remonstrated that they "do not agree that we should be slow to get deeply involved . . . The United States is already deeply involved." Army leaders were not as anxious to become heavily involved in Vietnam as were those in the other services, but by the end of the year they were carried along. For the first half of 1964, the majority of the President's civilian advisers (with the exceptions of Ambassador Henry Cabot Lodge and Rostow) favored postponing coercion of North Vietnam through overt military force, while the Joint Chiefs regarded the covert operations authorized as militarily inadequate. Five times between February and June the Chiefs recommended a direct campaign of air strikes against North Vietnam, but cautioned in March that if the government chose such a course, it would have to resolve to carry it through successfully, regardless of cost.[20]

By the time of the August 1964 Gulf of Tonkin crisis (in which there was unanimity for retaliation), the disagreements between civilians and soldiers were not over increasing direct United States military pressure but over what form it should take. In May Mc-George Bundy had recommended force to President Johnson as the only path to success. But the civilian majority still favored the Office of International Security Affairs' limited-force approach; the military (except Taylor) favored rapid use of massive force. The Chiefs grudgingly obliged the civilians by providing scenarios and contingency plans for graduated pressure. But they criticized the lack of definition in United States objectives, claimed their duty was "to define a militarily valid objective for Southeast Asia and then advocate a desirable military course of action to achieve that objective," maintained that success required destruction of North Vietnam's capabilities to support the Vietcong, and complained that "some current thinking appears to dismiss that objective in favor of a lesser objective." They distinguished between destroying North Vietnamese capability and "an enforced changing of policy . . . which, if achieved, may well be temporary." After Tonkin Gulf they resubmitted their massive bombing proposal, recommended bombing in Laos, and reemphasized their disagreement with the reprisal concept. As the situation deteriorated, the civilians edged closer to the Chiefs' position, or beyond (Rostow recommended ground troops in November 1964), but as Taylor said, the government in 1964 was "still not ready to bite the bullet."[21] When the Vietcong attacked the United States air base at Bien Hoa and bombed a Saigon billet on Christmas eve, the military recommended air reprisals. The President held off, but his options were dwindling.

For ten years the United States had been nibbling the bullet in Vietnam. By the end of 1964 it was no longer possible for the President to defer the decision to intervene in force.

In February 1965, with a consensus of advisers behind him, Lyndon Johnson ordered the bombing of North Vietnam. This decision also made the first token commitment of troops on the ground inevitable. The first troop units were needed to provide perimeter security for the Danang air base. General Taylor, by then the ambassador, opposed Westmoreland's request for two marine battalion landing teams two weeks after the bombing missions began, cabling Rusk, "Once this policy is breached, it will be very difficult to hold line." Commitment of a conventional combat unit would be a watershed decision, not comparable to sending another increment of advisers or logistics personnel, and it would be almost impossible to reverse. Initially troops were used to garrison specific areas, but the enclave strategy was abandoned when the bombing failed to produce desired results.[22]

Analysts reluctant to believe that liberal administrations could purposely have led the nation into the massive commitment that resulted by 1968 have considered the military the primary culprits.[23] But the record does not bear out these accusations. It shows instead that Lyndon Johnson took the lead in promoting infusion of United State troops, hoping partial measures might stave off defeat, despite military warnings that they would not succeed.[24]

In May 1965 the Vietcong launched their spring offensive, and General Westmoreland feared they were about to cut the country in half. In early June he asked for forty-four battalions and freedom to use them in offensive operations (the search-and-destroy strategy). Taylor, now more worried, shifted his position and agreed. The military leaders did not predict that forty-four battalions would solve the problem, however. When the President asked if that number of troops would lead the enemy to desist, Westmoreland said no, claiming only that they would reverse the balance favorable to the Vietcong by the end of the year. If the United States were to take the initiative, more troops would be needed later. The commander asked a prominent visitor to United States headquarters at Military Assistance Command, Vietnam (MACV) later in 1965 to tell everyone in Washington that if he received the troops he asked for and all the breaks he needed, it would take six or seven years to turn the tide decisively.[25]

When the major commitment was being considered in June, the marine commandant and army chief of staff estimated that victory in the classic sense would require a minimum of 700,000 men and perhaps as many as 1.2 million. When the President asked the chairman of the Joint Chiefs what would be required, Wheeler replied that the answer depended on the goal. If eradication of the Vietcong was the job, it would take up to a million men and seven years; to maintain stability, a major force might have to remain for up to thirty years. If only prevention of communist victory was the goal, fewer would suffice. The President dismissed the estimate as absurd.[26] The civilians hoped for better results with less effort and were less pessimistic. They may have written off such estimates as typical military alarmism, a cynical move to cover themselves for posterity, or a bureaucratic ploy to ask for more than they needed, knowing they would get less.

In October 1966 McNamara recommended both stabilizing the air war and putting ceiling of 470,000 on the troop level. The Joint Chiefs disagreed with all of McNamara's recommendations, but nevertheless the President approved them a month later. By spring 1967 Westmoreland had the 470,000 troops and was requesting an "optimum" increase beyond the approved program to bring the troop total to 680,000 by June 1968. As a fallback, Westmoreland asked for a "minimum essential" increase of two and a third divisions to bring the level to 565,000. When the President asked what would happen without any increase, Westmoreland told him the United States could hold on effectively, but the war could continue as a "meatgrinder" for five years, or indefinitely. With the full increment, he predicted two more years of war, and with the 565,000 number, three years. John McNaughton, Office of International Security Affairs, who opposed the increases, was shocked at the predictions. McNamara held the ceiling to 525,000—40,000 fewer than Westmoreland's minimum. Part of the problem for the civilians in evaluating the estimates was that while pessimism drove military recommendations, good news characterized military reports. The contrast between Westmoreland's caution about the future and boastful good cheer about past accomplishments was remarkable.[27] With different stimuli to respond to, the civilians could still hope for the best.

Clashes over the air war were more acrimonious. The scope of bombing was extended slowly, following the gradualist strategy of the Office of International Security Affairs. To most military, they always received too little, too late. When McNamara rejected the Joint Chiefs' bombing plans at the beginning of 1965 and requested a less severe alternative, they suggested an eight-week program of graduated strikes. Air Force Chief John McConnell was especially adamant, however, that this alternative would not be successful. Within a month of the beginning of sustained bombing (the Rolling Thunder campaign) the Chiefs and the administration were again in opposition. The Chiefs asked to strike the first surface-to-air missile site that went up near Hanoi before it became operational. McNaughton claimed the sites would not be activated and opposed the move, fearing Russians might be killed. McNamara forbade it. The missiles were used after all and began taking a heavy toll of United States aircraft and crews. The Chiefs considered the early prohibition against bombing them almost criminally irresponsible.[28]

At the end of July McNamara was disappointed in the bombing's results and recommended to President Johnson that future bombing policy should emphasize threat, minimize North Vietnamese loss of face, and avoid undue risks of escalation. The bombing strategy then shifted to interdiction of supplies on the Ho Chi Minh trail. But the JCS remained committed to the by-then shopworn massive blitz approach. Beginning in September 1965, they issued, along with Commander in Chief, Pacific, U. S. G. Sharp, constant memos recommending strikes against industrial targets, especially oil supplies (POL). The initial proposal was rejected as a dangerous escalatory step, and the debate raged for more than nine months, while Rolling Thunder still failed to produce the overtures from North Vietnam that the civilians hoped for, before POL targets were finally authorized. In the interim, the Joint Chiefs, Sharp, and Westmoreland had all opposed the bombing pause from December 1965 to January 1966, maintaining that it gave North Vietnam time to recover, firm up defenses, and move massive amounts of supplies down the Ho Chi Minh trail unmolested. They also opposed the forty-eight-hour truce the following Christmas.[29] Limitations were gradually whittled away as the State Department and the Office of the Secretary of Defense's "carrot and stick" approach failed. Even more restrictions were lifted after the Senate air war hearings and McNamara's departure, but the Chiefs never got all the tactical freedom in targeting they sought until the end of American bombing in 1972.

The Tet offensive at the beginning of 1968 was the crest of the wave of American involvement. The shock it produced in Washington was amplified by the military request for reinforcement. This request catalyzed its own rejection. Because McNamara was leaving office, the pattern of internal negotiation was not repeated. The secretary did not go to Saigon to bargain with Westmoreland and shave requests to save the President from having to arbitrate between the professionals and the Office of the Secretary of Defense. Instead, JCS Chairman Wheeler went alone and brought pure military judgment back to the councils in Washington. If he had not done so, there might never have been the request for 206,000 new troops, the proposal that jolted the civilians and prompted the reassessment of policy.

To the military, Tet at first signaled different things. To Westmoreland in Vietnam it was comparable to the battle of the Bulge, the Vietcong throwing away all their best assets at once. To Wheeler in Washington it was the battle of Gettysburg, the Vietcong threatening to destroy the South Vietnamese regime. But to all of them it was an opportunity because they believed that now the President would have to loosen their leash and do what they had been pushing for: call up reserve units, replenish the empty stateside strategic reserve, ticket more troops to Southeast Asia, and escalate the war to include attacks on sanctuaries in Laos and Cambodia. Wheeler encouraged Westmoreland to make his request for 206,000 troops and then presented it in Washington as urgent without emphasizing the Chiefs' primary motive: to rebuild the stateside reserve. The gambit backfired. The civilian principals, who were initially disposed to a modest increase, were shocked by the magnitude of the figure, and the disillusioned assistant secretary–level working group began to make inroads on the principals' resolve. They converted the new secretary of defense, Clark Clifford, to their skeptical view and mobilized presidential consultants such as Dean Acheson and Generals Bradley and Ridgway to tell Johnson that strategy had failed and deescalation was the best alternative.[30] The President subsequently curtailed the bombing, held troop reinforcements to an emergency boost of fewer than 11,000, sought negotiations, and dropped out of the election race.

President Nixon began the first large troop withdrawals, but the withdrawal schedule forced a decision in spring 1970. If the United States was to attack North Vietnamese sanctuaries and logistics complexes in Cambodia, it had to act then. The military favored this move and top civilian advisers were more cautious, but the President made his decision to authorize the incursion basically alone. As Vietnamization unfolded after Cambodia, the administration was divided between Henry Kissinger and military leaders who favored slow withdrawal on one hand and Secretary of Defense Laird who favored rapid withdrawal on the other. Laird's military assistant, air force Major General Robert Pursley, was influential in convincing the secretary to push for faster stand-down. The Joint Chiefs and the command in Vietnam feared the withdrawal pace would destabilize the battlefield balance. Nixon compromised. In mid-1971 he accepted Laird's goal for numbers to be withdrawn within a year but privately let the military delay the resumption of the move for two months.[31]

By early 1972 the last United States infantry units were gone from Vietnam. When the North Vietnamese launched their conventional invasion of the northern provinces in the spring, no one considered sending United States troops back, although Nixon decided—with strong military support—to mine Haiphong harbor and resume American bombing. Most of the military leaders fought to the end to maximize United States aid to South Vietnam and minimize concessions in negotiations. According to one report, the Joint Chiefs and Commander in Chief, Pacific, Noel Gayler were the spoilers behind the collapse of the Paris negotiations after Kissinger's "peace is at hand" statement in October 1972, issuing grave warnings that the proposed agreement would leave the survival of a noncommunist regime in doubt. Haig, Kissinger's deputy, also complained privately that his boss was conceding too much. Most of the military were gratified, though, when Nixon authorized the intense bombing campaign against Hanoi in December—the closest they ever came to the kind of bombing they had recommended eight years earlier. After the peace accords, when debates on military assistance grew in the year prior to the communist victory, the top United States military representative in Vietnam, Major General John Murray, criticized aid cuts for causing ammunition shortages and increasing South Vietnamese army casualties. He was hustled home shortly thereafter, severely reprimanded in the Pentagon, and retired.[32] When South Vietnam collapsed in 1975 there was no military assistance command in Saigon to mourn the passing or to fulminate for more American resolve. The odyssey from firm military opposition to war on the ground in Indochina to bitter military resignation to defeat in just such a war had lasted more than two decades.

3 Professionalism, Position, and Power: The Background of Influence

With politicians, the question is whether they're going to use you, or you're going to use them ... To use them, you must begin by making them think they're using you.

Colonel Ross's wife, in
James Gould Cozzens, *Guard of Honor*

There was a time when military responsibility was appreciated, when the civilians trusted us to do our jobs. The civilians really began to move in after the Defense Department was created. But when McNamara and his boys came, thinking that amateurs could run the Pentagon better than we could, the military lost the last vestiges of meaningful authority. Those kids got to ordering two- and three-star generals around and the power went to their heads. I never saw the military more abject.

An air force brigadier general

THE potential for American military professionals to wield influence depends on the nature of their relation to superior executive and legislative authorities. At the same time, the different institutional interests of the President and Congress may lead one branch of political authority to encourage military behavior inconsistent with the demands of the other. To understand military influence on use of force, it is necessary to understand systems of civilian control that administrations have imposed and avenues of redress that disaffected soldiers can exploit.

PROFESSIONALISM AND EXECUTIVE AUTHORITY: BUREAUCRATIC POLITICS AND CIVILIAN CONTROL

Traditional administrative theory posits a dichotomy between politics and administration: elected leaders and political appointees establish policy; politically neutral career bureaucrats execute the politicians' decisions. The conception is identical to the traditional military principles discussed earlier. The corollary of these assumptions in civil-military relations theory is Samuel Huntington's model of objective civilian control, which prescribes keeping the soldiers politically neutral by segregating political and military roles in government, restricting military participation in policy making to advice about the military implications of decisions. Civilian authorities accomplish the integration or balancing of the military implications with differing political, economic, or social considerations. The alternative to this system is subjective control through the fusion of military and political roles, coopting and identifying the military with the administration's political goals and the values of society at large. "Subjective control is fundamentally out of place," according to Huntington, "in any society in which the division of labor has been carried to the point where there emerges a distinct class of specialists in the management of violence."[1]

Traditional administration theory has been challenged, especially since the vast growth in bureaucracy following the New Deal, by those who argue that a division of labor between political and administrative roles is impossible. Programs and decisions are so numerous, top political leadership so overburdened and lacking in information, and the relations between policy and implementation so entangled that career bureaucrats and professionals are inevitably political actors rather than neutral executors. In this view, a President who tries to live by traditional administrative wisdom, such as Eisenhower, cedes the effective power to subordinates who deal with details, becomes the prisoner of decisions made below him, and is only an arbiter, not a leader. The model of presidential political control, according to this theory, is Franklin Roosevelt, who dominated his burgeoning bureaucracies by politicizing them, by placing trusted lieutenants in middle-level positions, and by encouraging overlapping of jurisdictions, proliferation of communication channels, and bureaucratic competition and conflict to force issues to the top, maximizing the President's range of choice. To this school of thought, which I call bureaucratic revisionism,[2] objective control can be only an impracticable illusion that threatens to weaken a President against his military subordinates. Because of the complexity of defense and foreign policy, political, diplomatic, and military functions are inevitably fused. Political and military roles cannot be segregated without endangering presidential control of the outcomes of his decisions.[3] Some form of subjective control is the only astute strategy for a President who wants his generals to serve him rather than constrain him.

Both traditional administrative theory and bureaucratic revisionism are stark ideal types of the policy-making process, and reality can lie along the continuum between them. Toward which end of the continuum it lies, however, determines which system of civil-military relations—objective or subjective control—is most plausible. Moreover, although there are limits to how close an administration can come to one system or the other, it can move in either direction with its organizational choices. The critical problem is how the roles of professional experts and political generalists interact.

Within the government, various agencies' interests differ from each other, and career professionals' perspectives may conflict with the political interests or ideologies of the President and his appointees in the bureaucracy. Traditional administrative theory can allow some autonomy to professionals because they are subordinated to political appointees in the administration who enforce the chief executive's policy. These appointees combine partisan loyalty and authority; the professionals combine loyalty and expertise, which can be applied to dictated ends. By subordinating the latter group to the former, democracy subordinates bureaucracy and technocracy. Objective control is practicable because the political leaders are free to reject specialized professional advice on generalized political grounds, and the politicians keep the professionals honest by their direct authority over them. The professionals can compromise this control, though, to the extent that their indirect power (control of information and expertise) makes their superiors dependent on them—which is a vast extent, in the bureaucratic revisionist view. For these reasons, objective control theorists see the postwar trend in military influence as a decline since their direct influence over foreign policy has declined. Bureaucratic revisionists point to a rise, since they focus on indirect influence, which has increased. For the same reasons as well, military influence on escalation decisions is often higher than on intervention decisions, since during war the military have more of a monopoly of information and intelligence than they do in prewar situations. McNamara recognized the political importance of information and expertise and deliberately institutionalized analytical staffs in the Office of the Secretary of Defense with advocacy status independent of the military.

In the Eisenhower administration, most of whose political executives had previously been in business, the secretary of defense and his subcabinet lacked confidence in their military expertise and exercised their control mainly through fiscal limitations and broad policy guidelines. The professionals were left to adapt the details of strategy within these constraints. This method accorded with Eisenhower's traditional administrative style, which maximized delegation of authority. The President reserved his attention and discretion to issues that reached the National Security Council level. He did not compromise the chain of command by asking lower-echelon officials for opinions or information, as his successor was known to do, and he even resisted resolving disagreements among the Joint Chiefs, demanding instead that they settle their own disputes. In the Kennedy and Johnson administrations, the secretary of defense was an activist who determined to lead rather than judge with a large corps of executives who had confidence in their ability to make military decisions. These men came from areas not widely tapped by the preceding Republicans. They included operations research specialists, systems analysts, and academic strategic theorists (who acted mainly as consultants). More importantly, Kennedy could draw on a corps of in-and-outers—executives who move back and forth between private life and government service—with Pentagon experience such as Roswell Gilpatric and Paul Nitze. Backed by McNamara, all these people enlarged the scope of political direction at the expense of that of professional authority.[4] National politics made this organizational strategy possible. In 1961 only eight years had elapsed since the last Democratic administration. In 1953 the Republicans had been out of power for twenty years—a generation in chronological terms and an era in military terms—and Eisenhower had fewer political executives with relevant experience from whom to choose. In 1977 President Carter had the same opportunity and flexibility as Kennedy.

The Kennedy-McNamara approach assumed the fusion of political and military roles. The corollary for military advice on use of force, inspired in part by the President's irritation with the failure of the Joint Chiefs to speak out against the Bay of Pigs plan, was a presidential National Security Action Memorandum (NSAM 55) instructing them to consider political and economic factors when making recommendations. "I look to the Chiefs . . . to be more than military men," Kennedy enjoined. Lyndon Johnson later reaffirmed this directive. Except for Taylor, however, the Chiefs did not accept this mandate with enthusiasm. They preferred to be no more— and no less—than military men, respected in their jurisdiction as generals rather than patronized as generalists. Reticence to accept a political role went hand in hand with resistance to being dispossessed within the Pentagon in management and strategic planning by McNamara's civilian analysts. As subsequent years came to show, the Chiefs did not fully adhere to the logic of the directive; rarely did they temper their military perspective with political judgment. In 1962 Earle Wheeler still ignored the interdependence of political and military factors, arguing, "It is fashionable in some quarters to say that the problems in Southeast Asia are primarily political and economic rather than military. I do not agree. The essence of the problem in Vietnam is military."[5]

Fusion of roles in the 1960s was a qualified success. McNamara's managerial fusion, injecting civilians into previously military functions in the Pentagon, did work. But the attempt to extend fusion in the other direction by enmeshing the professional soldiers in the political directorate of the administration did not. The soldiers became substantial political actors without becoming substantially politically conscious. The administration imposed effective control over the Defense Department but did not get the military support for policy that it wanted. And while political executives could successfully reduce their dependence on subordinates, they could not eliminate it.

Since professionals operating at the policy level of an administration do not come in laterally as do political executives, it is impossible to guarantee either their political identification with administration political goals or their sensitivity to domestic political constraints. Political perspectives are unavoidably tempered by professional perspectives. For example, General George Brown's notorious comments about the Israel lobby in 1974 were both unprofessionally political and professionally impolitic. They probably were rooted more in professional realpolitik uneasiness about the drain on American resources and commitment in the Middle East than in anti-Semitism and reflected both responsiveness to organizational interests and external strategic interests, along with insensitivity to domestic social values and political imperatives. Similarly, most of the anti-Zionist opposition by foreign service officers to the partition of Palestine in 1947 probably was rooted in perceptions of external diplomatic and economic national interests rather than any domestic political interests of the Truman administration.

Professionals differ as much from each other, though, as they do from politicians. The divergence in military and diplomatic responsibilities can lead to different views of the same crisis. The ambassador and regional assistant secretary of state may not agree with the chief of the military assistance advisory group and chairman of the Joint Chiefs of Staff. Such differences, in turn, can serve the interests of the political leaders just as intramilitary disagreements do. They increase the range of both analysis, evaluation, and alternative advice on which the President can base a decision and of political leaders' choice by reducing the leverage of the professionals, whose disunity may allow the political executives to dominate them and win.

Diplomats value flexibility and seek to resolve crises through negotiation. In the view of military men, foreign service officers tend to feel that if force becomes necessary they have failed; military intervention is a reflection of the inadequacy of the State Department. Diplomatic success, though, may require making military threats to deter adversaries or bluff them into coming to terms. Military men, however, value certainty, are wary of bluffs, and oppose making threats that will not be enforced if the bluff fails. They consider superior combat capability the best means of deterrence. Diplomats prefer to avoid a decision to use force until the last moment; military officials prefer an early decision on action so that operational efficiency can be maximized and units can be alerted, readied for deployment, and positioned, so that if force has to be used, it can be done before the enemy has time to firm up defenses and the military odds for success diminish.[6] As one aggressive chief of naval operations put it, State Department officials try to postpone action so that "maybe the problem will go away. And the hell of it is, sometimes it does."[7] Both soldiers and diplomats participate in decisions on the use of force as reporters and advisers, but the critical difference between them is the additional military responsibility for operational implementation. If intervention is decided, the primary diplomatic job is done; the primary military job is just beginning. This difference in priorities and perspectives can make military advisers seem more aggressive than diplomatic advisers, more timid, or even both at the same time. There were instances after World War II when the diplomats were more bellicose than the generals, such as when Yugoslavia shot down an American plane in 1946. Major General Lauris Norstad complained to Defense Secretary James Forrestal that "contrary to public impression—it was usually the military people who had to hold back the sporadic and truculent impulses of political people and diplomats who do not realize the consequences of aggressive action."[8]

Franklin Roosevelt distrusted the foreign service and squeezed the State Department out of an important role in the decisions of World War II. He placed soldiers in important diplomatic positions (including ambassadors to the Soviet Union and China and a secretary of state) during the war, as Truman did later. Many military officers became top-level diplomats in the Department of State (Dean Rusk was among them). These changes made some military men apprehensive, including Norstad, who feared that the trend would damage the military. The State Department regained its previous position of importance in the late 1940s, in one view because of the increased number of foreign service officers who were often more strongly anticommunist than the military. The result, however, was a disjunction of foreign policy and military policy: demobilization coincided with rising U.S.-Soviet tension. The soldiers were caught between diplomats who increased their commitments and budget cutters who pruned their resources.[9] Later, in the 1961 Berlin crisis, there were no significant military-civilian cleavages on the Berlin task force, the special planning unit established to monitor the problem. But the military members were more conservative and cautious because of their sensitivity to the operational complications implicit in any scenario of possible conflict and their responsibility for implementing any tactical operation. The civilian planners were more interested in the need to show firmness and the political signals a limited military move would convey.[10]

Military concern with enemy capabilities rather than intentions occasionally creates an ambiguous situation where diplomats advocate a middle-road action between two extremes of ambivalent military advice. In an April National Security Council meeting in the Laos crisis of 1961, one week after the Bay of Pigs fiasco, most civilian participants tentatively favored a limited show of force in Southeast Asia, which they hoped would produce diplomatic results. Averell Harriman supported the proposal of Walt Rostow, who wanted to send 25,000 troops to Thailand ready for deployment to Laos so that he would have some bargaining chips in the coming Geneva negotiations on Laos. The Joint Chiefs, on the other hand, seemed to waver between timid opposition to any military intervention and a frightening proviso that they be given the option to use tactical nuclear weapons if United States force was committed. Actually the military—especially Army Chief of Staff George Decker—wanted to avoid a show of force or a limited action which could end in disaster. They wanted either massive commitment sufficient to win or a complete avoidance of military entanglement.[11] Their concern with operational success took precedence over a concern with political signalling. The ultimate impact that their equivocal stance had on the decision was dovish, though some civilians saw it as recklessly hawkish because of the mention of nuclear weapons.

What seemed like military indecisiveness in this case contrasts with the common image of military advisers as overly confident and certain, so much so that they seem to dwarf less crisply efficient State Department personnel. The speed of military planning and presentation of options typically did outstrip the more viscous pace of the State Department in the 1960s. (This is a significant fact because bureaucratic revisionists tend to argue that the *availability* of military options induces political leaders to choose them.) The military have this advantage in presenting options in part because there is no analogue in the State Department for either the Joint Staff or the Joint Chiefs of Staff. State's Policy Planning Staff was designed as an elite group of creative thinkers, not a program-planning organ. The line of demarcation between professionals and political executives is also drawn much less explicitly in the State Department than in Defense. But the de facto distinction is not all that much clearer among the military than among the diplomats.

In traditional administration theory, there is a clear demarcation between political officials and professionals. The second Hoover Commission recommended that the line be established just above the bureau chief level.[12] The professionals are kept clear of political influence by being low in the bureaucracy, and they maintain a preserve of authority because the politicians remain high in the bureaucracy. Bureaucratic revisionists would add two more types between these extremes: political appointees with professional experience and expertise and career professionals with political skill and involvement (see figure 1). A revisionist administrative strategy extends political control further down by making political appointments at low levels in the bureaucracy and by expanding the size, purview, and authority of cabinet staffs (McNamara's Office of the Secretary of Defense) or White House staffs (the National Security Council under Kissinger until 1973). Development of a corps of in-and-outers with enough experience to have pretensions to real

FIGURE 1. Politicos, professionals, and the gray area.

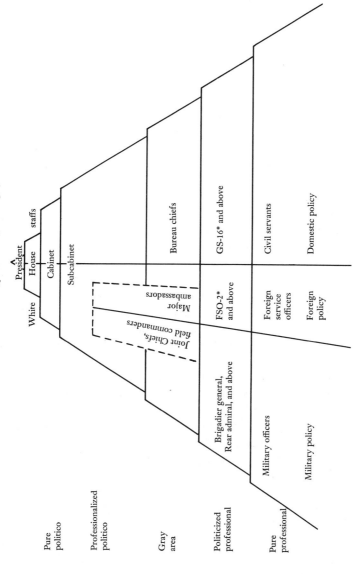

* Ranks in foreign service and civil service just below the highest career level (FSO-1 and GS-18).

professional expertise also blurs the distinction between political executives and professionals within the bureaucracy, and the tendency to appoint people experienced in government service to political posts is most pronounced in the State and Defense departments.[13]

Bureaucratic revisionists stress the antagonism between the President, responsible for ranking priorities and reconciling tradeoffs between competing interests, and parochial bureaucrats, unable to distinguish their partial organizational interests from the general national interest. The problem with this formulation is that it is both too bureaucratic, overemphasizing the parochialism of top (cabinet-level) officials, and not bureaucratic enough, glossing over the differences between political appointees and careerists in a department.

Cabinet members are much more likely to be attuned to presidential interests and to share a broad political perspective than are their respective subordinate professionals.[14] Miles' law—"Where one stands depends on where one sits"—is least valid at the top of the hierarchy and most valid at the bottom.[15] Careerist professionals are more likely to have a narrow range of opinion than generalist political appointees. Middle-level administrators with strongly vested organizational interests are more likely to be special pleaders than are in-and-outers whose rewards come from the White House. Military men are all careerists, but some are less parochial than others. Research indicates, for instance, that among officers serving in the Pentagon, opposition to civilian viewpoints was highest among low-ranking officers and lowest among the high ranks.[16]

The Joint Chiefs of Staff are likely to be less parochial than colonels or others lower in rank. They recognize that their decisions and recommendations have political impact, even if they resist making political decisions themselves. But because their latent political function is still secondary to their manifest professional identity, they are more parochial than the top civilians in the Pentagon. They rarely admit a conflict between their organizational interests and ideologies and their political responsibility. Military men tenaciously favor the traditional administrative theory of roles and usually see themselves as objective professionals, brought into political controversy by the incompetence of amateurs in authority.

Political executives and career professionals have contrasting perspectives, responsibilities, and interests; these differences occasionally bring them into conflict. But the administrative process is not one of victimization of one group by the other; it is more a sinuous process of mutual manipulation. Objective control theory stresses the extent to which political leaders domesticated military professionals after 1940; bureaucratic revisionism stresses the extent to which careerists tame naive political executives. Objective control theorists focus on the acquiescence of military leaders to liberal civilian strategy in World War II and the leadership of civilian strategists in the containment era. Revisionists look at the ways in which political officials' inexperience makes them dependent on subordinate professionals and can cite, for example, the extent to which service secretaries become spokesmen for service interests as well as enforcers of departmental and presidential priorities.[17] Bureaucratic revisionists are more concerned about how the professionals constrict the choices of the politicians than the reverse because organizational parochialism in concert with organizational autonomy threatens presidential power and control of policy; broad political control is more important than narrow professional efficiency. Traditional administrative theory fears overcentralization of authority in the hands of presidential minions because these political lieutenants lack the substantive expertise of the professional generals.

Both problems are real, which is why both the political appointees and the professionals see their proper authority threatened by the other. At issue is the tradeoff between control and expertise. Imbalance on either side may have positive or negative effects, depending on the particular values and expertise involved. James Thomson, a former official, criticized the "banishment of real expertise" in Vietnam policy making; important decisions were made by political generalists without the benefit of the knowledge and opinions of professional Asian specialists.[18] He might be surprised, though, to find that military men agreed in principle but believed that it was *their* expertise that was improperly discounted by political executives. Similarly, some Democratic bureaucratic revisionists who chafed at the subversion of political leadership's goals by officialdom's inertia in the 1960s welcomed such inertia in the 1970s when an activist Republican President trying to centralize administrative authority in the White House had inherited a bureaucracy full of New Dealers, New Frontiersmen, and Great Society recruits who lacked enthusiasm for administration policy. In this context, "civilmilitary relations" may be subsumed under "political-professional relations." In the 1960s military professionals felt degraded and dispossessed by the so-called whiz kids in Defense, while Secretary McNamara felt the services obstructed him within his department and undercut him on Capitol Hill. In the early 1970s, Nixon distrusted the diplomatic professionals in the State Department bureaucracy and centralized foreign policy in Kissinger's National

Security Council committees, which led the foreign service officers to feel excluded. This disfrancisement of professionals by political leaders in both cases reflected a desire of the President to exercise greater control, as well as the lack of awe for professional expertise felt by top political executives (McNamara and Kissinger).

Bureaucratic revisionists may justly criticize traditional administration theorists for overemphasizing the significance of formal authority as a means of policing the professionals, but they tend to overstate the degree to which military experts imprison their political superiors by controlling information and narrowing options. This happened more under Eisenhower than in succeeding administrations. Moreover, the image of entrenched experts whose years of experience in a job make a political generalist no match was erroneous in Democratic administrations. The average tenure of service chiefs was only marginally longer than that of political executives, and the rotation system, which limits the time an officer spends in a Pentagon job usually to a maximum of three years, combined with the bureaucratic experience of many Democratic political executives, tends to equalize the manipulative ability of political executives and military professionals in many administrations.[19] Complaints by critics of the military that civilian control of the Pentagon is an illusion are more hyperbole than analysis, just as traditional administration theory's emphasis on role distinction and formal authority discounts indirect sources of influence and power too much. Whatever the antagonism between the interest and ideologies of the professionals and political executives may be, the battle of civilian control within the executive is more of a standoff than either military critics or apologists will admit.

What complicates the problem of discerning and institutionalizing the proper relations between professionals and politicians is that the politicians—specifically, the executive and Congress—are not all on one side. Because of the growth of the executive power after Hoover, Congress's role shifted increasingly from legislative initiative to oversight of the executive. Only recently did congressional reforms and aggravation of legislative-executive tension by the division of party control of the two branches under Nixon and Ford reverse this process. The legislators found that placing checks on presidential power or policy may require protecting experts from the whims of an administration, preserving the independence of the service chiefs and careerists who can criticize or provide alternative perspectives on executive programs. The Joint Chiefs in the cold war found themselves in the middle of the executive pyramid administratively and at one end of a constitutional triangle politically.

Divided Loyalties:
The Military and Congress

Although Congress has a smaller role in foreign policy than in domestic issues, it does have budgetary power over the military. The State Department budget is negligible, but the size of military appropriations and the legislative authorizations required for procurement programs give legislators a veto over executive policy and enhance the lobbying function of Congress in the process of executive legislation of strategy. Legislators can be either antagonists or allies of the President where professional soldiers are concerned. As Max Weber wrote:

> There are born politicians, but they are rare. The monarch who is not one of them becomes a threat to his own and to the state's interests if he attempts to govern by himself, as did the Tsar ... However, this temptation—nay, necessity—arises inevitably for a modern monarch if he is confronted only by bureaucrats, that means ... If there is no powerful parliament, the monarch is today dependent upon the reports of officials for the supervision of the work of other officials. This is a vicious circle. The continuous war of the various ministries against one another ... is the natural consequence of such allegedly "monarchic" governments without a *political* leader.[20]

Congress and the President can have this common interest in Congress's oversight capacity in periods when the policy divisions pit politicians against professionals or when military policy is relatively unimportant, as before World War II. But James Madison and the other founding fathers had other concerns and did not envision a federal bureaucracy of thousands of officials. A strong Congress can help a weak President control the military, but it obstructs a strong President, one of Weber's "born politicians," who embodies bureaucratic revisionist virtues. When there are policy differences between the President and Congress, the harmony of interest breaks down. This was periodically the case in the late 1950s, when congressional liberals favored higher military spending than the administration;[21] more so in the late 1960s, when conservative Armed Services Committees looked askance at the power of the Office of the Secretary of Defense and trusted the Joint Chiefs more; and in the early 1970s, when congressional liberals favored lower defense spending than did the administration. The pattern in the first days of the Carter administration was mixed; the Senate Foreign Relations Committee supported the President's first initiatives on arms control by rallying behind the nomination of Paul Warnke to direct the Arms Control and Disarmament Agency, while the Armed Services Committee gave more support to critics who shared the military's alarm over the Soviet strategic buildup.

The situation is most awkward when there is a disagreement between the military and the administration and the military are supported within Congress. It is most likely to occur when there is a realignment of basic national security strategy that contradicts service interests or ideologies. This problem arose under Eisenhower, when the New Look defense policy imposed budgetary and strategic constraints that hurt the army, and under Kennedy and Johnson, when the flexible response policy reduced the importance of the strategic missions of the air force and navy. The legislative-executive relations problem was less severe in the first case because there was only minority military disaffection (one service), because low budgets accorded with the congressional economy norm, and because Eisenhower could use his personal military prestige in imposing limitations on military spending. Legislative reaction was stronger in the 1960s because there was majority military disaffection from administration strategy (two services in the early 1960s and all services in the late 1960s), and because McNamara's centralization of power in the Office of the Secretary of Defense threatened the legislative-executive balance of power by increasing congressional reliance on the civilian secretariat for information and evalution. In 1966, for example, the House Armed Services Committee attacked McNamara's selection of weapons systems, which had roused the ire of the air force and navy, and stipulated in the defense procurement and research authorization bill that the secretary was prohibited from eliminating any major system without first reporting all details to Congress. The committee report accused McNamara of overruling "sound military recommendations" by the Joint Chiefs, misleading Congress about the Chiefs' proposals, and harboring an "almost obsessional dedication to cost effectiveness [which] raises the specter of a decisionmaker who ... knows the price of everything and the value of nothing."[22]

Under these circumstances the committees rely on and encourage "end runs" by the military leaders around their executive superiors, that is, public disagreements, such as LeMay's testimony for manned bombers and Anderson's testimony against the TFX airplane, both of which contradicted administration procurement policy. This ability of the Chiefs to undercut the administration in turn prompts the President to try to keep them under control (ideally) or at least to disarm them in public debate. Kennedy reminded the reluctant Chiefs, two years after his post–Bay of Pigs directive, that they were to consider the political benefits in deciding whether to endorse the 1963 limited test ban treaty. Because of the presidential pressure, they did back the treaty, only to have Senator Bourke Hickenlooper criticize their stand because it was based on political grounds. The President can also try to prevent end runs, by exhortation as Johnson did by telling Curtis LeMay not to do against him on the Hill while he was President what he had done for him when he was in the Senate (prime members to ask questions that would require a response critical of administration policy). But his only sure means of discipline is retaliation by firing a chief, which is a rare and politically costly step. The means at the President's disposal for silencing the Chiefs are limited because the National Security Act in effect mandates end runs by reinforcing military access to Congress, and because congressional leaders exact commitments from the Chiefs in their confirmation hearings to keep Congress informed of their disagreements with the administration.[23]

This congressional concern with preventing administration suppression of professional opinion is an old one. Immediately after Truman relieved MacArthur in 1951, following, among other actions a letter by MacArthur to House minority leader Joseph Martin, a law was passed providing that no member of the armed forces could be prevented from communicating with any member of Congress. In 1958, Eisenhower asked the House to delete provisions from pending legislation that would have allowed service chiefs to make proposals to Congress on their own initiative, which he considered "legal insubordination." In Senate hearings Arleigh Burke, chief of naval operations, supported the bill against the President, and Senator Richard Russell demanded assurance that no reprisals would be taken against Burke or any other officer who opposed the President's view. "Legal insubordination" was exactly what many legislators wanted. (The final bill, the Defense Department Reorganization Act of 1958, watered down the controversial House provisions.)[24] This tendency to limit presidential control of the military is a natural extension of constitutional checks and balances in a situation where the executive branch has outstripped Congress in size and analytical resources. Congress oversees the executive by dividing it against itself. In the face of this situation, the President has few options at his disposal to discipline service chiefs short of replacing them. This forces the Joint Chiefs into a tenuous position between presidential and congressional demands. Thus, Congress has a political interest and the military have a professional interest in ensuring job security for the Chiefs while the administration interest is to preserve the maximum discretion of the President to replace them. In this context, controversy over the tenure of service chiefs was almost inevitable.

Military rotation, combined with the development of the retirement system, has produced a tradition of regular turnover of service chiefs in this century. Chief of staff became a term assignment, but with the exception of legislation fixing the term of the commandant of the marine corps, this was by custom rather than statute until the past decade. In 1967 Congress legislated four-year, nonrenewable terms for service chiefs and two-year terms, renewable once, for chairman of the Joint Chiefs. The President retained the right to fire a chief for cause. This legislation, designed to safeguard the objectivity of the Chiefs by guaranteeing their security and removing the temptation to curry favor with the administration, capped a long-standing controversy over JCS terms.

The dispute had begun years earlier. Army Chief of Staff J. Lawton Collins criticized Eisenhower for reducing the normal term for service chiefs from four years to two, arguing that the short term forced a Chief to campaign for reappointment, pressured him to conform to administration policies, and inhibited frank and honest professional judgment. Most officers seconded Collins's views. President Kennedy continued Eisenhower's short appointment pattern, feeling that "compatibility with the President's thinking was as important in the Joint Chiefs...as in the head of any civilian department." But several incidents in Kennedy's handling of Joint Chiefs of Staff appointments provoked some House Armed Services Committee members to push for mandatory four-year terms in 1963. Chairman Lyman Lemnitzer, Chief of Staff of the Army George Decker, and Chief of Naval Operations George Anderson were not reappointed, and air force Chief Curtis LeMay was reappointed for only one year. Carl Vinson then introduced legislation providing nonrenewable four-year terms for Chiefs and the chairman. The bill was supported heavily by active and retired service chiefs and opposed vigorously by Deputy Secretary of Defense Roswell Gilpatric and Secretary of the Army Cyrus Vance in hearings. Kennedy planned to veto the bill if it passed. Ten committee Democrats supported the administration position that the measure would impair the President's commander-in-chief powers, though, and the bill died in committee.[25] Four years later at the height of the Vietnam War, with some congressmen worried about the President's muzzling of dissent by the Chiefs, the bill was resurrected and passed, with the change differentiating the length and renewability of the chairman's term from that of the service chiefs. Civil-military relations were a secondary issue in this controversy. Congress, the weaker branch of the political estate, was maintaining its power by allying with the professional estate, constraining disagreeable presidential policy by compromising the integrity of the chain of command. This triangular tension consequently gives the President an incentive to ensure loyalty of the Chiefs by subjective control, appointing men who share his political values and perspectives and who are personally committed to his programs. This presidential control in turn increases congressional attempts to keep the Chiefs independent. If the President aims for fusion of military and political identities in his military advisers, Congress tries to preserve military leaders' professional autonomy.

Divided military loyalties were usually no problem in intervention decisions because use of force before the 1973 War Powers Act was an executive decision. Congress was usually not consulted in the postwar era, except as individuals. There are also only rarely cases where consulted congressmen and military chiefs together opposed an administration decision, and when it happened it had nothing to do with legislative-executive rivalry. Examples of such divisions were the 1954 Indochina crisis, when consulted congressmen such as John McCormack and Lyndon Johnson joined the army chief of staff and naval chief in opposition to an air strike, and the 1962 Cuban crisis, when consulted congressmen, including J. W. Fulbright and Richard Russell, agreed with the military in advising much stronger measures than the blockade. But there are relatively few cases in which legislators are willing to recommend a specific course of action.[26]

The military-congressional connection can be a problem in regard to escalation decisions in an ongoing conflict. Three examples are the 1951 MacArthur hearings, the 1966 Fulbright Vietnam policy hearings, and the 1967 Stennis committee air-war hearings. In the first case, some military officers opposed administration strategy in Korea and recommended escalation, while others (the Joint Chiefs and Secretary of Defense Marshall) supported the President. Nevertheless, the administration continued its limited strategy, and the soldiers who supported it suffered when the Republicans came into office and adopted the philosophy of the military dissidents in its new defense policy. In the second case, no military testimony opposed administration policy, although retired Lieutenant General James Gavin recommended restraint and consolidation rather than escalation. The result was politically neutral, since the political consensus on war policy had not yet fully disintegrated. In the third case, all military spokesmen opposed administration limits on bombing targets. As it had done in Korea, the administration continued its limited policy, but the Chiefs did not suffer blame when the Republicans came to power a year and a half later because they had not been administration partisans. The Democratic administration in 1951 had more to fear than the one in 1967 from hostile congressional investigations because vocal opinion favored the dovish side more in the Vietnam case, which might have countered the leverage of congressional and military hawks against the administration. President Johnson did not fully realize the ramifications or he placed more weight on opinion polls showing that the disaffection of the intellectuals was not paralleled in the public as a whole.[27] Like generals preparing to fight the last war, he prepared to win the last election. He saw right-wing demands for escalation as a greater threat than the antiwar left until the Tet offensive and the 1968 New Hampshire primary. Shortly before Tet he decided to replace McNamara, whose doubts about continued bombing of North Vietnam had widened the cleavage between him and the Joint Chiefs and had surfaced visibly in the air-war hearings. The lesson Johnson drew from Korea and McCarthyism was that a congressional-military alliance protesting tactical restraint and rejection of military judgment was more dangerous to an administration than liberals complaining of too much military influence.

Congress can help the administration and both branches of government can be partners in civilian control of the military when the common political interests of the politicians vis à vis the professionals outweigh the differences in institutional interests of legislative and executive branches. Or the executive does not have to worry about divided military loyalties if the administration and Congress differ on military policy but Congress does not support service interests, as in the early 1970s when the administration's position was between the services and antimilitary or economy-minded legislators.[28] But when Congress's stance lies between administration policy and military interests, the military-congressional connection is destructive of the goals of both objective control and bureaucratic revisionism because both of these theories, while disagreeing on means, share the end of subordinating the military to executive political control. Objective control theory recognizes the constitutional tradeoffs between intrabranch political control of administrators and professionals and interbranch political checks and balances and accepts them as the price of democracy. And those who value a strong Congress would not see military-congressional collusion as uniformly harmful. Bureaucratic revisionist theorists, on the other hand, have rarely considered in detail the problems of legislative oversight. With their focus on the desirability of strong presidential control of subordinates, congressional critics seeking to subvert the chain of command are usually considered destructive.[29] A revisionist administrative strategy of identifying military leadership with the administration in power serves to blunt the leverage the soldiers can obtain from their relationship with Congress. One significant difference between objective control theorists and bureaucratic revisionists is that the latter see few virtues (if any) in professional autonomy and think that subjective control—ensuring presidential power over careerists by placing presidential agents in crucial military offices—is a useful and valid method of civilian control of the military.

MILITARY AND POLITICAL ROLES:
THE CHOICE AND COSTS OF INTEGRATION

Integration or separation of military and political roles is a choice that depends on the goals to be served. At one pole is the principle of objective control and segregation of roles, which maximizes professionalism to minimize the dangers of military politicization. At the other extreme is the alternative of subjective control and fusion, which invests the soldiers with political responsibility to minimize the dangers of narrow professionalism. Administrations have instituted civil-military relationships at different points between these extremes. Either alternative poses costs and benefits, and the choice depends on beliefs about the ability to distinguish policy from tactics in international relations, the quality and reliability of military expertise, and the competence of civilian administrators to challenge military judgment on operational matters. Rather than preventing military involvement in politics, subjective control presupposes it, argue Samuel Huntington and other traditionalists. To the revisionists, that is exactly the point.

The primary cost of objective control is the danger of too much military autonomy. The Nixon administration salved the military's alienation under President Johnson over strict civilian control of bombing target selection by relaxing the rules of engagement and civilian clearances required for tactical operations. A result was that the Seventh Air Force commander, General John Lavelle, was able to conduct twenty unauthorized bombings between November 1971 and March 1972, which apparently sabotaged administration negotiating strategy by provoking Le Duc Tho to cancel secret talks with Kissinger. Though the evidence is weak and incomplete, there is reason to believe that there was military complicity in these bombings at levels higher than Lavelle's headquarters. The incident led the administration to tighten up command and control, virtually to the former Johnson-McNamara level.[30] Notwithstanding suspicions that the administration had known about and tolerated military disregard of the bombing ban, the Lavelle affair resurrected traditional fears of a "man on horseback" with too much professional autonomy. To those who believe in objective control, cultivation of professionalism is a prerequisite for political neutralization of the military, but for critics of the theory who cite Lavelle, it is the prime threat to neutralization. Samuel Finer argues, for example, that professionalism is not automatically consistent with civil supremacy because the military may think their loyalty is due to the transcendent state rather than to the transitory government.[31] The prime American example of this problem in the postwar era was Douglas MacArthur, who complained after Truman fired him:

> I find in existence a new and heretofore unknown and dangerous concept that the members of our armed forces owe primary allegiance to those who temporarily exercise the authority of the executive branch, rather than to the country and its Constitution which they are sworn to defend.[32]

Men with these attitudes have not been a major problem of postwar civil-military relations, however. MacArthur was replaced in Korea by Ridgway, who asked himself "Why are we here?" and wrote in response to his own question:

> The answer is simple and conclusive. We are here because of the decisions of the properly constituted authorities ... The answer is simple because further comment is unnecessary. It is conclusive because the loyalty we give, and expect, precludes any slightest questioning of these orders.[33]

But neither of these extremes is representative. In reality, most cold war military leaders were less fused in the civilian political mold than objective controllers feared or bureaucratic revisionists wanted and were both less autonomous and less influential than liberals feared and conservatives wanted. Most often they floated in a limbo between professionalism and fusion. Their ambivalent role in Vietnam policy reflected their problem. The Kennedy-Johnson Chiefs did not adapt well to Kennedy's directive to consider political factors in their recommendations, but in trying to do so they forfeited their professional integrity. Ridgway, a model professional, had warned unequivocally of the high price of intervention in Indochina in 1954 and indicated he would resign if the administration decided to commit American combat troops. A decade later when military planners were similarly pessimistic, estimating a need for up to 1.2 million American troops in South Vietnam if the country were to be pacified, they supported the administration, settling for limited measures. Although they protested, they remained loyal. A mass resignation might have served the nation better.[34] Rather than provoking irresistible pressure for the massive escalation the military wanted, the million-men figure might have jolted the public and catalyzed the reassessment and withdrawal decision, which had to wait for the 206,000 troop request in 1968. The costs of insufficient professionalism and insufficient insistence on their own autonomous judgment by the Chiefs in 1965 may have been as great as the costs of excessive demands for autonomy by MacArthur in 1951.

The choice between the two extreme conceptions of how civil-military relations should be organized is impossible to resolve by a simple formula. Neither extreme is realistic because government has inconsistent interests. There is an inevitable tension between expertise and political control; to enshrine one is to corrupt the other, and government needs some measure of both. Finding the balance is complicated by the check of legislative oversight. And while the separation of powers interferes with the ideal of objective control, the professional selection system usually prevents effective subjective control.

4 Choosing and Using the Chiefs: Structuring Influence

One other thing I would like to clear up. I was referred to here yesterday as the President's witness. I thought I was the committee's witness.

I would like to point out that I am neither a Democratic [sic] nor a Republican. I think it would be improper if I were, in my position. I have never voted . . .

General of the Army Omar N. Bradley, 1951

It's good to have men like Curt LeMay and Arleigh Burke commanding troops once you decide to go in. But these men aren't the only ones you should listen to when you decide whether to go in or not. I like having LeMay head the Air Force. Everybody knows how he feels.

John F. Kennedy, 1961

IN traditional theory, military advisers are supposed to be non-political professionals. In practice, they rarely can be. Bureaucratic revisionists believe the reason is that the administrative process is intrinsically political. Objective control theorists think politicization is fostered by the essence of the Constitution: the separation of powers. The degree of political significance of military advice varies just as does military influence, but politicization of military roles implies the politicization of the selection process for the men who fill those roles. If the military's role is minimally political, the administration can afford to ignore considerations of political loyalty and make professionalism the only criterion in appointment. But if the adviser's role is highly political, the administration risks subverting itself if it does not screen prospective appointees politically.

POLITICIZATION OF MILITARY ADVICE

The military figures with by far the most important, sustained, and institutionalized relationship to the President are the Joint Chiefs of Staff. The Joint Chiefs were constituted by Franklin Roosevelt in 1939 and served directly under him. The 1947 National Security Act institutionalized the JCS and reduced their intimacy with the President by interposing layers of Defense Department civilian authorities, although it did envision a need to prevent the secretary of defense's domination of the Chiefs by providing them the legal right of direct access to the President. Legally the Chiefs are nonpartisan professionals; practically they are often political actors with potential leverage against their superiors in the administration.

The Chiefs can be politicized in two directions. Positive politicization—support and advocacy of administration policies—characterized them under Truman; negative politicization—opposition to administration policies—characterized them under Johnson. Mixed politicization prevailed under Eisenhower and Kennedy. The Chiefs under Nixon and Ford came closest to political neutralization primarily because no service's basic strategic mission was compromised to the same extent as in the administrations with mixed politicization; the Chiefs were happier with the administration's Vietnam policy, tactical controls, and managerial philosophy than they had been in the early 1960s; and Congress had come to be more of an antagonist than an ally with appropriations cuts more a threat than administration budget limits. The administration had become a buffer against Congress and the public rather than the reverse. Early indications of the situation under Ford's successor were unclear. There was no evidence of dissent from the Chiefs in the first days of the new administration, before the President had set national policy firmly. But Carter's confident view of the strategic balance with the Soviet Union, his rhetorical commitment to abolition of nuclear weapons, and his installation of a civilian team in the Pentagon reminiscent of the McNamara regime were likely to worry many of the professional military and could preface a negative politicization of the JCS.

The first and most serious embroilment of the Chiefs in partisan controversy came during the Korean War when Senator Robert Taft attacked them for being "absolutely under the control of the administration" and for making their recommendations "what the administration demands they make." The cauldron in which this controversy boiled over was the Senate investigation of General MacArthur's dismissal. These hearings went on for weeks featuring the whole panoply of pro- and antiadministration military and civilian officials and receiving intense national coverage. The Joint Chiefs, along with Secretary of Defense George Marshall and Secretary of State Dean Acheson, carried the burden of explanation of administration war policy and faced the most hostile Republican questions.[1] The proadministration Truman Chiefs suffered the most from their politicization because their administration put them in the position of spokesmen for policy. (Johnson did not put his wartime chiefs in the same spot. In the 1966 Fulbright hearings, Maxwell Taylor, who was officially retired, filled this role. Johnson and McNamara successfully kept their increasingly disgruntled Chiefs quiet until the Stennis hearings on the air war.)

To mollify Taft and because he planned a revision of national strategy, President Eisenhower replaced the Chiefs and chairman in 1953 shortly after he took office and made clear that he would review the appointments of the new chiefs after two years. Republican politicians had protested the implicit politicization of the Truman Chiefs; professional soldiers who had supported their view of national strategy now criticized Eisenhower's more explicit politicization of the institution. Taylor complained that a "new ambiguity was given to the position of the Joint Chiefs of Staff."[2] Actually the ambiguity preceded Eisenhower's changes, and was institutionally built in, deriving from the tension among three potentially conflicting military loyalties: to the commander in chief, to professional standards, and to Congress acting in its oversight capacity. Eisenhower intended to ensure the primacy of the first loyalty and to meet the different needs of his administration. Kennedy dealt with his inherited chiefs in a more circuitous but similar way. Disappointed with their performance and political insensitivity, he first circumvented them by hiring another source of more responsive military advice; he brought Maxwell Taylor out of retirement to the White House in the specially created job of military representative of the President. As soon as the old Chiefs' terms were up, Kennedy replaced them and appointed Taylor as chairman. The Chiefs who served under Johnson kept a low profile politically, considering their disagreement with strategy in a war in progress. Having been chosen for their cooperativeness, in contrast to the obstreperous Chiefs of the early 1960s, they remained an unhappy but loyal internal opposition.[3]

An administration can ensure that the JCS chairman will support the President, but it is more difficult to do so with the service chiefs. Two major problems frustrate attempts to make career generals into political lackeys: political cost and professional obstacles. Service chiefs are unique among high executives in the foreign and national security policy field. They are career officials but hold positions at a level of importance usually reserved to political appointees. In de facto importance, a chief of staff ranks higher than a service secretary, and a JCS chairman equals a deputy secretary of defense. Yet all other appointments at such levels—and several levels lower—are political appointments; they are people trusted by the President and secretary to enforce presidential priorities enthusiastically on a career service. The statutory basis of the Joint Chiefs does not facilitate this kind of political selection. The Chiefs are enjoined to report fully and frankly to Congress as experts more than as administration spokesmen. The President can ensure the support of the Chiefs by appointing people loyal and devoted to his programs, but he must pay a political price for such a move. The services would be embittered, always sensitive to corruption of professional autonomy and derangement of normal career advancement standards that are threatened by politicization of promotion, and reaction would then come in turn from Congress, which has an institutional interest in preserving professional military independence from partisan executive control. This problem is more of a danger to an administration at odds with the armed services committees or vulnerable to charges of not being strong enough on national security issues than to one that is not. The pre-Watergate administration could elevate Kissinger's deputy Alexander Haig to the position of vice-chief of staff of the army in 1972; a liberal Democratic administration would have more difficulty making a similar move. More of a limitation than the potential political criticism, however, is the fact that it is usually impossible to find a political minion who is qualified to be a service chief in terms of seniority, expertise, and military achievement. Most candidates for appointment have been determined by a thirty-year process of intraservice selection, not by a history of partisan identification. The executive has some freedom of choice among the candidates but usually only in a prophylactic sense by ensuring that the chief is not an enemy of administration policy or strategy. Even this degree of discretion is not always possible, particularly in administrations that make strategic changes affecting the missions of services, as demonstrated by the cases of Ridgway and Taylor under Eisenhower and LeMay under Kennedy. In some instances civilian leaders do not know in advance what resistance their military appointees may offer on future issues.

Postwar JCS appointments have followed three general patterns. In the first, *routine-professional*, the executive exercises negligible choice and does not make compatibility with administration political goals his central consideration in selection. This is the most common method used, but men picked in this manner have less power within the administration than those selected by the next two methods. *Professional-political* appointments compromise between the first and third variants. The President does not appoint a close political follower, but he broadens the field of selection beyond the normal candidates. The President and secretary of defense may move down a substantial distance in the seniority list or select officers with atypical career backgrounds. The third pattern is *exceptional-political*. An officer gains the complete confidence and admiration of political leaders and becomes a member of the inner circle of the administration.

The first method is the simplest manner of selection for the executive and exacts the fewest immediate political costs in terms of military and congressional opposition. But it poses the greatest potential political costs to the administration since this type of Chief will respond more to professional and organizational loyalties, which may conflict with administration priorities, than will an appointee chosen on political grounds. Conversely, the third method is the most difficult (there may not be any political devotees in the ranks when a President wishes he had them), and it poses political costs that are high in the short run but low in the long run. These constraints reflect the crux of the problem: the Joint Chiefs of Staff is an institution with political import, but an administration cannot easily control its membership politically.

Table 1 shows that Presidents have made few political military appointments. Most military advisers incur an administration political role but retain an organizational political orientation. There is little difference in the tendency of Democratic or Republican admin-

TABLE 1. Modes of military appointment.

	Chairman, Joint Chiefs of Staff	Chief of Staff, Army	Chief of Naval Operations	Chief of Staff, Air Force	Commandant, Marine Corps	Other
Routine-professional	Bradley Twining Lemnitzer Moorer Brown	Eisenhower Bradley Collins Ridgway Taylor Lemnitzer Decker Westmoreland Abrams Weyand Rogers	Nimitz Denfeld Sherman Fechteler Carney Anderson Moorer McDonald Holloway	Spaatz Vandenberg Twining White LeMay McConnell Ryan Brown Jones	Vandegrift Cates Shepherd Pate Greene Chapman Cushman Wilson	Haig (military assistant to the assistant to the President for national security)
Professional-political	Wheeler	Wheeler Johnson	Burke Zumwalt		Shoup	Norstad (SACEUR)[a] Haig (deputy assistant to the President for national security)
Exceptional-political	Radford Taylor				Cushman	Taylor (MILREP)[b] Haig (vice-chief) Haig (SACEUR)[a]

[a] Supreme Allied Commander, Europe.
[b] Military Representative of the President.

57

istrations to politicize appointments although Republicans may be slightly more political, perhaps because they have felt less vulnerable to accusations of not being strong enough on national security policy. It is obvious as well that the overwhelming number of military appointments have been from the routine-professional track. The Chiefs who embarrassed, obstructed, or disappointed the administrations that appointed them also were all products of that same mode of selection. The least politicized method of selection yields to an administration the most negative political results. Thus, the least political of the appointment processes deserves the most political analysis.

THE ROUTINE-PROFESSIONAL ROUTE: APPRENTICESHIP VERSUS POLITICIZATION

The most common way to appoint service chiefs is to select the senior officer considered to have the highest professional stature within his service.[4] In practice this often means appointing the outgoing Chief's understudy, the vice-chief of staff, or one of the principal field commanders. In the army, vice-chiefs are usually chosen in peacetime, while combat field commanders are always selected during or immediately after a war.

Accession of vice-chiefs usually means that the political executives exercise little choice, essentially ratifying professional judgment. Civilian involvement in selection of a vice-chief is normally minimal, since he is usually the chief of staff's personal choice. Generally there is an inverse relation between elevation of vice-chiefs and conscious political selection. (The same holds for JCS chairmen; most have been promoted from among the service chiefs. The only ones brought in from outside were the exceptional-political appointees, Radford and Taylor.) The air force in particular was adept in controlling succession. From 1948 until 1972, every Chief selected had been the vice-chief. The army followed the same pattern, but to a lesser extent. One-third of the postwar army chiefs of staff succeeded from the vice-chief job. The navy, on the other hand, did not use the vice-chief of naval operations position in the same way. Denfeld was the only CNO to succeed from the vice-chief position. Arleigh Burke, for instance, chose vice-chiefs who would challenge him and serve as devil's advocates rather than likely candidates for succession.[5]

There is a pattern of rotation from one top job to another, which reflects the carefully designed professional system of apprenticeship at all high levels. This system even operates in wartime, when the seniority norm and the usual rotation patterns are more flexible than in peacetime. When General MacArthur was relieved of his command, he was replaced by his subordinate Eighth Army commander, Ridgway. In Vietnam the apprenticeship system, from field to chief of staff, was remarkably consistent. The three army chiefs of staff from 1968 to 1976—Westmoreland, Abrams, and Weyand—all passed through the same sequence of assignments: deputy commander, United States military assistance command, Vietnam; commander, United States military assistance command, Vietnam; chief of staff. In peacetime, when the immediate importance of the field command is diminished, it is more common for such a commander to become a vice-chief before chief of staff. The route for Lemnitzer and Decker was: commander in chief, Far East; vice-chief of staff; chief of staff. During the period immediately after the end of a limited war and the beginning of tenuous peace, the succession can go either way. Taylor went from the command in Korea straight to the top post; Frederick Weyand was vice-chief briefly between closing down the command in Vietnam and becoming army chief of staff. There is no necessary contradiction between this kind of a field of candidates and an administration's political interest, but the range of executive choice and discretion in high military appointments is very limited if restricted to normal selection standards.

Some officers boost themselves into contention for service leadership by a feat of brilliance. Frederick Weyand was not a West Point graduate and had served in an intelligence assignment, credits that do not normally enhance advancement to top positions. As a field force commander in Vietnam at the beginning of 1968, however, he made a judgment that helped prevent a crushing victory by communist forces in the Tet offensive. Weyand convinced Westmoreland to pull United States troops in from the remote border areas and redeploy them nearer the cities, just in time for the onslaught. The analysis impressed Westmoreland and higher command. Weyand subsequently was put in line for succession when he was made deputy commander in Vietnam.

Another unusual route is succession by default. When Chief of Naval Operations Forrest Sherman died in 1951, the only one of four admirals in line for succession who had not been tainted by testimony against the administration in the controversial hearings on B-36 bomber procurement was William Fechteler, who was subsequently chosen. More frequently a history of consistently outstanding performance in key assignments determines candidacy. The important posts on the way up are not always commands, especially in the army. The view that staff positions and unconventional assignments do not lead to advancement has been exposed as myth. Janowitz differentiates these adaptive career routes to high position from the generally prescribed route of operational commands. Many postwar army chiefs had adaptive backgrounds: a mixture of command, staff, and unusual jobs. Ridgway, Taylor, and Lyman Lemnitzer had important diplomatic assignments or performed secret missions during World War II and were noted for their ability with foreign languages. George Decker, although he had the United Nations command in Korea, held mainly administrative posts, including two fiscal management positions in the Pentagon. Earle Wheeler, except for brief tours as a division and corps commander in the 1950s, also rose through a succession of staff assignments. The trend away from the prescribed combat command pattern of succession toward the managerial staff or adaptive track, however, has not been consistent. Westmoreland and Abrams rose almost exclusively through airborne and armored commands. The traditional command route has been much more dominant in the navy and air force.[6]

Excellence is not a sufficient condition for military advancement. The personal connections a soldier develops with influential higher officers can be crucial. The chiefs of naval operations who came into office after the National Security Act had worked closely with the top commanders during the war. Robert Carney was chief of staff to Brett Halsey; Forrest Sherman was deputy chief of staff to Chester Nimitz. Later naval chiefs were comparably attached to the leaders of the postwar generation. George Anderson had been both chief of staff to Pacific commander Felix Stump and special assistant to JCS Chairman Radford. In the army the central patron-client system in this century was George Marshall's.[7] Many of the officers who rose to eminence in World War II were the ones Marshall had noticed in Tientsin, China, and Fort Benning, Georgia, in the 1920s and 1930s. Marshall himself had risen in part because of his connection with General Pershing as a planner in World War I, which offset the effect of Chief of Staff Douglas MacArthur's lack of esteem for him. Protégés of Marshall—as well as of Eisenhower and Bradley—were Ridgway and Lawton Collins. Marshall kept Collins from resigning in 1936 when he was demoralized at having been a lieutenant for seventeen years by telling him that he was marked for important advancements in the future. Collins in turn developed his own protégés. While he was chief of staff, Ridgway, Alfred Gruenther, and Maxwell Taylor all served under him as deputy chiefs. Similarly, Lemnitzer, George Decker, and James

Gavin had top Pentagon positions under Ridgway. Some officers do not wait to be patronized and insert themselves into a network. William Westmoreland began his surge to the top in Sicily in 1943, where he took the initiative to drive to Ridgway's Eighty-second Airborne divisional headquarters, present himself, and offer his artillery battalion and the much-coveted trucks that went with it if Ridgway took him into the Eighty-second for the campaign. Maxwell Taylor was the division artillery commander at the time and made note of Westmoreland.[8]

Some officers are so exceptional that they have no competition. MacArthur, for example, distinguished himself as a prodigy in the early 1900s, a precocious division commander in World War I, and a youthful chief of staff in the early 1930s. Such exceptional men may ease the problem of choice for political executives if the administration is looking only for the officer with highest professional standing. Thomas Moorer had been carefully prepared by preceding naval chiefs and was purposely given the choicest assignments (he was the first officer ever to command both the Atlantic and Pacific fleets). When a successor for David McDonald had to be chosen, according to Paul Nitze, "There was only one person considered—Moorer." A situation in which there is one particularly outstanding candidate can leave the administration with virtually no choice. In 1961 Curtis LeMay was the unanimous candidate of the air force hierarchy; any other selection would have been an affront to the service. The administration reluctantly appointed LeMay, who quickly proved to be the most troublesome of the Joint Chiefs.[9]

In most instances, however, there are several possible appointees who have been noticed and prepared since the middle grades. These officers are sponsored by chiefs of staff who are constantly looking for potential leaders of the next military generation. Taylor, for example, spotted three special officers while he was chief of staff of the army: Westmoreland, Andrew Goodpaster, and Bernard Rogers. The chiefs monitor and guide these officers' careers, making sure that they are given assignments that provide the experience and responsibility appropriate for future chiefs.[10]

The early career choices an officer makes within his service may determine how he advances at much later stages. Until very recently, if a soldier elected a branch other than one of the combat arms—for example, if he entered the chemical corps, military intelligence, or became a quartermaster specialist—he almost certainly never rose higher than colonel. If he chose the prescribed track of operational command or the adaptive track of staff work and military diplomacy, he had the same chance for reaching the elite as most of his other colleagues. If, however, he invested in a military growth stock, he wound up by World War II with a head start on his traditionally oriented cohorts. There were three major examples of such career stocks in the twentieth century: the army air corps, naval aviation, and airborne infantry (paratroops), which were once obscure or disfavored branches of the services. Officers who became pilots in the early 1920s were making a risky choice because the air services were underfunded and underappreciated. But World War II reversed priorities, and the small corps of aviation veterans flew to flag rank while their academy classmates took the slower surface routes. (Before Pearl Harbor Curtis LeMay was a lieutenant; within four years he was a major general.) All of the leaders of the air force when it was separated from the army in 1947 and the dominant leaders of the postwar navy were men who had chosen ascendant branches early in their careers. Chairmen Radford and Moorer and Naval Chiefs Sherman, Anderson, McDonald, Moorer, and Holloway were all naval aviators. Surface sailors Carney, Burke, and Elmo Zumwalt were appointed chiefs of naval operations when Radford and Moorer were chairmen in large part to balance the membership of the Joint Chiefs, restraining the dominance of the fliers. Radford, Anderson, Moorer, and McDonald also had important prewar staff positions in the development of naval aviation. Postwar Commanders in Chief, Pacific, Radford, Felix Stump, Harry Felt, and Noel Gayler were aviators (ironically, CINCPACs U. S. G. Sharp and John McCain, who ran the air war against North Vietnam, were not). In the army, paratroop units were not even formed until after the war in Europe had begun, but charter members of the airborne club dominated the service in succeeding decades.

In most routine military appointments, Presidents are not personally acquainted with the men they nominate. The name a President sends to Capitol Hill is one passed up through the civilian chain of command after solicitation of recommendations from the service elite. In the past each service had a board of officers that forwarded recommendations to the service secretaries. In some cases the basic choice was then made by the service secretary and ratified by the secretary of defense and President. George Anderson was originally made chief of naval operations principally on Secretary of the Navy John Connally's recommendation. A JCS chairman, unless he is the President's exceptional-political choice, is usually the secretary of defense's preference. George Brown, for example, was James Schlesinger's personal selection.[11] Recommendations of the outgoing chief usually carry great weight, as the high rate of selection of vice-chiefs in some services attests. The lower number of vice-chiefs of naval operations who become chief does not imply, however, that navy chiefs' choices are more often disregarded.[12]

The most important clearances are from outside the chain of command. The secretary of defense usually checks a list of possible nominees informally with congressional armed services committees before he forwards them to the President for decision. Congressional preferences naturally affect Pentagon civilians' consideration of candidates. In Eisenhower's case Senator Taft influenced initial JCS appointments. In Kennedy's case, LeMay was inevitable because the administration was caught in between LeMay's professional constituency in the service and his political constituency on the Hill. This preemptive leverage of powerful congressmen is one reason that service chiefs' confirmation hearings are usually perfunctory.[13]

As a five-star general acquainted with the top echelons of the armed services, President Eisenhower could have been expected to dominate the military by appointing friends to the Joint Chiefs. He did not. The one consciously political appointment he made was Radford, with whom he had had considerable differences. His two other nonroutine appointments, Burke and Norstad, were approvals of recommendations passed to him from the Pentagon. The only real crony he appointed was his former chief of staff at NATO headquarters, Alfred Gruenther, to the post of supreme allied commander in Europe. One reason behind the President's abstemiousness was his traditional hierarchical administrative philosophy, which dictated maximum delegation of authority and the right of officials to pick their own subordinates. The other factor was Eisenhower's desire to deemphasize his military image and background. He resolved not to act as his own secretary of defense.[14] Most of Eisenhower's appointments were routine, but he did accede to the invigoration of service leadership. Prior to the 1950s, seniority had been the prime criterion of selection of peacetime service chiefs, but in in the nuclear age it seemed necessary to dip further down to get the best leadership. This occurred in the selection of Gruenther's successor Lauris Norstad and Carney's successor Arleigh Burke, and was a slight consideration in choosing David Shoup to replace Randolph Pate.

THE PROFESSIONAL-POLITICAL ROUTE: COMPROMISE CANDIDATES

A professional-political appointment differs from an exceptional-political choice in that the officer is appointed not because of his personal identification with the administration or his eagerness to

propagandize for it on the Hill but because of his professional
excellence. It differs from a routine-professional selection in dispens-
ing with the traditional professional norms of seniority and restriction of choice to the vice-chief and major commanders. Political
executives discover these less obvious candidates in several ways.
One is by the professional grapevine passing the judgment of the
service to the civilian executives, as in the case of Arleigh Burke.
Another is for a service secretary to notice an outstanding officer
and groom him, just as the professionals groom their own protégés.
A third way is through chance encounters that impress the President
or secretary of defense, such as special briefings.

"I never heard of Burke, but the Navy is your responsibility and
if he is your choice it is all right with me," Eisenhower told Secretary of the Navy Charles Thomas in 1955. Burke had helped plan
the so-called admirals' revolt of 1949 against the cancellation of
Navy supercarriers. But like Arthur Radford, Burke overcame
General Eisenhower's prejudice against the navy rebels and eventually became one of President Eisenhower's confidants despite
occasional clashes with administration policy. He served three two-
year terms, more than any other service chief since World War II.
Burke's elevation was the initiaitive of Pentagon civilians, who were
in turn following the lead of the service, which made choosing the
junior rear admiral over ninety-two seniors politically acceptable.
Under Secretary of the Navy Thomas Gates had queried officers
throughout the service on who should succeed Carney, and Burke's
was the name he heard most.[15] When marine Commandant Pate's
term was up, the administration chose Shoup, who had become well
known as a reformist head of the Parris Island depot following a
major scandal over training deaths. Shoup was almost a routine
choice, given his qualifications, but was not quite senior enough to
be among the normal candidates.

Elmo Zumwalt was an example of the second way. He was a desk
officer at International Security Affairs in 1962–1963, when Paul
Nitze was the assistant secretary there, and Nitze took a special interest in him. As secretary of the navy, Nitze worried that the
admirals who were becoming chief of naval operations were too
old. He picked three young rear admirals, Zumwalt among them,
and gave their career development special attention. Zumwalt particularly impressed Nitze with his swift and efficient engineering of
the Vietnamization of naval forces when the admiral was in-shore
naval commander in Vietnam. By the time Moorer left the naval
chief job to become chairman of the Joint Chiefs, a new administra-

tion was in office, and Nitze judiciously refrained from lobbying for Zumwalt, fearing that as a Democrat, his involvement would be counterproductive. Nitze's earlier attention had already given the vice-admiral the chance to make his mark, though, and when the time came Laird and Navy Secretary John Chafee picked him despite grumbling from retired admirals.[16] Zumwalt jumped over a host of seniors and in 1970 became the youngest naval chief in modern times. The problem with this method of selection is that the time lag between the identification of potential candidates and the chance to put them in major positions usually cuts across administrations. Republicans appointed the officer Nitze had helped, and Democratic executives Joseph Califano and Cyrus Vance first recommended Alexander Haig to Kissinger. (As Haig's case shows, an officer can rise through all three routes of selection.)

Lyman Lemnitzer, who had been on General Eisenhower's staff in North Africa, made a favorable impression on President Eisenhower years later during a briefing that Chief of Staff Taylor would have given had he not been out of town. Lemnitzer was already vice-chief of staff, however, and any effect of the meeting was probably just to bias the routine mode of choice in his favor. A better example of this sort of entrée was the selection of Earle Wheeler, the army officer who briefed President-elect Kennedy on military affairs in 1960. In these sessions he impressed Kennedy, who also soon became concerned that too many of the senior officers were close to retirement age, and his choices for appointments ranged only among men close to sixty years old. Kennedy subsequently instructed McNamara to provide him a wider choice of potential appointees in the future. McNamara, who had liked Wheeler's work as director of the Joint Staff, recommended him to replace Decker in 1962. Kennedy also altered the autonomous service systems for selection of flag officers. Secretary of the Army Vance, for instance, chose the men on the selection boards. (Under Laird the boards reverted to the traditional control of the regulars.)[17]

Congressional sensitivity, which Eisenhower's personal military prestige could neutralize, was more intimidating to a Democratic administration. Some Kennedy administration executives wanted to choose service chiefs from even lower ranks than they eventually did. The President himself, impressed by Westmoreland on a 1962 visit to West Point, reportedly wanted to name him to succeed Decker until he was convinced that (in peacetime, at least) it was impolitic to make a very junior major general chief of staff. Two years later Cyrus Vance backed Major General Creighton Abrams for army chief after working with him in controlling racial confrontations when southern universities were integrated. In both cases, though, the administration chose from among juniors, but not as far down as the two-star level. Wheeler had attained three-star rank only two years before he became chief of staff, and his successor, Lieutenant General Harold Johnson, was jumped over forty-three seniors (because, according to some disgruntled officers, McNamara had to go that far down to find someone who had never disagreed with his policies).[18] David McDonald was twenty-eighth in seniority among vice-admirals when he was promoted to admiral shortly before becoming naval chief, but he was not nearly as junior as Burke had been.

President Kennedy did not delegate his choices entirely to Secretary of Defense McNamara, despite his high confidence in him. He made sure that three or four months before a vacancy opened on the Joint Chiefs he had a chance to meet the candidates informally, a practice Lyndon Johnson continued. McNamara supported the President's inclination to deemphasize seniority and experience in the field, and he took part in the search more than earlier defense secretaries had.[19]

THE EXCEPTIONAL-POLITICAL ROUTE: JOINING THE ADMINISTRATION

Although both the Eisenhower and Kennedy administrations sought to improve military leadership by compromising the seniority system and encouraging military leaders to develop political sensitivity, they limited their consciously political military appointments to one man each.

President Eisenhower had two incentives to name Arthur Radford head of the Joint Chiefs. A defensive reason was that the new administration wanted a new military policy that would be both firmer and cheaper than the old one, and Radford was willing and able to lead the Chiefs in devising the appropriate strategy. Indeed, the admiral captivated Secretary of Defense Charles Wilson during their first meeting because of his well-thought-out plans. But the President had one reason not to appoint Radford: he disliked him intensely. The two had clashed in the interservice debates of the late 1940s to the extent that Eisenhower once refused to attend a JCS meeting because Radford was present. But as President-elect, Eisenhower changed his opinion of the admiral on his trip to Korea when Radford entranced him with crisp and convincing monologues on Asian problems and world strategy.[20] Eisenhower buried the old feud and made Radford his principal military official.

John Kennedy had a high regard for Maxwell Taylor even before the new administration came into office because of the polemical attack on Eisenhower's policy—*The Uncertain Trumpet*—that Taylor had written after retiring as army chief of staff. Kennedy offered the general a choice of two civilian posts, ambassador to France (which went to Taylor's airborne rival James Gavin) and director of central intelligence, both of which Taylor declined.[21] Instead Taylor returned to uniform, first as Kennedy's special military representative in the White House and a year later to the chairmanship of the Joint Chiefs of Staff. His ardor in promoting and organizing the administration's new flexible-response policy placed him in a political light and alienated most of the Joint Chiefs.

Both Radford and Taylor were so eminent that they could have been routine choices had they not been so controversially identified with doctrines suppressed in one administration that a new Administration wanted to adopt. Robert Cushman also had the normal qualifications to be picked as marine commandant, but it is uncertain that he would have been had he not earned a claim on Nixon's patronage as assistant to the vice-president for national security affairs from 1957 to 1961. Cushman thus qualified for his post as both a routine and exceptional choice.

The officer who rose through all three modes of military appointment and ultimately became the most blatant military political appointee in over half a century was Alexander Haig. Haig had an extremely adaptive early career. He worked on MacArthur's staff in Japan and Korea and was later an assistant to the secretary of the army and the deputy secretary of defense in the Johnson adminstration before getting his command credentials with brief service as a battalion and brigade commander in Vietnam. His rise was meteoric under Nixon and Kissinger, to whom he proved himself a devoted aide. Haig rose from lieutenant colonel to four-star general in fewer than five years, exceeding even Douglas AacArthur's prodigious promotion rate. The only comparable jump in this century, other than in time of general war, was Theodore Roosevelt's promotion of John J. Pershing from captain to brigadier general over 862 seniors. Haig's selection as vice-chief in 1972 was the boldest civilian political military appointment in the postwar era but was exceeded two years later when he retired from the most politically controversial civilian appointive post in the country—chief of staff in the Watergate White House—to return to uniform as supreme allied commander in Europe.[22]

CONTROLLING THE CHIEFS

An administration can try to control the Joint Chiefs by making exceptional-political appointments, but such candidates are rare. Given scarcity, exceptional appointees have been placed where they can do the administration the most good: at the top. The JCS chairmanship was created in the 1949 amendments to the National Security Act to simplify communication between the President and the Chiefs and to coordinate the work of the group. The chairman controls the Joint Staff, the organization under the JCS that is the largest research, analysis, and planning staff in the government. Members of Congress have been wary of the amount of authority they grant to the chairman, often citing the danger of creating a "man on horseback." Nevertheless Congress has reluctantly but steadily authorized periodic increases in both the scope of the chairman's authority and the size of his support establishment.

When he retired as army chief of staff under Eisenhower, Maxwell Taylor charged that the chairman of the JCS "has come to be a sort of party whip."[23] The enthusiasm with which Arthur Radford enforced administration policy, however, is not a necessary condition of the job. The chairman can serve a minimally political function— as the service chiefs, the legislators, and traditional administrative theory would have it—if he operates as a neutral communication channel between the Chiefs, secretary of defense, and President. Or he can be maximally political, moving from coordination toward control of the service chiefs—as a strong President and bureaucratic revisionists would have it—if he uses his position to impose administration views and requirements on the services. In the twenty-five years since the chairmanship was created, there have been only two "whips" (Radford and Taylor); the other chairmen have approximated the ambassador model to various degrees (Twining and Wheeler were somewhat closer to the former however).

As a dissident in 1959, Taylor attacked Radford, especially since the chairman's lash had fallen most often on army interests. He also complained that in the JCS "the chairman's side nearly always wins," an assertion he illustrated with statistics. Three years later when he became chairman, Taylor told McNamara that he would not try to force the Chiefs into partisan support of administration policy, but he did in fact come to be a whip of sorts.[24] He dominated the meetings of the Joint Chiefs, which became less open than they had been, and pushed administration innovations vigorously. As a result, much of the senior leadership came to distrust Taylor, feeling that he was a lackey to McNamara; some of the service chiefs also lacked confidence that Taylor adequately represented their views to the President.[25] Service chiefs naturally resent politicized appointees as chairmen because such men are strong chairmen with leverage against dissenters. Strength, deriving from the mandate of civilian leadership, goes hand in hand with politicization in the chairmanship. The President benefits from a strong chairman, and the service chiefs lose. Congress is therefore wary of politicized choices. A chairman closer to the ambassador model may have both executive and legislative confidence, as well as the confidence of the Chiefs. Earle Wheeler was such a chairman, and he had the longest tenure in history: six years. His appointment was extended twice by special legislation (by Johnson in 1968 and by Nixon a year later). Wheeler's tenure also interrupted the tradition of rotating the chairmanship among the services. What was more important than this tradition, for the Johnson administration faced with a senior military leadership growing increasingly restive, was that McNamara and Wheeler got along well and worked effectively together. The manuevers, frustration, and lost sleep required by this delicate balancing act were so debilitating, however, that Wheeler's health was ruined.[26]

Unlike service chiefs, a chairman cannot fulfill his function and remain in consistent opposition. At most he can be a lobbyist for his colleagues. Because his power derives from the administration, the appropriate spectrum of politicization for him is shorter, from activist leader to neutral ambassador. Whatever the cooperation of the chairman, the Chiefs remain potential independent political powers within an administration. When they fail to support administration policies, a President who intends to affirm his own control must either reform them (which is virtually impossible), replace them (which is politically costly), repress or ignore them (which is inefficient and awkward), or transform them.

Making a military appointment is hard enough for an administration. It is even more difficult to get rid of an unwanted service chief. In almost all cases Presidents have allowed nettlesome chiefs to complete their terms before replacing them, even though the President has the right to fire them. President Truman replaced CNO Louis Denfeld in 1949 because of his role in the controversy over B-36 bombers and supercarriers, but more discreet internal opposition to administration programs is not usually considered politically solid ground on which to dismiss a chief. The furor that engulfed the Truman administration when MacArthur was relieved in 1951 also established a precedent that deterred firings in later years. When George Anderson defied McNamara, testifying against the TFX fighter plane and the military pay bill, the admiral was allowed to finish his term and was given another assignment rather than consigned to congressionally conspicuous retirement.

The establishment of fixed terms for the Joint Chiefs poses both advantages and dangers for an administration. Terms provide a softer alternative (nonreappointment) to firing, but the presumption against removal that accompanies a fixed term means that an undesired chief may remain in office for years. The two-year terms Presidents Eisenhower and Kennedy used made the first of these considerations viable and minimized the executive discomfort implied by the second. But the establishment of four-year terms created a greater potential problem for an executive faced with chiefs appointed by a previous administration. Truman avoided this problem because he had the opportunity to appoint all of his own chiefs soon after World War II. Eisenhower replaced the Truman chiefs, most of whom conveniently finished four years in office within a few months of the inauguration. Kennedy removed all of his inherited chiefs as soon as their terms had expired, but not reappointing those who had served only two-year terms was seen by some in Congress as the equivalent of firing; this reaction in 1963 inspired the four-year-term legislation.

Replacing holdovers does not necessarily end the problem of recalcitrance in the JCS. Given the constraints on political selection and screening, it is easy for an administration to find that one of its own choices is a mistake. This occurred with two of Eisenhower's initial appointees. Ridgway was let go because of severe disagreements with the administration's massive retaliation strategy, and Carney was not reappointed because of a number of administrative abrasions: an uncleared speech on the Taiwan Straits crisis that predicted war with China, a power struggle and personality clash with Navy Secretary Charles Thomas, conflict with Marine Commandant Shepherd, and a secret communication system used between Carney and Pacific commander Felix Stump that infuriated Secretary of Defense Wilson.[27]

Kennedy and McNamara found that their biggest embarrassments on the JCS were not the holdovers they eliminated but two of the men they picked to replace them: LeMay and Anderson. The President acceded to pressure to appoint LeMay in part because he "had the toughness Kennedy felt the country needed most" in the wake of the Bay of Pigs.[28] This toughness came home to roost in the missile crisis a year later when LeMay was vociferously in the vanguard of the extreme hawks, blithely unafraid of nuclear confrontation with the USSR. He also opposed the defense secretary's strategic innovations. But despite McNamara's objection, Kennedy reappointed LeMay in 1963 (though only for a one-year term) rather than open the administration to attack from the Right. For similar reasons President Johnson extended LeMay's term again the following year, but only for seven months, which prevented LeMay from speaking out for Barry Goldwater in the 1964 presidential campaign.[29] Eisenhower had the military prestige to replace Ridgway and Carney without repercussions, but Kennedy and Johnson felt too vulnerable to charges of stifling military experts.

Reappointing chiefs who have not fully supported the administration is surprisingly common. Taylor claims that Neil McElroy offered him reappointment in 1959, which he declined.[30] Some officials wondered why Nixon reappointed Thomas Moorer as chairman of the Joint Chiefs in mid-1972 when evidence was uncovered that Moorer had illicitly received documents from the National Security Council. The reason is that discharging a military official has a political cost (congressional or public reaction) unequal to the benefit, unless the man makes his opposition public by persistent leaks to the press or Congress. If a chief is clashing with the administration, it is easier to ignore him than to suffer criticism for replacing him. With such incentives, Kennedy could not oust LeMay. He did agree, at McNamara's insistence, to replace Anderson but ensured that elaborate efforts were made to find an attractive position for the admiral.[31] Thus Kennedy replaced all of the chiefs he had inherited and two he had appointed himself. Of those who had not completed normal four-year tours, only George Decker was summarily dropped; the administration muffled its purge. Lemnitzer and Anderson were let down gently by giving them new assignments that took them out of Washington: Lemnitzer to the prestigious NATO command and Anderson to the more modest post of Ambassador to Portugal.

Presidents have used lateral transfers frequently as a way to move unwanted officers out of Washington or out of field commands. This maneuver minimizes the embarrassment of the rejected general and forestalls protests by suspicious members of Congress. Such transfers are, in effect, bribes, because major field commands and membership on the Joint Chiefs of Staff are roughly comparable in prestige and responsibility. A chief of staff has vertical administrative jurisdiction over an entire service; a unified command has horizontal operational authority over an entire geographic area. A unified command may have more importance during wartime or a period when war is expected in the area, while in more quiescent periods the service chief may seem the more vital job. An example of the attractiveness that field command may have in opposition to service on the Joint Chiefs is the stir that Commander in Chief United States Naval Forces in Europe Admiral David McDonald caused in 1963 when he told Deputy Secretary of Defense Roswell Gilpatric, who had called him to Washington to congratulate him on his selection to replace Chief of Naval Operations Anderson, that he did not want the job and would prefer to remain in an operational role.[32] The purest case of a lateral shuffle occurred when Eisenhower had Truman's CNO Fechteler switch places with southern Europe NATO commander Carney.

The most important unified command usually held by the navy is the Pacific command and is the apex of an admiral's career. Only Chester Nimitz, Louis Denfield, and Arthur Radford went on from there to positions on the Joint Chiefs, and no CNO has later become CINCPAC. The supreme allied commander in Europe (SACEUR), however, a job usually filled by an army general, has been shuffled with Washington positions on several occasions, and it is just as political a post as chief of staff. President Eisenhower, who claimed that he only reluctantly became chief of staff in 1945 instead of retiring, willingly became SACEUR five years later (and then resigned to run for President).[33] Ridgway was then assigned the European command.[34] When Eisenhower made Ridgway chief of staff a year later, he was not so much promoting him as he was moving him out of the way so he could appoint his protégé Alfred Gruenther to the preferred SACEUR post. Sending Lemnitzer to NATO ten years later opened up the JCS chairmanship for the administration's favorite soldier, Taylor. Earle Wheeler, who had been sent to Europe as deputy commander in chief of the European command only a few months before to be prepared to succeed Norstad as SACEUR, was shuffled back to replace George Decker as chief of staff of the army. This process also served to remove Norstad, who had some differences with the administration.[35]

It is easier to remove a unified commander with minimal political criticism because his term is less fixed in length than a service chief's, and he is not confirmed by the Senate. Andrew Goodpaster, who did not want to retire as European commander in 1974, watched helplessly as President Ford combined the domestic political imperative of moving Alexander Haig out of the White House with his own gratitude to Nixon's White House chief of staff by appointing him to Goodpaster's post. The army chief of staff position was open at the time because of Creighton Abrams's death, but Ford acceded to anti-Haig sentiment in the army by sending him out of

Washington and avoided congressional opposition to Haig by appointing him to a post that did not require Senate approval.

A convenient expiration date in a service chief's term also provides a dignified way to relieve a combat commander. The shock of the 1968 Tet offensive jolted Lyndon Johnson into reassessing the strategy he had pursued through Westmoreland. The President was able to change commanders and still reward Westmoreland by appointing him to succeed Harold K. Johnson as chief of staff. When incumbents are moved from one post to another, the administration makes an assumption about which post is more important. Using a major field command to exile an unwanted service chief or JCS chairman happens only in peacetime, and using a chief of staff's position as a consolation for a rejected field commander happens only in wartime. The JCS chairmanship is the most important military position, so it is never used to soothe any soldier (though Eisenhower used it partially to soothe some Republican politicians). In wartime, confidence in the field commander takes precedence over relations with a service chief, and the selection problems apply as well when choosing the man who manages the war on the spot. Truman had trouble with MacArthur in Korea because he was burdened with a commander he had not chosen and one with a powerful professional reputation and a formidable public and congressional consistency. Kennedy and Johnson did not have this problem in Vietnam because Harkins and Westmoreland were administration choices. Although Westmoreland wanted more force than he got after 1964, he remained cooperative, making his recommendations but accepting their rejection or modification in good humor. This was less true of the men who ran the air war, who were routine appointments, such as Pacific commander Ulysses Grant Sharp.

Choosing the Method of Appointment

The alternative methods of selection of military leadership parallel the alternative administrative strategies discussed in chapter 3. The problem of choice remains between maximizing professionalism and expertise and maximizing executive political control. The choice depends on two values: the importance of professional expertise or independent influence vis à vis presidential power and the desirable constitutional balance of power between the President and Congress.

The routine-professional mode of service chief selection optimizes the values of professional standards but leaves more autonomy to the soldiers than do the more politicized methods of selection. Routine selection is most agreeable to the military establishment and to Congress. If there are no major strategic debates or policy cleavages between the military and administration, routine selection may also be agreeable to the executive as well. Exceptional-political appointments, on the other hand, derogate traditional professional standards of leadership selection and maximize executive leverage over military leaders. When policy is controversial, this approach cushions the administration against internal subversion. The professional-political mode of choice is a synthesis of these two extremes. Since either undiluted military autonomy or unbridled presidential domination of career services pose substantial costs, both are compromised. A professional-political choice is more congenial to an administration than a routine choice and raises fewer suspicions of corruption of professional standards than does an exceptional choice. This compromise is unlikely to upset anyone, other than the senior officers passed over. Compromise is also desirable because the dangers implicit in either high autonomy or military alienation are greater than traditionalists or objective control theory admit and less than bureaucratic revisionists fear.

It is clear that the routine method of selection predominates, even under activist Presidents known for the value they place on control of subordinates. This raises three problems. First, since the military leadership may have low rapport and identification with the administration in power, their perceptions of the requirements imposed by national policy may be problematic. These perceptions are salient determinants of their advice and therefore of their direct influence. Second, the constraints on judgment that organizational identifications and perspectives produce are likely to be important in the roles of military advisers in decision making because these perspectives are less moderated by partisan considerations than are the attitudes of most other major advisers. Third, although their direct influence may remain low, the political distance of the chiefs from their administration is likely to increase the importance of their indirect channels of influence.

5 The Range of Necessity: Policy and Strategy

The European War had just ended, and Eisenhower still felt warmly about the Russians. He spoke with respect about Zhukov, in whom he placed great hope for Soviet-American relations ... General Lucius D. Clay, who had just been appointed second in command to Eisenhower for German affairs, advanced a theory, which was by that time all too familiar to me, that the key to getting along with the Soviets was that you first had to give trust to get trust ... I told Clay that within a few months, or certainly within a year, he would become one of the officials in the American government most opposed to the Soviets.

Charles Bohlen, *Witness to History*

9 March 1946
The Soviet government is an ally of the United States of America ... I will not tolerate any disparaging remarks against our Allies ...
* Millions of Russian soldiers and civilians died to save our skins. Just remember that ... They died for* you too ... *by God I never want to fight again. Think it over. You have been warned.*
Frank W. Ebey
Lt. Col. CAC, Cmdg.
Letter order posted in an American
headquarters in Germany, quoted by C. L. Sulzberger

THE military's role in formulating foreign policy during the postwar period was marginal at best. The one exception was George Marshall, acting as secretary of state. Soldiers did, however, affect nuances of policy. These nuances were crucial for two reasons. First, the basic premise of policy—containment of communism—remained unchanged for over twenty years until the cold war consensus eroded when disillusionment over Vietnam weakened liberals' anticommunism and when bipolarity declined and a conservative President embraced détente and began to court China.[1] The second reason is that although the military do not make policy, they interpret it. Their views of the strategic and tactical implications of containment were often crucial when the use of force was an issue. In the past, the soldiers often turned out to be more wedded to policy than the politicians who established it, seeing strategy and tactics as clearly determined by policy guidelines. Where civilians often sought loopholes and room for maneuver in crisis decisions, the military were likely to pose starker alternatives and to couch them in terms of necessity rather than choice. Only the differences in military interpretations of necessity provided the flexibility that Presidents valued.

MILITARY CONSERVATISM AND ANTICOMMUNISM

Military officials were neither leaders nor laggards in committing the United States to the cold war. Their views of the USSR paralleled those of civilian leaders, and dissent within the military paralleled dissent among the civilians. Many in both camps were pro-Soviet in World War II and did not give up hope for postwar cooperation until well into 1946. As the balance of opinion within the government shifted, soldiers marched in step with policy makers. Together they prepared for general war with the Soviets, planned the defense perimeter in the Pacific, excluding Formosa and Korea, and reversed themselves in June 1950. Naive appeasers, paranoid jingos, and the dominant stance favoring containment could be found in roughly similar proportions in both groups. (One exception was a small flurry of proposals in the late 1940s by a few air force and navy officers favoring preventive war against the Soviets on the premise that war was inevitable and might as well be undertaken before the USSR broke the American atomic monopoly.)[2]

United States policy in World War II rested on unconditional surrender by the Axis powers and deferral of permanent political settlements and territorial adjustments to postwar negotiations among the Allies. In this spirit the Joint Chiefs blocked consideration of postwar boundaries at the Dumbarton Oaks conference. The military dimension of strategy superseded the political. The dominant military leadership concurred with President Roosevelt, in opposition to the British, who were more balance-of-power oriented, wanting to subordinate strategy to postwar Western political goals. Many in the top echelon of United States military leadership were more suspicious of British imperial designs than of the Russians. Omar Bradley remembered ruefully, "As soldiers we looked naively on the British inclination to complicate the war with political foresight and non-military objectives." Diplomat George Kennan saw strong pro-Soviet attitudes among soldiers quite frequently and considered them disgraceful. When President Roosevelt went to Yalta he took a joint memorandum from the Joint Chiefs and the State Department, which opposed "spheres of influence" as a conceptual basis for peace.[3]

There was a significant minority of anti-Soviet officers, including one with special entrée to the President—Admiral William Leahy—but few had a receptive audience. When Lauris Norstad, then a junior brigadier general, agreed with the British chiefs' proposal for a campaign in the Balkans and Eastern Europe to cut the area off from Soviet occupation, he was reprimanded by George Marshall and nearly courtmartialed. Albert Wedemeyer, one of the top strategic planners in the early part of the war, opposed Marshall's divorce of political considerations from strategy. He denounced unconditional surrender, which he believed prevented an anti-Hitler coup that could have led the Wehrmacht to lay down its arms in the West while stopping the Red Army short of the Vistula. Wedemeyer had favored keeping the United States out of the European war and directing the primary United States effort to the Far East until Germany and the USSR exhausted each other. He had attended the German War College from 1936 to 1938, claimed to view German expansionism as no different from British and French imperialism, and saw bolshevism as a greater threat than nazism. But he was eased out of planning and reassigned to the tertiary China-Burma-India theater.[4]

The dominant view of military victory as an end in itself was reflected in Eisenhower's decision to halt American forces on the Elbe River and allow the Red Army to take Berlin. Roosevelt, Marshall, and Truman delegated the decision to him, regarding it as a purely military prerogative of the field commander. Winston Churchill, who wanted to extend the Western Allies' lines as far east as possible before the German capitulation, protested. Eisenhower believed it militarily inadvisable to try to take Berlin from the west because he placed first priority on destruction of the German armies in the south and the Ruhr pocket and feared well into April Nazi plans to hold out in a redoubt in the Alps. This decision was no more a reflection of military insensitivity to the political dimension of strategy than of civilian insensitivity. Occupation zones for Germany had already been decided at the August 1943 Quebec conference. If the Western Allies captured Berlin, they were obligated to pull back, as they later did from the large section of German territory west of the Elbe, and share occupation of the city. Bradley estimated to Eisenhower that a United States breakthrough to Berlin might cost 100,000 casualties.[5]

Were the military success to offer a postwar political benefit, the issue would have been different, which the military recognized. Earlier they had seen that the Allies were advancing faster than anticipated on the western front. Eisenhower sent Bedell Smith to tell the Anglo-American conference on Malta that the armies would advance beyond the boundaries set by the European Advisory Commission. "We felt that if our political superiors agreed . . . they might decide to insist upon their right to occupy a greater portion of the German territory," Eisenhower later wrote, but Smith's presentation did not change policy. Churchill to the contrary, civilian views abetted the soldiers' disinterest in a race for Berlin. The only important general to advise Eisenhower to go for Berlin—and then "on to the Oder"—was George Patton.[6] As a result, the Western Allies ended the war with part of Berlin, isolated deep within the Soviet occupation zone, and a casus belli was born that threatened to ignite another world war several times from 1948 to 1962.

A clearer example of military pressure to subordinate postwar political goals to tactical economy was the soldiers' emphasis on securing Soviet entry into the war in the Far East to hasten the defeat of Japan. The Joint Chiefs were more concerned than the President to have the Russians intervene and emphasized the need through the first half of 1945. According to Forrestal even Mac-Arthur, despite his denial in later years, urged Soviet participation. By summer Admiral Ernest King had revised his thoughts, as had Leahy, but Marshall remained firm in recommending the advantages of Russian entry.[7]

These cases support neither right-wing revisionist charges of a "sellout" to the Russians nor left-wing revisionist charges of collusion by the Western Allies to deny the USSR the fruits of victory or compromise Soviet security. Rather they reveal the separation of tactical and political decision making and the primacy of the former. Even for months after the war, military leaders remained hopeful of cooperation with the Soviet allies. Eisenhower told a House committee in November 1945, "There is no one thing, I believe, that guides the policy of Russia more today than to keep friendship with the United States."[8] Suspicions grew, but not until 1946 did most military leaders shift to irrevocable assumptions of Soviet hostility and potential conflict in Europe. The Iranian crisis of that year solidified the disillusionment.

The cold war was not prompted by bellicose generals seeking conflict with the Soviets. Nor did the soldiers prevent the President from adopting an anti-Soviet strategy sooner than he did. There is little evidence of consistent differences in the recommendations of soldiers and statesmen. A near exception was China, where General Joseph Stilwell—whose view of Mao's communists was benign compared with his acid contempt for Chiang's government—was relieved by Wedemeyer, whose firm support of the Nationalist government set him apart from the American diplomatic contingent in the country. But even this case reflects the dominance of civilian views and the diversity of military opinion. Military advice on China was divided, during both World War II and the civil war. At first, one side included Stilwell and army Chief of Staff Marshall, who were concerned solely with reforming the Chinese army so it could help defeat Japan; Stilwell recommended military cooperation with Mao and a quid pro quo policy toward Chiang that demanded reforms in exchange for aid. In opposition was the theater air commander, Major General Claire Chennault, who believed an air offensive from China would be the best military strategy and whose close personal, emotional, and (according to some sources) financial ties to Chiang Kai-shek made him a strong supporter. Roosevelt leaned first toward Chennault, although all of the Joint Chiefs supported Stilwell, then toward Stilwell and Marshall, and finally in 1944—despite the disastrous backfiring of Chennault's military strategy—he gave in to the Chiang-Chennault axis and replaced Stilwell.[9]

Wedemeyer took the field and clashed with Marshall in December 1945, arguing that postwar cooperation between the Nationalists and communists was impossible. When he had realized that the USSR was not honoring the Sino-Russian treaty of the previous August, denying Chiang access to Manchuria and arming the Chinese communists, Wedemeyer recommended sending seven United States divisions to north China to protect Chiang's lines. The Joint Chiefs demurred but deployed two marine divisions along the Tientsin-Peking railroad with a directive, opposed by Wedemeyer, to avoid involvement in incidents. By the time of Marshall's 1945 mission to China, the Joint Chiefs, the marine commandant, the State Department, and the War Department were anxious to pull the marines out. The marine commander in China, Keller Rockey, supported the settlement Marshall sought and conceded the need to give the communists a large degree of control of the northern provinces. The troops were removed. Stilwell, who had resisted letting political considerations interfere with wartime strategy, had been replaced by Wedemeyer, who placed priority on the postwar political balance of power.[10] But Wedemeyer's extreme anticommunist strategy was rejected by both Marshall and Truman.

Once the cold war was underway, military attitudes again paralleled civilian alignments. Some became strongly right wing, some became dedicated but prudent anticommunists, and some remained more interested in the profession of arms than in ideology. Wedemeyer retired during the Korean War and became national chairman of Citizens for Taft in 1952. During the McCarthy period he joined Generals Clark, Van Fleet, Stratemeyer, and Almond and Admiral Joy in right-wing criticism of national policy. Such officers became the stereotype of the military viewpoint to most liberals. Other liberals identified with those army officers such as James Gavin and Matthew Ridgway who believed in polycentric rather than monolithic communism and the possibility of deterrence as an alternative to war with the Soviet Union. Still others identified with leaders like the gruffly apolitical Marine Commandant David Shoup. Faced with hostile cross-examination in Senate hearings by Strom Thurmond, who was concerned about whether the corps was indoctrinating recruits sufficiently against communism, Shoup retorted that the marines' job was not to worry about ideologies or teach troops to hate but to be trained and ready for combat against whomever national policy dictates.[11]

It is not surprising that liberals usually see the right-wing extremists as characteristic of military attitudes. Professional military life in itself is often assumed to be implicitly fascistic; the military is an authoritarian institution subject to stern discipline and deprivation of normal civil liberties. Contradicting the stereotype of soldiers as authoritarian personalities, however, some sociological research indicates that military training reduces authoritarian orientation. Statistically, authoritarian personalities tend to be selected out because they bungle assignments and are not promoted, and F-scale ratings (test measures of authoritarian orientation) are highest at the early cadet level and lowest among the high ranks. Other studies, however, suggest a correlation between authoritarian attitudes and choice of a military career. Military officers, for example, rank higher in doctrinaire cognitive style than foreign service officers

(60 percent high and 40 percent low versus 22 percent high and 78 percent low). It is difficult to be sure, though, where authoritarianism ends and conservatism begins. Surveys indicate that 70 percent of military leaders identify themselves as "conservative" and "hard line" in general foreign policy beliefs and 30 percent "liberal" and not "hard line." The proportions of foreign service officers' attitudes were reversed. This evidence contrasts with the immediate postwar pattern, when some diplomats were more anticommunist than many soldiers. In the Dulles period as well, there were instances when State Department officials argued that the communist military threat in certain areas was greater than the Joint Chiefs believed. Under budgetary pressure in the mid-1950s, the JCS wanted to reduce the American-funded Laotian army from 32,000 men to 15,000, which they considered an adequate number. State protested and forced a compromise reduction to 23,650.[12]

Military conservatism, according to Morris Janowitz, is "more a conservatism of form than it is of content," implying support of the status quo. Leading soldiers identify as conservatives because this allows them a political perspective that preserves nonpartisanship. Samuel Huntington goes further, asserting a consistency between ideological Burkean conservatism and the basic standards of military professionalism.[13] In any case, conservative military attitudes did not produce a consistent split between military and civilian leaders on cold war policy. To understand the civil-military differences that affected crisis decisions, it is necessary to look beyond formal policy to the ways in which policy is translated into strategy and tactics.

THE MILITARY MEANINGS OF CONTAINMENT

The end of American isolation in 1941 found the United States faced with war on two broad fronts. The dominant group within the military considered victory in Europe the first priority. A clique that resented the secondary status of the Pacific war developed around the theater commander, Douglas MacArthur, who never forgave the administration or the Joint Chiefs for the 1942 decision to abandon the Philippines.[14]

As Soviet-American cooperation disintegrated after World War II, the dispute over geographic priorities continued, with the Europeanists still dominant. The pro-Asia group complained that economic and military aid were not given to Nationalist China on the same scale as to Greece. Ironically it was the Europe First policy of the liberal Roosevelt and Truman administrations that helped lay the basis for the Vietnam War (the priority of shoring up the weak government in Paris prevented the United States from pressuring the French to give up their Indochina colonies), while the Asia-oriented group, so identified with reactionary domestic politics, championed Asian nationalism and opposed European imperialism in the Far East.[15]

The Korean War raised the standing of the Asia Firsters because it was the only theater of combat, and they argued for victory. The Joint Chiefs, however, stayed with the Europe First principle. During the month before Chinese intervention in 1950, the Chiefs wanted to cut back supplies and reinforcements intended for the Far East command so that two divisions could be shifted to Europe to meet North Atlantic Treaty Organization commitments. In the second and third years of the war, the Chiefs maintained their commitment to limited goals in Korea.[16] MacArthur scoffed at their logic and the notion that the number of troops available for Korea was limited because they were "needed in Germany where there was no war." He also maintained that Soviet deployments in Eastern Europe were clearly defensive. MacArthur's historical theory and interpretation of Soviet strategy were antithetical to that of the Joint Chiefs and the administration:

> There was a failure to understand that the global panorama has long encompassed three great areas of potential struggle: in the center, Europe; in the flanks, Asia to the North and Africa to the south. The free world apparently conceived of the center as the area of supreme interest and potential struggle; that if it could be held safely, all else would fall into place . . .
> What the Soviets sought were the economic frontiers of the world . . . the world's potential wealth in raw resources. The center represented little in economic advance, the flanks everything. The Soviet strategy was merely to defend in the center, but to advance by way of the flanks, to cause the free world to concentrate its resources at the center to the neglect of the vital ends. It has worked even beyond wildest expectation.[17]

The Asia-oriented soldiers who had been submerged under the Democrats gained greater status under the Republicans. In both Roosevelt-Truman and Eisenhower cases, however, the dominance of one group over the other reflected the politicians' control of policy. The military did not convince Roosevelt of the importance of Europe any more than he convinced them. When the Chiefs momentarily wanted to redirect efforts to the Pacific after the 1942 continental invasion plan was resisted by the British in favor of the North African campaign, Roosevelt refused and made them re-dedicate themselves to the indirect campaigns in the Mediterranean. Political leaders decided basic strategic priorities and picked military men who shared those views. When Eisenhower, who had been a Europe Firster, became President, he elevated the Asia Firsters in deference to the Taft and Knowland Republicans who wanted to change geographic priorities. In general, though, he did not tip the balance completely but sought a higher degree of equality of the two theaters.[18] In terms of the use of force, the commitment to use United States troops against communist attack remained absolute only in Europe and Japan. The revised strategy in Asia was based on air and naval power and avoidance of commitment on the ground.

The Europe versus Asia dispute abated in the years following the Korean War but did not disappear. The MacArthur legacy was taken up less by his own service than by the navy and air force. But overall, the Europe first principle remained the rule for most of the postwar period, despite the fact that two wars were fought in the Far East, while no armed combat ever took place between NATO and the Warsaw Pact. The air force remained riveted to the mission of strategic nuclear retaliation against the USSR until the late 1960s. The army was relieved to return to its European mission after the frustration of Vietnam and as the beginning of détente with China reduced tension in the western Pacific. And as the Soviet navy expanded and the Near East gained in strategic importance in the 1970s, the American navy turned its attention increasingly west-ward to the Mediterranean, the Persian Gulf, and the Indian Ocean.

Because the priority of European defenses was determined and enforced by civilian leadership, it was in Asian crises that military advice was most salient. Given firm civilian commitments to the one theater, political leaders had less reason to rely on military advice in situations on which there was a consensus about the need for resistance to communist advance (such as Berlin) than in those where the commitment was less clear and where interests were more marginal. In some of the latter cases the limits of military resources also dictated caution. Whatever the aggregate level of military capabilities and force levels, the tendency in Asian crises was to subtract the amount required for European contingencies from the total and then to examine the feasibility of using force in terms of whatever was left over. Given strategic priorities, conventional capabilities for European defense were determined by military neces-sity, while military necessity in Asian crises was determined by available capabilities. Military advice is less salient in establishing basic policy and strategy than it is in evaluating tactical capabilities, and therefore interpretations of capabilities have been their major channel of influence. At the same time, however, military views of the marginal costs of intervention or nonintervention and their recommendations on what level of force is a reasonable response to a crisis derive from their interpretation of what civilian-defined policy requires and from their own philosophical convictions about the functions of force in international relations.

Conceptions of the nature of military conflict can be broken down into two broad schools of thought. The absolutist school views war as a punitive crusade of good against evil, with no room for compromise. Once the decision to resort to force is made, victory—complete defeat of the enemy—should be the government's goal. Deterring an enemy requires the threat of complete destruction as the consequence of any aggression. The pragmatic school is oriented to balance-of-power considerations and sees deterrence and defense as problems of relative interests rather than absolute values. Force should be measured and applied in proportion to costs and benefits. Limited aggression may be met by limited retaliation. In this view not all interests are important enough to require war. The use of force may successfully coerce an enemy, but it can also be counterproductive. These two sets of attitudes, combined with variations in the definition of the concept of containment, formed the range of postwar strategic debate in the cold war. The absolutist approach overlapped with the Asia First identification and was dominant in the air force throughout the cold war, in the navy intermittently, and was a minority faction in the army.[19] (There was a resurgence of absolutism at the top levels of all the services in the late 1960s because of the frustration of the Vietnam experience.)

The extreme version of the absolutist view was the evanescent rollback policy that surfaced in John Foster Dulles's 1952 speech in Buffalo, which pledged that the new administration would use "all means to secure the liberation of Eastern Europe." This crusade-like policy was supported by some military men such as retired General Lucius Clay, one of Eisenhower's closest advisers in the transition period. Clay wanted a more active policy that would warn the Soviets that the United States would not allow the Russian army to intervene in a revolt by a satellite nation. This alternative to containment was also considered in Operation Solarium, a conclave of top soldiers and diplomats in the first days of the Eisenhower administration to discuss foreign policy options. The consensus that emerged from Solarium, however, reaffirmed containment.[20] As a policy, rollback was only briefly declared and never practiced. In crises, President Eisenhower always took less extreme options. In Korea he chose not to bear the costs of marching to the Yalu again. This decision to settle for the status quo disappointed Arthur Radford, who favored military pressure on communist China. Soviet suppression of the East German riots of 1953 and the Hungarian revolt of 1956 sealed the casket of the liberation policy. There is no evidence that American counterintervention was ever considered seriously in these crises. The only area in which hope of liberation lingered was the Far East, where the most devoted anticommunists continued to hope that Chiang would return to the mainland.[21]

Containment reigned, but its operational meaning remained ambiguous. As a posture, administration policy leaned toward the absolutist doctrine, standing for complete containment of communism within the bounds of 1950. Massive retaliation was posed as the response to communist territorial advances. Eisenhower and Dulles reserved the option to counter communist threats in peripheral areas by striking Moscow itself rather than intervening in the besieged area. Administration military leaders became more wedded to this view—with the exceptions of Army Chiefs Ridgway and Taylor—than the President and secretary of state because they saw less room for a gap between verbal posture and actual policy. Radford and Air Force Chief Nathan Twining supported massive retaliation enthusiastically, as did Navy Chief Carney, though not so strongly. But in action, the administration failed to live up to its rhetoric. Eisenhower accepted partition of Vietnam and exercised restraint in the first Taiwan Straits crisis; some of the offshore islands, the Tachens, were in fact evacuated and ceded to communist China.

Even more restrained than the administration's action policy were the views of pragmatic army officers (usually Europe Firsters) who even before the civilian leaders and JCS majority recognized disunity in the communist world. They eschewed Dulles's and Radford's rhetoric about the "Sino-Soviet bloc" and "Moscow-Peiping axis" and asserted an American interest in exploiting differences among communist powers. In the early 1950s army leaders supported military aid for the independent communist government of Yugoslavia. When the chief of naval operations, the air force chief of staff, and the marine commandant recommended in 1954 that the United States should retaliate against China "if it is determined that Communist China is a source of armed aggression, either direct or indirect," Ridgway filed a remarkable dissent in a memo to the secretary of defense. He advised that the United States should try to divorce China from the USSR; avoid at all costs a war against both China and the Soviet Union; reject the view that China must be either appeased or destroyed; recognize that the attainment of United States global objectives did not require destruction of Chinese military power; and try to induce communist China into friendly relations. "I challenge any thesis that destroying the military might of Red China would be in our long-range interests," he wrote later. "We would create there, by military means, a great power vacuum. Then we would have to go in there with hundreds of thousands of men to fill that vacuum." These were unorthodox views, ahead of government policy by two decades.[22]

The rationale behind the pragmatic logic of containment was that prevention of communist territorial expansion was desirable but conditional on the costs of each case. Wider dimensions of the balance of power should be considered, and marginal communist territorial advances were not worth preventing if nuclear war resulted or if conventional forces and national resources were extended too far. This meant that automatic use of force to ensure complete containment was less desirable than assigning priorities to where United States power would be committed and limits to how much of it should be invested in any situation. It also meant, in opposition to Eisenhower's policy, that limited war capabilities should be preserved and expanded to provide more military options short of resort to nuclear weapons. The first point led retired officers such as Ridgway and Gavin to oppose escalation in Vietnam after 1965. The second point, when President Kennedy adopted it, provided the means by which pragmatic active duty officers such as Maxwell Taylor could deemphasize the first point.

Attention to sources of national power other than forces in being (as opposed to those that could be mobilized after a war began) was less characteristic of active army leadership in the 1960s, a period of expanding budgets and rising force levels. The Republicans had sought to protect the economic base of the country by reducing expenditures through the massive retaliation strategy: maximizing commitments while minimizing options ("strategic monism"). Presidents Kennedy and Johnson, given a higher rate of economic growth, paid less attention to the danger of economic drain and sought to maximize both commitments and options through the flexible response buildup ("strategic pluralism"). The Gavin view was intermediate: maximize options by pluralism in forces but guard against the drain of strategic power by limitation of commitments. He believed that spending $30 billion per year in Vietnam damaged America's strategic position by sapping its resources and told his

FIGURE 2. Policy, strategy, and constituencies.

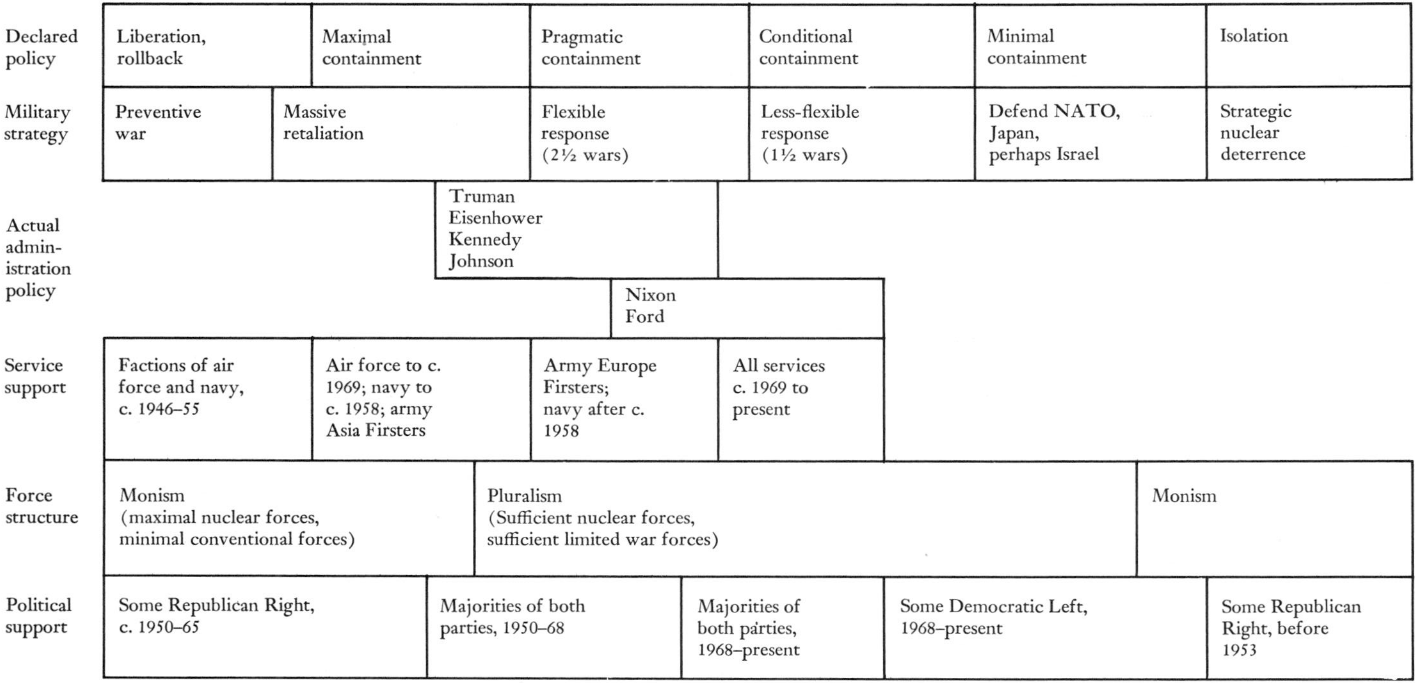

	Liberation, rollback	Maximal containment	Pragmatic containment	Conditional containment	Minimal containment	Isolation
Declared policy	Liberation, rollback	Maximal containment	Pragmatic containment	Conditional containment	Minimal containment	Isolation
Military strategy	Preventive war	Massive retaliation	Flexible response (2½ wars)	Less-flexible response (1½ wars)	Defend NATO, Japan, perhaps Israel	Strategic nuclear deterrence
Actual administration policy			Truman Eisenhower Kennedy Johnson	Nixon Ford		
Service support	Factions of air force and navy, c. 1946–55	Air force to c. 1969; navy to c. 1958; army Asia Firsters	Army Europe Firsters; navy after c. 1958	All services c. 1969 to present		
Force structure	Monism (maximal nuclear forces, minimal conventional forces)		Pluralism (Sufficient nuclear forces, sufficient limited war forces)		Monism	
Political support	Some Republican Right, c. 1950–65		Majorities of both parties, 1950–68	Majorities of both parties, 1968–present	Some Democratic Left, 1968–present	Some Republican Right, before 1953

active military friends that they were helping the communists by being in Vietnam.[23]

The absolutist and pragmatic attitudes have been competing strands of military doctrine for years, but the groups have not always been consistent. Postwar right-wing absolutists such as Wedemeyer opposed any accommodation with the USSR or China, but viewed World War II as a failure that might have been salvaged if the Western Allies had not demanded unconditional surrender; limited war strategy was desirable before 1945 but not after. Wartime absolutist liberals who sought unconditional destruction of fascism, on the other hand, were more likely later to take a flexible view of containment of communism. Absolutist antifascists became pragmatic anticommunists and vice versa. Containment policy in administrations before and after Eisenhower was pragmatic in both word and deed, and the dominant military advisers were Europe oriented. The Eisenhower-Dulles containment policy was publicly absolutist, rejecting limited war as a strategy that would drain and ultimately defeat the West by forcing it to fight on communist terms, and the administration's dominant military advisers were air power–oriented Asianists. Given their premise that the Soviets controlled the initiative behind challenges in peripheral areas such as Korea and Indochina, massive nuclear retaliation against the Soviet Union seemed a credible threat or deterrent. They did not perceive autonomous local revolutionary movements as distinct from Soviet-orchestrated aggression. American invulnerability to nuclear attack from the USSR was also short-lived. The fatuity of the premises behind massive retaliation and the gap between declaratory policy and action policy were revealed by the early crises the administration faced in the Far East when the President tilted toward the pragmatic views of the minority of the Joint Chiefs against Radford and Dulles.

THE PSYCHOLOGY OF NECESSITY:
DETERMINISM AND SYMBOLISM IN STRATEGY

Diplomatic maneuver is a sinuous process that seeks to maximize the choices open to leaders. Military combat depends on clear coordination of complex technical functions. While political leaders try to avoid constraints on decision in a crisis, military leaders seek simple and reliable standards by which to implement decisions. For politicians, policy and strategy are tentative and malleable; for soldiers, they are more often definitive and determining. Military professionals were more prone to see an absence of choice in cold war crises. Determinism eased their burden of calculation. As Arthur Radford put it, "A decision is the action an executive must take when he has information so incomplete that the answer does not suggest itself." But because the strategic implications of containment remained uncertain, different soldiers saw different necessities.

The first level of determinism is strategic, involving decisions about whether the United States should resort to force to achieve the goals of policy. The military can see response in a crisis as determined either positively (requiring use of force) or negatively (precluding force). In the first Taiwan Straits crisis, for example, Commander in Chief, Pacific, Felix Stump and JCS partisans of absolute containment believed that strategy required a positive United States commitment to help Chiang hold the offshore islands (Carney even opposed evacuating the Tachens). The Joint Chiefs voted three to one in September 1954 to bomb inland China to prevent a communist landing on Quemoy and Matsu. Ridgway, assuming a more pragmatic containment strategy, believed United States interests determined the situation negatively: war with China over insignificant pieces of territory with no objective value would benefit none but the Soviet Union. General Walter Bedell Smith, as under secretary of state, argued vigorously with Ridgway against Radford. The President, formally though not firmly committed to a policy of maximal containment, compromised between both extremes, evacuating the Tachens but planning to back up Quemoy and Matsu.[24]

The argument of military necessity, in keeping with the principles of professional autonomy, is most strenuous at the second level of determinism—operational tactics—which concerns issues of how to fight once the strategic commitment is made. Military views of tactical determinism caused only minor friction in the crises of the Eisenhower administration. As an ex-general the President empathized with the military view. "What he referred to always," recounts Andrew Goodpaster, who served with him in the White House,

> ... was the fact that when we got just about to the moment of decision, the crucial period, some of those ... who had recommended the operation to him began to get nervous about it, after we had committed ourselves. And his answer to them ... was that the time to have had those thoughts was before we started down this course, that if you at any time take the route of violence or support of violence ... then you commit your-

self to carry it through, and it's too late to have second
thoughts, not having faced up to the possible consequences,
when you're midway in an operation.[25]

Military leaders, especially in the navy, sometimes asked the President to delegate prior authority to commanders to respond forcibly
to a specified contingency or demanded that the political leaders
make the decision about using force earlier than they wanted to. In
the 1958 Quemoy-Matsu crisis, Eisenhower complained, "I was
continually pressured—almost hounded—by Chiang on one side and
by our own military on the other requesting delegation of authority
for immediate action to United States commanders on the spot in
the case of attack on Formosa or the offshore islands . . . asking
authority for the United States Air Force to support the Chinese
National Air Force in the event of a major landing attack on the
offshore islands . . . I insisted that I would assess developments as
they occurred."[26] In the Lebanon crisis of the same year navy Chief
Arleigh Burke persistently sought assurances that he would be given
sufficient warning if the National Security Council decided for intervention so that logistics, communications, and sailing time would
not delay landing beyond the time the civilians decided they wanted.
Burke wanted twenty-four hours of warning; Dulles agreed to guarantee thirteen; then Eisenhower called and asked if he could do it in
seven. Burke said he could. The President gave the authorization.
Then there were some second thoughts among the policy makers,
and some asked when Burke could halt the operation. It was too late,
he said. "This thing doesn't start and stop. It's like a missile. You let
her go, it's gone."[27]

Alleged tactical necessity—if the politicians believe the military—
can thus alter the conditions of decision and constrict the President's
choice and control. Operational procedures can also lead to politically provocative exercises. This happened in rescue searches in
both of the Taiwan Straits crises. In July 1954 China shot down a
British airliner near Hainan, mistaking it for a Nationalist plane. At
Radford's urging, two United States aircraft carriers were dispatched
to search for survivors. The search lasted an abnormally long time.
Then just as Peking radio was broadcasting an apology to the
British, American planes downed two Chinese fighters thirteen miles
off the mainland. Several years later the Chinese shot down an
American reconnaissance plane twelve miles off the China coast.
Burke ordered the Seventh Fleet to conduct search operations ex-
actly three miles from the coast, adhering to United States-recognized

territorial waters but violating the twelve-mile limit claimed by the Chinese. He then informed Dulles who reacted with alarm and opposed the closeness of the search. They decided to take the issue to the President, who initially had the same reaction as Dulles, though he finally allowed the search to continue.[28]

The Kennedy administration resolved to monitor operations carefully after the disaster at the Bay of Pigs. But the Cuban affair had hardened military attitudes about tactical determinism. Thus, the narrow gap in attitudes between politicians and professionals in the Eisenhower administration widened markedly under his successor. Tension over tactical determinism prevailed throughout the crises of the 1960s. Even in the 1965 Dominican intervention, a small and simple operation, tactical necessity temporarily threatened the success of negotiations to end the civil war. The diplomats had developed a plan that was gaining wide popular support when a firefight erupted, and the Inter-American Peacekeeping Force advanced fifty square blocks into the constitutionalist zone of Santo Domingo. Even when the ceasefire was restored, the troops did not got back to their former lines. The commanders convinced Ambassador Bunker that the new positions were needed to keep the constitutionalists from using the high-rise buildings in which they had placed snipers earlier.[29]

Strategic determinism may contradict tactical determinism. In Korea, field commanders were looking "through a gunsight," Mark Clark's metaphor for the narrower concerns of the soldier on the spot. To defeat the Chinese armies tactically would have required up to eight additional United States divisions and nuclear weapons, in the view of Taylor, the last field commander during the war, and a naval blockade of China and bombing of staging areas in Manchuria. For Europe Firsters, these tactics would have endangered the United States strategic position by draining resources away from the North Atlantic Treaty Organization. (From 1965 to 1967 there was no such contradiction between strategic and tactical priorities because there was less fear of imminent Soviet attack in Europe and because the flexible response buildup enabled the United States both to maintain force levels in Europe and to send increasing numbers of troops to Asia.) When a contradiction does occur, general strategic necessity takes precedence over specific tactical necessity. (Tactical determinism takes precedence only if it is negative, that is if capabilities are inadequate. Surface sailor Robert Carney agreed with Radford and Twining's strategic views more than with Ridgway's, but he shared the army's skepticism of the ability of an air strike alone to save the French position at Dienbienphu.)[30] Strategic necessity, however, is even less objectively calculable than tactical requirements.

At first glance, strategic requirements appear to be clearly implied by national goals and enemy strength. Military forces are quantifiable and comparable. The conventional logic of strategic rationality in war also dictates that forces should not be committed where there is no hope of securing a territorial objective, especially if the objective is insignificant in terms of terrain, population, and resources, or usefulness to the enemy. But policy may require military commitments that are not militarily rational if they achieve political goals that outweigh military costs.

Before June 1950 the government considered neither South Korea nor Formosa strategically vital, and Acheson and the Joint Chiefs explicitly excluded them from the United States defense perimeter. Military conflict, it was assumed, would come as a general war. The North Korean attack shattered this perception, and both areas were put back inside the perimeter. The attack touched nerves still raw from Hitler's salami tactics of the 1930s, suggesting the communists would attempt to conquer the free world in piecemeal steps. The domino theory and fear of appeasement cast strategic necessity in a subjective light. The Munich analogy came to underpin commitment to defend areas that lacked strategic military significance but that had symbolic political significance. Absolutists saw defense of Taiwan as vital in strategic terms. Even before the Korean War MacArthur's intelligence chief, Charles Willoughby, denounced its exclusion from the defensive perimeter. Radford described it as "the key to our entire defense system in the Western Pacific" and predicted its loss would imperil the Philippines, Okinawa, and Japan. Pragmatic soldiers, however, were more equivocal. A year after the war had begun, Bradley said Taiwan was important but not vital. Major General David G. Barr enunciated the symbolic ingredient when he testified that "the strategic value of Formosa to the United States is principally in not letting the other fellow have it."[31]

Taiwan and South Korea were major pieces of territory and were militarily defensible without resort to nuclear weapons. There were two areas, however, that exposed the symbolic dimension of strategy starkly: Berlin and the Chinese offshore islands of Quemoy and Matsu. The United States went to the brink of war for them despite the fact that they had no military value; in fact militarily they were a burden. Berlin, despite President Kennedy's morale-boosting hyperbole in 1961 comparing the city to Bastogne, was militarily indefensible, and the military were the first to admit it. The First

Battle Group was sent to reinforce the Berlin garrison not because it would prevent the Russians from taking the city but as a symbol of Western resolve. Quemoy and Matsu could be held but only by using nuclear weapons or landing an American army on the mainland. Yet Eisenhower decided to defend both territories, risking war with the USSR or China.

These commitments were made, not born. When the Soviets blockaded Berlin in 1948, top professional soldiers were far from sure that the Western Allies should stay in the city. General of the Army Marshall and upper echelons of the Defense Department considered evacuating, and Air Force Chief Hoyt Vandenberg reluctantly instituted the airlift Truman ordered. The Joint Chiefs vetoed the proposal of Military Governor Clay and his state department adviser Robert Murphy to send an armed convoy. Truman was more willing than the Chiefs to take the risk, according to Murphy, and offered to approve Clay's plan. Only the steadfast opposition of the JCS prevented military action in the ground corridor to the city. Even members of Clay's military staff urged leaving Berlin.[32] The airlift and the breaking of the blockade, however, enshrined Berlin as an outpost of freedom, which the United States was committed to defend. When the Soviets put pressure on the city a decade later, no military officials considered leaving. When communist troops detained three United States trucks at an autobahn checkpoint for over eight hours in November 1958, Norstad, the allied commander in Europe, planned to send a test convoy that he would extract, if the Soviets stopped it, "by minimum force necessary."[33] In the first offshore islands crisis in 1954–1955, the army opposed supporting their defense, but the crisis subsided without a test. In the second crisis four years later, there was no vocal military opposition to their defense even from the army—only an equivocation by the Joint Chiefs at one point and some muted misgivings communicated by leaks or by retired spokesmen.[34]

Crisis, and its successful weathering, invested these European and Asian outposts with strategic significance (although in the 1960 campaign John Kennedy still quoted Admiral Yarnell, former fleet commander in the Far East, that the islands "are not worth the bones of a single American").[35] Psychology and morale rather than objective military utility assigned to these territories political value worth the risk of war. Military judgment was not distinguished from political judgment. Psychological symbolism became strategic determinism. The absolutist Asia First wing of the military eagerly adopted this standard, even outdistancing political superiors in assessing the value of the disputed territories. Others, particularly pragmatic army officers, lagged behind, and remained more dedicated to defending the European symbol (Berlin) than the Asian one (Quemoy). In congressional testimony Pacific commanders Stump and Felt emphasized Nationalist morale as a critical reason for defending the offshore islands. Admiral Burke said, "I told Mr. Eisenhower then, 'They don't mean anything, it's a purely symbolic thing, they don't mean anything except, who's daddy? Who runs that part of the world...?' "[36] Eisenhower recalled that Ridgway was the only service chief who did not concur. To Ridgway, Quemoy and Matsu represented "no more than listening posts" and "had little value."[37]

Radford's definition of decision, like his conception of strategy, was simplistic and overstated. Presidents almost never faced situations, even where information was virtually complete, that they considered determined, in part because advisers usually disagreed about what constituted necessity. Policy was a malleable generality that evolved and allowed ample room for differing interpretations of the strategy dictated by objectives. And even in cases where strategy seemed clearly to recommend a response, the desire to use force had to be weighed against the capacity to do so.

6 The Range of Possibility: Capabilities and Choices

I remember when I was Secretary of State I was being pressed constantly ... to give the Russians hell ... at this time, my facilities for giving them hell—and I am a soldier and know something about the ability to give hell—was 1⅓ divisions over the entire United States. That is quite a proposition when you deal with somebody with over 260 and you have 1⅓.

General of the Army George C. Marshall

Capabilities created to increase the government's options by generating information and alternatives that would otherwise be unavailable, also, and of necessity, create interests in, and lobbies for, the use of these capabilities. The creation of a capability brings with it officials commissioned to search for instances in which that capability might be appropriately used ... [and] groups with interests in the exercise of that capability ... Ready options dominate potential but not-so-available alternatives ... Capabilities create demands ... Capabilities can create temptations.

Graham T. Allison

MILITARY assertions of negative tactical determinism are more influential for civilian leaders than any other kinds of advice. No President in the cold war era ever ordered an intervention when at least one top military official recommended firmly against it. And without exception, negative military recommendations were based primarily on doubts about the adequacy of available conventional forces to accomplish the mission. For a soldier to endorse, or a President to approve, use of force when capabilities were problematic would be reckless. Consequently soldiers are most negative in their attitudes toward precipitating a general war for which they rarely consider capabilities sufficient and for which they want more time to prepare. This was the attitude of the Joint Chiefs in 1941 and 1951. They are most positive and confident, or indifferent, when minor interventions are concerned, such as the Dominican Republic in 1965. But it was in precisely these situations, in which soldiers had the fewest reservations, that their advice was least heard and least salient; civilian leaders had no constraints to prevent them from making the decision on purely political grounds. Finally, military advice is least coherent, consistent, and certain in situations that fall between the above extremes—such as Vietnam—when different estimates of capabilities or assumptions of goals confuse the military or put them at odds with each other.

OBJECTIVES AND OPTIONS

In theory, foreign policy determines military strategy. Reality is rarely so simple. Foreign policy and the conventional military capabilities to enforce it have sometimes been out of phase, such as in the late 1940s and 1950s when domestic political and economic constraints contracted defense budgets. Another reason for confusion of the policy-strategy relationship is the complexity and occasional inconsistency of the requirements of diplomatic maneuver and military efficiency. Differences between the President and his military advisers on preparations for entry into World War II illustrate this problem. President Roosevelt denied general staff requests for a balanced force buildup in 1939 and 1940 and focused on ambitiously high aircraft production goals because he believed aircraft were a crucial lever on the European diplomatic situation. At the same time the military advised against full assistance to Britain because it detracted from the buildup of American defenses; the President overruled them. The military view of national policy, which they derived from executive declarations, was still oriented in large part to hemispheric defense. They were concerned with the capability to defend existing commitments once war began (the army had recently argued for withdrawal from the Philippines, in opposition to the navy). The President was in the process of nudging United States policy toward intervention in Europe, against domestic opposition, and focused on the problems of diplomatic manipulation and bluff, both at home and abroad. The military adapted to Roosevelt's policy goals, but because assistance to Britain was retarding United States preparation, they opposed new commitments at every stage and advised against provoking the Japanese. The Army War Plans Division warned that in the event of a Far Eastern crisis, the United States would find that it was not yet prepared and would not be for several years. Civilian leadership overruled the military and instituted an oil embargo against Japan in July 1941. "Roosevelt's gamble failed. The Japanese were not deterred . . . and the United States found itself in the very predicament that Roosevelt's military chiefs had feared. War on two broad fronts came suddenly and disastrously upon an America only partially prepared and everywhere overextended militarily."[1] The Philippines fell, and United States forces were pushed back to the eastern Pacific.

During the cold war military capabilities were always less than ideal compared to the general goal of containing communist control of territory. Specific policy goals often came to depend on the level of capabilities rather than to determine it. Except for later stages of war in Korea and Vietnam, each crisis also had to be handled with forces in being. This meant that military officials' task was not simply to study a policy, deduce the appropriate strategy and forces to implement it, and recommend the results to political leaders for procurement and deployment. Instead they were often in the position where their advice on what could be achieved was to determine what would be achieved. This led to situations that irked both military and diplomats, where neither side wanted to make a firm recommendation without guidance from the other. The army chief of staff during the Korean War complained,

> In our regular periodic meetings with representatives of the State Department the Chiefs constantly tried to pin down at any particular time after the Chinese intervention, just what our remaining political objectives were in Korea, but our diplomatic colleagues would always counter with the query "What are your military capabilities?" . . . the age old question of the chicken and the egg. The Chiefs could only deduce that

our State Department co-workers ... wanted us to attain the maximal military results within our military capabilities. But the military would have to assume all the responsibility if things went wrong.[2]

Eisenhower described a similar dialogue between his principal advisers: "Military plans for the area could be more specific if the Department of State would tell the Joint Chiefs what was likely to happen in the Middle East," snapped JCS Chairman Radford. Secretary of State Dulles retorted, "If I knew in advance what our capabilities were, it would help a great deal."[3] This tendency for political leaders to try to get as much diplomatic leverage as possible from military capabilities suggests two basic questions: in terms of indirect military influence on use of force, what role do uniformed officials have in developing the force structures available for employment in a particular crisis? In terms of direct influence, do military advisers in a crisis always recommend utilization of a military capability when it is available?

The military forces that can respond to a contingency are the product of prior analysis of likely threats, constrained by domestic politics and limited economic resources. Under Presidents Truman and Eisenhower, strategy was the child of the budget; the services had to divide a finite amount provided by the administrations. Under Presidents Kennedy and Johnson, the military budget was supposed to be the child of strategy; the principle of sufficiency took precedence over financial constraints, and there were supposed to be no arbitrary expenditure limits. The frugal Eisenhower administration relied primarily on nuclear weapons, which provided few conventional options. The army declined from approximately a million men in 1954 to 870,000 by 1959. Dienbienphu, Quemoy and Matsu, and difficulties in the Lebanon operation showed the weakness of United States capabilities for limited intervention, and field exercises in 1958 and 1960 showed weakness in NATO forces. Secretary of Defense McNamara developed a more pluralistic force structure, providing options for a wider range of contingencies.[4] Within a few years the United States had some of the extra divisions that Ridgway had lacked, and ground intervention in Asia became possible.

Eisenhower's military strategy, at least formally, was irrational. Administration anti-communism produced ambitious foreign policy goals that it could not back up militarily because of the economization dictated by fiscal conservatism. Thus capabilities were inconsistent with declared goals. (Truman's administration had a similar problem, though containment goals before Korea were more modest, and Soviet capabilities were lower.) The succeeding Democratic administrations' foreign policy and military strategy were more consistent. Containment goals did not differ significantly from Eisenhower's, but in the period following the 1961 crises the administrations paid the price to develop forces more attuned to combating communist advances without resort to nuclear weapons. The Nixon doctrine (and left-wing Democrats at the same time) tried to attain a rational force structure *and* minimal intervention by reducing containment goals and the armed forces. The first Nixon administration cut military manpower by more than a million and decreased defense expenditures substantially as both percentage of federal budget and percentage of the gross national product.

The military role in determining budgets and force structure has varied. The JCS majority under President Eisenhower acceded to budget limits because they believed strategic air power could enforce national policy effectively. By delegating decisions on force structure to the Joint Chiefs within these financial limits, the administration deflected their pressures for new weapons or manpower into interservice bargaining. Intramilitary fights substituted for civilian-military fights. McNamara's combination of bigger budgets, cost-effectiveness criteria for procurement, and greater civilian intervention in program decisions changed this pattern. With the constraint of arbitrary fund ceilings officially gone, the Joint Chiefs fought secretarial intervention in force structure decisions by burying their own feuds and presenting a united front. The number of unanimous JCS recommendations on procurement increased under McNamara.[5] Civilian-military cleavage was the price of reducing military autonomy and financial constraints at the same time. The military appetite for larger defense expenditures thus came to frustrate liberals more in the 1960s than earlier.

Liberals have no better reason than conservatives, however, to view military pressures for more arms as malevolent. The soldiers' responsibility for national security means that they can never be satisfied with the level of preparedness. There is always an additional increment of power to be gained by spending more. For soldiers to show no interest in gaining additional means to meet future contingencies would be unprofessionally complacent.[6] This natural professional appetite, ideally, can be restrained and denied by political authorities, who establish the point of diminishing returns and consider competing national interests. This view is the ideal of the traditional theory of administration. The fact that military officials have almost never advised against use of force when they considered capabilities adequate is considered desirable, as evidence of restriction of judgment to professional military considerations. Unlimited options maximize choice for the politicians. Bureaucratic revisionism, though, sees this ideal as impractical. Enabling the military to support use of force creates pressure on political leaders to use force. Options erode political choice.

CAPABILITIES AS TEMPTATIONS

There are roughly three perspectives from which military needs are judged. One extreme is the pole of worst-case analysis and pessimism about external threats, which suggests maintaining maximal military capabilities in order to meet any contingency. Acquisition of forces high in quantity and quality is a prophylactic against situations where the government finds itself unable to achieve what it wants to. This logic is close to the professional military viewpoint. The opposite is the pole of pessimism about internal threats to policy-making rationality and fears that easy availability of military options encourages authorities to use them in a crisis rather than to search energetically for diplomatic solutions. To forestall adventurist impulses, capabilities should be limited to those clearly necessary for serious and probable contingencies. Deprivation of tactical options can prevent situations where officials may want to achieve something forcibly because they are able to. This logic is not far from that of bureaucratic revisionism. In practice, neither extreme corresponds to actual opinion on procurement. Most government debates on budgets, force levels, and weapons systems take place within the broad limits of the intermediate view, which assumes that a high level of military security is desirable but, given the constraints of economic resources and competing nonmilitary interests, a compromise must be made short of worst-case preparedness. The essential problems are determining the scope of policy goals that are to be enforceable and the acceptable margin of uncertainty about what threats may have to be countered.

Military pessimists point to those situations where lack of capabilities prevented use of force when it was desirable. In early 1948 conventional forces had been reduced to skeletal form and the military believed commitment of a division anywhere would require partial mobilization. For this reason they opposed dispatching American forces to Greece. General Marshall warned Secretary of Defense Forrestal that the United States was in danger of becoming involved in conflicts without sufficient forces. Later, when North Korea attacked, the United States was still unprepared to intervene efficiently. The first American unit into Korea, Task Force Smith, was badly mauled because it was under strength, not equipped with modern antitank weapons, and plagued by inadequate supporting logistical capacity. In the first month of the war the Joint Chiefs could not meet General MacArthur's requests for the estimated number of troops needed to repel the invasion because the manpower was not available.[7]

Despite President Eisenhower's reduction of conventional forces after Korea, the only overt military intervention that he undertook —in Lebanon—seemed to occur smoothly. Some military men did not see the incident in such complacent terms, though, pointing out that if any heavy fighting had occurred, reinforcement of the United States expedition would have been problematic. The navy's Military Sea Transport Service had lost a hundred ships to budget cuts and had none ready in the Atlantic when landings were ordered. Even if the ships had been available, the navy would have needed nearly a month to load and move an army division from the United States to the eastern Mediterranean. At the same time, tension in the Taiwan Straits left military leaders fearful that United States conventional capabilities were inadequate to cope with threats in both theaters. The low level of conventional ammunition stocks in the Far East and the small number of combat aircraft rigged to carry nonnuclear ordnance alarmed Pacific commander Harry Felt, who warned that in the event of conflict in the Pacific United States forces would have to use nuclear ammunition at an early stage.[8]

In Europe shortly later Supreme Allied Commander Lauris Norstad's recommendations for reinforcement of low NATO manpower, as Khrushchev's Berlin deadline approached, failed to turn Eisenhower from further reducing the size of the army. This action left the United States committed to respond to a Soviet move on Berlin by going to nuclear war. At a press conference the President said, "We are certainly not going to fight a ground war in Europe."[9] Two years later Kennedy faced a similar problem; but unlike his predecessor, he took the military advice. The European comand and JCS chairman convinced him that the weakness of conventional capabilities left the United States with few options if the Soviets closed the corridor to Berlin. An armed probe down the autobahn could be contained by East German and Soviet forces, leaving few means other than nuclear weapons with which to counter; the military officials therefore reiterated their recommendations for augmentation of ground forces. The weakness of conventional capabilities was also underlined by the shocking unreadiness of the two national guard divisions that President Kennedy mobilized to replace two regular divisions slated to reinforce the Seventh Army in Germany (the regulars were not sent because of the problems with the guard divisions). Years later, after Vietnam had drained the United States reserve, the Joint Chiefs warned after the *Pueblo* seizure that the United States did not have the power to make the threat of an extra war against North Korea plausible. In the 1970 Jordanian civil war, they again opposed intervention because the United States had no staying power unless the standby reserves were mobilized. As a JCS leader put it, "We were pointing out to Nixon that we couldn't do it for free." When high State Department officials asked the Chiefs if the United States could establish a credible deterrent to Soviet intervention in Jordan, they were told "not really."[10]

Low force levels did not always plague decision makers. Military weakness in the first year of the Korean War prompted the JCS to oppose escalation, but military buildup following the outbreak enabled Mark Clark to argue by the time he made his recommendations for escalation, "America was far better prepared to call the tune than in 1950. In the intervening two years we had pumped more than $100 billion into our military establishment, sharply reducing Russia's temptation to start World War III, or our danger of losing it." Whereas Eisenhower's conventional force reductions had left Kennedy with few nonnuclear options for Laos in 1961, the flexible-response buildup provided a wide range of capabilities for dealing with later crises.[11] In both cases the buildup eroded military reticence about escalation or intervention and thus reduced the reasons for the President to avoid commitment of American forces. This situation strikes pessimistic analysts of bureaucracy as unfortunate. Halperin suggests that procurement of capabilities creates direct incentives to use them. He applied this argument to an attack on Secretary of Defense James Schlesinger's selective retargeting for flexible nuclear response, asserting that counterforce capability will prompt military leaders to recommend a nuclear strike in a crisis.[12]

The thesis that capability encourages action is plausible, since use of force has correlated with high levels of capabilities and abstention has correlated with low capabilities. Ability to intervene, however, is only a necessary, not sufficient, condition. At most, the availability of capabilities has tipped the balance in favor of intervention when policy makers were uncertain. Indeed, capabilities were increased at the times they were because administrations wanted, as a matter of policy, to be able to use force in situations just such as those in which they eventually did. Nor does development of capabilities always lead the soldiers who advised their procurement to recommend their use. Ridgway and Gavin were among the most vigorous proponents of increases in limited war forces, but they did not recommend escalation in Vietnam. The circumstances where capabilities loomed largest in decision makers' deliberations were those where they were absent, that is when insufficiency precluded intervention.

This argument, admittedly, says no more than that Presidents have used force where they wanted to. But it is useful to question the extent to which bureaucratic revisionists argue that means determine ends. This view that tactical options drive policy decisions is not entirely inappropriate if the purpose of the analysis is actually to criticize the substance of policy as well as the dynamics of the policy-making process. Given premises that intervention in Laos would have been a mistake, and that intervention in Vietnam was a mistake, it is fortunate in retrospect that the administration did not clearly have the capability to intervene in the former case and unfortunate that it believed it did have the capability in the latter. In either case, though, it is still primarily the policy goals rather than the tactical options that should have been different. The real salience of bureaucratic revisionist pessimism lies in the extent to which Presidents cannot be trusted to make decisions that are rational in terms of their own policy goals, the extent to which dependence on professional evaluations reduces the possibility of analytical objectivity in decision making, or the extent to which military capabilities may be overestimated and alternative diplomatic solutions ignored. Reality is usually midway between the images of bureaucratic revisionism and traditional rational strategic analysis. Capabilities have rarely determined decisions on intervention, except negatively. Vietnam escalation decisions, though, were more affected by availability of apparently appropriate capabilities because a decision to use such means seemed easier than a decision to give up and withdraw. Even in these cases, however, capabilities matched executive political preferences; they did not distort them. Nor were the civilians coerced; their decisions for escalation always came long after the military recommendations.

This compromise view thus lies a bit closer to the "rational actor" and traditional administration theory pole of analysis than to the pole of organizational determinism. It does not, however, answer which predisposition—worst-case military strategy pessimism or bureaucratic revisionist decision-making pessimism—is an appropriate guide to decisions on force structure and options because design of forces must rest on prediction of future threats. Given opportunity costs and competing nonmilitary interests, this determination cannot be objective. The size of the cautionary hedge against hypothetical dangers depends on the value placed on military goals and the amount of confidence in the predictability of the environment. Both the ideal types of conservative military pessimism and liberal bureaucratic revisionism agree that means should be consistent with ends, but they divide over the scope of ends and the acceptable margin of uncertainty about prospective threats. From a purely rational and strategic point of view, with conservative assumptions about the extent of the external threat or radical assumptions about how aggressive United States policy should be, prophylactic procurement of maximal conventional capabilities is desirable because it reduces the number of contingencies to which the United States would be unable to respond forcibly; too many options are better than too few. From a political and subjective stance with optimistic views of low external threat and conservative views of how activist United States policy should be, some bureaucratic revisionists argue that a modest spectrum of capabilities is appropriate because such prophylactic deprivation guards prudent policy by precluding adventurous tactics; additional options only risk tempting leaders to escalate their goals or avoid recognizing the insolubility of a problem if apparent military means are at hand. This argument is least persuasive if national policy is maximal containment of communism (as it was for most of the postwar period) and most persuasive if government goals are less ambitious (as they have been since 1970).[13] The argument is even more important once the debate extends beyond conventional capabilities to nuclear weapons.

NUCLEAR OPTIONS

Conventional capabilities governed decisions on the use of force after 1945 although the use of nuclear weapons was not ruled out. But nuclear weapons were never used when military leaders recommended their employment and the only time they were, the military advisers had little to say about the decision. Truman said that the atomic bomb was "nothing else but an artillery weapon" and considered the decision to drop it "a purely military decision." But he would have paid more attention to military advice than he did in fact if this had strictly been the case. The Joint Chiefs never discussed the atomic bomb at any of their meetings prior to its use in 1945, and MacArthur was told of its existence only five days before Hiroshima. Marshall reportedly opposed dropping it without forewarning the Japanese so that they would have a chance to surrender first. Eisenhower claimed he recommended against using it, and all of the Joint Chiefs were reluctant to use it, saying the war could be ended satisfactorily without it. By June 1945 the President's civilian advisers were unanimous on favoring use of the bomb, though, and the President did not solicit the views of the military or naval staffs.[14]

The first postwar instance in which nuclear weapons were considered was the 1948 Berlin crisis. Advisers unaimously agreed that the bomb would be used if war broke out, and as a signal to the Russians Truman ordered sixty B-29 bombers to Britain. But few in the military believed that the United States nuclear monopoly could guarantee victory against the Soviets. Existing bombs were limited both in supply and destructiveness—perhaps fewer than a hundred low-yield warheads. The heavy Soviet civil defense program and the prospective attrition of aircraft by air defenses led many United States officers to believe through 1950 that the USSR could survive a nuclear attack on the homeland—of total proportions less devastating than the destruction German cities suffered from conventional bombing—while the Red army marched to the English Channel.[15]

The Korean War brought more active consideration of nuclear weapons. After Chinese intervention threatened to push United Nations forces out of the peninsula, President Truman caused public outcry when he suggested that atomic bombs might be used. Even earlier, when the original North Korean attack pushed American troops into the Pusan perimeter, air units were alerted (on a contingency basis only) for a nuclear strike. At that time James Gavin also went to see Ridgway, who was deputy chief of staff, and urged that he ask Chief of Staff Collins to recommend to the President use of nuclear weapons in order to prevent defeat. Maxwell Taylor remembers:

> I had expected a mushroom cloud to rise from the battlefield at any moment . . . But I found in Washington that there had been cogent military reasons, apart from political, for having withheld atomic weapons . . . we had too few of them at the time to risk their expenditure so far from the major threat . . . in Europe . . . the mountainous terrain of Korea would have limited the effectiveness of these weapons . . . Finally, it was feared that their employment here might reveal shortcomings which would have diminished their deterrent effect elsewhere.[16]

These tactical uncertainties continued to reinforce political inhibitions after the front stabilized. MacArthur considered atomic bombs as a means to cut Chinese supply routes in North Korea, but his successor Ridgway told JCS Chairman Bradley that he saw no need or justification for them. Ridgway's successor, Mark Clark, recalled that from time to time there were discussions about possible use, but they could find no targets that could not be handled by conventional explosives. One officer who reportedly favored nuclear attack on China was Major General Emmett O'Donnell, head of the Far Eastern bomber command, who was relieved early in 1951.[17] When Eisenhower took office in 1953 MacArthur and Radford advised him to think about using nuclear weapons to end the war. He decided to force a settlement in Panmunjon by hinting to the Chinese, through third parties, that the United States would move "without inhibition in our use of weapons, and would no longer be responsible for confining hostilities to the Korean peninsula." Neither the outgoing nor incoming army chiefs of staff, nor General Clark, were consulted about or knew of the atomic threat.[18] The decision was closely held and was made essentially by the President alone.

The only way to get the "bigger bang for the buck" which the new Republican defense policy contemplated was to reduce expensive conventional forces and rely more heavily on atomic capability. In 1953 the President approved a National Security Council paper authorizing the Joint Chiefs to plan on using nuclear weapons whenever their use was militarily desirable. Military leaders thus believed they would have the nuclear option with relatively few political constraints.[19] Within a year of the Korean armistice the administration was considering intervention to save the French in Indochina. French Premier Georges Bidault claimed that Secretary Dulles offered three atomic bombs to France for use against supply lines near the Chinese border, which Bidault refused (Dulles denied he had made the offer).[20] The French military staff was also certain that Radford's Operation Vulture plan was based on use of atomic bombs, and, according to a member of the JCS, Radford indeed argued vociferously for use of the weapons. (Radford later issued equivocal denials of a direct recommendation.)[21] Air Force Chief Nathan Twining recalled that the State Department told the Joint Chiefs that it was imperative to save Dienbienphu and that he and Radford agreed that the only way to do so was by the use of three small nuclear weapons. Curtis LeMay, then commander of the Strategic Air Command, later told an interviewer that indeed he had drawn up a plan for the tactical nuclear bombardment of Dienbienphu. When the interviewer asked what would happen to the French garrison, LeMay answered, "Well, I guess they'd have gotten it too."[22] Not surprisingly, Vulture was never implemented.

Later in 1954 the military stipulated the option to use nuclear weapons as the condition for the defensibility of Quemoy and Matsu. Dulles and the President agreed that small-yield bombs probably would have to be used against the surrounding mainland air fields. Several years later when the islands were threatened again, Eisenhower once more resolved that use of atomic weapons might be necessary—a view seconded by Commander in Chief, Pacific Harry Felt—which made some military appraisers uneasy about agreeing to defend the islands. Nevertheless eight-inch howitzers capable of firing atomic rounds were installed on the islands. After 1958 the only policy-level discussion of use of tactical nuclear weapons in Asia was during the 1961 Laos crisis. During the siege of Khesanh in late 1967, Westmoreland commissioned a study of the possibility of using tactical nuclear weapons to relieve the marine position but he never proposed doing so.[23]

The last instances where first use of nuclear weapons was a lively issue were the Berlin crises between 1958 and 1962. The conventional inferiority of NATO forces meant that the Western allies would find it difficult to break through a blockade to Berlin with conventional forces alone. This prompted the popular misconception that General Norstad favored a probe down the autobahn, in the event of a blockade, to bring about conditions that would allow the United States to use nuclear weapons. In fact Norstad was much more cautious. As early as 1957 he had been appealing in vain to Eisenhower for conventional "shield" forces of thirty divisions precisely in order to avoid use of nuclear weapons to meet a Russian attack. In 1959 he warned privately that it was wrong to be too tough on the Berlin issue because limiting nuclear war would probably be impossible, and he announced publicly that if hostilities began over Berlin there would not be an automatic western nuclear reaction. Rather NATO would use ready forces to compel a "pause" which would force the USSR to consciously go to general war.[24] (This contrasted with LeMay's view that "the pause idea is one of the most idiotic to come out of the Pentagon.")[25]

Absolutist doctrine after 1945 saw permanence and continuity in the character of war. Arthur Radford declared, "We have reached a state where atomic weapons are now conventional." For two decades after Hiroshima, most air force leaders believed, in contrast to the prevalent view that nuclear exchange was unthinkable, that it was likely and could be fought and won if the United States maintained superiority in strategic forces. Even before he left office Curtis LeMay reportedly advocated a nuclear attack on China.[26] Pragmatic doctrine, which came back to the fore after Eisenhower, saw nuclear weapons as revolutionary. Mutual nuclear deterrence

would force East-West conflict into conventional modes. To Maxwell Taylor the Cuban missile crisis "exposed the fallacy of a shib-
boleth of the previous decade that it would be impossible to have a
nonnuclear conflict between the United States and the USSR." He
believed American and Soviet strategic forces neutralized each other
and allowed the American conventional advantage in the Carribean
to decide the issue.[27] Limited war was possible not in spite of nuclear weapons but because of them. Naval leadership in the postwar
period was divided on this issue, leaning to air force absolutism in
the early and middle 1950s and toward army pragmatism in later
years. These doctrinal divisions were matched by disagreements
among civilian strategists. Different nuances and priorities, however, sometimes differentiated the dominant wing of the military
from dominant civilian views.

Statesmen and soldiers are partners in preventing war and fighting
it. The primary job of the politicians and diplomats, however, is to
ensure that the unthinkable does not happen, that deterrence does not
fail. The primary job of the soldiers is to make the best of the unthinkable if deterrence does fail, to limit damage and win the war.
These can be complementary or contradictory tasks, depending on
the theory of deterrence that governs strategy. As nuclear strategic
doctrine evolved within the government in the 1960s, some issues
separated the opinion of the military, which wanted to maintain
United States superiority and capability to fight a nuclear war if
deterrence failed, from the dominant civilian opinion, which wanted
to limit strategic arms deployments and to fortify deterrence by
eliminating the perception that either side could win a nuclear war
in any meaningful terms. The principles that formed the basis of the
first strategic arms limitation talks (SALT) agreement differed substantially from traditional military principles in that most of the
arms control advocates believed stabilization of deterrence required
relative equality of United States and Soviet strategic forces and
elimination of defensive systems, such as the antiballistic missile
(ABM). In this view, parity prevents the incentives to catch up that
fuel a spiral of reactive arms deployments and permits stabilization or
reduction of expenditures. Not deploying ABM systems reinforces
the threat of mutually assured destruction, which precludes a rational
decision to strike first and also retards the spiraling of offensive sys-
stems required to penetrate a screen of ABMs. Military orthodoxy,
however, considered United States superiority the best guarantee of
deterrence and viewed ABMs as desirable because minimizing expenditures is less important than maintaining security, which is increased if the enemy knows it is inferior, and because professional

soldiers do not believe armaments in themselves are the cause of international tension.[28] If deterrence fails, damage should be limited by any means possible, even if only marginally effective.

The leaders of the Strategic Air Command were most consistent and vociferous in opposing arms control. In 1956 its commander told Congress that deterrence could not be achieved without quantitative superiority in offensive strategic force. A decade later his successor agreed, maintaining that deterrence requires "assured superiority" and "assured war winning capability."[29] Army leaders were less vehement in attachment to the principle of superiority, in part because the view that strategic nuclear exchange was unthinkable enhanced the mission of the ground forces. But even Earle Wheeler told Congress in the early 1960s that the concept of parity was fundamentally contrary to all military precepts. The army also had an organizational interest in development of the antiballistic missile.[30]

Until the first strategic arms limitation talks most military leaders sought to maintain United States nuclear superiority, quantitative as well as qualitative. When the military's battle for strategic superiority was lost in SALT I, many turned to counterforce targeting strategies (that is, planning options for attacks on enemy weapons rather than population centers) as a means of preserving a warfighting capability, a fallback position from the assured destruction deterrence system. A limited variant of this strategy was adopted under Secretary of Defense James Schlesinger and provoked opposition from arms control theorists who believed it undermined deterrence. The new nuclear flexible response program compromised between the arms control view and concerns of former air force leaders: it rejected both the need for superiority and the position that capability to destroy enemy cities is sufficient for deterrence or as a credible response to a limited Soviet nuclear attack. Implicit in this controversy was the crux of the contradictory civilian and military priorities. Military pessimists are unwilling to place all reliance on deterrence because there is always a worst-case scenario in which deterrence can fail, and they deny any contradiction between deterrence and war-fighting capability. Arms control theorists remain uncomforted by assurances that enabling limited strategic exchange actually increases the credibility of deterrence, and they point to the costs of worst-case hedging, which can become self-fulfilling. With numerous exceptions, arms control proponents are unwilling to take chances in compromising the stability of mutual deterrence, and military authorities are reluctant to foreswear the capability to fight a nuclear war and limit damage in the event the deterrent system breaks down.

Development of tactical or theater nuclear weapons for battle-field use in a limited war was the army's answer to the air force's devotion to massive retaliation in the 1950s. Army pragmatists saw these weapons as the only way to defend Europe against superior Soviet conventional forces without resort to strategic thermonuclear attacks on the Soviet homeland that would provoke mutual annihilation. Absolutists were skeptical. They believed limited tactical use of nuclear weapons against China was feasible because the Chinese lacked intercontinental nuclear capability but believed war in Europe would inevitably be unlimited and would require full strategic assault against the USSR. Thus, in attitudes on tactical nuclear weapons in the 1950s air force radicals and army conservatives seemed to switch their usual stances: the former tended to agree with civilians who deprecated the possibility of limiting nuclear war once the threshold was crossed, and the latter seemed more adventurous in their confidence that theater nuclear weapons could be employed with discrimination and restraint on the battlefield. (It was civilian scientists seeking alternatives to the hydrogen bomb, though, who were the major force behind initial development of tactical nuclear weapons, not the military.)[31]

As chief of army research and development, Lieutenant General James Gavin argued that nuclear weapons had not been strategic since the Soviets had developed similar capability and that intercontinental missile forces were useful only for deterrence. But he argued against the insistence that West Germany not get tactical nuclear weapons because, he said, they had become standard equipment of a modern army, as much as gunpowder had been earlier.[32] The Lebanon operation subsequently suggested the limits of nuclear-based forces. When army units that included Honest John rocket batteries as standard equipment landed, a Pentagon official realized at the last minute the political significance of introducing nuclear weapons into the volatile Middle East and ordered that the missiles be left on board ship. After this experience, the army, which had replaced a large amount of divisional artillery with the Honest Johns, began putting conventional howitzers back into its divisions.[33] Army leaders, however, remained committed to the usability of tactical nuclear weapons despite the skepticism of some civilian strategists of the early 1960s. One incident that contrasts the confidence of the pragmatic soldiers with the nervousness of the pragmatic civilians was a debate over the Davy Crockett, a virtual nuclear bazooka that two men could operate. Staffers in the White House, especially Carl Kaysen, wanted to get rid of it. When General Taylor asked why, Kaysen said, "Well suppose a corporal

and a sergeant get cut off from their regular unit and become sur-
rounded—do we really know enough about them, about what's
going on in their heads, to give them a nuclear weapon?" Taylor
responded that he'd commanded troops and had never lost touch
with any unit under his command. Kaysen was stupefied, remem-
bering the fragmented units of Taylor's division that were scattered
across the French countryside on D-day.[34]

As one military intellectual put it, a soldier worries less about how
he is going to be killed than whether he is going to be killed, which
makes him instinctively more receptive than civilians to the view
of an atomic bomb as intrinsically no worse than an ordinary
weapon. But military men have had to recognize the prevalent
concept of a firebreak, or stark dividing line, between conventional
war and first use of nuclear weapons and accept the salience of the
concept for policy makers. This recognition, though, has not kept
them from lobbying against the inhibition. North Atlantic Treaty
Organization alliance problems have periodically encouraged consideration of quick resort to low-yield tactical nuclear weapons in
the event of European war. In 1974 Taylor even recommended
reducing the American garrison in Europe because prolonged conventional defense had become impossible since 1966 when DeGaulle
removed France from the NATO lines of communications, leaving
United States forces vulnerable to quick Soviet penetration. The
former commanders of NATO and the Seventh Army also spoke
out against the firebreak concept (which they saw as serving Soviet
interests) and for the need to modernize the tactical nuclear weapon
stockpile and plan better options for use of tactical nuclear weapons, despite widely held civilian views that political realities would
keep them from ever being used. Many military men, however,
opposed the position embodied in Barry Goldwater's 1964 presidential platform plank that field commanders should have authority to
decide when to use tactical nuclear weapons, recognizing that
such a decision would be profound and should be made by political
authority.[35]

The majority of military leaders' views of schemes for limitation
of nuclear arms stockpiles have been skeptical, but on occasion
grudgingly and conditionally supportive. Eisenhower's first chairman of the Joint Chiefs of Staff opposed any arms control agreement with the Russians and was rebuked by the President. Radford's view contrasted with Ridgway's and Taylor's, and within the
military the army undertook initial staff planning for nuclear disarmament at a time when official policy still opposed it.[36] In general
the army has been least receptive to proposals to limit antiballistic

missiles or reduce tactical nuclear weapon stockpiles but most receptive to limits on offensive strategic systems; the air force has been least receptive to strategic arms limitations.

Military suspicion of civilian control of nuclear policy began early when the Joint Chiefs opposed a 1948 proposal to put atomic bombs in the custody of the Atomic Energy Commission.[37] Some soldiers were also uneasy about creation of the Arms Control and Disarmament Agency (ACDA) in 1961, fearing it as a wedge for influence by utopian and irresponsible disarmers. Military supporters in Congress limited the agency's autonomy by placing the director under the secretary of state and later made the chairman of the Joint Chiefs a member (instead of adviser) of the arms control policy Committee of Principals. They ensured that military officers, both active and retired, were well represented in the arms control agency's personnel complement. The Joint Chiefs also sought to delete a provision in the legislation providing for the agency director's direct access to the President (comparable to the right of direct access guaranteed the JCS in the National Security Act). The Chiefs wanted at least to be assured the right to review and comment on any disarmament recommendations before they went to the President. They lost on both counts. In fact the first head of the Arms Control and Disarmament Agency, William Foster, told the Senate he would get his military advice from the secretary of defense rather than from the Chiefs.[38]

Conservatives in Congress and the executive believed military officers serving in ACDA might be checks on the suspect agency. Liberals worried that the officers would be a fifth column. Neither fear was borne out. The most salient impact of military officers posted to the agency may have been their indirect influence through control of data. Until the 1973 reorganization, 95 percent of the active officers in ACDA were in the Weapons Evaluation and Control Bureau, which prepared the agency's quantitative analyses. In 1972 military officers comprised twelve of seventeen professionals in the operations analysis division, the largest analysis unit engaged in arms control. This presence cut two ways, though, and benefited the civilians as well. In the early 1960s, the Defense Department occasionally denied certain information to the agency, and the resident officers proved helpful in acquiring it from friends in the Pentagon who could help locate data.[39]

The first real test of strength on arms control for military leaders came in 1963, when the Joint Chiefs opposed a comprehensive nuclear test ban (along with retired leaders White, Radford, Twining, Burke, and Power). They eventually agreed, with varying degrees of reluctance, to endorse a limited test ban treaty; Chairman Taylor and Marine Commandant Shoup were instrumental in convincing the other members to agree. The navy opposed the treaty less adamantly than did the air force, and the army's major reservations were that the agreement might compromise tactical use of nuclear weapons in a war and might adversely affect ABM development. Despite their official endorsement the Chiefs' reluctance came out in congressional hearings and was considered sympathetically. Senate Armed Services Committee leaders worried about the lack of administration consultation of the miltary, particularly the exclusion of military advisers from the negotiating mission in Moscow, and implied that the Chiefs should be able to veto proposals during decision making and negotiating. Nevertheless, Secretary McNamara relied on his own staff for advice on the issue, rather than on the JCS or Joint Staff, and Assistant Secretary John McNaughton alone represented the Defense Department at the Moscow negotiations.[40]

Military influence on the test ban treaty thus was less than overwhelming. The administration could play one set of professional experts off of the other. In August 1961 a panel of scientists under Jerome Wiesner and Wolfgang Panofsky met with the President and the National Security Council and reported that there was "no urgent technical need for immediate resumption" of United States nuclear tests. The Joint Chiefs attacked the report, but their rebuttal did not convince White House officials. President Kennedy also later coerced the Chiefs into backing the treaty by meeting with them individually and admonishing them to factor the political as well as military implications of the issue into their calculations. The Chiefs did manage to forestall acceptance of the principle of strategic parity and successfully demanded four conditions for endorsement of the treaty.[41] The Joint Chiefs were an obstacle in getting the United States planning for SALT off the ground, but again not an insurmountable one: "Nothing about the preparation for the SALT talks in 1968 was so remarkable," writes Newhouse, "as the willingness of the Joint Chiefs to accept restrictions that could not be verified with full reliability." In exchange for exclusion of both a testing ban on multiple independently targeted reentry vehicles (MIRV) and an ABM limit, the JCS (with one dissent from Chief of Naval Operations Moorer) accepted the original negotiating package developed by Secretary Clifford's Office of International Security Affairs. Although military leaders' conservatism has led them to be reluctant about arms control, they have been coaxed along by civilian bureaucrats and politicians so that negotiable terms could be developed and agreements reached. Younger military men tend to be less obdurate and less distinct in their attitudes from civilian strategists. One recent survey of advanced officers showed marked diversity in military outlooks on arms control and a virtual absence of officers completely opposed to arms limitation.[42]

7 Organizational Doctrines and Incentives

The advent of air power, which can go straight to the vital centers and either neutralize or destroy them, has put a completely new complexion on the old system of making war ... The result of warfare by air will be to bring about quick decisions ... a long-drawn-out campaign will be impossible.

Colonel William Mitchell, U.S. Army
Air Corps (Ret.), *Skyways*

After it gets dark, the Army can't fly back to Guam.
An army chief of staff

MILITARY men often disagree about what is necessary or possible in a crisis. Their perceptions of what choices are advisable flow not only from their interpretations of policy but also from attitudes instilled by lifelong identification with their own professional organizations. Where officers stand often does depend on where they sit, but soldiers sit in different places.

INTERSERVICE DIFFERENCES:
INTERESTS, IDEOLOGIES, AND INTERVENTION

Although civilian analysts frequently criticize interservice rivalries for the divisiveness, inefficiency, and confusion they cause in defense policy, these disagreements can often help civilians keep the maximum number of choices in their own hands. In the first fifteen years of the cold war, interservice controversy enhanced civilian control by deflecting conflict away from civilian-military lines.[1]

Military disunity increases administration choices in intervention decisions just as it does in budgeting and procurement decisions. To understand the miltary's impact on crisis decisions, therefore, it is necessary to understand the interaction of organizational interests (status, force levels, and missions) and ideologies (strategic and tactical doctrines) in the four services.

The fundamental principles that guided air force officers' advice in cold war decisions on use of force were that strategic bombing can cripple an enemy in its homeland, aerial interdiction of supply lines can cripple an enemy army at the front, and either form of bombing is an effective coercive tool independent of other military operations. These views made air force attitudes the most consistently radical of those of all the services in the cold war.[2]

The radicalism of postwar air force ideology derived from prewar air corps interests. For years the army air corps had fought for autonomous status as a separate service. In the 1920s the air officers felt aviation was disastrously underappreciated and underfunded. The court-martial of Billy Mitchell and his demotion from brigadier general to colonel was a traumatic and bitter experience for the young officers who became the leaders of the air arm in the 1940s. Organizational interest and doctrinal radicalism fed on each other. To make strategic bombing the dominant form of warfare required autonomous status, and the claim to autonomy was justified by the logic of the strategy.

In World War II, the goal of service autonomy dominated planning for the postwar period. By conceiving strategic bombing task forces as the International Police Force (in the period when it was believed the United Nations would have its own collective security military branch, composed principally of United States forces), preemptive attack as a strategy against threatening aggressors, and the need to rely on forces in being rather than mobilization, air corps planners justified the need for an independent air force that would be the dominant service within the military establishment. This orientation coincided with two tendencies among air force leaders in cold war crises: absolutist views of the conflict with the Soviet Union (consistent with the primacy of the strategic nuclear war mission, which was the service's preserve) and the overselling of service capabilities. Ideology, however, remained more extreme than interests required. Autonomy was achieved and assured in 1947, yet air force leaders—particularly in the Strategic Air Command—clung to the assumption of the omnipotence of air power. Britain's Royal Air Force, in contrast, developed pragmatic doctrines and learned many lessons from World War II about the limitations of air power which were lost on American air corps. The RAF had achieved autonomy long before and did not need dogmatism to serve organizational interest.[3]

The air force overemphasized the efficacy of air power in the quest for service independence, and this radicalism outlived the incentives that had spawned it. The lag between the change in conditions and the change in attitudes was evident in the fact that more realistic and prudent air force officers emerged predominantly in the lower ranks, where the fight for autonomy had not been a formative generational experience. These officers did not begin to take over the leadership of the service until after 1970. Recent chiefs such as George Brown and David Jones have had backgrounds more diverse and balanced than did their predecessors. Lieutenant General Brent Scowcroft, who in 1975 became assistant to the President for national security, is another example of the better educated and more moderate breed of Air Force leaders, as was Robert Pursley. As military assistant to the secretary of defense, Pursley was instrumental in helping Melvin Laird convince Nixon and Kissinger not to launch a retaliatory air strike after North Korea had shot down a United States EC-121 reconnaissance aircraft in 1969. Similarly General Brown sided with Secretary Schlesinger in the 1975 *Mayaguez* incident, arguing successfully against Kissinger's preference for using B-52 bombers in punitive raids against Cambodia.[4] These were the first instances since the 1948 Berlin blockade in which air force officers gave advice more conservative than some of the principal civilians.

Convergence of air force views with those of the other services still may not be complete. A 1974 poll of students at three war colleges indicated that army and navy officers approved of détente with the Soviet Union but air force officers did not.[5]

Although the marine corps has always been an autonomous service, it had to protect its status in postwar unification debates. To ensure survival, it exploited the romantic mystique of toughness and elitism —the tradition of the nation's shock troops embodied in the slogan "first to fight"—that appealed to supporters in the public and in Congress. This combat mystique, in turn, did not depend on a *grand strategy* or highly complex functional mission. Mystique served the marines as doctrine served the air force. The only substantive doctrinal point separating the marines from the army was the corps' emphasis on the continuing importance of amphibious landing operations. The marines were not burdened with all of the concerns of army strategists because their orientation was tactical; their function was simply to serve as assault troops. The marines were not responsible for the massive logistical coordination, sustained large-scale operations, and mopping up that the army always had to accomplish (though in practice in Korea and Vietnam marines did have essentially the same missions). The marine corps is always an adjunct in a major war, or the cutting edge in a minor intervention, but it has a mission in either case. As a result, marine commandants' advice in cold war crises depended less on organizational interests than did the advice of other service chiefs, had less ideological consistency, and depended more on the personal inclinations of the individual commandants.

After World War II the army thought a separate marine corps was outmoded, and it resented the corps' overblown status. As chief of staff, Eisenhower argued for reducing the strength of the marines and complained of their aggrandizement of the army land war function. This move was a threat to marine leaders, and they mobilized opinion to preserve their strength, independence, and access to highest authority. Senate liberal Paul Douglas (who at more than fifty years of age had been a combat marine during the war) achieved these goals through legislation that fixed the peacetime strength of the corps at not less than three divisions and three air wings and gave the commandant conditional representation on the Joint Chiefs of Staff. The bill was passed against the opposition of Secretary of Defense Marshall and Army and Navy Chiefs Collins and Sherman. The Chiefs' opposition was lessened only by the special language in the bill restricting the commandant's role to participation "on matters pertaining to the Marine Corps."[6]

In practice, however, by the 1960s the commandant's position on the JCS had evolved into one of equality, and commandants since Shoup have participated without inhibition. The army had also opposed marine representation on the JCS on the grounds that the corps was a subordinate component of the navy, equivalent to the army's engineers, armor, or artillery components. This premise was invalidated and the marines further secured their independence when Secretary of the Navy Robert Anderson was convinced to remove the corps from the jurisdiction of the chief of naval operations, having the commandant report directly to the service secretary. Since then the chief of naval operations has never exerted much authority over the corps.[7]

The marines had to lobby so vigorously for these measures because in strict military terms they were functionally redundant. There were no significant operations that they alone were equipped and trained to perform (the army developed amphibious capability in World War II). Justification for survival as a significant force led to stressing the marines' traditional reputation for extra toughness and unique suitability as quick-reaction forces, although army airborne and ranger units had the same (but less publicly visible) reputation. While there was no objective reason for the structural autonomy and prominence of the marines, there were powerful subjective ones. One flag raising on Mount Suribachi was worth a hundred congressional votes.

In short, the two major results in the cold war were that first, the marine corps achieved a position of near equality with the other services in the councils of war and second, secure autonomy combined with the absence of either *structural* constraints against use of force or incentives for use of force to allow marine commandants great personal discretion in advice they gave about use of force.

Because the marine corps has no integral strategic planning capability comparable to the staffs of the other services, some commandants (Lemuel Shepherd and Randolph Pate) have been demure in giving advice in crises.[8] The secure status ensured in the 1950s allowed another commandant (David Shoup) to play the role of skeptic, gadfly, and dove in the 1960s. The fact that the marines' assault mission did not entail the follow-up mission of the army to occupy territory and reach a military decision made it easier for another (Wallace Greene) to play the role of hawkish goad in the early Vietnam decisions on ground force commitments.

In contrast to air power advocates in the navy and air force, army officers were the most consistently conservative and cautious

military advisers in cold war crises. Army doctrine has held that
bombing cannot obviate the need for ground combat to reach a
military decision in war. The service stresses the need to maintain
high ground force levels and a strong central reserve. In the postwar
years the air force had a vested interest in organizational and strategic
change; the army's interest, in contrast, was stability, and it asserted
that the atomic age did not make conventional warfare obsolete.
Once the unification debates and the Korean War were over and
defense spending was contracted, the army and air force fought each
other tenaciously for shares of the budget. In a world of scarcity
the contradiction between their interests became a major policy
problem. Expansion of airpower and reliance on massive retaliation
could be achieved economically only by cutting army force levels.
The opposition of interests was matched by opposition of doctrine,
and both were reflected in splits in advice on the use of force in the
crises of the 1950s. As the Eisenhower administration progressed,
steadily reducing conventional forces, the army found its own
mission withering away. One response, similar to the navy's several
years earlier, was the so-called colonels' revolt of 1956 in which
army staff planners established liaison with sympathetic Democratic
senators and leaked documents critical of air force doctrine. This
gambit failed, and shortly after the army was threatened with
further reduction by the secret Radford plan of July 1956, which
proposed scaling down army deployments to small atomic task
forces. The plan was discarded only when it was revealed in the
New York Times, triggering frenzied protests from Allied governments.[9]

From a formal strategic perspective, the air force's primary mission is deterrence and the army's is defense. In the cold war, however, service leaders' attitudes did not always seem consistent with
these priorities. Air force officers were much more willing to use
their war-fighting capabilities in international crises than were army
officers. Air officers' aggressiveness followed from a high presumption of air power's competence; army caution grew from a low
presumption of competence largely because of cuts in service
capabilities. When a service has received a fair amount of what it
has requested, it cannot easily be reticent in a situation where use
of its capabilities is an option. Having oversold capabilities, air
officers could hardly denigrate their capacity to handle a crisis.
Being concerned with preserving force levels rather than gaining
autonomy, army officers could undersell capabilities. When a service
does not have the resources it has claimed are necessary, aggres-

siveness would be foolhardy, and reticence buttresses its case for getting the additional resources.

Resource allocation is not the sole determinant of military militancy, but, combined with the intrinsic differences in combat tasks, it explains much of the difference between air officers' and army officers' advice. Air force and naval air power, because of their structure and missions, are always readier for action than the army is. Complex and cumbersome logistical requirements are an overriding feature of army operations. Training, equipping, moving, maintaining, and supporting large numbers of men in sustained ground combat in unfamiliar terrain is a task that army leaders believe few outside the service understand or appreciate. "What throws you in combat is rarely the fact that your tactical scheme was wrong . . . but that you failed to think through the hard cold fact of logistics," wrote Ridgway, discussing the mission of the survey team he dispatched in 1954 to analyze the terrain, port facilities, road net, and climate conditions United States troops would have to cope with if they went into the Red River delta of Vietnam to rescue the French.[10] Army leaders also consider a high proportion of support forces relative to combat troops to be the inevitable price of a modernized military organization. Civilians rarely sympathize with this view, more often considering army estimates padded and extravagant. (In the first year of massive intervention in Vietnam, Westmoreland had to resist pressure from President Johnson and Defense Secretary McNamara, who wanted to move large numbers of troops into the country as fast as possible. The commander protested that the civilians' failure to authorize the logistic buildup needed made it impossible to absorb troops as fast as they wanted.)[11] High estimates of the number of ground forces required for success in crisis interventions also seemed suspect to many civilian leaders, particularly in the 1965 decision to send ground troops to Vietnam.

Army leaders also stress the imperative of maintaining a large strategic reserve. (The "strategic" or "central" reserve should not be confused with "the reserves." The former is the group of standing divisions held in the United States for emergency deployment to trouble spots. The latter are the trained but inactive forces that can be called to duty from civilian life by the President, but require much more time to assemble and retrain before they can be ready for action.) Army generals cautioned and restrained civilian leaders contemplating use of force most in the instances when the strategic reserve was weak or virtually nonexistent, such as the late 1940s, the first half of 1961, and the 1970 Jordanian crisis. Wheeler was not so cautious in the 1968 Tet offensive, but his aggressiveness was designed to provide an excuse to reconstitute the depleted reserve.[12]

Army officers also approach their job with more fatalism than do most air power enthusiasts. Ground officers are more sensitive to enemy strength and capacity for retaliation because outside of Europe, the major enemies the United States has engaged (North Korea, China, and North Vietnam) have had substantial ground forces but negligible air and naval power. In addition, while evidence of success in bombing is often ambiguous, criteria for success on the ground are clear and unrelenting: control of territory and population. Failure to achieve a mission is always more obvious for the army than for the air force. The marines sometimes share the same concerns. Around the time of the missile crisis Commandant Shoup became annoyed by the cavalier way in which the invasion option was being discussed, and he undertook a demonstration to a group of officials. On a map of the United States Shoup superimposed an overlay map of Cuba, which surprised his audience. The comparison made Cuba seem much larger; it stretched all the way from New York to Chicago. Then Shoup placed another overlay on the two maps: a microscopic red dot. When his subjects turned and asked what the dot was, Shoup said, "That, gentlemen, represeents the size of the island of Tarawa, and it took us three days and 18,000 marines to take it."[13]

Commitment of the army is normally the last and most serious conventional military option authorities can choose and thus implies that the situation is desperate when it is undertaken. Bombing can be used as a limited measure, such as in the 1964 Tonkin Gulf reprisal raids, without implying complete commitment. In both Korea and Vietnam the decision to commit ground troops was made after the decision for bombardment and because bombardment had not succeeded in containing the communist advances. War on the ground is also a more debilitating enterprise than the kind of war fought by the navy and air force. The ground forces take much heavier casualties, and war disrupts their organizational structure and coherence much more than it does to the other services. The army has to expand much more and much faster than the other services, and it has to contract much more after a war. In addition, promotions are initially faster but are much slower after the war is over. Personnel standards and professionalism decline, organizational élan and stability crumble, and authority and troop discipline erode. None of the other services face these problems to the same degree.

Naval doctrine cannot be summarized as clearly as that of the air force or army because at different times the navy has supported all of the principles of the other services. In organization, capabilities, and missions, the navy is involved in every major aspect of defense. Unlike the army, it has a major role in strategic deterrence through its nuclear submarine missile force. More than the air force, it has a major role in intervention operations by virtue of its capacity for projection of power in remote areas by carrier-based aircraft (and, in Vietnam, with in-shore riverine operations). Unlike any of the other services, the navy has exclusive responsibility for military operations at sea. As a result, "The Navy's postwar strategy ... remained more an argument in behalf of maintaining a variety of capabilities, what Air Force General White disparagingly called 'a little bit of everything,' than a positive prescription for fighting any particular kind of war."[14]

Naval leadership shifted from opposition to massive retaliation strategy in the late 1940s (when its interests contradicted those of the air force) to support for the same strategy in the mid-1950s (when their interests converged under the new budget ceilings). Even then, however, the navy retained the primary limited-war role. After Arthur Radford left the JCS chairmanship and the State Department began to abandon massive-retaliation strategy, naval leaders moved away from air force thinking and back toward the army. By the time of the Lebanon intervention and the second Taiwan Straits crisis, Chief of Naval Operations Burke was warning Congress that nuclear deterrence would not prevent "creeping aggression." At the same time that the navy moved doctrinally toward the army position in favor of strategic pluralism, however, the CNO's personal philosophy remained close to that of the absolutist anticommunism prevalent in the air force. When army leaders resisted intervention in Laos in 1961, Burke lobbied vigorously for it, and when he retired shortly thereafter, he said, "We must aim to destroy the sources of communist power in any country where the communists have provoked so-called 'wars of national liberation,' and impose upon ourselves no other limitation than the decision not to apply means more violent than necessary."[15]

In this way naval organizational interest united with the army's in terms of force structure and capabilities, and naval leadership's ideology agreed with the air force's orientation to unremitting and unconditional opposition to communist advance. The combination of air force strategic monism and ideological absolutism often gave aggressive air force advice the air of bluster because use of nuclear weapons was not a realistic option in postwar crises. The combination of army strategic pluralism and ideological pragmatism often made army advice appear to be timid forebearance. The navy combination united advocacy of limited-war forces with advocacy of their use. Adapting pragmatic means to absolutist ends made the dominant naval attitudes in this period more aggressive than those of the army but more rationally aggressive (in terms of logical consistency in relating means to ends) than those of the air force. But while the combination made naval advocacy more reasonable, that advocacy rarely prevailed in crises.

The critical factors in military calculations on the use of force tend to be the relative importance of different policy objectives and the character of the proposed use of force. In the 1954 Indochina crisis, for example, there was military consensus on neither the objectives of intervention nor the options. This lack of agreement reduced military influence on the final decision. During the Cuban missile crisis, on the other hand, not intervention but the kind of intervention that should be used to get the missiles off the island was the issue. The military, which opposed the blockade option as insufficient and dangerous, proposed the alternative of massive bombing, but for different reasons. Chairman Maxwell Taylor claims that he favored a surprise air strike because he wanted to avoid invasion.[16] He was more optimistic than Ridgway and earlier army leaders had been about the possibility of using bombing effectively without a follow-up occupation by troops.[17] The air force, on the other hand, believed a follow-up invasion might be necessary to guarantee that the strikes had made the missile sites inoperable. All agreed that the limited surgical air strike favored by Dean Acheson and, tentatively, by President Kennedy, was not feasible. When these differing military opinions were matched against political calculations, the President was led to the intervention option least favored by any of the military.

A fundamental point is that a service's interests are not always served by employment of the service's forces. This is most true of the army. The interests and ideologies of all the services might conceivably have been indulged to a fair extent in Vietnam without the massive troop deployments that occurred from 1965 to 1968. Air force and naval bombardment could have satisfied those services; limited coastal combat for base security might have satisfied the marines; and provision of advisers, technical personnel, and training teams might have satisfied the army. These options were, in fact, not far from what the service chiefs were recommending in 1964. The problem in 1965 that was the immediate impetus to escalation on the ground was the interdependence of air and ground intervention that Ridgway had feared a decade earlier. The first ground units were introduced when the bombing campaign began to protect the perimeter at Danang, from which the bombing missions were being flown. Even the above options for indulging service interests, though, would not have solved the field commander's problem. His success would not be measured by maintaining a stalemate but by defeating communist forces. It was Westmoreland who pressed for landing the first battalions and later for abandoning the enclave strategy and moving to offensive operations. It was the fact that the Vietcong were winning—not military organizational interests—that prompted escalation.

Future service attitudes are difficult to predict because the evolving changes in the international system in the past several years imply that future strategic problems will differ substantially from those that existed throughout the cold war. The uncertain prospects for United States–Soviet détente, relations with China, accommodation in the Middle East, Sino-Soviet relations, and the world economy will determine the range of threats and American goals, and domestic politics and economics will determine the force structure and force levels available. Some extrapolations from past patterns can be made, but they are certain to be modified by global and domestic developments. The army, by the mid-1970s lower in manpower than at any other time since before the Korean War, will probably remain averse to any Third World entanglements of even a fraction the scale of Vietnam or Korea. This does not mean, however, that the service will lapse back into the position of beleaguered internal opposition that it had under Eisenhower because the scope of United States commitments and goals has contracted substantially from what it was then; the imbalance between ends and means is not as clear. Schemes for oil imperialism, proposed in the wake of the 1973 Arab embargo,[18] should not appeal to the army either and would be vigorously resisted unless the hypothetical intervention were restricted to a miniscule area. But this possibility is not likely to be a problem. Despite Kissinger's overblown remark about intervention not being ruled out in the case of Arab strangulation of the West, it is obvious that the government did not consider the threat probable or the option plausible (especially since the United States has trained Saudi military forces to protect their oilfields).

Strategy was dominated by the air force from 1945 to 1961, and by the army from 1961 to 1970. Depending on developments in Asia and the Near East, the navy is likely to dominate strategy in coming years. But this change suggests no clear new divisions in military alignment. Since 1970 service attitudes on the use of force have become increasingly homogenous. Recently retired military leaders tend toward absolutist explanations of the reasons for failure in Vietnam, but they, current leaders, and the rising generation of officers lean toward pragmatic predictions about future military engagements. Détente and the decline of bipolarity are hardly as conducive to absolutist attitudes toward force as was the cold war. The differences in service interests are also not as stark as they were under President Eisenhower. In the aftermath of Vietnam none of the services felt starved while others gorged; they *all* considered themselves on short rations in the early and middle 1970s.

The only changes likely to upset this equilibrium are extremely hypothetical. If the mutual and balanced force reductions negotiations succeed beyond what anyone expects and United States forces are reduced to negligible proportions in Europe, the army would lack a major mission. If manned bombers are phased out and land-based missiles considered so vulnerable that the whole strategic deterrent should be moved to sea, the air force would panic. If United States policy maintains pretensions to a forward presence and combat capability in the Middle East and Asia but reduces the naval ship complement (which in 1975 was at levels the lowest since 1939), the navy—like the army two decades ago—would balk at the gap between its responsibilities and resources. Barring such developments, two significant changes from the cold war era are likely, and in terms of civilian control of the military one neutralizes the other. First, the cleavages among services that differentiated military advice in cold war crises and thus increased civilian choice have declined and should remain less extreme than they were for the first two decades of the cold war. Second, this decline in itself will probably not signal a rise in direct military influence, or a rise in the likelihood of intervention abroad, because the importance of the military security dimension of national policy (apart from the strategic nuclear balance) seems to be in even greater decline. Whether either of these trends accelerates or changes direction will depend on the evolution of international and domestic politics. In any case, changes in service interests and ideologies are more likely to derive from civilian policy changes than to determine them.

INTRASERVICE DIFFERENCES

Cleavages among services have been complemented by divisions within services. Some are informal transitory groupings, such as the entourages of leading personalities.[19] The more enduring bases of internal identification are the separate combat branches or specialties.

In the army, for example, elite officers spent most of their careers before becoming generals in the combat arms: infantry, armor, artillery, or airborne. Divisions in the navy have been between surface sailors, aviators, and submariners. In the air force the major groupings have been the Strategic Air Command (SAC), the Tactical Air Command, and the Military Airlift Command (formerly Air Transport Command). Just as the services have their own professional journals (*Army, Air Force, Seapower, Leatherneck*), so do the subservices (*Armor, Ordnance, Naval Aviation News*).

Some branches are significant for the extent to which they suppress competitors, dominate the elite nucleus, and govern the doctrine of their services, thus shaping or distorting the service leaders' perspective and advice in crises. The Strategic Air Command is a prime example. One analyst has pointed out that an autonomous air force places excessive value on strategic rather than tactical forces, "particularly in an early period of intense struggle for an assured status. An emphasis on strategic competence ... is congenial in the struggle for autonomy and prestige."[20] This orientation accounts in great part for the prevalence of absolutist attitudes among air force leaders. Prior to gaining autonomy, there was a relative absence of debate and rivalry within the air corps. All energies were focused on the fight for autonomy, and fighter doctrine—which challenged the omnipotence of bombers—was suppressed in favor of proving the decisive role of bombers.[21] The fixation carried over into the postwar air force as SAC broke the tradition of preparing military leaders as generalists, encouraging extreme specialization instead. The absolutist attitudes in the air force have been attributed to this narrow experience, which did not provide SAC officers the background of varied assignments that might have made them more sensitive to the complexity of the political dimension of warfare.[22] The SAC elite attained leadership by flying heavy bombers, not by reading Clausewitz.

After the air force was established, SAC became the best path to advancement. Curtis LeMay, SAC's first and longest commander, was succeeded as chief of staff by John McConnell and John Ryan, who had been vice commander and commander of SAC, respectively, and both of whom had spent most of their postwar careers in assignments within that branch. Only since the Vietnam War has SAC's dominance within the service been reversed. David Jones was the first chief of staff in more than two decades to have a background in tactical air units. The minority of pragmatic officers who did rise to positions of power within the air force during the cold war, indeed, were mostly those who had served in fighters and tactical air support, such as Elwood Quesada, Hoyt Vandenberg, Lauris Norstad, and Otto Weyland. It was Tactical Air Command officers (along with some in the Air Transport Command) who were more interested in graduated deterrence than was SAC. Eisenhower fought continuously with air force leaders to convince them to develop more tactical air combat and conventional bombing capability. Previously in the Korean War, even though the overwhelming proportion of air force combat in that conflict was tactical, most of the expansion in service expenditures went for increases in strategic air power. The overweening power of SAC and massive retaliation strategy's emphasis on nuclear weapons also led the Tactical Air Command, especially under the leadership of F. F. Everest, to aim for a nuclear delivery role, trying to emulate SAC rather than to complement it. In this context it is not surprising that military counterparts in the Soviet Union made the FBS issue— whether forward based systems of NATO tactical aircraft should be counted in totaling strategic nuclear delivery vehicles—a sticking point in SALT negotiations.[23]

Other service branches are significant, in contrast to the SAC example, in terms of their failure to capture a service and provide its leading advisers. The army's Special Forces are a good example. The reasons why the Green Berets, the principal counterinsurgency forces in the military, did not sustain an influential role in a counterinsurgency war—Vietnam in the 1960s—are more understandable in terms of the case study of airborne and airmobile warfare that follows it. Indeed, counterinsurgency and airmobile warfare were the only novel tactical doctrines to emerge in the army in the 1960s, and although the first withered after an initial vogue, the second prospered for a longer time. This contrast between a clique that failed and one that succeeded shows in turn why conventional combat unit commitment in 1965 was a natural choice and why the Vietnam War unfolded as it did.

Tradition versus Innnovation: The Rise and Demise of Counterinsurgency

The evanescent heyday of the Special Forces illustrated the hazards of trying to combine military and political functions in military doctrine. Counterinsurgency, a fusionist doctrine, was primarily the creation of civilian strategists in the Kennedy administration. As a tactical doctrine, an ancillary component of normal military force structure, which did not detract from building up conventional forces, it was tolerated by the service; indeed the army encouraged it in an effort to please its political sponsors and to prevent other agencies from being given the unconventional warfare mission and moving into army jurisdiction. But the military high command was unwilling to concede strategic significance to counterinsurgency, in contrast to civilians such as Walt Rostow, Robert Kennedy, Roger Hilsman, and the President himself. As the lonely dove of the Johnson administration, George Ball, later wrote, "The military did not push us into Vietnam half so much as the civilian theoretitians with theses to prove—doctrines of counterinsurgency and guerrilla tactics all reeking of the lamp."[24]

Events that catalyzed development of counterinsurgency theory were Fidel Castro's 1958–1959 guerrilla victory against an American-equipped conventional army, the failure of the Bay of Pigs operation, and the French political decision in 1962 to give up Algeria even though the rebels had been defeated militarily on the battlefield. Before Kennedy assumed office, the Special Forces were a nearly extinct group of fewer than 2,000 men, primarily East European émigrés. Their official mission, a remnant of the late 1940s, was to serve as guerrilla organizers behind Soviet lines in a European war. The new administration reversed the mission, turning the units into counterguerrilla forces, and expanded their number nearly fourfold in less than two years (and ultimately to a strength of 12,000). With specific support from the President, Brigadier General William P. Yarborough invigorated the Special Warfare Center at Fort Bragg, and additional centers were established in Panama, Okinawa, Vietnam, and Germany.[25] President Kennedy also established a high-level administration committee, the Special Group for Counterinsurgency, and by the end of 1962 counterinsurgency training programs involved 50,000 military and civilian officers.

Once the President had made clear the importance he placed on guerrilla war, the services rushed to see which could accommodate him fastest. The marines claimed that they were designed for counterinsurgency, so there was no need for other services to do anything. Marine leaders believed they had a unique understanding of insurgency from their interwar experience in interventions in the Caribbean and Central America. In response to the Special Forces buildup the navy created the Sea/Air/Land Teams (SEALS), and the air force started the Special Operations Forces. Some air force officers touted conventional air power as the key to counterinsurgency, citing British use of the Royal Air Force against the Mad Mullah in the Mesopotamian desert. Soon the army was protesting usurpation of its antiguerrilla mission.[26] Energy in developing counterinsurgency capabilities was no indicator of service priorities; most at the four-star level of the army fought the vogue, viewing the Green Berets as a theatrical distraction. They particularly did not approve the elitist image of the group sponsored by the civilians. When the President ordered restoration of the distinctive beret headgear (which had been banned in the 1950s, ironically, by Chief of Staff Taylor, who oversaw the counterinsurgency program under Kennedy), he did so over JCS objections. After a trip to Vietnam in early 1961, newspapers printed a leak that Chairman Lemnitzer felt the administration was "oversold" on the importance of guerrilla warfare.[27]

Counterinsurgency doctrine was not developed primarily at the Leavenworth staff college, in the prescribed way, but informally at Fort Bragg, and its biggest proponent within the military was not an army regular but the unconventional air force officer Edward Lansdale. Toward the end of the Eisenhower administration, Lansdale had had a small, devoted coterie of Special Forces officers and like-minded air force and navy people on his Pentagon staff develop plans for counterinsurgency capabilities. In trying to get the army to approve a new Special Forces mission, they met resistance. Their initiatives were sidetracked by instructions to go through the correct procedures and channels. Lansdale tried to expedite the process and encouraged his staffers to write up their own mission. The Lansdale group then took a risk and arranged for top civilians—the secretary of defense, White House staffers, State Department personnel—to visit Fort Bragg around the presidential transition period. There Lansdale's officers gave a demonstration, based on their as-yet unapproved new mission and evoked enthusiastic response from the civilian leaders. Army officials privately charged Lansdale with having arranged the blackmail of the army.[28]

The reason that counterinsurgency was never enthusiastically adopted by the military elite was that it was not a thoroughly military mission and was incompatible with their conception of professionalism. The essence of counterinsurgency theory was paramilitary civic action, a delicate interweaving of political and military functions—the kind of fusion that irritated so many of the military elite who preferred a clear line of demarcation between the two spheres. The ideal Green Beret was supposed to be an ambassador, propagandist, medical and economic aide, applied anthropologist, and surrogate ward heeler for the client government. He was to inspire loyalty, confidence, and anticommunist nationalism in remote peasant villages and serve as an intelligence agent. His military role was limited: training irregular native troops and conducting isolated ambushes with the small-unit tactics that seemed trivial to a conventional professional soldier. Some army leaders scoffed at the notion that American soldiers could or should be paramilitary politicos, seeing this function as the natural responsibility of host-country forces. Exemplary of the backwardness of the counterinsurgency tacticians, in the eyes of some service leaders, was the development of a modern cross-bow as a basic antiguerrilla weapon (it was later discarded). The army elite preferred conventional strategic concepts and division-, brigade-, or battalion-size operations to the small-scale, squad-size tactics of Special Forces teams.

The prime advocates of the counterinsurgency vogue were civilian advisers, such as Rostow and Robert Kennedy. It was not surprising, then, that the army sabotaged Assistant Secretary of State Roger Hilsman's "Strategic Concept for South Vietnam," a plan that envisioned, as one option, thousands of Special Forces in Southeast Asia rather than conventional troop units. When the tour of the chief of the military assistance advisory group in Vietnam, Lionel McGarr, ended in 1962, some of the civilian policy makers lobbied to have an unconventional warfare officer replace him. Yarborough and Colonel William R. Peers were suggested, but the selection of an officer so junior in rank would have antagonized service leadership. Hilsman believed that the President would have had more freedom to make such an appointment if the State Department had supported the idea vigorously, but Secretary Rusk considered the choice of the military commander in Vietnam to be solely the responsibility of the Defense Department. Taylor's conventional protégé Paul Harkins was selected.[29] At command headquarters in Saigon, in turn, Harkins relied on traditional staff officers, such as Brigadier General Gerald Kelleher, rather than the extraordinary staff of counterinsurgency specialists that had been established there earlier. Harkins's entourage seemed immune to the logic of counterinsurgency. When guerrilla war theorist Douglas Pike tried to educate Kelleher on the limited effectiveness of conventional tactics in Vietnam, the general simply kept repeating that all the United States needed to do was kill more Vietcong.[30]

The marines made more energetic attempts at pacification in Vietnam, even prodding the army to do the same, but they too *conventionalized* the concept of counterinsurgency. David Marr recalls:

As a young Marine Corps intelligence officer ... the only Vietnamese speaking American among 550 Marines ... I was surprised to discover that my immediate superiors were only interested in classical combat intelligence, not the "new" counterinsurgency varieties taught by Trager, Lansdale, Fall or Valeriano . . .

Reassigned to the United States Pacific command headquarters in Hawaii in Mid-1963, it was a revelation to me to discover that not only the colonels, but also the generals and admirals were fundamentally bored by the political complexities of Vietnam . . . they cut my regular political analysis in half, a mere five minutes out of a one-hour briefing . . .

When I left the Marine Corps in June 1964 it was already obvious that enforcement of physical security—convenient rhetoric for violent repression—had become the overwhelming theme in counterinsurgency.[31]

General Lew Walt, who commanded the marines in Vietnam for two years, later confessed that he did not comprehend the nature of guerrilla warfare when he went to Vietnam, and, like other military officials, he conceived the war in terms of World War II and Korea. His bewilderment was capsulized in the title of his Vietnam memoir: *Strange War, Strange Strategy*.[32]

This fading of counterinsurgency action beneath a façade of counterinsurgency rhetoric was paralleled in Washington. Lansdale, the primary military missionary for the doctrine, came favorably to the President's attention through Rostow early in 1961 and was slated for a major role in Saigon, possibly to replace the ambassador. In April, however, State Department objections to giving him authority succeeded in cancelling his key role. From that point on Lansdale was shunted from work on Vietnamese problems, and his influence evaporated. His unit in the Office of the Secretary of Defense lost importance as the action in counterinsurgency planning shifted to the special assistant to the Joint Chiefs of Staff for counterinsurgency and special activities, Major General Victor Krulak of the marine corps. Lansdale retired within two years and returned to Vietnam as a civilian assistant to Ambassadors Lodge and Bunker from 1965 to 1968, after the war had left the counterinsurgency phase and United States conventional units were in the country in force. The Special Group for Counterinsurgency also withered away.[33]

The original appointment of Taylor to oversee counterinsurgency was curious and contributed to the destruction of counterinsurgency theory in Lansdale's view. Taylor turned to Lansdale for advice at first, but then to Joint Chiefs and Krulak because Lansdale was too unconventional, garrulous, and independent for him. As this change happened, the basic conception of counterinsurgency became narrowed to military considerations of applied force, reducing the emphasis on political, economic, and psychological factors.[34] The standards for Special Forces also declined as they were expanded. From a small corps of committed men, the Green Berets were transformed into just another job, something for an officer to qualify in and rotate through but not a vocation an ambitious officer would stay with. Special Forces were known to be a dead end for anyone who aspired to high rank. In the view of one ex-Green Beret, it also became a "scrap heap" for rejects from regular units.[35] As the military advisory effort grew in Vietnam after 1961, army leaders played down the civic action aspects of the strategic hamlet program, fearing they might detract from the preferred program of building up the conventional South Vietnamese army. Military Assistance Command, Vietnam and the Joint Chiefs also opposed the advice of British Brigadier Sir Robert Thompson, who advocated a police-style counterinsurgency strategy in opposition to the conventional military approach.[36]

As the Vietnam War grew in intensity the Special Forces became a marginal component, relegated primarily to training Montagnard tribesmen. This change in role compounded the Green Berets' estrangement from the powers that ran the war, since the Saigon government and Montagnards hated each other. The close links between the Green Berets and the Central Intelligence Agency further alienated them from the army mainstream. All Special Forces units were removed from Vietnam in 1970 and 1971, well before the last infantry and air cavalry units left. Counterinsurgency's prime boosters in the early stages of the war had been liberal civilians, who became the prime critics of the war in its latter stages. The Special Forces thus became an orphaned anachronism, an embarrassment to disillusioned civilians, a nuisance to embittered military leaders. By the mid-1970s they still had a few semisecret missions in Latin America advising on antiguerrilla campaigns, but otherwise they functioned more often as paramedical and public works construction teams. By 1974 there were fewer than 5,000 Green Berets, and the Special Forces' mission was further conventionalized and largely taken over by World War II-style Ranger battalions. By 1976 their mission, status, and size had reverted to what they were before Kennedy. The Green Berets survived, but they did not prosper. William Yarborough retired in 1971, symbolically, to Southern Pines, North Carolina, on the outskirts of Fort Bragg, rather than to Washington like so many other generals. The passing army elite's resentment of the Special Forces means that future army leadership will have a conventional background.

CONVENTIONAL INNOVATION: THE
AIRBORNE CLUB AND AIRMOBILE WARFARE

As the Special Forces' mission waned, another new component rose in importance. The army took the need for innovation seriously as the Vietnam War became serious to it. To the professional soldier that meant change that improved and facilitated the combat deployment of large troop units and the concentration of modern firepower. The development of an airmobile division—a standard infantry division with organic helicopter transport—was seen as a step forward, relying on technology and conventional force structure, rather than a step backward that relied on cross-bows. The success of the airmobile doctrine, however, was largely the result of its sponsorship by the dominant clique in the postwar army: the airborne club. (*Airborne* refers to paratroops; *airmobile* refers to helicopter-borne troops.)

The principal land warfare innovation of the twentieth century was the development of armored (tank) warfare, which began in World War I and matured later when it was revolutionized by the Germans early in World War II. The major tactical innovation that emerged during World War II was airborne warfare: infantry assault behind enemy lines via mass paratroop landings. The Germans also pioneered in this area, but the concept was embraced most enthusiastically by the American army. The leaders of the army in the cold war were the men who had led airborne divisions in World War II. At one point in 1943, three future chiefs of staff were serving in one such division at the same time—Ridgway, Taylor, and Westmoreland—as was James Gavin, another influential service leader in the postwar period.

That airborne doctrine should have achieved such prominence is curious because it proved less than an unqualified success in the war: casualties in airborne operations were always astronomical, and the operations often failed to achieve their objectives. In the 1943 Sicily landings, the operational plan went completely awry. Troops who made it to the drop zone were widely dispersed, and many wandered lost, helpless, and isolated in the countryside. Some were dropped at sea, some shot down by American naval antiaircraft batteries. This fiasco shocked service leaders in Washington, who wanted the paratroops' mission to revert to small-unit landings for sabotage. Only vigorous lobbying from airborne generals, especially Ridgway, prevented such a change. Nevertheless, in Normandy some of the same disasters occurred, and casualties were enormous.[37]

Despite these problems, higher command was impressed with airborne performance in Normandy (in contrast to Sicily, objectives were achieved in this case) and decided to form an airborne army under Lieutenant General Lewis Brereton. But the only other airborne operation of the war—"Market-Garden" at Arnhem—was a disaster. One of the main reasons the operation was mounted, in fact, was simply that the supreme command felt it had to do something with the capability it had developed. Market-Garden offered the chance to use the idle airborne resources. Even Ridgway admitted that the principal objectives of the operation were not attained. Taylor admitted the same, yet paradoxically still maintained that the Arnhem drops demonstrated the effectiveness of airborne troops.[38]

Indeed, the American army did not draw the lessons from airborne experience that its enemies did. The Russians had been the first to develop paratroops, in 1925, but their use in Finland in 1940 proved so disastrous that they were never used again (although the Red Army does continue to maintain airborne divisions). The invasion of Crete by paratroops struck the Germans as so costly that they decided to discontinue airborne operations for the rest of the war. But ironically Crete impressed the United States Army so much that it decided to increase the number of its own airborne divisions in 1942. In Korea, airborne operations were minimal and questionably effective,[39] and in the mud and jungle of Vietnam the only major jump—Operation Junction-City—was essentially a failure. Aside from tentative contingency plans for a parachute drop onto the Palestinian-held airfield in the 1970 Jordanian crisis, there have been no other significant instances where airborne operations have been considered either useful or feasible.

Airborne units nevertheless continued to be the elite units in the army. Airborne training became virtually a required qualification for any ambitious officer. Although the service tentatively phased airborne operations out as a tactical concept in the early 1970s, it still trained 5,000 men each year as paratroops. The reason for this vitality is that airborne embodies the tradition, morale, and mystique associated with the central values and images of the service: toughness, courage, and the other psychological attributes of the ideal combat soldier. The rationale is that anyone willing to jump out of an airplane is someone who can be depended on to fight tenaciously in the worst situations. Airborne training thus serves as a rite of passage, a socializing and bonding agent that transcends tactical utility. For similar reasons paratroop units have been the elite of foreign armies, particularly the Soviet, French, South Vietnamese, and Israeli. Another reason that enabled airborne officers to ignore the concept's short-comings in postwar years, as Edward Katzenbach suggests, is that "nothing is more difficult to test than a weapon's effectiveness." Evidence often appears ambiguous, mitigating circumstances or saving graces can always be found.[40] Army officers' unwillingness in World War II to admit airborne's cost ineffectiveness parallels air force officers' resistance to recognition of the limitations of strategic bombing.

In this respect airborne resembles its predecessor, the cavalry. Horse cavalry, incredibly, survived well into this century, and rationales were developed to justify its mission in spite of modern technology and mechanized warfare. The charge was continued as tactical doctrine even after World War I, "because the cavalry liked it. In virtually all countries the cavalry was a club, an exclusive one . . . the home of tradition, the seat of romance, the haven of the well-connected." During World War II one tactically obsolete basis of elite identification was superseded by another; the paratroopers were lineal descendants of horsemen. Similarly, helicopter mobility theorists a generation later found support among paratroopers.[41] Lieutenant General Hamilton Howze, who was most responsible for initiation and development of army helicopter doctrine, had an extensive background in airborne commands when Defense Secretary McNamara appointed him to direct an investigation of army battlefield mobility and aircraft requirements in 1962. The Howze board concluded that helicopter-borne troop units were superior in effectiveness to airborne or any other infantry units and recommended that one-third of the service's infantry divisions should be airmobile and that the rest should have substantial helicopter support. Early in 1963 McNamara authorized the testing of an air assault (airmobile) division.[42]

Early in 1965 as the prospect arose that United States troops might be committed in Vietnam, Army Chief Harold Johnson decided to send the still-experimental Air Assault Division rather than a conventional infantry division. In June 1965 McNamara activated the test division as the First Cavalry Division (Airmobile) and sent it to Southeast Asia.[43] This was the step that marked the transition of American involvement in Vietnam from advice and counterinsurgency to full-scale intervention. The division's cavalry designation and the 1969 conversion of the 101st Airborne to a dual airborne-airmobile capability signified the related progression of doctrinal innovation, branch elitism and clique dominance within the service, and tactical advice to civilian leaders.

Intraservice branches and subcultures thus indirectly influence the military recommendations and solutions offered to civilian authorities. (Intraservice differences also interact with interservice disagreements: SAC dominance of the air force caused the downgrading of tactical support and airlift missions in that service, which in turn caused the army to develop its own competing capabilities in those areas.)[44] In Vietnam, a theoretically appropriate doctrine (counterinsurgency) was shunted aside, and its supporters—middle-level soldiers and high-level civilians—lost their influence as the enemy threat grew because army leaders thought the war should be fought with large units and as much firepower and technology as possible. An irrelevant tactical doctrine—airborne warfare—became indirectly influential by having permeated attitudes and established loyalties within the service elite, thus helping to channel innovative impulses in a conventional direction. The inclusion of Major General William B. Rosson (special assistant to the chief of staff for special warfare) on the Howze board signified the relation of airmobile capability to counterinsurgency, but airmobility did not enhance counterinsurgency as much as it superseded it. With hindsight, airmobile tactics were in fact hardly more useful in the war than were the Green Berets. Brigadier Thompson, the counterinsurgency theorist, has attributed the failure of American strategy to helicopters because they were "wonderful pieces of gadgetry" that "proved a fatal fascination" and made possible the mistaken search-and-destroy attrition strategy.[45] By providing extra mobility, helicopters also reduced contact between military forces and the populace and "tended inevitably to draw the Saigon regime even further away from the humdrum realities of creating political and social credibility at the local level."[46] Moreover, just as the army approached the final stages of withdrawal from Vietnam the first sure signs of airmobile doctrine's obsolescence appeared. The major problem was the advent of the small shoulder-fired Russian Strela missile, which shot down massive numbers of helicopters in the 1971 South Vietnamese army invasion of Laos. Overreliance on helicopters, which became less usable in combat and led the South Vietnamese army to abandon much of the intricate system of interlocking firebases that bracketed transportation routes, was one of the many factors contributing to South Vietnam's eventual defeat. By 1975 the 101st was the only U.S. airmobile division; the pioneering First Cavalry became an armored division as the army backtracked in its plans to universalize airmobility.[47]

The contrast between the fortunes of the doctrines of counter-insurgency and airmobility was the problem of United States policy in Vietnam writ small. Probably neither could have worked, probably there was no way to win the war at an acceptable moral or material price. In some ways the conventional war was militarily successful anyway. After the Tet offensive and until the conventional North Vietnamese invasion across the demilitarized zone in 1972, control of the countryside by the United States and South Vietnamese army did increase. Ultimate defeat derived more from the political aspects of the war. And counterinsurgency, as naively ambitious as it may have been, had been a fusionist doctrine for a war where military and political functions were tied more closely than in any other war the United States had ever fought. In terms of professional military advice and influence, this was precisely the problem. Resisting civilian unconventional war doctrine, military leaders recognized the political complexity of the war but insisted on dividing the labor, leaving the politics to the civilians and concentrating themselves on actual combat. They had looked as an example to their formative experience in World War II, a total war which was conceptually simple because political considerations interfered hardly at all with strategy and tactics and the highly destructive technology of fighting the enemy did not detract from the mission of winning the war. To these soldiers, mass operations were natural and congenial and could be recommended and pursued with more confidence and energy than the bizarre tactics of the Green Berets.

8 Positions, Preparations, and Prejudices

Winston Churchill once said that the secret of the survival of the British Empire was that they never trusted the judgment of the men on the spot. I never understood that until recently.

John F. Kennedy, 1962

MILITARY organization does not break down only along
lines of services or service branches. Two other important structural constraints on the military advice
given to civilian leaders sometimes transcend these divisions. One is the position of the field commander in an area in
which a crisis occurs. His responsibility, and hence his perspective,
differs from that of his cohorts in Washington. Another is the
military planning process, especially the combined planning in the
Joint Staff under the Joint Chiefs of Staff.

The Chain of Command and the Men on the Spot

Military decisions in Washington are made by high officials who
depend on the skill and responsibility of those closer to the problem
to furnish them information on which choices can be based. Between the President and operational units in action, there are major
field commands, such as the United Nations command in Korea or
the military assistance command, Vietnam (MACV). Larger geographic unified commands, such as the Pacific command in Hawaii
or the allied command in Europe, usually participate more in decisions on use of force than do functional specified commands such
as the Strategic Air Command (SAC), because strategic nuclear
preemption (the option on which SAC's recommendation would
be most salient) has never seriously been considered in a crisis. In
Vietnam, MACV was nominally subordinate to the commander in
chief, Pacific, and reported formally through him, but Westmoreland often conferred directly with the Joint Chiefs, the defense
secretary, and the President.

In the nineteenth century American naval officers sometimes made
foreign policy as much as they executed it. Lack of communications often left the initiative for gunboat diplomacy in the hands of
ship captains who seized territories in the Pacific or coerced small
nations such as Korea sometimes in cooperation with local American
consulates, sometimes in conflict with them. The American military
traditionally grants greater authority to field commanders than do
other nations. In World War II the Joint Chiefs sometimes allowed
Eisenhower to represent them in meetings with the British chiefs,
delegating to him complete authority to make binding decisions—
to the astonishment of the British. Modern electronic communications have increased the potential for command and control from
the top. In Korea, battalion-level operations were monitored by the
JCS.[1] The Joint Chiefs nevertheless continued throughout the cold

war to adhere to the principle that a commander should have a wide latitude in his choice of tactics. The Chiefs in Washington overrule their subordinates in the field only rarely: when there is a clear difference in strategic analyses, when forces have not yet become engaged, and when the field commander is clearly junior to the Chiefs, as when the Joint Chiefs differed with General Clay over breaking through to Berlin on the ground in 1948; when the priority of another theater conflicts with the needs of the field command, as in Korea; or when a commander makes a costly blunder or is insubordinate, as in the case of MacArthur.

In the first months of the Korean War, the Joint Chiefs were reluctant to overrule MacArthur. Though he was nominally subordinate to them, he was a five-star general, outranking all but Omar Bradley, to whom he was still nearly two decades senior. The Chiefs previously had risked their credibility by challenging MacArthur's plans for the Inchon landing behind North Korean lines, considering it extremely dangerous. In a conference in August 1950 MacArthur managed to overcome the objections to the plan. The Inchon operation turned out to be such a stunning success that it confirmed the legend of MacArthur's genius and embarrassed the Chiefs. As Army Chief of Staff Collins wrote, "The Chiefs hesitated thereafter to question later plans and decisions of the general, which should have been challenged." Thus even though the Chiefs were uneasy about MacArthur's command arrangements for the attack across the thirty-eighth parallel and were alarmed by the exposed position of the Tenth Corps as United States forces approached the Yalu, they again conceded the tactics as the commander's prerogative. MacArthur's certainty that the Chinese would not intervene overrode the growing fears of intelligence staffs in Washington, and the JCS did not exercise their prerogative to go to the President with their doubts. It took the debacle of Chinese intervention and the near defeat of the Eighth Army to destroy MacArthur's credibility and make it easier for the Chiefs to support his dismissal. Nevertheless Army Chief Collins did not question the principle of field command autonomy. Instead he chastised MacArthur for not adhering to it himself by relying on his own staff in Japan and by failing to consult his subordinate commander in the field when issuing tactical directives.[2]

In Vietnam there was no friction between Westmoreland and the Joint Chiefs. Defense Department civilians criticized their failure to consider alternatives to Westmoreland's attrition strategy and their reluctance to do an independent analysis of the war. But the Chiefs saw their function as backing up the commander rather than dictating to him, and they transmitted Westmoreland's views rather than assessing them in depth. Yet it is unclear that the failure to challenge strategy, tactics, and the ambiguity of operational goals was much more a failure of the Joint Chiefs of Staff than of their superiors. The civilian principals had dismissed the 1965 million-range military estimates of troops required for victory, and they had imposed the restrictions on troop levels and bombing targets that limited military results. Their expectations of what intervention on the ground would accomplish were as tragically muddled as those of the soldiers. Years later McGeorge Bundy admitted in a Council on Foreign Relations meeting that the administration had not properly articulated the military mission and that there had been a "premium on imprecision" in administration instructions. General Ridgway as well, consulted from retirement by President Johnson at the height of the Tet offensive, noted the lack of clarity in operational goals.[3]

With few exceptions, field commanders have been more aggressive and more optimistic than their superiors in Washington about their particular military situation. This optimism and aggressiveness reinforce each other: one minimizes the costs of action; the other holds out the prospective benefits of action. In some instances civilian officials in Washington are also more optimistic than the Pentagon military, who then find themselves outflanked on both sides.

In the spring of 1948, for example, a telegram from Lucius Clay, military governor in Germany, combined with the Czech coup, sparked a war scare in Washington. A top civilian diplomat, however—George Kennan—criticized the overreaction of the military leaders and military intelligence in the capital. When more tangible evidence of impending conflict became available as the Soviets blockaded Berlin a few months later, General Clay was certain the Soviets were bluffing and was more bellicose and less fearful than the Joint Chiefs. First he decided on his own initiative to begin the massive airlift. Then he recommended sending an armed convoy to the city, assuring the army department that war was unlikely.[4] The Chiefs overruled him.

In the first days of the North Korean invasion in June 1950, the most confident statements came from the man on the spot with the most parochial perspective, Korean military advisory group commander Brigadier General William L. Roberts, who predicted (incorrectly) that the South Koreans would have no trouble repelling the attack. After American intervention, MacArthur was more optimistic than the Joint Chiefs. At the Wake Island conference with Truman, he boasted that the war would be over by Thanks-

giving and United States troops would be back in Tokyo by Christmas. During most of the Korean War the major commanders in the
field—MacArthur, Clark, Almond, Walker, and Van Fleet—were
more aggressive than the Joint Chiefs. Only Ridgway and Taylor
disagreed minimally with the Chiefs. Ridgway reasoned in 1951
that driving the Eighth Army back to the Yalu would not be worth
the cost from "the purely military standpoint." To do so would
have shortened Chinese supply lines and lengthened those of the
United Nations forces, and guerrilla warfare would have remained
a severe problem behind the advancing lines. He turned down Van
Fleet's proposals for limited counteroffensives in 1951–1952. At one
point early in his command, however, Ridgway did ask the Chiefs
to delegate to him authority for maneuver in China if it became
tactically necessary. His more generally moderate stance came from
his Europe First views and from his wider responsibilities. He held
two posts concurrently: the theater command with responsibility
for the defense of Japan and the Korean command. This double-hat
was the one factor which had made MacArthur ambivalent, when
he complained to the Joint Chiefs that he did not have sufficient
forces both to prosecute the war in Korea and guarantee Japan
against invasion. The dual responsibility lay behind MacArthur's
vacillating in the desperate winter of 1950–1951, between escalating
dramatically or evacuating the peninsula.[5]

Thus there is a rough inverse relation between scope of responsibility and aggressive optimism of major military officials. (The
total pattern is more like a bell-shaped curve. Low-level soldiers in
the field, such as local advisers in Vietnamese provinces, were often
less optimistic and confident than their commanders in Saigon.) As
United States support for the French in Indochina grew in the early
1950s, the soldier on the spot, Lieutenant General O'Daniel, reported
confidently that the French Navarre plan would accomplish the
decisive defeat of the Vietminh by 1955. The Joint Chiefs were
more cynical and skeptical. In August 1959, while military opinion
in Washington was divided, officers at the headquarters of the
commander in chief, Pacific (CINCPAC), were the most vigorous
proponents of aggressive action in Laos. In fall 1961 Lionel McGarr,
chief of the military assistance advisory group, reported confidently
that the situation in Vietnam was progressing well, while the mission from Washington headed by General Taylor reported that the
war effort was in dismal shape. In fall 1964 CINCPAC Sharp and
Westmoreland at MACV requested provision for deployment of
marines and army units for air base security, but the Joint Chiefs
disapproved, preferring to avoid commiting United States forces at

that point. In the 1965 decisions to send troops to Vietnam, Westmoreland was more aggressive than Army Chief Harold Johnson, who told reporters in February that he dreaded going to war in Vietnam. After early June of that year, the impetus came from the Saigon command and the JCS were caught between Westmoreland's demands and the opposition his request for forces had provoked in Washington. In the 1968 Tet offensive Westmoreland was unworried while JCS Chairman Wheeler was alarmed.[6]

Mark Clark, who chafed under restrictions as commander in Korea, had realized this tendency of the central government to be more fearful than its local commanders when he was serving as United States high commissioner in Austria, and he recognized the need to lobby his superiors from the field. When Washington hesitated to approve a major buildup of the South Korean army, in part from fear that the country's economy would be destroyed by taking too many men from the labor force, Clark directed his own staff in Korea to produce a manpower study. It concluded that the South Koreans could support twenty divisions.

It is common for the field to produce uncritical studies and reports because the environment of a commander's staff is not conducive to questioning the mission, tactics, or success of the commander. Loyalty takes precedence. Mission-motivated estimates are more common in intelligence sections of overseas commands than in the Pentagon. In Vietnam the tendency was extreme. When Paul Harkins arrived in Saigon in 1962, he told the press that he was an optimist and intended to have optimists on his staff. Harkins's persistent reassurances to Washington, as the situation actually deteriorated, disturbed Secretary McNamara, who eventually replaced him. Westmoreland succumbed to the same tendency. Despite his frequent warnings about how long success would take without the requisite number of troops, he issued a steady stream of confident reports about progress in the war throughout his tenure from 1965 to 1968.[7]

Such aggressive optimism may pose indirect problems of political control because local commanders can exercise substantial discretion. This authority could have been most dangerous in Berlin since conflict over that city always had the latent possibility of escalation to general war. In late August 1961, shortly after the wall went up, the East German government banned western personnel from approaching the wall closer than a hundred meters. The Allied commandants met and, without referring their decision to their governments, ordered a full alert of Western forces in the city, sending a thousand troops with tanks inside the hundred-meter span. Fearing an incident, Washington later ordered United States forces to pull back from the wall. There was an atmosphere of tension and crisis in Washington, but senior military officers in Germany were less concerned, denigrated the notion of crisis, and believed that Kennedy overreacted when he mobilized reserve units and dispatched troops to reinforce the Berlin garrison.[8]

At this time, the President sent retired General Lucius Clay back to Berlin as his personal representative. Even before he got to the city Clay began worrying government officials. On the flight over, he told Charles Bohlen that if he were still commander in Berlin, he would have ordered troops to tear down the East German barricades and barbed wire. This made Clay the only adviser, military or civilian, to consider tearing down the wall. JCS Chairman Lemnitzer thought the United States was in no position to take any offensive action in Europe and believed destroying the wall would constitute an attack on the Soviet zone. United States Army Europe commander Bruce Clarke agreed. Clay was more confident. When he reached Berlin, the first thing he did was to make a provocative helicopter flight to Steinstücken, a tiny Western enclave cut off from the rest of West Berlin by a sliver of East German territory, and he announced assignment of a military police detachment and continuation of daily flights to the area. The East Germans threatened to shoot the helicopters down, but they backed down. He next resumed United States military patrols of the autobahn, which had been discontinued years earlier because of Soviet harassment.[9]

Clay's actions began to alarm Washington officials. One of Taylor's aides recalls heated phone conversations between the general and Clay, with Taylor worrying about what provocative scheme the envoy might concoct next.[10] Ten days after Clay's arrival in the city, General Clarke visited Berlin and told garrison commander Albert Watson that he could not use American forces to counter communist moves without clearing each action with headquarters— a direct attempt to subdue Clay. Soon after, when the Soviets challenged the resumption of the autobahn patrols, Washington forced Clay to rescind them. Nevertheless, within a month there was an incident at the Friedrichstrasse checkpoint (guards stopped United States Deputy Chief of Mission Allen Lightner and demanded identification, which the diplomat refused), and Clay succeeded in getting the Berlin command to act on its own initiative. A squad escorted Lightner through the checkpoint with fixed bayonets. Four days later a similar incident at Checkpoint Charlie escalated to a tense sixteen-hour confrontation of United States and Soviet tanks, again alarming Washington. Watson was subsequently given new and even more detailed directives, over Clay's protest, which left him virtually no discretion at all as tactical commander. In February 1962 when the Soviets began harassing United States planes in the Berlin air corridor, Clay recommended fighter escorts and was turned down. Soon after, he resigned and left the city in frustration over the restrictions placed on him.[11]

It was because of such problems that the McNamara regime in the Pentagon put so much emphasis on preventing subordinate links in the chain of command from taking initiatives that might have dangerous political ramifications. To some military men the institutionalization of tight command control from the top seemed to go so far that it cowed commanders and prevented them from living up to their responsibilities, as in the 1968 *Pueblo* case. A retired admiral wrote:

> I feel sure that by the time this book is published, there will be some half-assed "explanations" from the Defense Department as to why the *Enterprise* didn't send planes. The real explanation is simple—nobody had the guts to do it without orders from Washington—and orders never came.
>
> In the chain of command that afternoon there were two four-star and one three-star admirals. I should think at least one of them would have issued shooting orders to help the *Pueblo* on his own authority. If Washington disapproved, the worst that could happen to him would be retirement a few years early—on three-fourths pay. But no one was willing to stick his neck out that day . . .[12]

INFORMATION, INFLUENCE, AND FRAGMENTATION OF AUTHORITY

Many cold war crises occurred in countries where United States forces were not stationed in strength. In those areas United States military representatives are middle-ranking officers whose primary impact on crisis decisions is not through direct advice but through the way in which they tell government officials about the situation. In such communications there is a hazy line between objective reporting and personal recommendation. Theoretically, the opinions of these military representatives have a neutral effect on policy because they are not valued as highly as those of an ambassador. Soldiers in an embassy country team are supposed to function as neutral conduits for intelligence. In practice, however, the sources from which information is gathered, the extent to which it is selectively reported to Washington (or to the ambassador), and the tone in which it is transmitted may give military assistance advisory group chiefs or military attachés an indirect influence on policy. Reporting from the field conditions the premises of decision in Washington. This organizational constraint takes on higher relative importance in minor interventions, such as in Lebanon and the Dominican Republic, because in these cases where United States military capabilities are not in doubt, civilian leaders pay scant attention to high military advisers in Washington.

Military attachés occasionally have influence disproportionate to their rank because they act as intelligence agents and diplomats. They have been particularly important in Third World countries where they are the American representatives in most intimate contact with the host country's armed forces, which are often key actors in crises. This was the case in the 1958 Lebanon intervention in which a United States attaché transmitted the information about a proposed Lebanese army coup against the American-supported President Camille Chamoun. In addition a naval attaché functioned as the ambassador's liaison with the United States assault force when radio links with the fleet were broken at a point when the tactical mode of implementation of United States intervention— the timing and location of the landings—threatened to have dangerous political ramifications.[13] Lebanon was a case where military reporters were important, but in this instance they played a neutral role of informing civilian decision makers rather than influencing them.

The 1965 Dominican Republic case is less clear. Theodore Draper claims in his analysis that the American attachés and the military assistance advisory group encouraged the right wing of the Dominican military in its resistance to the forces favoring the return of Juan Bosch, that American officers were active in pressing their projunta views on their superiors, and that they exerted an aggressive and independent influence in the development of the crisis. It is difficult to determine how accurate this view is, since the answer depends on the subjective nuances of reports and unverifiable but plausible suspicions and rumors about the attachés' activities. The most exhaustive study of the crisis, however, casts doubt on this interpretation. Lowenthal notes that in the early stages of the crisis, the attachés did not encourage the Dominican chiefs to expect United States support, that the civilians in the embassy decided unanimously themselves to support the junta and did so more vigorously than their superiors in Washington or presidential envoy John Bartlow Martin desired, and that Ambassador W. Tapley

Bennett reported the country team unanimously supported landing the marines when the Dominican junta leader requested United States intervention. President Johnson's memoirs confirm this interpretation. The attachés had a critical role as liaison between the embassy and the Dominican military and as agents in arranging and chairing negotiations between the contending parties, but there is no clear evidence that they did not scrupulously avoid political initiatives of their own. In this light, the soldiers were simply fulfilling their proper reporting function. To differentiate this function from influence, though, is difficult. The alarmism that the united country team conveyed to Washington was based on the suspicions of the attachés about the motives of the rebels who were asking for a cease-fire. Washington also placed special weight on the reports of the military assistance advisory group because of the belief that the military mission had better information by virtue of its special entrée to Dominican government.[14]

The Bay of Pigs is a clearer example of improper influence. In this case the zealotry of officers on the scene led them to dangerous overconfidence and, at least according to testimony of exile soldiers, criminal deception and deliberate insubordination. The most important figures were two colonels on detached duty with the Central Intelligence Agency, working with the Cuban exile brigade-in-training in Guatemala prior to the invasion. The day after President Kennedy's press conference precluding use of United States forces to invade Cuba, a cable went to a marine colonel with the brigade, asking if he had changed in any way his favorable evaluation of the exiles' capabilities. The colonel replied, "My observations have increased my confidence in the ability of this force to accomplish not only initial combat missions, but also the ultimate objective, the overthrow of Castro." Confidants of the President later testified that it was this message that overcame the last of Kennedy's doubts and prompted him to give final authorization to the operation.[15]

The more shocking example was the other officer, from the army, code-named Colonel Frank. Despite the President's prohibition of direct American intervention, the colonel assured brigade leaders that United States support would follow their establishment of a civil government on the beachhead within three days of the landing. He implied naval as well as air support. The colonel's deception of the brigade conceivably could have been innocent, since the confused plans for the operation vaguely envisioned recognition and support sometime after the exile force had established possession of a major part of the island, and it also assumed neutralization of Castro's air force by air strikes. Even if it was, however, his plan to deceive his own wavering superiors was not. Frank reportedly told two of the exile leaders at the end of March that there was talk within the administration about cancelling the invasion and that he would tell them if he received such an order. The exiles claim Frank told them that if that occurred, they should stage a rebellion, pretend to imprison the American advisers, and continue the program on their own. On the Friday before the landing, Frank told an exile leader that if he was ordered to stop the invasion after the ships had embarked he would send a radio message directing them to return, and that they should ignore that message.[16] What happened to Colonel Frank's army career after the Bay of Pigs is not in the public record.

In areas where crises erupt, soldiers may be caught between conflicting military and political responsibilities. What the ambassador demands may be inconsistent with what the Pentagon directs. In this situation, however, the military chain of command has the advantage. As a result, force and diplomacy can become disjoined, and implementation can distort policy.

In the Lebanon operation the ambassador wanted United States troops to land unobtrusively on the docks in the harbor to avoid the bad public-relations effects of a spectacular amphibious landing. The military feared that this maneuver could trap the marines and prevent them from advancing to the positions specified in their orders. Because sanctity of the chain of command is one of the most important military values, the commander at sea prevailed over the ambassador, and the marines went in over the beaches. Ambassador Robert McClintock later complained about the unhelpful navy captain who, when asked to delay the landings, "answered that he was subject to the orders of the commander of the Sixth Fleet, who was under the instructions of CINCNELM, who in turn was responsible to the Chief of Naval Operations, who in his turn was under the direction of the President of the United States. This sort of brass-bound answer torn from the naval regulations did not exactly fit the needs of an emergency situation."[17]

Shortly after this problem came another. The ambassador wanted to honor President Chamoun's request for troops to protect the palace from a coup, and he sent his air attaché to the Beirut airport, already occupied by the marines. The battalion commander in charge, however, considered himself bound so rigidly by his orders that he refused to endanger the tenuous beachhead by releasing a company to defend the palace. No coup took place, however, and American policy was spared a costly embarrassment.[18]

A third crisis almost occurred during this time when Lebanese armor and artillery units took up positions along the road from the airport, preparing to resist the American marines. Ambassador McClintock asked Brigadier General Wade to delay entry into Beirut in order to avert a bloody encounter. Wade hesitated because of his orders but finally agreed to delay deployment for an hour until the Lebanese units were calmed down.[19] After the delay the entry to Beirut proceeded without incident. In all these instances, the combination of tactical determinism and the difference in authority between military and diplomatic officials only narrowly missed precipitating political disaster.

Military officers are reluctant to be placed in positions where they are answerable to people outside their normal chain of command because this reduces the clarity of their responsibility. In the Dominican intervention Lieutenant General Bruce Palmer was extremely agitated about being subordinate to a foreign military commander (the head of the inter-American peacekeeping force), a position he believed was unprecedented for an American commander.[20] As military governor in Germany, Lucius Clay received instructions through the Department of the Army; State Department messages were only suggestions.[21] Soldiers do not like to have this situation reversed. In his 1954 mission to Vietnam, Colonel Edward Lansdale initially communicated directly to Washington through CIA channels, which infuriated the President's envoy General Collins, and prompted a severe confrontation between the two.[22] In the country team, as in the foreign affairs community at home in Washington, ambiguities in the channels of authority and responsibility can complicate the implementation of policy.

Fragmentation of authority was a problem in Laos where the covert military mission in 1959–1960 was independent. Brigadier General John Heintges established separate communication channels to the Pacific command and the Pentagon, enabling him to circumvent Ambassador Brown. Only when Brown threatened to resign over the issue were the separate arrangements terminated. In May 1961 the President decided to bring the fragmentation in country teams under control, but he still deferred to the military norm that integrity of the operational chain of command should not be compromised. Kennedy sent personal letters to all ambassadors, giving them authority over all missions in their embassies, including service attachés. The one exception was the control of regular United States military forces, which would remain under Defense Department authority. This meant that military advisory groups would retain their independence of ambassadors. Maxwell Taylor supported this exemption because he wanted General Harkins to have autonomy in Saigon. But when Taylor himself became ambassador several years later, his first action was to arrange revocation of the military assistance command's separate authority and issuance of another directive giving him control of the military forces in Vietnam.[23]

The most divisive force in some United States missions abroad before 1961 was not the military but the Central Intelligence Agency, which occasionally managed to avoid ambassadorial control of its station chiefs. In Laos Ambassador Smith demanded the transfer of CIA chief Hecksher, who had engaged in covert political action without Smith's approval, but Washington transferred Hecksher only at the end of his normal duty tour, and then to Thailand, from where he could still direct some operations in Laos.[24] One aspect of the CIA station's independence, which persisted even after it was placed under the ambassador, was the way it used some members of the military against others as well as against the ambassador. An example is the efforts of Ambassador William Sullivan and his air attaché to limit the bombing of villages in Laos in 1967 with the specific assistance of a control group of air force officers in a unit under the attachés code-named Project 404. The Project 404 group monitored targeting and restrained CIA officers who wanted wider bombing. According to one of the air force targeting officers, the CIA managed first to circumvent the project controls and arranged for other units to bomb targets that the ambassador had in fact proscribed. When the ambassador and project officers tried to prevent such raids, CIA personnel were able to gain more control of targeting responsibilities and managed to have the project moved to Udorn, Thailand, where its actual control weakened with distance from the scene.[25]

This is but one example of CIA penetration of the military. The air force colonel who was focal point officer between the CIA and Pentagon in the early 1960s claims that JCS Chairman Lemnitzer and Marine Commandant Shoup were both shocked when they found out inadvertently the extent of the use of military units as CIA covers.[26] As the case of Colonel Frank suggests, the CIA operations directorate's use of military personnel did less to militarize the CIA than to compromise the professional integrity of the military.

The military chain of command usually manages to maintain its separate "back channel" communications network—intraorganizational communication lines not normally monitored by political superiors—despite ambassadors' uneasiness. This system is what led

Draper to suspect that attachés in Santo Domingo during the 1965 crisis were coached by superiors in the Pentagon about what to do with their contacts in the Dominican military. The back channel allows military leaders in Washington to caucus with subordinates abroad without their discussions being overheard by other members of the government. CNO Carney and CINCPAC Stump developed this technique to a fine art in the mid-1950s to keep messages from wide circulation to assistant secretaries in the departments of State and Defense. They went as far as to develop a secret code for the back channel, enraging Secretary of Defense Wilson when he discovered it.[27]

The government as a whole, at cabinet or presidential level, can use the back channel device politically, such as by engineering announcement of important events from the field in order to invest the incident with importance or to give the report the authenticity of the men on the scene. In the 1964 Gulf of Tonkin incident, the first alleged attack on the U.S.S. *Maddox* was announced at the Pacific command headquarters in Honolulu but only after the statement had been approved in Washington and transmitted to Hawaii. That the announcement came through CINCPAC surprised newsmen who were used to centralization of news dispatches under President Johnson. To cap the incident, the Pentagon made a subsequent announcement that quoted Hawaii.[28] Political manipulation of the back channel for public relations purposes, however, is of less interest than professional use of the system to deceive policy makers. The back channel undercuts ambassadors' authority in the field and also permits military officials to act as advisory puppeteers. Prompting a military man on the spot about what to report to the President, a military official in Washington can double the impact of his own recommendation. A single agency can use the technique to produce within the government an echo of its own recommendation from another agency or to gain the attention of influential members of other agencies. The Central Intelligence Agency operations directorate was reportedly adept at this technique. It has been claimed that the CIA often prepared reports in Washington and sent them to Vietnam, where they could be retransmitted to Washington with the Saigon dateline. Agencies have been known to have their representatives in a country team brief the ambassador in order to have him or her forward from the field the recommendations that the agency in Washington favors.[29]

The back channel, or even personal visits of a Washington official to the field, can be exploited when a combatant in a bureaucratic debate uses it as a ploy to get men in the field to back him up. Wheeler did this in cajoling Westmoreland to make the 206,000 troop request in February 1968. In the most dramatic case, Taylor had used the back channel to keep personal control of military assessments. In September 1963 President Kennedy asked for reports on progress in the war from Saigon. Ambassador Lodge's assessment was grim, but General Harkins's was optimistic. Harkins's report, however, sounded strange. It was phrased in a way that made it seem as if it was based on the debate in Washington more than on the situation in the field. Suspicious White House aides noticed a reference in the report to a cable from Taylor. They sent to the Pentagon for it and found that the cable had explained to Harkins the divisions in the government at home and coached him on which questions to address and how to answer them. The civilian aides decided to have cable machines installed in the White House in order to prevent this sort of maneuver. The military cheerfully complied, fourteen machines were installed, and reams of routine cables churned out every day; the civilians were hopelessly over-whelmed by sheer volume. Unable to monitor the flow, they gave up and had the machines taken out.[30]

The back-channel phenomenon detracts from the thesis that men on the spot are more aggressive than those at home. It also de-emphasizes the autonomy of field representatives and reaffirms that the most crucial policy battles are within the Washington com-munity. Nevertheless, the phenomenon amplifies the importance of indirect mechanisms of influence. Another indirect influence in crises is the limitation on choice of options that prior operational planning may pose.

PLANNING:
CONFINING THE CONDITIONS OF DECISION

The military establishment has the largest organized capability for planning in the United States government. At the apex is the Joint Staff. Each service also has its own planning staff, as does each unified and specified command. Most general strategic planning is done in Washington, and most of the contingency planning for local problems is done in field command headquarters. These groups generate massive amounts of material that may provide the only ready options available to civilian leaders searching for solutions and facing deadlines in a crisis.

The danger of insufficient or inappropriate planning is obvious: a government may find itself unprepared to cope with a challenge or unable to meet diplomatic commitments. In 1914, for instance, the Russians had promised the French that they would commit to battle whatever forces they had ready within fifteen days after mobilization began, even though mobilization would not be completed. But the Russians had not made plans sufficient to meet this contingency and they had to improvise at the last moment. The mobilization process was disorganized, and the chaos contributed to the German rout of the Russian army at Tannenberg, which in turn helped bring the German General Staff's Schlieffen plan perilously close to success in the West. When the United States entered World War I, in a more extreme example, the army general staff had no plans for mobilization. President Wilson, on political grounds, had forbidden the service to make contingency plans for the European war.[31] Faulty planning was again a problem in 1950. Having prepared in the late 1940s for general war, the government and the services were caught off guard by the North Korean attack in June. Defense Secretary Louis Johnson admitted in the first top-level conference on the crisis that his department had no war plan for Korea and thus no recommendation. The Joint Chiefs as well did not attempt formal estimate of the military situation in Korea, and they were not sure what would be required to mount United States military operations in the area. At first they could do no more than reiterate their earlier position that Korea was not strategically important. When President Truman decided that a response was necessary and the second conference's decision for use of American military force was transmitted to the commanders in the Far East, MacArthur and Vice-Admiral C. Turner Joy were not prepared for the reversal of the policy that had excluded Korea from the American defense perimeter, and they had no applicable contingency plans.[32] As a result, intervention had to be improvised, with disastrous results. The first troops sent in suffered heavy casualties, and United States and South Korean forces were nearly pushed into the sea at Pusan.

Less obvious than such constraints on action posed by gaps in planning are constraints on decisions posed by too much planning. Contingency plans can push options as well as preclude them, constricting the decisional premises of political authorities who rely on professional advice. Planners also shape the perspectives of the prime military advisers themselves. The Joint Chiefs, for example, depend on briefings and data prepared by lower-level officers on the Joint Staff. When a crisis erupts, the relevant contingency plan may be as unfamiliar to the Chiefs as to the secretary of defense or the President. When no one knows what to do in a crisis, a contingency plan can virtually set the terms and focus the decisional debate. Advocates of an existing plan have an advantage over opponents who do not have one of their own.[33]

Plans may orient and organize the military machine in directions that reduce the political room for maneuver of government leaders. The Schlieffen plan, for example, governed German diplomatic decisions before World War I, and the inflexibility of Russian plans was one of the precipitants of war. The czar's general staff could not provide partial mobilization without disorganizing the mechanism of general mobilization. The German general staff also had not foreseen a limited war and the organizational rigidity of the plans on both sides contributed to the escalation of the Austro-Serbian conflict into general European war. Such constraints can be Machiavellian as well as mechanistic. Professionals can manipulate the problem to prevent politicians from faltering. General Moltke falsely claimed the rigidity of plans as an excuse to refuse a last-minute change in strategy to concentration on the Russian front in August 1914. Alternative plans that could have implemented the shift toward Russia actually did exist. If the kaiser had asked General Staab, chief of the railway division, he would have found out about the possibility.[34]

In the Cuban missile crisis, President Kennedy did not make the same mistake. And in this case a ready military plan for bombing Cuba did not subdue civilian opposition but instead catalyzed the search for alternative options. When Chief of Staff LeMay and the air staff maintained that a "surgical" air strike on the missiles alone was not feasible—as opposed to the massive strike against multiple targets, toward which the contingency plan was oriented—the President went further down the chain of command and asked Walter Sweeney, head of the Tactical Air Command, who convinced him. In one view, however, this military report that the surgical strike was impossible was false and was a strategem to gain approval of the desired larger air strike. The Bay of Pigs had inspired the Chiefs' conviction, according to Graham Allison's analysis, that Kennedy could not be trusted in a crisis to follow through with necessary tactical authorizations once an operation had begun. The JCS therefore resolved that if the politicians wanted military action in the missile crisis, they would have to agree to use massive force. The service planners had a previously coordinated contingency plan for action against Cuba. When considering the air strike, the Air Force based its recommendation on the previous plan, rather than directly addressing the limited surgical option the civilians were really interested in.[35]

On this basis Allison argues that inappropriate contingency plans, which produced incorrect military advice, led the President to decide against a surgical strike on erroneous grounds. The evidence as a whole, however, does not indicate that the President was deluded. In fact, he understood the reasons behind the air force advice. The military plan called for bombing airfields, surface-to-air missile sites, nuclear warhead storage depots, and artillery batteries opposite the United States base at Guantanomo. The justification was the need to reduce United States aircraft losses and casualties from a Cuban attack on Guantanomo. Dean Acheson, the prime advocate of the surgical strike, dismissed these considerations as petty. But Robert Kennedy certified that the President was aware of the air force reasons by the time he talked to Sweeney.[36]

A second reason for the air force refusal to endorse the surgical strike was its contention that it was impossible to guarantee more than 90 percent destruction of the missiles with limited bombing.[37] This assessment was atypical of the more frequent inclination to overstate bombardment capabilities, but it came from the Tactical Air Command, the more pragmatic branch of the service. Given the poor record of bombing accuracy before the advent of precision-guided munitions in the 1970s, this hedge of 10 percent uncertainty was prudent. In short, while contingency plans may have distorted the initial consideration of the air strike option, they did not deceive the President; instead they functioned as a form of tactical determinism. The President understood the air force's reasons for insisting on wide collateral bombing and declined to dismiss them for political reasons. Instead he vetoed the whole bombing option on political grounds. Presidents may have their flexibility in decision narrowed artificially by contingency plans, but only if they take military recommendations at face value without probing the assumptions behind them.

There was more danger of being imprisoned by plans in the Eisenhower administration than under those of Presidents Kennedy and Johnson because formal planning was more institutionalized in the National Security Council at that time. The problem for the Eisenhower administration was that some of the early challenges it faced were not congruent with the general strategic plans that had been developed, and specific tactical planning, such as the 1954 Ridgway report based on his Indochina survey team's analysis of intervention requirements, precluded implementing strategic plans. Ridgway seized upon the planning mechanism to develop arguments against intervention. No one ordered him to make the staff study, and he took it to the President himself to prove the infeasibility of using force. Under Eisenhower, the National Security Council was organized to plan rationally—deducing specific policies from consistent general goals—while decision making at the departmental level proceeded more through ad hoc bargaining. Under Kennedy the pattern was reversed: McNamara rationalized Defense Department planning by institutionalizing program budgeting and systems analysis, while the formalistic rationalism of the National Security Council was abolished. Kennedy dismantled the NSC's planning board and operations coordinating board and substituted ad hoc consultation and temporary planning task forces to deal with crises. Direct military participation in decisions declined, and the politicians' scrutiny of plans and options increased. The Nixon administration established a compromise between the Eisenhower and Kennedy styles. It took crisis planning out of the NSC itself and put it into the Washington Special Action Group, a permanent committee.

One point on which civilian and military officials agree is that in a crisis the Joint Chiefs will have a plan prepared before the Department of State does. Military officers are frequently frustrated by diplomats' failure to have crisp solutions thought out in advance of a crisis, and they are impatient with civilian representatives' circuitous modes of analysis. Part of the reason for this difference is that the foreign service traditionally emphasizes the skills of representation, negotiation, and reporting more than making detailed operational plans for alternative contingencies, while military staff work is much more attuned to these functions.[38] The problem is that the same techniques cannot be used for diplomatic planning and military planning. Political goals and trade-offs cannot be programmed like tactical operations or weapons procurement. The latter functions are clear, tangible, quantifiable, and verifiable, while the former are more inchoate, ambiguous, inconstant, and uncertain.

Military planners and the Joint Chiefs who rely on them usually have a preference for formulaic solutions that reduce problems to manageable terms, clarify responsibilities and calculations of capabilities vis-à-vis objectives, and maximize certainty and efficiency. Thus at the strategy-making level, they tended to prefer the Basic National Security Policy (BNSP) paper procedure of the Eisenhower National Security Council, which articulated administration goals and encouraged the JCS to base long-range plans on them, to the informality and tentativeness of the Kennedy style of consultation. At the operational level, comparably, soldiers assert tactical determinism of implementation. Policy-making civilians' instincts, though, are to avoid formulas that can commit the government to certain actions before other options can be considered.

This difference between military and political responsibility exploded in the post–Bay of Pigs recriminations. Administration leaders criticized the Joint Chiefs for not having pointed out strongly enough the military infeasibility of the operation. The Chiefs took refuge in their prior evaluation of the invasion plan and their previously stated conditions for its success, which were not met. One condition had been the neutralization of Castro's air force, and the military agreed unanimously that the cancellation of the second air strike was irresponsible. Another condition the Chiefs had posited for the success of the final invasion plan was that it be backed up either by United States military force or a popular Cuban uprising. The latter, they claimed, was not their business to predict but rather the responsibility of the Central Intelligence Agency or State; the former they agreed was a political decision—also not their responsibility.[39]

Fundamental to the view of the Joint Chiefs was that the planning process had been irresponsible. First, the plan for the invasion had been tightly held by the President and the CIA, and the Chiefs had not even found out about it until January 1961 (Shoup had discovered it accidentally, when he tracked down mysterious arms transfers from one of the marine depots to the CIA). Second, the plan the Chiefs originally had approved as having only a 50 percent chance of success was for a landing at the Trinidad area on the Cuban coast. But the State Department had vetoed this option because Trinidad was near a town, and the diplomats feared seizure would be too dramatic and lead to protests in the United Nations. When the Bay of Pigs site was chosen, the Chiefs estimated the chances of success as less than 50 percent. Third, the Chiefs thought the plan was so carelessly constructed and revised so frequently and erratically that it violated all military canons of proper procedure. In fact, they never saw it in final form until the day of the first air strike. Finally, they protested that they could not properly evaluate the plan because they were prohibited from staffing it—that is, they were not permitted to inform their principal assistants, the vice-chiefs, or the Joint Staff logistics experts. After persistent complaints each chief was allowed to take one field grade officer into his confidence to help keep the papers in order.[40]

The different civilian and military attitudes to planning and the informal procedures in the new Kennedy National Security Council contributed to a breakdown in communication and differences in perception that led each group to feel that it had been victimized by the other. One of the JCS papers questioning the feasibility of the operation had been sent to Secretary of Defense McNamara, but it was shuffled aside amid the activity of administration changeover.

It later became obvious that the President was not aware of the Chiefs' reservations, and he blamed them for not having presented them more forcefully. In discussions, the civilians thought the Joint Chiefs had endorsed the final invasion plan.[41] The Chiefs, for their part, were adhering to the procedures of the former administration. They did not volunteer their opinions unless they were asked because the CIA was obviously in charge of the operation. They claim to have thought that they were being consulted, as had been usual, as briefing officers more than as advisers. They did not understand the new administration's freewheeling style of policy making. Nor did the two groups have the same semantic frames of reference. The language the President had used had indicated clearly to the Chiefs that he had decided to invade Cuba (while in fact his decision was still tentative), and this made them mute their opposition to the final plan. As Burke put it, "Our big fault was standing in awe of the Presidency instead of pounding the table ... We set down our case and then we shut up and that was a mistake." Another service chief told his successor that his greatest mistake during his tenure on the JCS had been failing to convey his opposition to the Bay of Pigs to the President.[42]

Thus where the Eisenhower planning system had problems of flexibility, relevance, or matching capabilities with objectives, the Kennedy system initially posed problems of intragovernmental communication. The system adapted better in the crisis of the following summer when State, Defense, and White House personnel worked smoothly together on the Berlin task force. The task force planners concentrated on alternative sequences of response for prospective crises, which bridged the gap between the diplomats who focused on political analysis and the military members who looked at action options.[43] In general, however, military planning is inevitably better than civilian diplomatic policy planning because of the intrinsic difference in the nature of military and diplomatic functions, because of the size and resources of military planning staffs, and because of the linkages between planning and operations in military activity.

Most decision analysts agree that the influence of planning staffs varies directly with their involvement in operations. Military planning is more closely linked to operations than is planning in the State Department. Least influential is long-range planning conducted by autonomous groups with no operational responsibilities. This linkage of effective planning with operational involvement leads bureaucratic revisionists to conclude that useful planning in foreign policy, as an autonomous function, is impossible.[44] In the State

Department, the planning function is vested in a small autonomous staff—the Policy Planning Staff—which has rarely been influential unless the secretary has chosen to use it as a personal source of ideas on immediate program issues (such as the Marshall plan or NSC-68). In the military planning staffs are larger and closer to the chain of command. The Joint Staff grew to gargantuan proportions during the cold war. In 1955 it consisted of 155 officers. The 1958 defense reorganization act raised its authorized strength to 400 officers (not including a comparable number of enlisted and civilian employees). McNamara was unsatisfied with the response of the Joint Chiefs, who were handicapped by the inadequate size of the Joint Staff in trying to provide the vast number of studies demanded by the civilian secretariat, so he assigned officers to the staff in excess of the legal limit. When the number reached 1,200 he sought legislation to raise the ceiling to 800 and was turned down by Congress. The law was circumvented by creating the Organization of the Joint Chiefs of Staff, which employed up to 2,100 individuals when Melvin Laird became secretary.[45]

The military's natural professional impulse is toward worst-case contingency planning for any conceivable disaster. The standard rationale is that enemy intentions cannot usually be perceived with certainty, and even if they are, they can change abruptly (such as in a cabinet or presidium shuffle), while lead-time requirements mean that enemy capabilities cannot be matched in a comparably short time. Political leaders, on the other hand, have to be more sensitive to competing nonmilitary needs. Their natural tendency is to "satisfice" rather than optimize, to shave as much as possible from the military estimates of their requirements. Because scarcity prevents providing resources for all hypothetical contingencies but because paralysis of policy is also undesirable, political authorities may sometimes be more prone to take risks by selecting options that have only a probability of success rather than a guarantee. In terms of strategic planning, the military instinct is moot if the services are subjected to politically imposed budget ceilings (as before 1961). If leaders try to deduce sufficiency rationally from external international constraints (as was supposed to be the case under McNamara) rather than politically from internal fiscal constraints, there may be extra friction between the military and civilians because the professionals have more room to maneuver with their worst-case rationales.

When it comes to tactical options in a specific case, however, military recommendations are less likely to diverge from those of civilians. In a crisis, the issue is not what forces to produce for future contingencies but rather what to do with those forces currently available. Worst-case hypotheses are not relevant in this situation, as opposed to strategic planning, but existing tactical contingency plans are. The desire of advisers to be influential by having a solution to offer can dampen reticence if the costs of forebearance appear high and compelling evidence is lacking that an option will fail. In these cases soldiers have as great an incentive as civilian leaders to gamble that the worst case will not occur. Immediate intuition may overcome prior analysis.[46] When a crisis is a reality instead of a hypothesis, military chiefs have to provide as many useful options as are reasonable.

In preparing for the worst, long-range strategic planning thus tends more naturally toward pessimism and more preparedness than may be necessary, and in so doing it also serves organizational interests by placing a claim on greater resources.[47] Short-term tactical contingency plans, however, tend less toward pessimism because their purpose is to offer a solution by which a job can be done with available means. Hence, they are less likely to constrain civilians from choosing a forcible option than they are to encourage force, except when the service is certain it lacks adequate capabilities (as with the 1954 Ridgway Indochina report) or a contingency plan serves organizational interest and doctrine by precluding a limited option in favor of a comprehensive and more forceful one (as with the Cuban missile crisis air-strike plan). Thus the kind of plans most likely to inhibit use of force are those that are usually least relevant in a crisis, and those plans most relevant in a crisis are usually the ones least likely to discourage military action.

Worst-case analysis has most effect when the issues are prospective or when advisers have reason to fear failure, and it has least effect when issues are immediate and costs of abstention seem certain while costs of action seem lower. In the missile crisis, the issue was immediate, and the chief of staff of the air force argued strongly for the necessity of attack. "When the President questioned what the response of the Russians might be," Robert Kennedy recalled, "General LeMay assured him there would be no reaction. President Kennedy was skeptical."[48] In 1964 the issue was prospective, and civilians in the Office of International Security Affairs supported a program of limited pressures—selective bombing—if the President decided for more direct United States intervention in Vietnam. The Joint Chiefs disagreed, favoring a heavy bombing program, on the grounds that the civilian planners were unrealistically optimistic in hoping that limited strikes would induce North Vietnam to change its policy permanently. The Chiefs said that forcing the North Vietnamese to come to terms would require destruction of their capabilities to wage war.[49] In early 1965, Under Secretary of State George Ball kept emphasizing the absence of any real contingency plans for failure. Other civilian leaders continued to hope that limited escalation would work. Former Eisenhower aide Emmett John Hughes discussed the problem with McGeorge Bundy:

> "We're just not as pessimistic as you are," Bundy told him. But what, Hughes asked, if the North Vietnamese retaliate by matching the American air escalation with their own ground escalation? ... "We just don't think that's going to happen." Just suppose it happens, Hughes persisted, just make an assumption of the worst thing that could happen. "We can't assume what we won't believe," Bundy answered ...[50]

If Bundy had believed either of the contrasting arguments of the Chiefs or Ball, it is conceivable he might have recommended no bombing rather than a little bombing. Liberals usually criticize worst-case analysis as a frame of mind that risks becoming a self-fulfilling prophecy. But in Vietnam it was the absence of worst-case planning that yielded disaster.

9 Precedents and Personalities

Some wars are the kind that timid young men achieve manhood in, while others are the kind that make tough guys throw up every-time they think of it for ten or fifteen years.

James Park Sloan, *War Games*

THE constraints of policy, strategy, capabilities, organization, and doctrine are usually well recognized in decision making. The effects of careerism and distortion of intelligence are much more latent, and their impact on policy is less recognized. In the middle are a pair of influences more apparent than the latter set but less predictable or consistent than the former. One is the role that experience plays in shaping advisers' attitudes. Another is the subtle way in which an adviser's style and personality determine his efficacy and influence on the advisory process. More refined understanding of the function of military advice requires looking beyond doctrine to experience and beyond offices to the people who fill them.

THE CONTRADICTIONS OF EXPERIENCE

A standard critique of military thinking is that professional soldiers prepare to fight the last war, relying too much on experience. The reverse complaint is that the generals fail to learn anything from the last war, ignoring experience. Trying to use the lessons of the past correctly poses two dilemmas. One is the problem of balance: knowing how much to rely on the past as a guide and how much to ignore it. The other is the problem of selection: certain lessons drawn from experience contradict others. On the first count, a mean has to be found between "grooved thinking" or excessive devotion to precedent at one extreme and planning in a vacuum in order to avoid that mistake at the other. Finding this balance is complicated by the dilemma of selection. For instance, the failure of the South Korean army to repulse the North Koreans in June 1950 was a rude shock to the United States advisory group that had trained it. The army had been organized more as a constabulary than as a conventional fully militarized force (in part from fear of providing Syngman Rhee the means to invade the north). When Lawton Collins, army chief of staff during the Korean War, went to South Vietnam as Eisenhower's special emissary in 1954, he had no intention of making the same mistake. Edward Lansdale recalled that the first chief of the military assistance advisory group, Lieutenant General Samuel Williams, also concentrated on preparing the new South Vietnamese army for a surprise invasion across the demilitarized zone in opposition to Lansdale's prediction of gradual guerrilla infiltration; he attributed Williams's orientation to his being a veteran of Korea.[1] One of the prime complaints of civilian strategists a decade later was that the army should have been trained as a constabulary counterguerrilla force—in short, as the South Koreans had been trained before 1950.

The feedback effects from military involvements can be positive (encouraging intervention) or negative (discouraging it); they can be short term (from recent events) or long term (from past incidents); they can be particular (from specific incidents) or general (from major wars). When the merchant ship *Mayaguez* was seized by the new Cambodian revolutionary government in 1975, for instance, the decisions were influenced by feedback encouraging intervention that was long term and particular (from the embarrassment of the 1968 *Pueblo* seizure) and short term and general (from the just-completed debacle of the fall of Saigon, Pnom Penh, and the final collapse of American policy in Indochina). In 1961, President John Kennedy told a reporter that he had been ready to intervene in Laos but changed his mind after the fiasco at the Bay of Pigs.[2] For the civilians, the negative results of the recent Cuban disaster were a powerful disincentive to use of force. Cuba also influenced the military, smarting under the blame for having failed to veto the Bay of Pigs plan. They resolved not to leave themselves open to the same criticism of underwriting an operationally risky proposal. Army Chief George Decker went to such lengths to discourage intervention in Laos that he warned of the dangers of yellow fever to the troops (Dean Rusk, who had been head of the Rockefeller Foundation when it had successfully promoted eradication of yellow fever in Southeast Asia, did not tolerate this excuse for nonintervention).[3] State Department representative Roger Hilsman believed the Joint Chiefs were trying to "build a record" so they could not be subject to blame this time.[4]

The event that had produced such negative instincts, however, had itself been encouraged by a positive lesson. Richard Bissell, the CIA deputy director for plans in charge of the Bay of Pigs invasion, recalled that before the 1954 operation against the Arbenz government in Guatemala, agency personnel had estimated the chances of success as less than 50 percent. That coup turned out to be amazingly easy. In projecting the odds for the Bay of Pigs, CIA planners believed they were better than they had been for Guatemala.[5] The Guatemala venture had also been a key incident in the career of Thomas Mann, who was Lyndon Johnson's key adviser on Latin America during the Dominican crisis of 1965.[6] In that case when the Bay of Pigs lesson that covert, ill-prepared military operations were to be avoided was combined with the principle of preventing the spread of communism in the Western Hemisphere, overt con-

ventional intervention emerged as the logical solution. The successful Dominican operation also occurred just before acceleration of
combat deployment to Vietnam was considered and may have com-
forted Johnson when he made that decision.

Positive experience—especially an intervention that proves un-
expectedly easy—lessens fear when future interventions are considered. Although there were logistical difficulties and other problems
apparent only to those on the spot, the 1958 Lebanon operation
appeared to most Washington authorities to be a smooth success.
But before embarking on the venture, military officials had been
haunted by the possibility that once troops landed they might become embroiled indefinitely. JCS Chairman Nathan Twining had
warned that troops might be there for ten or more years.[7] This
consideration had certainly been a disincentive to intervention in the
Chinese civil war. But restraint in that case had yielded the "loss"
of China, while action despite the threat of entanglement yielded
easy success in Lebanon. Colonel Lansdale's spectacular success
against the Filipino Huk guerrillas in the early 1950s and in groom-
ing and promoting Ramon Magsaysay as a popular and effective
nationalist leader, also led to the hope that he could do the same
for Diem in Vietnam. And in the mid-1950s, he almost did. Given
these successful experiences, policy makers would have difficulty in
being reticent about intervention in Vietnam in the 1960s.

The most pervasive and influential effects of experience on cold
war decisions on resort to force came from major involvements
(wars, not incidental crises) that were professionally formative or
traumatic experiences. Three wars have provided guides for American policy makers since 1945. Primary were the lessons of World
War II—appeasement, the Munich analogy, and the threat of salami
tactics (precursors of the domino theory)—which impressed civilian
and military leaders in roughly equal proportions. Secondary were
the lessons of Korea, which had greater impact on the soldiers than
on the politicians. It is difficult to overestimate the impact of World
War II on military consciousness, especially in reinforcing absolutist views of conflict and opposition to limitations on tactics once
intervention was undertaken. The total war of World War II was
where the leaders of the 1950s and 1960s achieved their professional
manhood; the agonizing war in Korea, on the other hand, frustrated
them for years afterward. The third set of lessons are those of Vietnam, which have been seized upon more vigorously by the civilians
than by the military but that demoralized both camps to the same
extent. The 1973 War Powers Act was in some ways the civilian

counterpart in sentiment of the so-called Never Again Club of the army in the 1950s.

Since 1968, Vietnam has been seen as a watershed, and politically it was. It shattered the cold war consensus and marked at different times both the apex and nadir of United States commitment to containment. For impact on military thinking, however, Vietnam was matched by the Korean War: the late 1960s led many Americans to seek to prevent protracted war by contracting containment goals; the early 1950s had led many air force and navy officers to try to prevent indecisive and wasteful combat by threatening massive retaliation. For the dominant wing of the army, though, Korea posed a dilemma: the need to avoid a repetition of the costly stalemate combined with the need to prepare to fight a limited war again. The 1961 all-or-nothing recommendation of the Joint Chiefs on Laos reflected this dilemma. The tragic paradox was that consciousness of the need to avoid another Korean War was not sufficient in itself to prevent the war in Vietnam.

The year after the Korean armistice General Mark Clark wrote, "Never, never again should we be mousetrapped into fighting another defensive ground war on that peninsula. Never should we commit numerically inferior American troops . . . against numerically superior forces of the enemy's second team unless we are prepared to win."[8] Sentiment against involvement in another limited land war in Asia characterized much of army leadership in the 1950s and made bedfellows of both pragmatists and absolutists. The absolutists wanted unconditional victory, and the pragmatists wanted to avoid unnecessary and draining entanglements. The premise of the Never Again Club was conditional: the United States should never again intervene in Asia unless it was prepared to fight an all-out war.[9] (Thus even Douglas MacArthur lectured President Kennedy in 1961 about the need to stay out of a land war in Asia, realizing by then that going all the way to what he saw as the root of the problem in Peking was practically out of the question.) At the end of 1964 army officers with Never Again sentiments recommended bombing North Vietnam as an alternative to sending in ground troops.[10] When this option was tried and failed to halt the deterioration, "the Never Again Club was hoist by its own petard, for when the President went along with its proposals to bomb the North, the Army generals lost the means of saying no to . . . ground troops."[11]

The failure of bombing still does not explain why army skeptics fell into line on Vietnam. In the early 1960s, Vietnam already seemed déjà vu, but the problem was which precursor was the most salient: the Korean War or the Chinese civil war. The lessons of both experiences were in conflict, and both the administration and the army were torn by the uncertainty. If the United States was to avoid another frustrating stalemate but also avoid decisive escalation, which would risk much wider conflict, foregoing intervention altogether would have been desirable. But avoiding war threatened to erode containment. (The army may have been more sensitive to the political dilemma than the other services because it, along with the State Department, had been among Joseph McCarthy's prime post-Korea targets.) The policy makers were faced with two contradictory rules: do not lose another country to communism versus do not fight another land war in Asia.[12] Until 1965 the government tried to accommodate to both rules by providing supplies and assistance to the Saigon regime and by limiting direct intervention to covert operations. When these solutions proved insufficient, the first rule took precedence over the second.

Economic aid and military assistance had been a major issue in the recriminations over the communist victory in China. Wedemeyer complained that he had drawn up a plan for a military advisory group of 3,600 officers and men for Chiang's forces, but only a small group was established, and it was not allowed to enter combat areas (as were advisers in the Greek civil war). Marshall claimed that Wedemeyer's estimate was higher (about 10,000 men) and could not be met because of demobilization. In December 1949 the Joint Chiefs recommended an assistance program for Chiang on Formosa, but President Truman ruled against it and did not reverse the decision until the Korean War broke out.[13] Earlier, in 1946, Seventh Fleet commander Vice-Admiral Charles Cooke had made a case very similar to the reasoning of military officers fifteen and twenty years later at the Pacific command and MACV. As Forrestal recounted,

> He expressed the view that the Chinese had within themselves the making of a great nation—that they were very much like ourselves in the degree to which they prized personal liberty and the freedom of the individual, but that they have not yet learned the principles of management necessary to provide a cohesive administration which would give a stable order within which individual people could really have the benefits of freedom ... America's contribution to China would be the training of the Chinese in the business of management and administration [while maintaining United States military power in the area].[14]

When asked by Senator Alexander Wiley in the 1951 hearings what he would have done in China in 1945, MacArthur answered that he would have provided aid sufficient "to have checked the growing tide of communism. A very little help and assistance ... at that time, would have accomplished that purpose." Senator Estes Kefauver asked if the United States should put more advisers in if the situation deteriorated and suggested the scenario of the slippery slope of incremental containment. The general said no: "I can conceive of no strategic or tactical position where I would put in formed units of American ground troops in continental China. So far as the technicians and others are concerned, we had about a thousand officers and men that were on the Republic's side all during the civil war. That did not involve us in anything that led to ground troops going in."[15] Air power could substitute for American troops.

By 1965 the United States had taken MacArthur's advice on China, applied it to Vietnam, found it wanting, and moved down the slope Kefauver had worried about. In the intervening years, the radical wing of the military had remained absorbed with liberating China or destroying its power, although most agreed that only air and naval power—not troops—should be used. But in time this preoccupation lessened, and the old China fixation was transferred to Indochina. For such radicals the lessons of Korea and China reinforced each other and dictated an early crippling blow against North Vietnam. For the pragmatic strategists who dominated the army and the administration, however, the lessons suggested a trade-off: the need to contain communism had to be balanced against the costs of imbroglio on the ground. As the military situation in Vietnam deteriorated, they hedged their bets and turned to a "coalition" general to assume the command in Vietnam: Westmoreland was both a protégé of Matthew Ridgway and Maxwell Taylor and an Asia-oriented admirer of MacArthur.[16] Vietnam soon turned into a longer, more difficult, and more unpopular war even than Korea, and military frustration grew apace.

The lessons of Vietnam are still taking shape. In one sense, military men are anxious to forget it and to write it off as an aberration. Westmoreland himself came to regret the ways in which the war had lowered service professionalism, distorted army doctrine, and engendered an inappropriate static defensive mentality among the service's infrastructure that would require massive retraining. Others, taking over the leadership of the services as Westmoreland's generation passed, considered the war to have been fought in vain. As Marine Commandant Louis Wilson said, Vietnam gave the services experience, but "It's not the experience I would like to have." "Never Again" sentiment is resurgent. And as with Korea, some soldiers have adopted a "stab in the back" theory, arguing that domestic dissent gave North Vietnam what it could not win on the battlefield and that the United States could not win the war because military power was shackled. As after Korea, these attitudes are more prevalent among air force and naval aviators. Army officers are more modest and fatalistic. Sidney Berry, one of the new army leaders, admitted that the United States could not have won in Vietnam not simply because of the tactical restraints but because "the political understanding and staying power of the Communists ... were greater than those of our forces."[17] Vietnam showed the civilian veterans of policy making that they were naive to have thought the United States could translate its military power into political leverage in a revolutionary war. Vietnam showed the military that the United States was naive to have thought it could succeed in waging a protracted war in South Vietnam or that it could succeed by coercing the enemy in North Vietnam rather than by crushing him.

THE IMPACT OF INDIVIDUALITY

An office orients its occupant in certain directions. No air force chief of staff will recommend a 10 percent reduction in air force appropriations, although some members of a congressional budget committee might; no Arms Control and Disarmament Agency director will recommend cancelling strategic arms limitation negotiations, though a Pentagon hardliner might. These same people, though, may find that their outlook and recommendations change when they switch jobs. As Secretary of State George Marshall became much more anxious to use aid as leverage to force Chiang Kai-shek to reform the Chinese Nationalist government than he had been as army chief of staff.[18] Those in the same office, however, sometimes differ sharply in their views simply because they are different people. Consider the contrast between MacArthur and his successor as commander in Korea, Ridgway, or Marine Commandant David Shoup, who was strategically conservative, in comparison to his successor Wallace Green, a bellicose proponent of sending troops to Vietnam. The office an individual holds is not determinative; it sets limits to his view of an issue but leaves ample room for different opinions. In contrast with the Marshall example, for instance, Lawton Collins felt no difference in outlook when he became a diplomat in South Vietnam, believing that there is no such thing as a unique "military mind" except in the mind of the beholder.[19]

Another reason that an office or role is not a reliable predictor of its incumbent's advice is that officers at the upper echelons sometimes serve in more than one office at once and have conflicting responsibilities. MacArthur and Ridgway, for example, felt uncomfortable balancing the respective demands of their double responsibilities for war in Korea and defense of Japan. In the 1958–1962 Berlin crises, Lauris Norstad also had a divided role as both head of the international NATO command (SACEUR) and commander in chief of the United States European command (CINCEUR). In his American job, he took part in the crisis contingency planning kept separate from NATO (since Berlin was technically a problem for the occupying powers rather than the full alliance), but he was cool to the idea of using force because of NATO allies' trepidations.[20] The members of the Joint Chiefs of Staff are also the chiefs of their services, simultaneously responsible for advising on general issues of national defense and protecting the needs of their own separate organizations. Just as overlapping associations and crosscutting cleavages moderate conflicts in pluralist society, they blur the lines of division in pluralist bureaucracy.

Previous roles may also influence an individual's orientation in an office. Two naval members of Eisenhower's first JCS had less in common with each other than with the chiefs of the other services: naval aviator Arthur Radford supported airman Nathan Twining and surface sailor Robert Carney often agreed with Ridgway of the ground forces. On the other hand there is no necessary correlation between personal background and personal recommendations. Combat-oriented "heroic" types of the Janowitz model do not always turn into belligerent JCS members, and staff-oriented "managerial" or intellectual types are not necessarily more pacific. Shoup and Ridgway were among the first type but cautioned against the use of force; Wallace Greene and Thomas White were in the second category but were very aggressive.

The contribution of bureaucratic revisionism to international relations theory has been to disaggregate the unitary government, for analytical purposes, into constituent interest groups in the decision process. Refinement of bureaucratic analysis logically pushes the disaggregation further than the departmental level. "The Pentagon" is scarcely a more useful category than "the government" for tracing military policy decisions. Roles and perspectives differ not only between the Department of Defense and other agencies but within the department as well. The ultimate disaggregation of decision constituents is to the individual level. This is especially true for high-level decision making, where roles are less confining and participants have a wide sphere of concern.[21] Thus James Forrestal "liked to insist that he was not as much interested in the diagram of organization as he was in the names in the little boxes."[22] Offices may gain or lose influence in the councils of decision depending on the interpersonal relations of the officials and authorities. State's first director of policy planning, George Kennan, had a special entrée to policy under Secretary of State Marshall but lost most of his influence under Secretary Acheson, with whom he had less rapport; when Kennan was succeeded by Paul Nitze, whose style and outlook were more congenial to Acheson, the post rose in importance again.

A strong personality can also mold his office or avoid its normal constraints. MacArthur went into the Korean War as if the unification reforms of the late 1940s had never occurred. He did not use a joint staff, and he regarded his theater command as the independent one it had been in World War II rather than as the unified command established by the National Security Act.[23] But he ultimately took too many liberties and stretched his role too far, so he was dismissed—but not until well past the point at which he had begun to usurp prerogatives. Averell Harriman believed MacArthur should have been relieved two years earlier because of clashes with Washington over policy on the occupation of Japan.[24] The mandate of an office presents a range of discretion and choice within which an incumbent can indulge his personal values, impulses, and judgments. This range is small for low-level functionaries with a small scope of authority and large for high-level advisers who are close to the President. The amount of leeway depends on the confidence, concerns, and demands of the President.

Finally, some people have an impact on policy not because they succeed to an existing office but because they create roles that would not otherwise exist. Taylor did this when he convinced Kennedy to create the post of military representative of the President for him. A less visible but more striking example was Edward Lansdale. Lansdale did not fill a conventional slot that some other soldier would have filled if he did not. If Lansdale did not exist, he would not have been invented. He was a politico-military entrepreneur, weaving in and out of intelligence assignments. His early successes convinced his administrative superiors to give him wide freedom of action.

Lansdale was not a professional soldier so much as a professional

missionary of American democracy who used the military as a
vehicle. In a sense he was the T. E. Lawrence of Southeast Asia.
Like Lawrence he identified with his Third World clients, was fired
by idealistic zeal united with a talent for using violence, and experienced both spectacular success and failure. Journalists are fond of
pointing out that Lansdale was the model for both Colonel Hil-
landale in Lederer and Burdick's *The Ugly American* (a compli-
mentary portrait of a competent United States operator among a
swarm of embassy idiots) and Pyle in Graham Greene's *The Quiet
American* (a devastating portrait of a naive and dangerous provincial who threatens to destroy those he wants to uplift). Lansdale
entered the military late, at thirty-three, going from the advertising
business to the Office of Strategic Service (OSS), then to army
intelligence. After World War II he decided to remain, he claims,
because he was attracted to the American military's role in establishing democratic institutions in Japan and Germany during occupation. He transferred to the air force when it was created because
he believed fresh ideas would be more readily received in the new
service. He professed a spiritual kinship with Thomas Jefferson and
Tom Paine, which he wanted to share with Asian nationalists. (This
led French officers in Vietnam in 1953 to see him as "a dangerous
revolutionary" and to oppose his inclusion in General O'Daniel's
military mission. The Dulles brothers came to see him as excessively
visionary and idealistic, but they nevertheless gave him a generous
rein in Vietnam because of his exploits as Magsaysay's eminence
grise in the Philippines. Though only a colonel, Lansdale dealt
directly with both of the Dulleses as early as 1953 because of the
intimacy he had with Asian leaders.[25]

Lansdale's techniques were not militarily orthodox. He built his
reputation by rejecting the purely military approach to defeating
the Huk movement in the Philippines and by stressing the importance of political, economic, social, and psychological factors. He
had little use for military discipline or the sanctity of the chain of
command; his behavior toward General Collins in South Vietnam
was virtually insubordinate. Lansdale's independence coincided with
a reputation for bluntness and candor (a JCS chairman once asked
him if his superior was telling the truth in a briefing). His explanation of how he was able to get away with his freewheeling behavior was that he made clear shortly after he became a regular officer
that he had joined the military for what he believed were patriotic
reasons and would easily quit for the same reasons.[26]

Lansdale's achievements in the Philippines and in Diem's early
years in Vietnam were unique. As a consequence he acquired a

legendary reputation that led, intermittently, to influence at the highest levels of government. His enthusiasm for making Asia safe for democracy helped fuel United States commitment in Southeast Asia. Although he impressed President Kennedy early in 1961, the State Department and Maxwell Taylor maneuvered to reduce his standing and after Kennedy's death he slipped from prominence. But he had a significant impact on Walt Rostow, who became one of the central powers in Vietnam policy making in subsequent years. If Lansdale had gone back to the advertising business after World War II, the United States might have become involved in Vietnam as deeply as it did anyway and the Kennedy administration might have become as devoted to counterinsurgency as it did, but perhaps not as much or in the same way. Lansdale's association with the Central Intelligence Agency, his role as Robert Kennedy's close adviser in the covert war against Cuba in the early 1960s, and his part in plots to assassinate Castro have led many observers to see him as a diabolical reactionary. What he really exemplified, and what is so difficult for many intellectuals to accept in retrospect, is the extent to which the excesses of the cold war were often fired by liberal idealism.[27]

PERSONAL STYLES AND INFLUENCE

Personalities are unique, but the impact of individual attitudes, characteristics, ambitions, consciences, and styles on the way in which officials influence leaders can be conceived in terms of several general categories. A few people's actions, advice, and influence are relatively unconstrained by the formal limts of their offices' purview. They inspire such awe and admiration that their opinions are persuasive on any subject of importance, and their reputations and appeal to public or legislative constituencies are so great that they are powers in their own right. Only two such charismatic soldiers appeared in the cold war: Marshall and MacArthur. Others may lack such extraordinary prestige or public support but transcend the limits of their roles because ideological zealotry leads them to see issues in Manichean terms and thus to see what are nonmilitary issues in the eyes of others as concerns within the sphere of their military judgment.

Other people do not transcend their offices. As roles can expand to accommodate initiative and ambition, they can contract to accommodate narrow self-conceptions or inertia and timidity. Men can have influence in certain situations precisely because they do not attempt to interpret their roles broadly but maintain a narrow military perspective. In some cases this means acting purely in the professional mode: giving expert military advice based on strategic security considerations unalloyed with ideological or personal motives, uncowed by the disagreement of colleagues or the displeasure of superiors. In such instances remaining professional may require risking one's status by vociferous support of an unpopular view. In contrast are organization men who try to keep a low profile when controversy arises. They define their roles narrowly because they are primarily attuned to the perspectives of their services, have risen by excelling as technocrats, and have little interest in politics or intrigue. They give extreme advice when service interests are at stake but otherwise are likely to couch their recommendations in untendentious or innocuous terms.

A third pair of types have influence because they take advantage of opportunities to increase their access and involvement in policy making or because they challenge the conventional wisdom of one constituency with the backing of another. The first are skilled bureaucratic manipulators who cultivate contacts and expand the circle of their patrons. The second are mavericks who either fight professional colleagues with the support of the President or fight the President with the support of professional or congressional allies.

Examples of both aggressive and cautious advice can be found within each of these categories, which are thus not neat predictors of behavior any more than roles are. (The categories also overlap.) They simply capsulize ways in which the idiosyncrasies of individuals come to bear on decision. The categories are roles within roles.

Two rival leaders dominated the army before, during, and after World War II. One was George Marshall, who was regarded with awe not only by the men who served under him but by the Presidents who served over him. To his colleagues he was brilliant, ascetic, olympian, humorless, dedicated, the epitome of selfless integrity. No one but Stilwell ever called him by his first name.[28] When the cold war intensified, Truman called him out of retirement to become secretary of state and engineer the recovery of Europe. When the Korean War broke, Truman decided he needed the best he could get for secretary of defense and again called Marshall from retirement. The National Security Act specified that regular military officers may not serve as secretary of defense; for Marshall, the legal requirement was suspended. With the tremendous influence his stature had gained him, Marshall acted cautiously on cold war crises such as China, Berlin, and Korea.

Marshall was charismatic in spite of himself: he did not seek power; power sought him. He impressed associates with integrity and intellect more than style or verve. His opposite was Douglas MacArthur, seen by many as a prima donna, by others as a mystic. He had an equal capacity to inspire deference and awe and regularly won over opponents with his dynamic self-confidence (as in overwhelming fears of the Joint Chiefs about his Inchon landing plan).[29] C. L. Sulzberger recalls a conversation with General Alfred Gruenther in 1950:

> Gruenther admitted that when he went out to Tokyo last summer, he had a preconceived prejudice against MacArthur, but by the time he left Tokyo, MacArthur's charm and personality had won him over. "How long did he take to get you in his pocket?" Al asked me. "About thirty seconds." "Oh," Al sneered, "it was about thirty minutes for me."[30]

General Collins recalls, "MacArthur always gave me the impression of addressing not just his immediate listeners but a larger audience unseen."[31]

In contrast to the strictly professional Marshall, MacArthur was a crusader. "The professional officer exists in a world of grays," as Samuel Huntington says. "MacArthur's universe was one of blacks and whites and loud and clashing colors."[32] MacArthur had no patience with Washington's timidity about bombing China during the Korean War. He condescended to the Joint Chiefs of Staff and to Truman, who was an unpopular President while MacArthur was a national hero. When he was cashiered after exceeding his authority in the field, the general was genuinely surprised. He had built his career on unconventionality and, in some instances, insubordination. Not only had he never suffered professionally for impudence, he had profited from it.[33] He had led a charmed life, was used to dominating everyone with whom he came in contact, and constantly had his sense of destiny reinforced by sycophants. In Ridgway's view he had a "tendency to cultivate that isolation that genius seems to require, until it became a sort of insulation."[34] MacArthur's charisma cowed his colleagues and deceived himself.

MacArthur's powerful popular appeal and support in Congress made it difficult to dismiss him, and for a long time those in government disturbed by his antics did not believe it could be done. The Joint Chiefs were as reticent as the civilians, but when pressed they finally recommended his relief in the spring of 1951. MacArthur came home to a wild public welcome, and in the Senate investigation he was handled gently, while Marshall and the Chiefs were questioned severely.[35] MacArthur had stepped beyond the bounds of his office, but his aggrandizement of authority had been tolerated much more than similar actions by a less eminent general would have been. The charisma stayed with him. Kennedy paid a courtesy call on him after the Bay of Pigs, and the general's shrewdness and eloquence made an exceptional impression on the President. Kennedy later consulted MacArthur in the White House and was intrigued when the general, who seemed to have mellowed since Korea, warned him against intervention in Southeast Asia.[36]

None of the later cold war military leaders had the stature, wide appeal, or base of support that Marshall or MacArthur had had. Some, however, exceeded even MacArthur's zeal to win the Korean War, liberate China, or contain communism absolutely. The most adept zealot was Arthur Radford (who inspired Fletcher Knebel's novel about an American military coup d'état, *Seven Days in May*). Radford had strong policy views of his own and did not hesitate to proselytize from his position as military adviser.[37] Although he impressed people he met, he did not always awe or convert them in the manner of a charismatic personality, and he did not have a base of power apart from the navy. He was taken on by a sympathetic administration; he did not lead the administration. His advice on use of force was rejected by the President in every crisis where overt intervention was considered.

A similarly blunt anticommunist zealot was Arleigh Burke, whom Eisenhower appointed to three terms as chief of naval operations; no other cold war service chief ever served that long. In most cases during his tenure, Burke recommended more forceful action than a majority of other presidential advisers favored. In an example of his aggressive vigor, Burke talked the reluctant Dulles into the provocative act of putting United States advisers on Quemoy and Matsu during the 1958 Taiwan Straits crisis. When Dulles worried they might be killed, Burke said they might, but that risk was part of their job. One of the first events in the previous straits crisis had been a communist artillery barrage that killed two United States military advisers on Quemoy.[38] In the Laos crises of 1959–1961, Navy Chief Burke's aggressiveness, in contrast to the caution of the ground forces, seemed humorous to McGeorge Bundy since Laos was completely landlocked.[39] Burke's attitudes were sufferable to Eisenhower but out of place in the New Frontier. His term ended early in the new administration but not before a flap over muzzling (one of his speeches was censored) or before he had become "the chief voice of the counterrevolutionary line within the government."[40]

The most inept zealot to serve on the Joint Chiefs of Staff was Curtis LeMay, whose fundamentalist anticommunism was matched only by his faith in the efficacy of the Strategic Air Command as an instrument to save Western civilization. He quickly came to be regarded as the most primitive thinker in the Kennedy and Johnson administrations, and Robert Kennedy cited his recommendations in the Cuban missile crisis as prime examples of military idiocy. Although he discomfited his superiors by undercutting executive policy in Congress, LeMay was utterly without influence within the administration. Whereas Radford and Burke under Eisenhower had been tolerated by the administration, Burke and LeMay under Kennedy were not. By the time his service as chief of staff ended, he was rebuffed, frustrated, disgusted, and bitter.[41] Of all these zealots, however, from Radford to LeMay, it is notable that although they had some influence on budget or procurement issues, none prevailed in decisions on the use of force.

More influential than those who advocated force were the soldiers who cautioned against reckless commitment of United States troops. Some of these recommendations were soft-spoken or equivocal because they came from organization men who sought to conform as much as possible to the interests of their services, the views of their colleagues, and the desires of their superiors. Army Chief George Decker was reluctant to risk the army in Laos in 1961 but he hesitated to advise unequivocally against it. He told President Kennedy that the army was ready to go wherever the President directed, but he hedged with so many warnings and conditions that his advice had the effect of a veto. To Decker he was doing his job: thinking prudently but trying to leave the President some choice.[42] Decker did not step beyond his role; he took refuge within it. Nathan Twining had sharply different strategic views, but he had also rarely been too forceful in the councils of policy while he was chairman of the Joint Chiefs of Staff; he did not dissemble but conceded the initiative in policy discussions to President Eisenhower and Secretary Dulles.[43] At the same time he steadfastly safeguarded the autonomy of the services.

The army chiefs who followed Decker in the mid-1960s also kept a modest profile and were chosen in part because they were efficient managers who would help McNamara rather than hamper him. They favored increasing the military support mission in Vietnam by sending more advisers because such a program would benefit the army and was consistent with national policy. They were cautious about endorsing direct intervention, but they were more so about resisting it. When bombing failed to produce quick results, Presi-

dent Johnson dispatched Army Chief Harold Johnson to Vietnam
in March 1965, giving him "a real dressing down ... right in front
of members of the general's staff," according to David Halberstam.
"All he heard from his generals, President Johnson said, was 'Bomb,
bomb, bomb ... Well, I want to know why there's nothing else.
You generals have all been educated at the taxpayers' expense, and
you're not giving me any ideas ... I want some solutions. I want
some answers.'" Westmoreland quotes the President's blunt instruc-
tion to the chief of staff: "You get things bubbling, General."
General Johnson complained privately to reporters about the prospect of war in Vietnam, dredging up all the old frustrations of
Korea. But he was not about to challenge the President. When he
returned, he recommended commiting one division.[44] Westmoreland
was another organization man. He had always been well regarded
by politicians, but because of his crisp military bearing rather than
his brilliance or outspokenness. When he was given a vaguely defined mission, beyond what many considered his military means, he
did not reject it and he was not abrasive in his requests for additional means to do the job. He was polite and pliant to the politicians
and reserved his anger for his memoirs.

The kind of caution more influential than Decker's or Harold
Johnson's was that which was forthright and outspoken from professionals who saw their roles as strictly military advisers but who
refused to temper their strategic analysis of capabilities and threats
with bureaucratic political prudence—men who did not hesitate to
go to the top and force stinging disagreements on colleagues or
superiors. The two best examples of this type in the cold war era
were Matthew Ridgway and David Shoup. Ridgway put his career
in jeopardy for the first time in World War II when he opposed
a plan to drop his airborne division on Rome before the Allied
Armies reached the city. During his brief tenure as chief of staff he
again vigorously opposed military recommendations to use force on
two occasions (the 1954–1955 Indochina and Taiwan Straits crises),
making sure his dissent reached the President.[45]

Shoup entered the military only because the Reserve Officer
Training Corps at De Pauw University paid thirty cents a day,
which he needed to pay his rent. Once in the marines, he established
a reputation as an archetypal combat leader, winning the Congressional Medal of Honor at Tarawa. Even soldiers whose views differed sharply, such as his successor Wallace Greene, vouched for
Shoup's uncompromising realism. Shoup never voted in a national
election, in the professional tradition that faded rapidly after World
War II, viewing partisanship as incompatible with responsibility to

the commander in chief. When the United States intervened in force in Vietnam a year after his retirement, Shoup spoke out publicly against the war. He had been Kennedy's favorite service chief and had the reputation as the only one of the Joint Chiefs the President trusted because he had staked out a position within the Pentagon as gadfly and devil's advocate. Shoup was a maverick professional, not a manipulator, and he considered himself a failure. He did not successfully influence his contemporaries on most issues, and some of his views were recognized as correct only in retrospect, after the mistakes had been made.[46]

Shoup was considered for the ambassadorship to South Vietnam after he retired from the marine corps, but the post went instead to a politically astute manipulator, Maxwell Taylor. Taylor was an intellectual and sophisticate (his favorite authors were Aeschylus, Balzac, and Goethe, all of whom he read in the original)[47] and a skilled bureaucratic politician. His tenure as chief of staff was similar to Ridgway's, embattled and rebellious. He was more adept than Ridgway, however, in arguing the army's case within the Eisenhower administration.[48] Some, such as Halberstam, also saw Taylor as more devious and prone to look out for himself, letting his subordinates expose themselves in the 1956 colonels' revolt, then standing off when the controversy broke, leaving them alone to be ruined.[49] Taylor became more highly politicized under Presidents Kennedy and Johnson, and was careful to control as many of the levers as possible on early Vietnam policy. Taylor did not shrink from power and he did not overstep the bounds of his office; he simply engineered the tailoring of his offices to his ambitions.

Lucius Clay was another politico at heart. He was the son of a United States senator from Georgia and had entered West Point only because his father's death had left family finances strained. He built his career in the army as an engineer and manager and was a favorite of Eisenhower. Clay was a major political adviser in Eisenhower's 1952 quest for the Republican nomination and in the personnel search of the new administration. He was a political rightist and opposed John Kennedy twice: once as a nearly uncontrollable envoy in the Berlin crisis and once in his role in an official review of foreign aid (he vociferously opposed United States support of public enterprise abroad).[50]

Mavericks are usually outmaneuvered by manipulators. In a clash on a particular issue a maverick may prevail because his case is so compelling (for example, Ridgway on intervention in Indochina). But over time only three things can happen to him: he becomes a manipulator himself, acquires sponsors and power, converts his superiors, and his position moves from being aberrant to being the new conventional wisdom (Taylor, maverick under Eisenhower and manipulator under Kennedy); he is institutionalized as an internal opposition and tolerated because he has powerful friends but is isolated from influence on most issues (LeMay, isolated politically by his administration superiors; Shoup, isolated professionally by his military colleagues); or he becomes too nettlesome and is eased out (Ridgway at the end of his first term). This can happen in the field as well. Joseph Stilwell was a classic maverick, known from his earliest years as a testy misanthrope who did not suffer fools lightly. He had no patience with the Byzantine politics, duplicity, and corruption of the Chiang Kai-shek regime, and he let everyone know it. His nemesis Claire Chennault was a classic manipulator, exploiting personal conduits to Roosevelt over Stilwell's head, currying favor with Chiang. Chennault's military position had also not been acquired in the normal professional manner of service and promotion. He had left the service in 1937 as a captain and had become an entrepreneur. Before Pearl Harbor (after which he was reactivated as a colonel) Chennault hired out to Chiang and organized the American volunteer group (the Flying Tigers), a collection of aerial soldiers of fortune who received bounties for each Japanese plane they downed. Chennault and Chiang succeeded in undermining Stilwell, overcoming the Joint Chiefs' support for Stilwell, and having President Roosevelt replace the commander with the more sympathetic Wedemeyer. (The Joint Chiefs, however, had the last word. Marshall and Arnold reorganized the theater command shortly before the end of the war and placed Stratemeyer as air commander over Chennault, who quit in a huff.)[51]

Most high-ranking military leaders since the onset of the cold war have been organization men in one form or another. Some leaned toward one or more other categories. Bradley and Collins were professionals as well because for them there was no contradiction between forthrightness and caution, or responsiveness to administration desires and organizational interests (except in the late 1940s when budgets were lean). For LeMay there was no contradiction between being a zealot and an organization man because the postwar air force was a radical organization, or between being an organization man and a maverick, because air force strategic doctrine was in opposition to administration strategy when LeMay was Chief. Few military leaders, however, have been strong and forceful personalities. Most were willingly subservient to their administrations. Those who were not were almost all counterbalanced within the military establishment by equally strong personalities on the administration's side. MacArthur ran up against Marshall, Ridgway and Taylor against Radford, LeMay and Burke against Taylor and Shoup. Presidents were rarely cursed with men on horseback against whom they had no troops of their own to send. In most cases Presidents got the strong men or the weaklings that they wanted.

10 Careerism, Intelligence, and Misperception

But for an officer it is particularly galling to be endowed with exceptional talent. The army will gladly pay tribute to a brilliantly gifted man—but only when his hand is already gasping a field marshal's baton. Till then, while he is still reaching for it, the army's system will subject his outstretched arm to a rain of blows. Discipline, which holds an army together, is inevitably hostile to a man of thrusting ability, and everything that is dynamic and heretical in his talent is bound to be shackled, suppressed, and made to conform. Those in authority find it intolerable to have a subordinate who has a mind of his own; for that reason, an officer of outstanding ability will always be promoted more slowly, not faster, than the mediocrities.

Alexander Solzhenitsyn, *August 1914*

"Well, three I was shooting at came apart but I guess every top turret and nose gun in our element was working on 'em too."

Prescott stepped over and turned the claim board toward Kane.

"Three more would make an even hundred, sir, our first . . ."

"There would still be time for a correction to make the Sunday papers at home, sir."

"Correction on claims, you mean?"

"Of course, sir. One hundred."

Kane pondered a minute. "Round numbers always sound suspicious, Homer. Make it a hundred and one. General Dennis, can you provide Homer and Brockie here with a place to write a press release?"

William Wister Haines, *Command Decision*

THE direct influence of military leadership on Vietnam policy decisions was low. President Johnson and Secretary of Defense McNamara felt no awe for the recommendations of William Westmoreland, U. S. G. Sharp, or the Joint Chiefs of Staff. The most significant impact of soldiers on decisions in the 1960s was indirect through the subtle ways in which the military reporting system controlled the flow of information from the field and conditioned the premises of decision. In this respect middle-echelon officers wielded influence that those at the most senior level did not. Analytic distortion of data at low levels may ramify into distortion of evaluation—and hence of decision—at high levels. The transmission of information transforms facts into judgments; each link in the chain of command "must take the judgments of lower echelons and use them as facts."[1]

The significance of indirect effects must be kept in perspective. Bureaucratic revisionists, apologists for the Kennedy administration, and critics of the military credit distortion of reporting as a major precipitant of United States escalation in Vietnam because it deceived civilian policy makers and led them blindly down the slippery slope of commitment. Others, such as Daniel Ellsberg, reject this view, emphasizing the cold and knowing rationality of the leaders, and place blame squarely on the President. Reality lies between these views, though closer to Ellsberg's.[2] Presidents and their principal advisers were never clearly deluded about prospects in Vietnam. But there were times when the combination of desperation, ambiguity or uncertainty in information, and the hope that optimistic reports reinforced that additional force might bring decisive results helped tilt the balance of choice and impel the leaders to gamble on another step in escalation. The effect of misreporting was marginal, but decision analysis is only relevant to the margins of policy anyway. And in war, marginal differences are important differences.

PERSONAL INCENTIVES FOR DISTORTION: CAREERISM AND THE PENALTIES FOR REALISM

Intelligence failures are usually explained as the result either of conspiracy or dysfunction. Blame falls on traitorous politicians or incompetent organizations. Neither explanation suggests complete solutions. There can be no guarantee that spies or evil, venal, or weak people will be kept out of positions of power, and no reorganization can immunize an information-processing system against breakdown. In the case of Vietnam reporting, both factors—fraud and dysfunction—played a mutually reinforcing role. The incentives of bureaucratic careerism (ambition, materialism, and the conception of being an officer as a job rather than a vocation) abetted the organizational dynamics of inaccurate reporting and overoptimism and contradicted the classic standards of military professionalism (realism, honor, asceticism, and sacrifice).

Careerism increased in the postwar era. In earlier years the small size of the standing army and navy slowed promotion opportunities, and pay scales were lower in real terms than after World War II. This turgidness of the promotion system and paucity of financial reward may have aggravated the careerist incentives to bellicosity that Tocqueville believed characterized democratic armies,[3] or it may have increased the proportion of mediocre men among the officer corps (by discouraging able men from staying in the military). But this system probably reduced the number of officers who were solely interested in personal advancement and remuneration. Ambitious materialists were more likely to leave the service; a higher proportion of those able officers who did stay were more likely to be idealists. When careerism is an easy option—which it became in the swollen military institutionalized by continuous cold war mobilization—there are apt to be more careerists, and competent ones, in the military. Professionalism in the classic sense varies inversely with the size of the military establishment.[4]

Vietnam was a routinized war, which made careerism particularly acute. United States forces were in action for more than twice as long as in World War II or Korea. For an aspiring officer Vietnam became a standard duty post, a slot to be rotated in and out of on two or three one-year tours. The routinization of Vietnam service was best capsulized in the term *ticket-punching* used to describe the scramble for brief command assignments. The ticket-punching pattern of rotation meant that officers rarely served in an assignment long enough to develop genuine familiarity with the local situation, and an officer who noted disquieting evidence of enemy success or South Vietnamese army failure had little incentive to make an issue of it; he would soon be gone. Rotation also reinforced optimism among province advisers that they would be able to accomplish a great deal. By the time an adviser had become disillusioned, his tour was finished, and another fresh optimist was ready to move in. This "shortness of institutional memory" limited military effectiveness, but the army nevertheless refused to extend the length of Vietnam tours.[5]

Promotion is the principal careerist incentive. The generation of pragmatic army officers who led the service after World War II were men who had spent their professional youth languishing in grade after World War I. Maxwell Taylor, Lawton Collins, Alfred Gruenther, and others spent between sixteen and seventeen years as lieutenants. They advanced rapidly once World War II broke, but it is doubtful that bright men who were especially egocentric or acquisitive or lacked emotional dedication to the profession of solddiering in itself would have remained in uniform during the interwar period. It would not be surprising if long years in low rank also instilled humility, pessimism, and modest expectation.

The type of general antithetical to this type was Douglas MacArthur, who was promoted exceptionally quickly throughout his career. Westmoreland, a type midway between the two, also had a rapid promotion rate. Absolutist air force officers especially were, in most cases, younger men who spent less time in the lower ranks and became generals at a much younger age. Promotion in the World War II air corps was much faster than in the ground army because it expanded at a much greater rate. Air officers were accustomed to high achievement at a comparatively early age. This fast advancement was more likely to reinforce subconscious attitudes of optimism and overconfidence and assumptions of competence. The more pragmatic group of air force officers who began to take over the elite of the service in the 1970s, in contrast, were those whose promotion patterns were similar to those in the army.

Careerist motives increase in wartime when the military expands and promotions are rapid. This pattern reinforced the odds that there would be a large number of careerists among the officers who collected, interpreted, and transmitted information from the field in Vietnam. The top civilians also encouraged a reporting system in their own image, all too often producing pseudo-rigorous analysis and answers that they wanted to hear. During a visit by McNamara to the field in 1965, for example, a marine colonel was giving a conventional briefing that left the secretary impatient. McNamara interrupted and interpreted the briefing in his own statistical terms. The colonel immediately perceived what McNamara wanted and spontaneously changed the script of the briefing, expressing everything in terms of numbers and percentages. To a correspondent present the performance seemed an unsubtle satire of the defense secretary's fascination with quantification. When the correspondent later tried to discuss the tactical situation with him, he found that McNamara had lost interest in the Vietcong and instead was absorbed with the excellence of the officer who had given the briefing. "That colonel is one of the finest officers I've ever met," said McNamara.[6]

The careerists knew they had no choice. They had as sobering examples the fates of those who told the disappointing truth to their superiors and who were rewarded with personal ruin.

Punishment of dissenters who challenge official strategy and doctrine, even when the challenge proves correct, is surprisingly common. In World War I French Marshall Joffre fired General Charles Lanrezac, who had obstinately warned against the nearly fatal underestimation of the German right wing under the Schlieffen plan.[7] When McNamara in 1967 insisted on criticizing the cost-effectiveness of the bombing of North Vietnam, Johnson replaced him. But when McNamara had been more optimistic a few years earlier, he himself had often ignored those who disagreed. One Central Intelligence Agency analyst, after presenting a briefing on progress in the war, based on favorable statistical indicators, told the secretary that as an observer who had dealt with Southeast Asia for years he was intuitively certain that United States tactics were not working. McNamara asked the agency to send him a different briefer next time.[8] Some military men can risk cautious realism when it is unpopular and survive, but these are usually general officers with assured status or most of their careers behind them, such as Ridgway or Shoup.[9] Middle-level officers serving as advisers in Vietnam in the early 1960s were not so lucky. The ones who kept their heads professionally often had them chopped off bureaucratically.

As the Diem government's war effort deteriorated in early 1963, the command in Saigon clamped down on defeatist reporting by American officers in the field, such as Colonel Wilbur Wilson, Lieutenant Colonel John Paul Vann, Lieutenant Colonel Fred Ladd, and Brigadier General Robert York. When Colonel Dan Porter, Vann's superior, filed a pessimistic final report, it enraged General Harkins, who blocked its dissemination. Harkins came down hardest on Vann, who had dared to call the mauling of his South Vietnamese army division at the battle of Ap Bac a rout, and to say it to the press. Thereafter Vann was ignored, and important visitors were steered away from him. When Vann left Vietnam, he found that the Saigon command had ordered that he not be debriefed in Washington, but he gave his briefing informally to friends in the Pentagon anyway. Gradually people at higher echelons began to listen to him. Eventually Vice Chief of Staff Barksdale Hamlett heard him and arranged a meeting with the Joint Chiefs. While Vann was waiting in Chief of Staff Wheeler's office on the day the briefing was scheduled, a call came in; Chairman Taylor had removed the briefing from the agenda. Vann retired from the service, returning to Vietnam a few years later as a civilian with the Agency for

International Development. Vann played a role similar to Lansdale's; he was an individualist whom the regulars could not suppress. Lansdale's leverage was his connection with the Central Intelligence Agency; Vann's was his following among journalists. In the process, Vann gained grudging respect even from many of the professionals. When Fred Weyand was given a field force command in 1967, he chose Vann as his senior civilian adviser.[10]

At a National Security Council meeting late in 1963, Rufus Phillips, a civilian directing the strategic hamlet program, challenged Major General Victor Krulak's contention that the war was going well militarily and brought out a report from a provincial adviser in Long An estimating 80 percent Vietcong control of the province. Subsequently Harkins's chief of staff, Brigadier General Richard Stilwell, launched an investigation. The major who had written the report was admonished, given a bad efficiency rating, and transferred to the least desirable job open, a National Guard training billet.[11]

The accuracy of many early intelligence reports and evaluations from the field was discouraged organizationally because pessimism became politically counterproductive. The administration had to justify its policy. As involvement grew, the bureaucracy became less responsible for reporting the truth than for making the war effort successful. As high policy makers became more committed, they developed a vested interest in optimistic readings of events, and the high officials' minions became increasingly susceptible to pressures to provide such interpretations where ambiguity allowed. As a division commander berated an American district adviser who insisted on reporting the persistence of unpacified Vietcong hamlets in his area, "Son, you're writing our own report card in this country. Why are you failing us?"[12]

Commanders created the conditions for their own deception. By the time United States combat involvement had begun in earnest, most officers had learned their lesson. In 1966, for example, William Lederer discovered evidence of major corruption in the South Vietnamese army hierarchy in one province, but the United States military adviser in the area refused to listen to him. The adviser knew that if he made an issue of the problem, the South Vietnamese army corps comander would complain to Saigon that the American adviser could not get along with Vietnamese, and the adviser would be removed in disgrace with his chances for promotion ruined.[13] In another area, American commanders were sometimes known to worsen the hamlet evaluation system statistics in their districts deliberately to allow room for improvement; initial pessimism was all right, as long as the trend was upward.[14] In addition, truthful reporting could cause other problems, even for a scrupulous officer. One district adviser told Congressman John Tunney:

> I work a 110-hour week. I downgraded four hamlets after the Tet Offensive and was immediately hit with a barrage of cables from Saigon demanding a full explanation for downgrading them. For the next couple of weeks I spent my time justifying the regress in those four hamlets. During that time I was not doing the things I should have been doing ... it may be a long time in hell before I downgrade another hamlet.[15]

Grim reports from advisers were also sometimes edited and made more reassuring on their way up the chain. A disillusioned adviser in the Vietnamization program who was selected to brief Army Secretary Resor in 1970 recalled, "I was told what to say. You know, polished. And I said, 'Oh yes sir, they're coming along just fine.' Real good soldiers and all that bull."[16]

One air force officer's experience led him to conclude that false statistical reporting was widespread even in peacetime management, for two principal reasons. One is that management information systems, which proliferated in the 1960s, are flawed evaluation devices because they often set unrealistic goals as standards. The responsible officer then has an incentive to lie (for example, about operational readiness rates of his aircraft) to make figures measure up to standards. Most significantly, commanders tend to blame and all too often punish bearers of bad news.[17] Captain Morris Blachman saw this fear at work in air force evaluations of bombing effectiveness in Vietnam. Interservice competition as well as the rewards and punishments of the promotion system also contributed to intelligence distortion. According to another participant, service loyalty was a force compromising the reports of the Defense Intelligence Agency:

> Many estimates have been changed or reworded because of an "Eyes Only" cable from a field commander. In one instance the Air Force Chief of Intelligence called my boss at DIA about a nearly completed estimate on United States bombing in Laos. He told him that he was sending a team down to change the wording of the estimate and that my boss had better remember what color his uniform was. Of course it was the same as the General's blue.

The estimate was changed.[18]

It is not surprising that the professional dissidents of the Vietnam War were scarcely to be found among general officers (except on the hawkish side), but rather among field grade officers. Neither is it surprising, because of the selection system, that many field grade officers provided congenial reports to protect their chances for advancement. Some observers see this pliant optimism as a characteristic difference between military and civilian officials in Vietnam. David Halberstam depicted corrupt reporting and overoptimism in the military and lauded the trenchant pessimism of some political officers in the embassy, and Ward Just attributed such a difference to both the naiveté and the operational responsibility of the soldiers: "A diplomat is trained to observe and report, and he is not responsible for the course of events; his career is not entangled in his reports ... It is the reverse for a military man ... a young major or lieutenant colonel could scarcely write of a deteriorating situation when, as military adviser, his superiors would hold him to account for it."[19] The difference in tendency does exist. When JCS Special Assistant for Counterinsurgency and Special Activities Victor Krulak and Joseph Mendenhall of the State Department made a joint visit to Vietnam in September 1963, the President asked wryly when he received their conflicting reports, "You two did visit the same country, didn't you?"[20] But the difference in tendency is only one of degree. Diplomats have in fact suffered as much as military dissidents for reporting strength in the communist camp and weakness in the client government. John Paton Davies, John Stuart Service, John Carter Vincent, and O. Edmund Clubb ruined their careers as foreign service officers by doing so in China, two decades before Vietnam.[21] When Roger Hilsman commissioned his deputy at the State Department's Bureau of Intelligence and Research, Lewis Sarris, to compile a report criticizing military estimates of Vietnam progress, Sarris did so brilliantly but infuriated Taylor, McNamara, and Rusk. Nudged by McNamara, Rusk ordered his subordinates in State not to challenge military estimates in the future. Sarris was not promoted; others who were less realistic were. Diplomats learned to be prudent in their reporting as well as the soldiers did. Social scientists have also noted the tendency among foreign service officers to avoid controversy and interpersonal conflict.[22] The problem of reporting incentives is universal for careerists, both military and civilian.

Diplomatic professionals share with military professionals two elements of a career system that encourage optimism in reporting: rotation, limiting service in any post to a few years (the military tour in Vietnam was one year, and officers usually spent no more than six months in a particular assignment), and efficiency reports, personnel evaluations filed by superiors that are crucial to promotion. Rotation minimizes the expertise that an individual can accumulate and bring to bear on a particular area, makes him dependent on local native officials, and limits his personal commitment and emotional investment in a given job and locale. It reinforces both indifference and naiveté. Efficiency ratings place a premium on success and on positive evaluations of progress by the officer being rated. Even at the top of the hierarchy in the field, diplomats such as Ambassadors Frederick Nolting and Graham Martin were often as optimistic as the soldiers.[23]

Not all officials are excessively optimistic about the situations in their areas and do not always support the host government. In the late 1940s George Kennan sent alarming reports home from Moscow, and his career was made by them. The pessimism of his so-called long telegram (the analysis of Soviet goals cabled home in February 1946) touched a receptive nerve in Washington, which was in the process of trying to decide what ought to be done rather than looking for indications of success in what was being done. And General Harkins's naive hopefulness in the time just before Diem's ouster was matched by General Collins's gloom a decade earlier about the capacity of Diem's government to survive.[24] It is much easier for a soldier in the field to tell his superiors a situation is deteriorating if United States troops are not involved and he has no operational responsibility or when disaster threatens and he needs to justify a major request for escalation.

SITUATIONAL INCENTIVES FOR DISTORTION

Advice and reports are often neither clearly positive nor negative. On issues of general principle—such as tactical autonomy and the need for a high level of preparedness—military attitudes are unambiguous. But in the interpretation of specific threats or operational results, the soldiers sometimes share the tentativeness or indecisiveness they deplore in civilians. There are some paragons of consistency, such as Curtis LeMay or Matthew Ridgway. In many instances, though, professional military officials oscillate between confident recommendations for force and sober advice to reconsider the feasibility of intervention—or between glowing reports of success and predictions of disaster. In some cases this wavering is an expression of conditional views, which see both advisability and feasibility of intervention as dependent on the scale and firmness of commitment. In many cases recommendations or nuances of confidence occur over time and reflect changes in the objective situation or stakes or in the adviser's perception of them.

Ambivalence often derived from the tension between the desire to act to meet the needs of national policy and contain communism, on one hand, and consciousness of the problems posed by any action on the other hand. Military reticence on Laos in early 1961 gave way to more aggressive recommendations soon after as the United States defense buildup increased the capability to intervene effectively. The administration's principal military official also vacillated on the issue of troop commitments as stakes changed. After his November 1961 mission to Vietnam, Taylor recommended commitment of 8,000 United States troops because the Saigon government appeared in danger of crumbling. But in March 1965 he opposed landing the first marine combat units because he was not convinced they were needed and feared that once the symbolic line between advisers and ground combat units was crossed, massive escalation would follow. Several months later he reversed himself again and thereafter favored heavy and rapid deployments. New North Vietnamese deployments had made the tactical situation critical, and the United States units engaged had to be supported and augmented in order to accomplish their mission.[25]

Dramatic shifts from optimism to pessimism may alarm and stampede civilian officials, but they are just as likely to anger them. In 1950 when MacArthur pivoted from confident assurances that the Korean War would be over soon, that China would not intervene, and that if Chinese forces did attack they could be contained, to what seemed to Bradley and Truman to be hysterical despair in predicting that the United Nations forces might have to evacuate the peninsula as the Chinese pushed south, both the President and the Joint Chiefs lost their awe of the general and grew increasingly exasperated with him.[26] When the stream of good news from Vietnam was interrupted by the Tet offensive in 1968, top civilians in the Pentagon rebelled at Wheeler's warnings of the need for new escalation.

Aside from changes in the objective situation, ambivalence can come from the contradictory incentives in estimating what is needed to achieve success in future operations and reporting on the success or failure of current operations. The incentives for the former task prompt pessimism; those for the latter prompt optimism. Military leaders rarely believe they have as much as they need to succeed in a prospective undertaking, but at the same time they do not like to admit failure in a job already underway. Under conditions of uncertainty, officers have reason to overstate threats in order to hedge against failure but also to overstate results in operations in order to prove their own competence. Military staffs and intelligence agencies are caught in the middle of these divergent impulses. Defense Intelligence Agency analysts were also torn between the Office of the Secretary of Defense and the Joint Chiefs of Staff. For the latter they felt pressed to present statistics that would support requests for more troops in Vietnam; for the former they were supposed to provide assessments of the strength of the South Vietnamese army, enemy body counts, and bombing results that could block such requests. In the first two years of ground combat in Vietnam, military leaders were particularly interested in evidence that would justify larger troop deployments, such as data on increased North Vietnamese infiltration. The Defense Intelligence Agency obliged them. But by 1967, the military was increasingly interested in proving the efficacy of United States operations, which meant demonstrating decline in enemy capabilities. Pulled in both directions, military advice during much of the period of combat involvement in Vietnam consisted of showing that the troops were effective but that they needed more help. In this context it is not surprising that Defense Department civilians and the President were cynical about the sincerity of military estimates or requirements. Such delphic hedges in intelligence estimates naturally make leaders impatient and distrustful.[27] President Johnson's failure to take seriously Wheeler's 1965 estimate of a million men as necessary for victory was both tragic and understandable.

This tension between the need to prevent future failure and to justify present performance also puts intelligence staffs in an awkward position in interpreting ambiguous indicators of enemy threats. In predicting imminent danger they can be damned if they do and damned if they don't. Military and civilian leaders in Washington never forgave MacArthur for his wishful thinking in failing to appreciate evidence that massive Chinese intervention was underway in Korea as troops approached the Yalu.[28] On the other hand, nervous predictions can cause diversion of resources. Allied intelligence fears of Nazi plans for a redoubt in the Alps in spring 1945 turned out to be a colossal mistake, but they helped prompt Eisenhower's decision not to drive on to Berlin.[29] Predictions that prove incorrect also foster a syndrome in whch leaders cease to take threat predictions seriously, dismissing the significance of indicators that recur without actually resulting in crisis. This happened to American and Israeli intelligence in October 1973. Thus the incentives to hedge make it common for military intelligence agencies to express caution in formal position papers and greater optimism in private briefings of top officials.[30]

The optimism of reporting from Vietnam was not simply an inversion of the military bias toward worst-case analysis and pessimism but a complement to it. Soldiers are naturally inclined toward the latter before operations begin and toward the former after they have begun. The problem in this kind of intelligence is one of timing. In Vietnam commitment was gradual and incremental, and operations took place within the dual context of what had already been invested and what the military desired additionally to invest. Pessimism and optimism went hand in hand. In time the ratio grew between the amount already committed and the amount still desired, so the optimism sometimes overtook the pessimism. In short, the total span of evaluation was often contradictory or muddled. If policy makers were more impressed, convinced, and influenced by the optimistic reports than by the negative codicils attached to them, their reaction was a normal one. Moreover, while predictions tend to be more pessimistic and cautionary than evaluations, it is the latter, which deal with what has happened, with apparent facts rather than misty speculations, that seem more certain to intelligence consumers, thus reinforcing the tendency for optimistic reports to take precedence over gloomy forecasts.

These contradictory incentives also explain some of the differences between analyses by military and civilian intelligence staffs. The intelligence community Office of National Estimates was an autonomous staff, dominated by the Central Intelligence Agency and charged only with analysis, while the Defense Intelligence Agency and service intelligence angencies were much more closely linked to the military chain of command and operational responsibility. As United States involvement in Vietnam unfolded, the Office of National Estimates tended to be more cautious and negative in interpretation of results and prospects in Vietnam—and with hindsight, more realistic—than were military analysts. The Central Intelligence Agency was more sensitive to the corruption of the reporting system. When Secretary of Defense McNamara expressed shock in December 1963 at the failure of the system to alert him to deterioration, Director of Central Intelligence John McCone arranged a covert CIA check of the in-country reporting apparatus. A team of CIA officials went to Vietnam, conducted a survey, and produced a critical report, but the report's impact was diluted. First, General Harkins issued a curious commentary accepting the facts in it but disputing its general conclusions. Second,

McNamara had stipulated conditions that weakened the CIA team's efforts; the mission was not to act as an inspector general and was to coordinate its work with other agencies. "It was indeed the mission of the group to set up checks," as the *Pentagon Papers* note. "But in the extent to which this system of checks was to be coordinated with the system as a whole, it risked losing some part of its independence of the accepted view. And it had been the accepted view that had been proved wrong."[31]

President Johnson preferred the optimistic estimates of the Joint Chiefs and resented what he saw as carping by the CIA that upset the delicate process of consensus building. CIA's station in Saigon predicted the Tet offensive, but most intelligence officers at the military assistance command headquarters scoffed; the command was in the process of reducing its estimate of communist strength as part of the effort to show United States success. It took Tet to shake the President's confidence in military reporting.[32]

Before the United States had begun to send military advisers in great numbers, however, the military intelligence agencies had been more careful. In estimates in June and December 1953, the CIA discounted Chinese intervention in Indochina, but military members of the intelligence community demurred and warned of higher chances of Chinese involvement. This prospective caution dampens military enthusiasm for force, just as the decision to intervene inflames it. At a National Security Council meeting in January 1954, State Department representatives favored United States action in Indochina, but the military representative refused to endorse American intervention and maintained that United States entry would demonstrate a bankruptcy of policy.[33] Absence of United States operational involvement and investment to that time allowed the military to indulge without equivocation their characteristic concern with enemy capabilities rather than intensions. For similar reasons the CIA has conversely tended to take a more relaxed view of Soviet strategic weapons development than have the military intelligence staffs.[34]

High estimates of enemy killed and favorable pacification statistics created the impression at high levels that enemy strength was plummeting in Vietnam by 1967. (In many respects such evidence was not contrived; after the Tet interlude, communist control in the countryside did decline until 1972.) But professional military officers were not as well equipped to judge progress in an unconventional revolutionary war as they were to evaluate conventional operations or the nuclear balance. The military reporting system produced an unfortunate brew of incentives and responsibilities. It was military reporting that was best tied to the highest echelons of policy making, and this dominance grew as the war effort increased. The same soldiers who had the motivation to offer positive evaluations of their own operations were the ones who dominated the flow of information.

Military intelligence agencies comprise more than 80 percent of the intelligence establishment, even since Congress slashed the personnel complement of the Defense Intelligence Agency in 1973. This preponderance is aggravated in wartime. In recent peacetime the dominance has also grown as the importance of traditional clandestine sources of intelligence has declined. Satellite surveillance is now the most crucial source of strategic intelligence, and satellite programs are under the jurisdiction of the Defense Department's National Reconnaissance Office.[35] Communications monitoring is done within the Defense Department, by service cryptologic agencies and the National Security Agency. Soldiers have also been prominent in the covert area as officers detached for duty with the Central Intelligence Agency or as military attachés in embassy country teams. One of the top two positions in the CIA (director or deputy director) was always held by a military officer until 1976.

Although professional soldiers have dominated intelligence, they have not always been well adapted to this role. Until recently the preferred career routes excluded intelligence assignments, and ambitious officers did not seek attaché duty for fear of harming their careers. After World War II, with the services top heavy in rank, there was pressure on army intelligence to find good jobs for generals, so some of the top attaché posts went to combat commanders. These assignments sometimes proved disastrous because the men had no training in or commitment to intelligence work. There were numerous examples of incompetent attachés who had to be recalled. In the most important of these posts, Moscow, there was an international incident over Major General Robert Grow's diary, which discussed war with the Soviet Union; Soviet agents photographed the diary and used it for propaganda. (Keeping a diary was in itself an elementary violation of intelligence procedure.) Yet Grow was replaced by another combat commander, J. W. O'Daniel, who also knew nothing of intelligence and reportedly performed no better.[36]

Only in recent years have the disincentives to intelligence work declined. Several leading army generals, such as William DePuy, William Peers, and Richard Stilwell, spent parts of their early careers with the CIA, and Noel Gayler, who headed the National Security Agency, went on to become commander in chief, Pacific. New initiatives to provide promotion incentives may attract more able officers to intelligence in the future. For most of the cold war, however, the traditional disrepute of intelligence assignments hurt the quality of military intelligence. In Korea Ridgway was unable to obtain intelligence specialists for nearly a year because no combat intelligence personnel had been trained in the service in the five years after World War II. After Korea, training was increased, and a separate military intelligence branch was created within the service. But in the early days of involvement in Vietnam, Harkins's staff organization at command headquarters in Saigon purposely merged the intelligence and operations components. Like civilians who regard war as too important to leave to the generals, the generals often regard intelligence as too important to leave to the specialists. In the field, intelligence officers in battalions or brigades were rarely from military intelligence because many commanders preferred to use combat arms officers on the assumption that they better understood tactics and operations. Even by 1968 not all division intelligence heads were military intelligence officers. An even more recent example of the tendency to discount the desirability of putting intelligence specialists in crucial intelligence jobs was Defense Intelligence Agency Director Vice Admiral Vincent De Poix's defense of assigning operational officers as military attachés.[37]

The prejudice of administrators against intelligence specialists and in favor of operational officers' opinions, despite the greater objectivity of autonomous intelligence staffs, is traditional. As the *Pentagon Papers* point out, senior officers in the operational line of responsibility in the field, civilian as well as military, accepted the more optimistic reports, while the "darker view was easier for those who lacked career commitment to the success of the programs in the form in which they had been adopted." The line operators' interpretations had more status at high levels. In July 1963 the Defense Intelligence Agency and the JCS special assistant for counterinsurgency and special activities reported favorably on military trends in Vietnam, while State's Bureau of Intelligence and Research presented a glum view, and in October it had an even less favorable assessment. Secretary of State Rusk immediately wrote a memo that it was not State's policy to issue military appraisals without consulting the Department of Defense.[38]

Rivalry between different operational groups can further degrade the influence of pure intelligence evaluators. The CIA had its origins under the tutelage of regular military officers who conceived of intelligence as a supporting staff function to coordinate and analyze information for the President. This initial development followed the wartime domination of intelligence by the military.

The Office of Strategic Services (OSS) had reported directly to the Joint Chiefs, whose Joint Intelligence Committee had coordinated most sources of intelligence, including the State Department's. Other officers (such as William Donovan, the reserve officer President Roosevelt had brought to duty to head OSS) agitated at the time of the CIA's formation for an activist anticommunist operational role for the new organization. According to one view, Donovan's clamoring for civilian control of the new agency was also a bid to attach the operational mission to the organization. In subsequent years this view of priorities was supported by young and ambitious military personnel assigned to the agency. The views of the regular officers who focused on the intelligence mission (such as Hoyt Vandenberg, the CIA's first director) were superseded by the views of political military men or young careerists who promoted the covert operations mission. Thus was born the division within the CIA between the objectivity and analytical orientation of its intelligence directorate and the tendency to wishful thinking and adventurism of its operations directorate The operational wing came to dominate the agency. These trends were illustrated by the Bay of Pigs operation where the intelligence directorate—which could have predicted that the necessary internal Cuban uprising would not happen—was not even informed of the planned invasion.[39]

The Bay of Pigs stimulated various proposals for reorganization of the intelligence community. The report of the President's foreign intelligence advisory board strongly criticized the Pentagon and encouraged adoption of plans to merge military intelligence activities into one defense intelligence agency. McNamara believed this change would eliminate wasteful overlapping and duplication of effort between army intelligence, air force intelligence, and the Office of Naval Intelligence. The secretary also saw unification as a way to extend his own control over information. To theorists of intelligence and bureaucratic revisionists, however, elimination of redundancy is dangerous rather than helpful: dispersion of responsibility among the several service intelligence agencies, as well as the CIA, the National Security Agency, and the Bureau of Intelligence and Research, could mitigate the stifling of information by hierarchy and centralization and increase the chances that alternative points of view would be considered at the policy level.

The theorists need not have worried—at least for those reasons. Because of military protests McNamara agreed to let the Defense Intelligence Agency report through the Joint Chiefs rather than a civilian assistant secretary for intelligence, which limited his control. It was not until after the report of the Blue Ribbon Defense Panel in 1970 that the agency was placed under an assistant secretary. Creation of the Defense Intelligence Agency also served the cause of redundancy qualitatively by creating a more powerful competitor to the CIA on the United States Intelligence Board where estimates were thrashed out, though it reduced redundancy quantitatively (under the old system there were six Pentagon representatives: one each for the secretary of defense, the Joint Chiefs, the National Security Agency, and the three services). Whether the centralization of service intelligence was an improvement or mistake, it was ephemeral. After DIA was created, the service agencies gradually regenerated themselves against the intent of the consolidation. The air force, for example, rebuilt much of its intelligence capability through its foreign technology division. Within a decade after DIA's inception, each service had a larger intelligence staff than it had before DIA existed.[40] The Defense Intelligence Agency's evolution had essentially accomplished the opposite of what it had been designed to do. Instead of increasing civilian control and reducing duplication, it increased both the military's weight in the intelligence community and the duplication.

Two basic points stand out about the military role in intelligence and reporting. One is that the scope of the military role within the intelligence community in the cold war, large to begin with, grew in the 1960s. The second is that the dynamics of careerism compromised the objectivity and quality of military reports and analyses. With the Defense Intelligence Agency burgeoning in the 1960s and with optimistic reports flowing from the field through command channels as United States commitment in Vietnam grew, there is nothing shocking in the President's apparent obliviousness to the pessimism of the Office of National Estimates.

Neutralization of Proof: Evidence and Ambiguity

The principal barrier to perfect rationality in decision making is the lack of clarity in goals and the inconsistency between certain goals. But even if goals and trade-offs could be calculated perfectly, complete rationality would still be impossible because the information by which the relation between means and ends must be judged is always imperfect. In some instances there is not enough information. In other cases, such as Vietnam, there is too much information. The flood of data from different sources—the Saigon command, the embassy, the CIA, the Pacific command, and the press—was overwhelming. There were hamlet evaluation statistics, body-count statistics, weapons loss ratio statistics, order of battle statistics. All the statistics, valid or phony, were more than any top-level generalist could digest. The overload of information meant that executives could not always distinguish which of the data they received were really relevant. In addition, they were dependent on the judgment of officials down the chain of command, who had to sift the flow, for the choice of data that they did get. The policy-level advisers of the President, and the President himself, had the problem of "noise" on a grand scale, and some important signals never got to the President.[41]

This information excess meant something else: a leader could find as much data as he needed to support whatever view of the war he wanted to believe in. Between 1965 and 1968, when the critical escalation decisions were made, President Johnson's closest advisers were able to avoid making difficult choices about changing the direction of policy momentum. While the Office of National Estimates produced pessimistic analyses that implied that the policy would not be successful, the President had only to turn to the Defense Intelligence Agency and the Joint Chiefs for data to show that escalation would work. Opposing sides could also see justification in the same documents, since written analyses usually presented both positive and negative data. On the 1961 Taylor mission report, the *Pentagon Papers* note, "Two people reading the full Report could come away with far different impressions . . . depending on which parts of the Report seemed to ring true." Redundancy in intelligence organization is two-edged. By increasing the number of viewpoints aired at the top, it serves the cause of "multiple advocacy," reducing the chances that responsible authorities will be unaware of relevant facts or opinions. But in doing so it may not help expose erroneous assumptions any more than it helps to equalize the empirical respectability of various viewpoints and to allow the President to believe whichever view accords with his preconceptions or hopes. Redundancy and data excess underwrite wishful thinking as easily as objectivity.[42] As military divisions in recommendations give greater freedom to civilian leaders to do what they want, intelligence differences allow the leaders to see what they want. Evidence is available for the taking by both hawks and doves, so true proof of which strategy best serves United States goals becomes problematic or impossible.

Predispositions among the consumers are as much a cause of intelligence pathologies as are dysfunctions in production and dissemination of estimates. President Johnson did not decide to escalate in 1965 because he was unaware of good arguments against doing so.

George Ball presented such arguments eloquently, citing the pessimistic analyses from the Office of National Estimates. Johnson simply chose to agree with Ball's opponents. By 1967 the President could still turn to the optimists who could supply data to show success. Special Assistant Walt Rostow was said to read over hundreds of incoming reports, select positive news, and publicize it.[43]

McNamara had a way to make rational cost-benefit calculations within the Pentagon: the program budgeting system. The Office of the Secretary of Defense did not run the war in the field, however, and command headquarters in Saigon and Honolulu did not process or evaluate their data by systems analysis techniques. Not only was the President a victim of selective channeling by his special assistant, but the assistant himself was the victim of misreporting and channeling from below him. Most fradulent were practices such as inflation of enemy body counts.[44] Channeling procedures were a more innocent form of deception but perhaps as significant. They determined the emphasis attached to certain pieces of information and, therefore, the impressions left with policy makers. For example in the first two years of the United States combat buildup, enemy infiltration data came in to the Defense Intelligence Agency in Westmoreland's daily cables, which had high priority, while reports of contacts with enemy units arrived in less important cables or by courier. As demonstration of operational success gained in importance on lobbying for the buildup, the procedure was reversed. Another example was air force assessment of bombing destruction. Accurate photointelligence techniques, which often failed to confirm destruction of targets, were disregarded in favor of the strike pilots' own visual reports, which were much less objective. Careerist incentives and service rivalry reinforced distortion. The commander of one military intelligence unit ordered his men not to exchange information with the nearby unit of another service, and the air force often withheld its bombing reports from the navy. Former intelligence evaluators and photo interpreters described numerous incidents of purposeful forwarding of misinformation and inflation of reports of bombing effectiveness.[45]

Proof that policy was or was not working was neutralized by the combination of fraud at the bottom of the chain of command, selectivity in processing data at the middle of the chain of command, and selectivity of perception at the top of the chain of command. Commitment to or against policy, apart from moral grounds, became as much a matter of faith as of calculation. Misperception occurred when it did because ambiguous evidence allowed it to do so. The temptation was natural to believe and to weigh more heavily apparently definitive evidence of casualties and battle contact in contrast to less rigorous indicators of Vietcong strength, weakness of the South Vietnamese army, and North Vietnamese ability to adapt to bombing. Overoptimism was not simply a matter of deception in the field producing illusion in the White House. There was enough of both to go around at both levels. But while opportunities for misperception abounded, it is important to keep responsibility in perspective. At most points along the way in Vietnam, the President and his advisers knew what they were doing; when they did not, they usually had themselves to blame. As Frances Fitzgerald writes:

> The neophyte journalists naturally assumed that these estimates were solely for their own benefit, but this was not the case. The officials made those figures for themselves. Each layer of officials added a new distortion with the result that the higher the official the less he usually knew about the situation on the ground. President Johnson, perhaps, knew the least of all . . .
>
> Clark Clifford . . . realized soon afterwards that this misinformation was only part of the problem. In his mettings with the President he would occasionally read the passages he considered significant from the reports of the CIA chief of station and the United States commander in Vietnam. Instead of objecting to those passages, the President would say, in effect, "Where did that come from? Why didn't anyone show me that before?" But the President had read those same reports already; he had merely overlooked those passages.[46]

The irony is that the highest military officials, the Joint Chiefs of Staff, have a vested interest in caution and pessimism. They have already arrived at their career destinations. They do not have reputations to make so much as reputations to *protect*. They have nothing to gain by overoptimism or making promises that cannot be kept. As Tocqueville wrote, "this blunting of ambition goes a stage further when he reaches higher ranks and thereby has more to lose . . . the least warlike and least revolutionary part of a democratic army will always be its leaders." But as Colonel Ross in *Guard of Honor* said, "In this life you succeeded when you were young because you never risked letting anyone do anything for you; and when you were old you succeeded, if you did, because you never risked doing yourself what you could pick someone to do for you." The company grade officers in action may have been cynical, and the top level civilian leadership had doubts inspired by political pressures, but the field grade officers in the middle were effective promoters.[47] The men with four stars were dependent on those below them for their understanding of the war. Unlike a conventional conflict such as Korea, where the army chief could look at where the lines stood on a map and judge the military situation himself, the generals of the 1960s had to rely on data about pacification, number of enemy killed, and bomb damage, data that lacked rigor or clarity. The lack of rigor made these data subject to coloration or suppression by the careerists trying to tell their superiors what they wanted to hear. Ambiguous information, filtered through selective perception, allowed the colonels to deceive the generals, the generals to deceive the President, and all to deceive themselves.

The tendency for opposing schools of thought to find self-justifying evidence in the same cases is illustrated by the recurrent debates over the miliary effectiveness of aerial bombardment, which go back to the days of Billy Mitchell. Since World War II the debates have pitted the air force, a majority of the Navy, and right-of-center civilians against the army, a minority of the navy, and left-of-center civilians. The former coalition has argued that bombing is more decisive and economical than a strategy based on ground forces and has not been decisive only in those instances where civilian authorities refused to let it be so by curtailing the scope and intensity of the air campaigns. The latter group has argued that bombing can only support the achievement of a military decision, which must be done primarily on the ground by occupying territory and controlling population and that air compaigns are not cost effective. Both theories have become articles of faith. The one cliché as popular as "air power can do anything" is "bombing doesn't work." These contending schools on bombing have found evidence for their opposing cases in the same source: the United States strategic bombing survey of World War II. Bombing skeptic George Ball and bombing enthusiast Walt Rostow both served on the survey. After he lost faith in Rolling Thunder, McNamara became irritated that the military chiefs advising on bombing seemed unaware of the negative conclusions of the survey or of studies that pointed out the limitations of air interdiction in Korea. Yet air officers confronted with the common civilian assumption that the survey proved the disutility of bombing responded that it actually proved their own case. Both sides in the B-36 debate of the late 1940s cited evidence from the survey and showed that there was no common perception of what it showed.[48]

Both sides used the same source to neutralize the arguments of the other because different parts of the document support each side. The survey does not prove simply either the efficacy or ineffectiveness of bombing. What it does show is that strategic bombing was effective under certain conditions—for example after the German interceptor force had been destroyed and attacks were focused on particular target systems that took months, rather than hours or days, to repair. The attacks on the aircraft and oil industries, and especially on transport systems, were very effective but attacks on the steel industry were not; precision bombing was effective, area bombing was not. Naval air power was crucial to the war in the Pacific in enabling the island-hopping strategy, but many naval and army leaders considered bombardment of Japan's home islands (including the atomic bombings) as less significant in forcing the Japanese capitulation than the naval blockade and Soviet entry. The survey was not decisive proof of the success of bombing because its evaluation was equivocal: "Allied air power was decisive in the war in Western Europe. Hindsight inevitably suggests that it might have been employed differently or better in some respects." Or as Verrier put it, the bombardment of Germany was only one of the crucial factors in World War II: "The bomber offensive was neither a victory nor a defeat. Its essential modernity is just that it lacks a decisive form."[49]

Within the military the army has been the most receptive to evidence of the limitations of bombing. (One of the army papers leaked to the press in the 1956 colonels' revolt was entitled "The Facts Versus Billy Mitchell.") Exceptions were the minority of Asia Firsters such as MacArthur, who asserted that removal of restrictions on the use of air power would enable him to destroy the Chinese armies in the fall of 1950. The Joint Chiefs took a dim view of this cavalier optimism. To most army leaders Korea proved that airpower failed both strategically and tactically. Lieutenant General Gavin referred to air force claims that air attacks on Manchurian bases could win the war as "the myth of the Yalu sanctuary." Operation Strangle, the interdiction campaign against supply lines in North Korea during the two-year negotiation period, also failed because the enemy munitions were not consumed fast enough at the front to strain the resupply train. The same problem occurred in Vietnam where interdiction of the Ho Chi Minh trail did not decisively constrict North Vietnamese and Vietcong resources. Factors limiting the impact of interdiction in both wars included enemy countermeasures such as air defense and dispersion of assets, the stalemated nature of the wars that left the tactical initiative to the enemy (which in turn did not force him to expend supplies faster than they could be replaced), and lack of effective night-attack capability.[50]

The air force historically refuses to recognize or admit the significance of negative evidence on bombing effectiveness. One example is the disparity between Chennault's claims in China and the strategic bombing survey's official assessment (see figure 3). Air-

FIGURE 3. Service claims versus external assessments. Comparison of Fourteenth Air Force claims and official assessment of Japanese shipping sunk by Fourteenth Air Force: August 1942–December 1943 (cumulative).

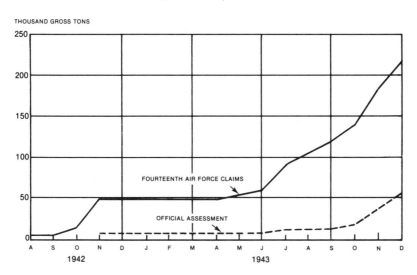

THOUSAND GROSS TONS

Source. Chart reprinted from Charles Romanus and Riley Sunderland, *Stilwell's Mission to China* (Washington, D.C.: Department of the Army, 1952), p. 338; constructed from data in U.S. Strategic Bombing Survey and Joint Army–Navy Assessment Committee studies.

power advocates and ground officers clash most vigorously over the limitations of tactical bombardment. The Operation Vulture bombing plans, which aimed to prevent French defeat at Dienbienphu, ignored the need to cut Vietminh supply lines, which would have required continuing sorties rather than the single strike contemplated, and they did not consider the possibility that the crucial Vietminh trench network could survive a conventional strike. In the dozen years between the end of the air war in Korea and the beginning of the air war in Vietnam, techniques to increase conventional

bombing accuracy scarcely improved because the massive retaliation policy concentrated on strategic nuclear forces and starved the
Tactical Air Command. Technological gimmicks developed during
the Indochina war, on the other hand, often broke down or proved
irrelevant because they were designed by nuclear-oriented generals
who were not attuned to tactical realities of guerrilla warfare. One
photo analyst estimated that the kill ratio for trucks on the Ho Chi
Minh trail was really only one in ten. There was also a dispute
between air intelligence and the Bureau of Intelligence and Research
over whether explosives could close Mugia Pass; the State Department people argued that bombing would widen it. The army was
sympathetic to this position, but the air force prevailed: the pass was
targeted, and it was widened. In other instances air force generals
resisted accepting clear photographic evidence that trucks could
traverse a road that had been cratered by simply driving around
the holes.[51] Challenges to air force bombardment doctrine failed
either to prevent or halt the Indochina bombing campaign. Westmoreland opposed bombing throughout most of 1964, but his views
on the subject were not solicited by the President or secretary of
defense. (Another example of continued army skepticism, even
after bombing began, occurred in July 1965 when a special national
intelligence estimate warned that extending air attacks in North
Vietnam probably would not hurt the Vietcong but cautiously indicated it might impede the enemy and prompt negotiations. Army
representatives on the United States Intelligence Board joined State
in dissent, rejecting even this modest hope.) Two other studies in
1964 also held out slim hope for results in a bombing campaign.
One was the JCS Sigma II war game showing that bombing would
not reduce Hanoi's ability to support violence in the South. The
other was a State Department study on bombing produced by a
staff under Robert Johnson, who disagreed with his superior
Rostow. The verdict was that bombing would not coerce the North
Vietnamese into coming to terms. The study was prescient in that
it predicted the bombing would cut off options and in effect imprison the American government itself.[52] This small, weak staff
challenged the logic of bombing early, to no avail.

When the powerful secretary of defense challenged the logic of
bombing much later he was replaced. His concern over cost ineffectiveness actually began in 1965 when he was distressed by low
damage assessments after the early raids. Nevertheless his July
review of the program that year gave Rolling Thunder modest
approbation. But by August 1967 McNamara was disillusioned, and
in congressional testimony he articulated the reasons why he had

not approved the complete JCS target list and his belief that additional air strikes would not shorten the war or weaken North Vietnam's will. Within a few months the President had authorized most of the fifty-seven unstruck targets that the Chiefs had complained about in the hearings and informed McNamara that he would be moved to the World Bank. It was the post-Tet political imperative, not the military cost-benefit argument, that induced Johnson to curtail and then stop the bombing in 1968, and he did so only after repeatedly seeking and receiving Seventh Air Force commander William Momyer's personal assurance that he could accept the halt.[53]

In the course of the war, military faith in bombing did not abate. Despite an intelligence survey and reconnaissance flights showing that there was not enough transshipment of war materiel in Haiphong to make bombing the harbor worthwhile, the military—especially Commander in Chief, Pacific Sharp—persisted in demanding that the harbor be struck. Despite evidence to the contrary, air force conventional wisdom and official history upheld the decisiveness of bombing in both Korea and Vietnam by pointing to the fact that North Korean and North Vietnamese negotiators came to terms immediately at Panmunjon and Paris after bombing attacks on special previously prohibited targets: the raids on the North Korean irrigation bridges in spring 1953 and the B-52 raids on Hanoi in December 1972.[54] The air force and navy answer those who denigrate the achievements of Rolling Thunder in two ways. First they argue that overall the bombing was effective; it hurt the enemy and reduced his capacity, even if only by degrees. In the first national security study memorandum review of Vietnam policy ordered by Kissinger at the beginning of the Nixon administration (NSSM-1), the CIA and the Office of the Secretary of Defense challenged JCS claims that bombing had destroyed 20 to 30 percent of North Vietnamese supplies on the Ho Chi Minh trail by pointing out that more than enough trucks still got through to keep the North Vietnamese army in ammunition. The air advocates could still argue that enemy activity would have been much greater if the supplies that the bombing did destroy had gotten through. Walt Rostow argued that the purpose of the bombing was to "impose an awkward inconvenience. Hanoi must run its economy and logistical system at a lower throttle." He also maintained that the bombing tied down 700,000 men in keeping the trail in operation. (This rationale was rejected by a 1967 Systems Analysis paper arguing that bombing actually increased the manpower supply in North Vietnam by releasing underemployed agricultural labor.) A naval aviator who served on the Joint Chiefs of Staff emphasized that despite the mass of statistics and studies generated by Pentagon civilians showing that the United States supposedly lost from the bombing in cost-benefit terms, the bombing was the one trump card the United States held in negotiations; it was the one thing the North Vietnamese wanted stopped and hence was politically worthwhile.[55]

The second argument is the military bitterness that the original JCS 94 Target Plan from 1965 for bombing key targets in North Vietnam in a quick blitz of a few weeks was never implemented. The air force and navy reasoned that the policy of gradualism ignored the military principles of mass, momentum, and shock effect and missed a good opportunity to accomplish the job when North Vietnam's air defenses were still weak and industrial capacity not yet dispersed. Not all of the targets had been struck even by the time the bombing was halted in 1968.[56]

Such air-power arguments are impossible either to refute or prove decisively since they hinge on different definitions of *effectiveness* and deal with what might have been rather than with testable reality. So the air force manages to maintain its faith in bombing, and civilian critics still have plenty of evidence by which to disbelieve. For the future, strategic bombing is increasingly outmoded. The B-1 probably represents the last gasp of manned bombers in the missile age. Tactical bombardment, on the other hand, is a different story. The technological revolution in electronic precision bomb guidance, which had its debut when television-homing "smart bombs" were used with devastating effectiveness in the 1972 bombing of North Vietnam and the 1973 Middle East war, suggests that future air force and navy claims in this area will be much more difficult for bombing critics to challenge. In future subnuclear crises, then, the air and navy will be better able than ever to offer bombing as a solution, and those opposed to bombing will have fewer arguments with which to refute military options on military grounds.

Conclusion

IF military advice were an undesired constraint on a President, there are several actions he could take. An antiinterventionist President could keep military capabilities lean rather than heavy, giving his advisers more reason for caution. He could organize the system of internal biases to reduce unwelcome internal pressures by raising the status of army advisers and lowering that of naval and air force advisers. He could listen more to the Joint Chiefs of Staff and less to field commanders. (A pro-interventionist President would do the reverse.) But this kind of administrative manipulation is too preciously Machiavellian, and it seeks irrationally to protect policy by precluding choice. It also would not work very well. Certain advisers unavoidably will be important depending on the nature of the crisis: external strategic constraints transcend internal organizational strategy. A President who favors air power cannot ignore army advice if the crisis involves use of ground troops. Conversely, a chief executive who seeks minimal intervention must consider air options before ground options. Irrespective of whether Presidents favor them, certain services and commanders are bound to be prominent in certain crises. Matthew Ridgway was influential in 1954 because he convinced Eisenhower the French position in Indochina could not be salvaged without United States troops; Chief of Naval Operations Arleigh Burke and Pacific commander Harry Felt were important in 1958 because the Pacific fleet would have been the cutting edge in a battle over the Taiwan Straits; Walter Sweeney of the Tactical Air Command was influential in Kennedy's decision against bombing the missiles in Cuba because Sweeney's planes would have had to do the job. In the immediate future strategic arms deployments and the naval balance will probably be the primary security issues. The air force will inevitably figure prominently in the first, the navy in the second. The army must inevitably remain preeminent in decisions about NATO.

There are no simple organizational solutions for dealing with direct military influence. A President at best can realize and use those aspects of the pattern of civil-military relations that have reinforced political control and discretion in the past. In his appointments he should seek individuals who will provide a broad spectrum of advice in the JCS and unified commands; diversity among professionals breeds choices for politicians. Most simply but most importantly he should be prepared to exercise his authority as commander-in-chief and reject military recommendations that do not suit his purposes. He must realize that the greatest pressure from professional soldiers will come not on whether to use force but on how to use it. In deciding on intervention a President must resolve either to use conventional forces without restraint or to suffer military displeasure. If he can afford neither, he cannot afford intervention.

But military advice in itself is not really much of a problem. The problem of military influence in decisions on use of force is not that Presidents either accept or ignore military recommendations too readily. When they followed or rejected military advice on intervention or escalation, they almost always did so with full awareness of the reasoning behind it. Within the negative constraints of capabilities, Presidents made their decisions on the basis of their own policy goals. Under the Constitution, this is as it should be. Indeed, pro-interventionists have more reason for distress than anti-interventionists. Military advice has been most persuasive as a veto of use of force and least potent when it favored force.

The real problem, as with other bureaucracies, is indirect influence and the extent to which it may condition the decision makers' frame of reference. A President who wants not only to control policy decisions at the top of the chain of command but outcomes at the end as well should not trust military subordinates' evaluations of strategy and tactics; or, rather, he should trust the military to be themselves, to see issues in their terms rather than his, and to adhere to the letter of presidential law more than the spirit. In deciding about the acquisition of military capabilities the President should discern the width of the margin for error in estimates prompted by military pessimism, and in evaluating the progress of ongoing operations he should recognize the impulse to positive assessments prompted by military vanity. In interpreting military intelligence, he should consider the filter of uncertainty and self-justification through which information flows up to him. He should especially be conscious that where there is ambivalence, as there was in the army when full-scale intervention in Vietnam was being considered in 1964 and 1965, there should be serious reservation.

There are three basic qualifications to the significance of these solutions. First, they are only hortatory homilies, and they deal with subjective inclinations rather than tangible reforms. A President is not elected on the basis of his cognitive disposition or his administrative style, and he is not likely to change either one very easily. Second, the proposed presidential behavior does not deal with the problem that military advisers may sometimes have too little influence. With benefit of hindsight, it is clear that the civilian leaders should have heeded warnings in 1965 that absolute victory in Vietnam would require twice as many troops as they ever had any intention of commiting. Less certain and less agreeable, but still possible, is that the reverse alternative might even have been better than what happened. The United States and the Vietnamese might have been no worse off if the President had authorized the air force 94 Target Plan, which promised decisive results. If that had been tried and failed, pressure for further escalation might have developed, but the failure itself would have destroyed the credibility of military promises; the air force would have had little left to offer other than nuclear weapons. Thus, the President might have had both an excuse and an incentive to disengage in 1965. As it was, the net devastation and suffering inflicted on Vietnam in three years of gradual escalation and more years of gradual deescalation was probably greater than it would have been under the 1965 air force plan. As the war unfolded instead, the responsible civilian leaders understood the immediate consequences of each step along the way, but managed to avoid facing the central issue of the ultimate limits of commitment and acceptable costs until those limits were actually reached in 1968.

Finally, even if adjustments in a President's operating style and perceptual tendencies are made, their effects will still be marginal compared to the overriding significance of basic policy goals. It is not possible to have good outcomes from poor policy or good policy from a poor President. The lack of clarity in calculation of the proportion between ends and means in Vietnam was disastrous. But the goals and perceived stakes of foreign policy in the cold war, especially in European crises such as those over Berlin, were models of precision compared with current conceptions of America's role in the world. The military security dimension of international politics seemed to be declining in the early 1970s as bipolarity waned and economic issues rose in importance. But there is no guarantee that the relevance of force will not remain or grow again. Disintegration of the North Atlantic Treaty Organization, military conflict between China and the Soviet Union, renewed war in the Middle East or Korea, and rampant nuclear proliferation are not implausible prospects for the last quarter of the twentieth century. The role of military influence in United States foreign policy may once again be significant as it was in the postwar decades. But if past patterns persist, the military will still bear less of the blame for intervening where the country should not—or failing to intervene where it should—than will those in whom the Constitution vests responsibility: the elected officials on Capitol Hill and in the White House.

Appendixes
Notes
Sources
Index

Appendix A:
Relative Aggressiveness
of Military Advisers

TABLES A–D present the data on which the analysis of the relative aggressiveness of professional military advisers is based. Tables A and B show the percentages of cases in which military officials gave recommendations that were more, equally, or less aggressive than the recommendations of principal civilian advisers. Tables C and D list the cases from which these percentages are derived. The cases include all cold war decisions in which the use of American forces in combat was considered by high-level policy makers. (Demonstrative deployments of forces for symbolic or diplomatic purposes, without the intention of committing them to engage in combat—such as the dispatch of the carrier *Enterprise* to the Bay of Bengal during the India-Pakistan War of 1971—are not included.) Covert uses of force, such as Central Intelligence Agency paramilitary operations, are excluded with the exception of the Bay of Pigs invasion of 1961. The Bay of Pigs is included because it was a major foreign policy incident that ceased to be covert once it began, and it involved some consideration of using U.S. forces when the operation began to fail.

It is important to note the limitations of the data presented here. The percentages in tables A and B are based on an uneven number of cases because some military officials, such as the chief of staff of the army, were almost always involved in decisions and some, such as the commandant of the marine corps, were seldom involved. Each percentage is based on the maximum number of cases (listed in the "number of cases" column) for which data were available on the official's advice. The percentages reflect numbers of decisions and do not discriminate between important interventions (such as Korea) and minor ones (such as the Dominican Republic). The figures do not give any indication of the differences between the views of various officers who occupied the posts listed at different times.

Forcing the data into the stark categories of the tables was inevitably a Procrustean exercise. In some instances evidence was fragmentary and officials' advice was tinged with ambiguity or ambivalence. In these cases I had to judge subjectively which category of relative aggressiveness best characterized the advice. (Evidence that prompted these judgments is cited at the points in the text where the cases are discussed.) The breakdown of the cases in table D was also slightly arbitrary. Similar recommendations on escalation were made repeatedly throughout the wars in Korea and Vietnam. For heuristic purposes I divided these wars in the tables into broad periods within which issues were similar and recommendations were consistent. The precision of all the tables can be subject to debate, but as illustrations of the general tendencies of military advice in comparison to civilian advice they are accurate.

TABLE A. Military aggressiveness on intervention decisions versus that of dominant civilian advisers.

	More aggressive than civilians (% of cases)	As aggressive as civilians (% of cases)	Less aggressive than civilians (% of cases)	No. of cases
Chairman, Joint Chiefs of Staff	11	79	11	(19)
Chief of staff, army	5	70	25	(20)
Chief of naval operations	43	50	6	(16)
Chief of staff, air force	25	63	13	(16)
Commandant, marine corps	10	70	20	(10)
Field, theater, unified commands	36	57	7	(14)
Other military	20	60	20	(5)

TABLE B. Military aggressiveness on tactical escalation decisions after intervention versus that of dominant civilian advisers

	More aggressive than civilians (% of cases)	As aggressive as civilians (% of cases)	Less aggressive than civilians (% of cases)	No. of cases
Chairman, Joint Chiefs of Staff	67	33	0	(9)
Chief of staff, army	67	33	0	(9)
Chief of naval operations	67	33	0	(9)
Chief of staff, air force	67	33	0	(9)
Commandant, marine corps	100	0	0	(6)
Field, theater, unified commands	90	10	0	(10)
Other military	33	33	33	(3)

TABLE C. Military aggressiveness on intervention decisions versus that of dominant civilian advisers: Cases

More aggressive than civilians	As aggressive as civilians	Less aggressive than civilians
	Chairman, Joint Chiefs of Staff	
Cuba 1962	Korea 1950	Laos 1961
Vietnam 1964	Indochina 1954	Jordan 1970
	Taiwan Straits 1954	
	Taiwan Straits 1958	
	Lebanon 1958	
	Berlin 1958	
	Laos 1960	
	Cuba 1961	
	Berlin 1961	
	Vietnam 1961–63	
	Dominican Republic 1965	
	Vietnam 1965 (bombing)	
	Vietnam 1965 (troops)	
	Pueblo 1968	
	EC-121 1969	
	Army chief of staff	
Cuba 1962	Berlin 1948	Indochina 1954
	Korea 1950	Taiwan Straits 1954
	Taiwan Straits 1958	Laos 1961
	Lebanon 1958	EC-121 1969
	Berlin 1958	Jordan 1970
	Laos 1960	
	Cuba 1961	
	Berlin 1961	
	Vietnam 1961–63	
	Vietnam 1964	
	Dominican Republic 1965	
	Vietnam 1965 (bombing)	
	Vietnam 1965 (troops)	
	Pueblo 1968	
	Chief of naval operations	
Taiwan Straits 1954	Korea 1950	Indochina 1954
	Lebanon 1958	

Continued

TABLE C. (Continued)

More aggressive than civilans	As aggressive as civilans	Less aggressive than civilians
	Chief of naval operations	
Taiwan Straits 1958	Cuba 1961	
Laos 1960	Vietnam 1961–63	
Laos 1961	Dominican Republic 1965	
Cuba 1962	Vietnam 1965 (bombing)	
Vietnam 1964	Vietnam 1965 (troops)	
Pueblo 1968	EC-121 1969	
	Air force chief of staff	
Laos 1960	Korea 1950	Berlin 1948
Cuba 1962	Indochina 1954	EC-121 1969
Vietnam 1961–63	Taiwan Straits 1954	
Vietnam 1964	Taiwan Straits 1958	
	Lebanon 1958	
	Cuba 1961	
	Dominican Republic 1965	
	Vietnam 1965 (bombing)	
	Vietnam 1965 (troops)	
	Pueblo 1968	
	Commandant, marine corps	
Vietnam 1964	Lebanon 1958	Indochina 1954
	Cuba 1961	Laos 1961
	Cuba 1962	
	Vietnam 1961–63	
	Dominican Republic 1965	
	Vietnam 1965 (bombing)	
	Vietnam 1965 (troops)	
	Field commands	
Berlin 1948 (Clay)	Taiwan Straits 1954 (Stump)	EC-121 1969 (Bonesteel)
Korea 1950 (MacArthur)	Taiwan Straits 1958 (Felt)	

Continued

TABLE C. (continued)

More aggressive than civilians	As aggressive as civilians	Less aggressive than civilians
	Field commands	
Berlin 1958 (Norstad)	Berlin 1961 (Norstad)	
Vietnam 1964 (Sharp)	Vietnam 1962–63 (Harkins)	
Pueblo 1968 (Sharp)	Vietnam 1964 (Westmoreland)	
	Vietnam 1965 (bombing) (Sharp)	
	Vietnam 1965 (troops) (Westmoreland)	
	Other military	
Berlin 1961 (Clay)	Indochina 1954 (Gruenther)	Vietnam 1965 (troops) (Taylor)
	Berlin 1961 (Taylor)	EC-121 1969 (Pursley)
	Vietnam 1965 (bombing) (Taylor)	

TABLE D. Military aggressiveness on tactical escalation decisions after intervention versus that of dominant civilian advisers: Cases

More aggressive than civilians	As aggressive as civilians	Less aggressive than civilians
Chairman,		
Joint Chiefs of Staff		
Vietnam 1965	Korea 1950–51	
Vietnam 1966	Korea 1951–52	
Vietnam 1967	Korea 1952–53	
Tet 1968		
Vietnam 1968–72		
Cambodia 1970		
Army		
chief of staff		
Vietnam 1965	Korea 1950–51	
Vietnam 1966	Korea 1951–52	
Vietnam 1967	Korea 1952–53	
Tet 1968		
Vietnam 1968–72		
Cambodia 1970		
Chief of		
naval operations		
Vietnam 1965	Korea 1950–51	
Vietnam 1966	Korea 1951–52	
Vietnam 1967	Korea 1952–53	
Tet 1968		
Vietnam 1968–72		
Cambodia 1970		
Air force		
chief of staff		
Vietnam 1965	Korea 1950–51	
Vietnam 1966	Korea 1951–52	
Vietnam 1967	Korea 1952–53	
Tet 1968		
Vietnam 1968–72		
Cambodia 1970		
Commandant,		
marine corps		
Vietnam 1965		
Vietnam 1966		
Vietnam 1967		
Tet 1968		
Vietnam 1968–72		
Cambodia 1970		

TABLE D.   (Continued)

More aggressive than civilians	As aggressive as civilians	
	Field commands	
Korea 1950–51 (MacArthur)	Korea 1951–52 (Ridgway)	
Korea 1952–53 (Clark)		
Dominican Republic 1965 (Palmer)		
Vietnam 1965 (Sharp)		
Vietnam 1966 (Westmoreland)		
Vietnam 1967 (Westmoreland)		
Tet 1968 (Westmoreland)		
Cambodia 1970 (Abrams)		
Vietnam 1968–72 (Abrams)		
	Other military	
Tet 1968 (Taylor)	Tet 1968 (Bradley)	Tet 1968 (Ridgway)

	Chairman	Chief of staff of the army	Chief of naval operations	Chief of staff of the air force	Commandant of the Marine Corps
Truman	(Fleet Admiral William D. Leahy, chief of staff to the commander in chief, 1942–1949)	George C. Marshall to November 1945	Ernest J. King to December 1945		Alexander A. Vandegrift to December 1947
		Dwight D. Eisenhower November 1945–February 1948	Chester W. Nimitz December 1945–December 1947		
		Omar N. Bradley February 1948–August 1949	Louis E. Denfeld December 1947–October 1949	Carl Spaatz September 1947–April 1948	Clifton B. Cates January 1948–December 1951
	Omar N. Bradley August 1949–August 1953	J. Lawton Collins August 1949–August 1953	Forrest P. Sherman November 1949–August 1951	Hoyt S. Vandenberg April 1948–June 1953	
			William M. Fechteler August 1951–August 1953		
Eisenhower	Arthur W. Radford August 1953–August 1957	Matthew B. Ridgway August 1953–June 1955	Robert B. Carney August 1953–August 1955	Nathan F. Twining June 1953–June 1957	Lemuel C. Shepherd January 1952–December 1955
		Maxwell D. Taylor June 1955–June 1959	Arleigh A. Burke August 1955–August 1961		
	Nathan F. Twining August 1957–September 1960			Thomas D. White July 1957–June 1961	Randolph McC. Pate January 1956–December 1959

	Chairman, JCS	Army	Navy	Air Force	Marine Corps
Kennedy	Lyman L. Lemnitzer, July 1959–September 1960				David M. Shoup, January 1960–December 1963
	Lyman L. Lemnitzer, October 1960–September 1962	George H. Decker, October 1960–September 1962	George W. Anderson, August 1961–August 1963	Curtis E. LeMay, June 1961–February 1965	
Johnson	Maxwell D. Taylor, October 1962–July 1964	Earle G. Wheeler, October 1962–July 1964	David L. McDonald, August 1963–August 1967	John P. McConnell, February 1965–July 1969	Wallace M. Greene, January 1964–December 1967
	Earle G. Wheeler, July 1964–July 1970	Harold K. Johnson, July 1964–July 1968	Thomas H. Moorer, August 1967–July 1970		Leonard F. Chapman, January 1968–December 1971
Nixon	Thomas H. Moorer, July 1970–July 1974	William C. Westmoreland, July 1968–July 1972	Elmo R. Zumwalt, July 1970–July 1974	John D. Ryan, August 1969–August 1973	Robert E. Cushman, January 1972–June 1975
		Creighton W. Abrams, July 1972–September 1974		George S. Brown, September 1973–July 1974	
Ford	George S. Brown, July 1974–	Frederick C. Weyand, September 1974–September 1976	James L. Holloway, July 1974–	David C. Jones, July 1974–	Louis H. Wilson, July 1975–
Carter		Bernard W. Rogers, September 1976–			

Notes

INTRODUCTION

1. According to Arthur Schlesinger, Jr., "Here surely lies a major cause of our imperial drift: the incessant pressure of the professional military... constantly demands... more military involvement, more military intervention." *The Crisis of Confidence* (Boston: Houghton Mifflin, 1969), p, 172. Schlesinger elaborates his argument in Richard M. Pfeffer, ed., *No More Vietnams?* (New York: Harper & Row, 1968), p. 10. See also John Kenneth Galbraith, *How to Control the Military* (New York: New American Library, 1969). Military influence concerns liberals and conservatives more than radicals of either extreme. Reactionaries see soldiers as pliant tools of the eastern liberal intellectual establishment; Marxists see the eastern conservative capitalist establishment as the governing elite. See Gabriel Kolko, *The Roots of American Foreign Policy* (Boston: Beacon Press, 1969), pp. 27–47.

2. Samuel Huntington writes, "War is more unsettling to military institutions than to any others. A Tsarist officer once said that he hated war because 'it spoils the armies,' and American naval officers complained that the civil war 'ruined the navy.'" The soldier is not a sheep in wolf's clothing; he "favors preparedness, but... never feels prepared." *The Soldier and the State* (Cambridge: Harvard University Press, 1957), pp. 69–70. Alfred Vagts distinguishes "militarism," which may affect civilians as well as soldiers, from the more prudent "military way." *A History of Militarism*, 2d ed. (New York: Meridian, 1967), p. 13.

3. Some analysts of international relations doubt the relevance of bureaucratic divisions for explaining foreign policy. Stephen Krasner argues that shared values and strategic objectives are the only crucial determinants of decision. This critique has merit, since part of the current allure of bureaucratic politics theory for liberal intellectuals may be the extent to which it absolves liberal civilian leaders of responsibility for consciously leading the United States deeper into the Vietnam imbroglio, vaguely articulated policy usually masks different conceptions of strategy and leaves ample room for intragovernmental debate on tactics. Alterna-

tive choices of tactics, in turn, often have significant ramifications for policy outcomes. The Cuban missile crisis decision for a blockade instead of an air strike, for instance, was a critical choice affected by disagreements within the circle of policy makers. Robert Art's critique is closer to the mark. Analysis of the influence of different groups within government rarely demonstrates that outcomes of policy were irrational or unintended by the President, but it does indicate how the President came to choose one option rather than another. Stephen D. Krasner, "Are Bureaucracies Important? or, Allison Wonderland," *Foreign Policy* 7 (Summer 1972); Robert J. Art, "Bureaucratic Politics and American Foreign Policy: A Critique," *Policy Sciences* 4, no. 4 (December 1973). Understanding military perspectives on use of force does not explain why the cold war happened or why Presidents believed in the need to contain communism, but it does help to explain why the United States went to the brink at certain times rather than at others.

1. MILITARY ADVICE AND THE USE OF FORCE

1. The civilian advisers involved in high-level decisions on the use of force varied, depending on the case, but usually included several of the following: secretaries of state and defense; subcabinet personnel such as the assistant secretary of defense for international security affairs or assistant secretary of state for the Far East; assistant to the President for national security affairs; ambassadors; and specific consulted congressmen.

2. On the missile crisis: Dean Acheson, "Homage to Plain Dumb Luck," *Esquire* (February 1969). Marine Commandant David Shoup was the one member of the Joint Chiefs of Staff to oppose the air attack, but not vociferously. Two military interviews. The exception mentioned was retired General Matthew Ridgway, consulted by President Johnson in 1968 at the time of the Tet offensive. But even here Ridgway's dovishness was supported by a large, growing, and ultimately triumphant civilian minority. Townsend Hoopes, *The Limits of Intervention* (New York: McKay, 1969). Ridgway was also the only exception to greater aggressiveness of field commanders as commander in chief of the United Nations command in Korea from 1951 to 1952.

3. Peter Beckman rejects this definition in "Influence, Generals, and Vietnam" (paper presented at the International Studies Association Convention, March 1971), using instead the extent to which the military can have their preferences included in policy. The problem with this definition is that it unavoidably inflates the image of military power by encompassing decisions that would have been made the same way, for other reasons, irrespective of military opinion.

4. Morton Halperin, "The President and the Military," *Foreign Affairs* 50, no. 2 (January 1972): 313; Don K. Price, *The Scientific Estate* (Cambridge: Harvard University Press, 1965), p. 230.

5. Morton Halperin, "War Termination as a Problem in Civil-Military Relations," *The Annals* 392 (November 1970): 94; Halperin and Leslie

Gelb, "Diplomatic Notes: The Ten Commandments of the Foreign Affairs Bureaucracy," *Harper's* 244 (June 1972): 36; and Halperin, with the assistance of Priscilla Clapp and Arnold Kanter, *Bureaucratic Politics and Foreign Policy* (Washington, D.C.: Brookings, 1974), p. 227.

6. Ridgway considered resigning if Eisenhower decided to intervene in Indochina. Tyler Abell, ed., *Drew Pearson Diaries: 1949–1959* (New York: Holt, Rinehart and Winston, 1974), p. 322. His eventual departure, however, was at the administration's behest rather than a move to embarrass the administration. In *Bureaucratic Politics*, p. 227, Halperin claims that the Chiefs threatened to resign in 1966 unless they got the new programs they wanted. One source he cites is Hoopes, *Limits of Intervention*, p. 90, which turns out to be a vague reference to a rumored threat by unnamed high military men to resign in 1967 in protest of McNamara's bombing policy. When asked whether there was such a threat General Wheeler dismissed the insinuation. Henry L. Trewhitt, *McNamara: His Ordeal in the Pentagon* (New York: Harper & Row, 1971), p. 245. A second source cited is an unpublished paper by Lawrence J. Korb, "Budget Strategies of the Joint Chiefs of Staff (Fiscal) 1965–1968: An Examination," which cites an interview with Chief of Naval Operations David McDonald. Yet the person who should know best vigorously denied that there was any plan or threat to resign in 1966. Military letter.

7. General William C. Westmoreland, USA (Ret.), *A Soldier Reports* (Garden City: Doubleday, 1976), pp. 262, 342–344; Ward Just, *Military Men* (New York: Knopf, 1970), p. 187.

8. "Navy Officer Quits over Infringement on Oil Reserves," *New York Times*, 13 January 1974, p. 30. My debunking of misconceptions about resignation should not serve to overemphasize the significance of the difference between retirement and resignation, but the leverage that a dramatic resignation, complete with press conference, is supposed to exert is absent when an officer leaves by filling out forms for his monthly retirement checks.

9. On the early Kennedy administration: two military interviews. On access during the Vietnam War: military interview; Hugh Sidey, *A Very Personal Presidency* (New York: Atheneum, 1968), pp. 204, 206; Hanson W. Baldwin, *Strategy for Tomorrow* (New York: Harper & Row, 1970), pp. 13–15. As Baldwin points out, low access of the Joint Chiefs to the President in the Vietnam years contrasts strikingly with Roosevelt's daily contact with Admiral Leahy and almost-as-frequent meetings with General Marshall and Admiral King. "In the crucial twelve months from June, 1965, to June, 1966, when large numbers of troops were committed to Vietnam and the bombing of the North was started, the Air Chief of Staff had about four private individual meetings with the President, the Commandant of the Marine Corps about the same number of meetings; the Chief of Staff of the Army saw the President privately twice." Ibid., pp. 14–15.

10. Neil Sheehan, "The Rise of Military Influence in the Nixon Administration," in D. M. Fox, ed., *The Politics of U.S. Foreign Policy*

Making (Pacific Palisades: Goodyear, 1971); John Leacacos, "Kissinger's Apparat," *Foreign Policy* 5 (Winter 1971–1972). On the bootlegging or "spying" controversy: U.S., Congress, Senate, Committee on Armed Services, *Hearing, Transmittal of Documents from the National Security Council to the Chairman of the Joint Chiefs of Staff*, 93d Cong., 2d sess., 1974, and Seymour Hersh's *New York Times* stories: "Report on Data Leak Said to Have Named Moorer," 14 January 1974, pp. 1, 13, and "Moorer Concedes He Received 'File' on Secret Security Papers," 19 January 1974, p. 1.

11. On the Bay of Pigs: Lyman B. Kirkpatrick, *The Real CIA* (New York: Macmillan, 1968), p. 198; military interview; General Maxwell D. Taylor, USA (Ret.), *Swords and Plowshares* (New York: Norton, 1972), pp. 186–187. On Berlin: Hugh Sidey, *John F. Kennedy, President* (New York: Atheneum, 1963), p. 236; Eleanor Lansing Dulles, *The Wall: A Tragedy in Three Acts*, Studies in International Affairs No. 9 (Columbia, S.C.: University of South Carolina Institute of International Studies, 1972), p. 78. On the Spanish-American War: Leonard D. White, *The Republican Era* (New York: Macmillan, 1958), p. 148.

12. Jack Raymond, *Power at the Pentagon* (New York: Harper & Row, 1964), pp. 285–286; Rear Admiral Daniel V. Gallery, USN (Ret.), *The Pueblo Incident* (Garden City: Doubleday, 1970), p. 21; Kenneth P. O'Donnell et al., *"Johnny We Hardly Knew Ye"* (Boston: Little, Brown, 1972), pp. 330–333.

13. Anderson and McNamara quoted in Graham T. Allison, *Essence of Decision* (Boston: Little, Brown, 1971), pp. 131–132, and Elie Abel, *The Missile Crisis* (Philadelphia: Lippincott, 1966), p. 156.

14. Johnson quoted in Rowland Evans and Robert Novak, *Lyndon B. Johnson: The Exercise of Power* (New York: New American Library, 1966), pp. 538–539. Wheeler speech quoted in Charles Moritz, ed., *Current Biography, 1965* (New York: Wilson, 1965), p. 451.

15. On the civilian decision to retain control of targeting, see U.S., Department of Defense, *The Senator Gravel Edition: The Pentagon Papers* (Boston: Beacon Press, 1971), 3:344. McDonald's comment reported in a military interview.

16. "Men who are bent on the accumulation of power do not consciously search for policy. They are likely to have fixed notions of what ought to be done. The constant concern with policy directives of the military is a testament to the reserve with which it exercises its influence." Morris Janowitz, *The Professional Soldier*, 2d ed. (New York: Free Press, 1971), p. 271.

17. Paul Hammond, "NSC 68: Prologue to Rearmament," in Warner R. Schilling, Paul Hammond, and Glenn H. Snyder, *Strategy, Politics, and Defense Budgets* (New York: Columbia University Press, 1962); General J. Lawton Collins, USA (Ret.), *War in Peacetime* (Boston: Houghton Mifflin, 1969), pp. 263–264.

18. U.S., Congress, Senate, Committees on Armed Services and Foreign Relations, *Hearings, Military Situation in the Far East*, 82d Cong., 1st

sess., 1951, pp. 68, 75–80, 84–87, 100–102; William Kaufmann, "Policy Objectives and Military Action in the Korean War" (Santa Monica: RAND Corporation P-886, June 1956), p. 6.

19. Wheeler quoted in Henry F. Graff, *The Tuesday Cabinet* (Englewood Cliffs, N.J.: Prentice-Hall, 1970), p. 128.

20. For an elegant theoretical elaboration of graduated response theory, see Thomas Schelling, *Arms and Influence* (New Haven: Yale University Press, 1966).

21. *Pentagon Papers*, 3:356, 407, 474.

22. Taylor, *Swords and Plowshares*, p. 418. To civilian strategists the graduated response limited war theory, which assumed the integration of force, diplomatic signaling, and political action, logically implied the integration of military and political roles in the war effort. This occurred in Vietnam. Although the takeover of the pacification program from State by Military Assistance Command, Vietnam (MACV) is usually seen simply as evidence of further militarization of U.S. programs, it is notable that when this occurred, civilians were integrated into the military chain of command, an unprecedented innovation. Westmoreland, *A Soldier Reports*, pp. 214–215.

2. CASES IN POINT

1. General J. Lawton Collins, USA (Ret.), *War in Peacetime* (Boston: Houghton Mifflin, 1969), p. 29; General Matthew B. Ridgway, USA (Ret.), *The Korean War* (Garden City: Doubleday, 1967), pp. 11, 16; Robert Sawyer, *Military Advisers in Korea: KMAG in Peace and War* (Washington, D.C.: Department of the Army, Office of the Chief of Military History, 1962), p. 37.

2. Alexander George, "American Policy-Making and the North Korean Aggression," in Allen Guttmann, ed., *Korea and the Theory of Limited War* (Boston: Heath, 1967), p. 71. U.S., Congress, Senate, Committees on Armed Services and Foreign Relations, *Hearings, Military Situation in the Far East*, 82d Cong., 1st sess., 1951, p. 376 (hereafter *Far East Hearings*); Glenn D. Paige, *The Korean Decision* (New York: Free Press, 1968), pp. 164, 174, 179. Truman quoted ibid., pp. 124, 148.

3. Harry S Truman, *Years of Trial and Hope* (Garden City: Doubleday, 1958), pp. 334–335; Senate Armed Services and Foreign Relations Committees, *Far East Hearings*, pp. 934, 1112; Courtney Whitney, *MacArthur: His Rendezvous with History* (New York: Knopf, 1956), p. 328; Major General Charles A. Willoughby, USA (Ret.), and John Chamberlain, *MacArthur, 1941–1951* (New York: McGraw-Hill, 1954), p. 357; Paige, *Korean Decision*, pp. 121–122, 151, 196, 238, 245–246, 250, 254, 260. Military interview.

4. On the decision to cross the parallel: Collins, *War in Peacetime*, pp. 82–83; Truman, *Years of Trial and Hope*, p. 341; Marvin Lichterman, "To the Yalu and Back," in Harold Stein, ed., *American Civil-Military Decisions* (Birmingham: University of Alabama Press, 1963);

Lieutenant Colonel James F. Schnabel, USA (Ret.), *Policy and Direction: The First Year* (Washington, D.C.: Department of the Army, Office of the Chief of Military History, 1972), pp. 179–180. On the controversy over the field commander's "misinterpretation" of his orders: testimony of MacArthur and Marshall in Senate Armed Services and Foreign Relations Committees, *Far East Hearings*, pp. 245, 340, and Collins, *War in Peacetime*, pp. 176–177, 179–180.

5. General of the Army Douglas MacArthur, *Reminiscences* (New York: McGraw-Hill, 1964), pp. 365, 379. On the recommendations and restrictions: Senate Armed Services and Foreign Relations Committees, *Far East Hearings*, pp. 82–83, 1722–24; William Kaufmann, "Policy Objectives and Military Action in the Korean War" (Santa Monica: RAND Corporation, P-886, June 1956), p. 9; Lichterman, "To the Yalu and Back," pp. 604–605.

6. For pro-escalation views see Senate Armed Services and Foreign Relations Committees, *Far East Hearings*, pp. 2294, 2567, 3342–49; Robert Murphy, *Diplomat among Warriors* (Garden City: Doubleday, 1964), p. 359; General Mark W. Clark, USA (Ret.), *From the Danube to the Yalu* (New York: Harper, 1954), pp. 3, 27, 81.

7. Collins, *War in Peacetime*, pp. 303–304. Bradley quoted in C. L. Sulzberger, *A Long Row of Candles* (New York: Macmillan, 1969), p. 638. See also Ridgway's secret testimony, declassified in U.S., Congress, Senate, Committee on Foreign Relations, *Executive Sessions of the Senate Foreign Relations Committee (Historical Series)*, 82d Cong., 2d sess., 1952 (Washington, D.C.: Government Printing Office, October 1976), 4:435, 439.

8. Collins, *War in Peacetime*, pp. 205, 206, 290–292; Ridgway, *Korean War*, pp. 48–49, 144–147. Two military interviews. Bradley, Marshall, Sherman, Vandenberg, and MacArthur statements in Senate Armed Services and Foreign Relations Committees, *Far East Hearings*, pp. 29, 354, 368–369, 482, 500–501, 731, 732, 744–745, 882–883, 886, 943–946, 1378–79, 1388, 1512–14. Admiral Arthur W. Radford, USN (Ret.), John Foster Dulles Oral History Project interview, Princeton University library. On recognition of the inadequacy of air force capabilities and the quid pro quo protecting U.S. installations, see declassified portions of Marshall testimony, in Arthur Schlesinger, ed., *Congress Investigates: A Documented History, 1792–1974* (New York: Chelsea House, 1975), 5:3615, 3704–3707. Eisenhower instructions reported in Clark, *From the Danube to the Yalu*, pp. 233, 267.

9. View of the Chiefs cited by Dean Acheson, *Present at the Creation* (New York: Norton, 1969), pp. 331, 361. Clark cited by Philippe Devillers and Jean Lacouture, *End of a War* (New York: Praeger, 1969), p. 216. Davis memorandum in U.S., Department of Defense, *The Senator Gravel Edition: The Pentagon Papers* (Boston: Beacon Press, 1971), 1:89.

10. Operation Vulture described in Melvin Gurtov, *The First Indochina Crisis* (New York: Columbia University Press, 1967); Jules Roy, *The Battle of Dienbienphu*, trans. Robert Baldick (New York: Pyramid,

1965), p. 244; *Pentagon Papers*, 1:97, 100. The *Pentagon Papers'* version is based heavily on the same source on which most analysts have drawn: Chalmers Roberts, "The Day We Didn't Go to War," *The Reporter* 11, no. 4 (14 September 1954).

11. Roberts identified McCormack in *First Rough Draft* (New York: Praeger, 1973), p. 114. Lieutenant General James M. Gavin, USA (Ret.), with Arthur T. Hadley, *Crisis Now* (New York: Random House, 1968), p. 41. Military interview. My evidence on the breakdown of advice of the Joint Chiefs is from one military interview, two military letters, and Dulles Oral History Project interviews of Radford and Twining. Confusion about Twining's support for the single air strike may have come from widespread knowledge that he opposed extended involvement in Indochina. See Devillers and Lacouture, *End of a War*, pp. 192–193, 217–218, and Tyler Abell, ed., *Drew Pearson Diaries: 1949–1959* (New York: Holt, Rinehart and Winston, 1974), p. 321.

12. Gurtov, *First Indochina Crisis;* Roberts, "Day We Didn't Go to War"; Ernest May, "Eisenhower," in May, ed., *The Ultimate Decision* (New York: Braziller, 1960), p. 220; U.S., Department of Defense, *United States-Vietnam Relations, 1945–1967* (Washington, D.C.: Government Printing Office, 1971), 9:367–369; four military interviews. The view of Dulles as secret dove is from a civilian interview. Robert F. Randle, *Geneva 1954* (Princeton: Princeton University Press, 1969), p. 64, suggests Dulles arranged the congressional briefing as a strategem to have Radford's plan vetoed, but Devillers' and Lacouture's sources said it was Radford who pressed for congressional consultation against Dulles and the President. *End of a War*, p. 80.

13. Department of Defense, *United States-Vietnam Relations*, 1:II-B-5, 6; *Pentagon Papers*, 1:444.

14. *Pentagon Papers*, 1:127n, 508; military interview; Gurtov, *First Indochina Crisis*, p. 123; David Halberstam, *The Best and the Brightest* (New York: Random House, 1972), pp. 143–144.

15. Department of Defense, *United States-Vietnam Relations*, 10:759–760, 771–774; *Pentagon Papers*, 2:408, 416, 431–432.

16. Lansdale memo described in Department of Defense, *United States-Vietnam Relations*, 2:IV-A, 52–77, and Walt W. Rostow, *The Diffusion of Power* (New York: Macmillan, 1972), pp. 264–265. JCS and McGarr recommendations in *Pentagon Papers*, 2:9–11, 48–49, 65–66.

17. Halberstam, *Best and Brightest*, pp. 150–151, 166; *Pentagon Papers*, 2:12–13, 73–74, 447.

18. *Pentagon Papers*, 2:13, 83–84, 87–92, 108–109, 652–654; General Maxwell D. Taylor, USA (Ret.), *Swords and Plowshares* (New York: Norton, 1972), pp. 227–228, 238–246; Marvin Kalb and Elie Abel, *Roots of Involvement* (New York: Norton, 1971), pp. 129–130; Stewart Alsop, *The Center* (New York: Harper & Row, 1968), pp. 162–163.

19. Henry L. Trewhitt, *McNamara: His Ordeal in the Pentagon* (New York: Harper & Row, 1971), p. 193. Halberstam, *Best and Brightest*, p. 209; *Pentagon Papers*, 3:1, 3, 113–114. In 1963 the disputes between the

State Department and the military were not over increasing U.S. involvement but over the form of support. Roger Hilsman and other diplomats favored concentrating on police tactics, static defense, and unconventional warfare, while the Joint Chiefs favored conventional military tactics. See *Pentagon Papers*, 2:128–129, 139–143, 146, and Roger Hilsman, *To Move a Nation* (Garden City: Doubleday, 1967), pp. 429–435, 438. The best example of interpretation of this period that differs from mine is Robert L. Gallucci, *Neither Peace nor Honor* (Baltimore: Johns Hopkins University Press, 1975), which views increasing involvement in the early 1960s as the result of pressure from the military and the failure of State's cautionary approach to prevail in decision making. Yet Gallucci admits: "It is not that State Department actors were 'doves,' for they issued prescriptions involving the use of American military troops, and they did not shrink from advocating violent means"; although the bounds of debate narrowed in 1964, creating momentum for military solutions, it was the President, in National Security Action Memorandum 288, who established the limits; and "The actual military actions undertaken during the fall of 1964 closely resembled those recommended by the State Department and differed most from those advocated by the Joint Chiefs." Ibid., pp. 31, 35, 37, 40. Eugene Windchy notes the pressure from the President, when he upbraided a group of admirals during the Tonkin Gulf crisis for the navy's poor performance against the North Vietnamese. *Tonkin Gulf* (Garden City: Doubleday, 1971), p. 5.

20. *Pentagon Papers*, 3:8, 9, 56, 106–107, 120, 126, 496, 550; Department of Defense, *United States-Vietnam Relations*, 3:IV-C-2 (a), 3; Taylor, *Swords and Plowshares*, p. 308. Military interview. The *Pentagon Papers* do not document disagreements within the JCS. On army reticence: Halberstam, *Best and Brightest*, 350; General Curtis E. LeMay, USAF (Ret.), with Mackinlay Kantor, *Mission with LeMay* (Garden City: Doubleday, 1965), p. 564; two civilian interviews. Gallucci reports a 1971 interview with Wheeler that dates the period of the Chiefs' agreement from November 1964; *Neither Peace Nor Honor*, p. 161n.

21. *Pentagon Papers*, 2:291, 3:13, 14, 110, 112–116, 126, 132, 134–135, 157–167, 172–173, 179, 628, 632; Taylor, *Swords and Plowshares*, p. 326.

22. *Pentagon Papers*, 3:418, 478–481; Kalb and Abel, *Roots of Involvement*, p. 184. Military interview.

23. According to Arthur Schlesinger, "at every point along the way, the generals promised that just one more step of military escalation would at last bring the victory so long sought." *The Crisis of Confidence* (Boston: Houghton Mifflin, 1969), p. 172. Doris Kearns attributes incremental involvement to JCS duplicity that lured the civilians gradually, not risking reversal of policy by making big demands in the beginning. *Lyndon Johnson and the American Dream* (New York: Harper & Row, 1976), p. 275.

24. *Pentagon Papers*, 3:406, 417, 485.

25. *Pentagon Papers*, 4:296; Halberstam, *Best and Brightest*, pp. 582–

583, 597; Westmoreland, *A Soldier Reports*, pp. 141–142; Taylor, *Swords and Plowshares*, pp. 348–349.

26. Military interview and civilian interview; Halberstam, *Best and Brightest*, pp. 595–597. These estimates may also have seemed unreasonable because four years earlier, when Vietcong and North Vietnamese activity in the south was at a much lower level, the Joint Chiefs had estimated that no more than 278,000 Southeast Asia Treaty Organization troops would be needed for any contingency. Department of Defense, *United States-Vietnam Relations*, 11:297–309, 312, 322, 327.

27. Halberstam, *Best and Brightest*, pp. 641–642; Westmoreland, *A Soldier Reports*, pp. 214, 227, 230; *Pentagon Papers*, 2:511, 4:6, 7, 279–280, 283–284, 456ff. Ambivalence also meant that on some days the soldiers' sanguine feelings overrode their caution and led to hopeful statements. Shortly after Westmoreland's minimal request was rejected in 1967, Army Chief Johnson reported that the United States was winning and that the latest 45,000 troop increase should be the last. *Pentagon Papers*, 2:303.

28. *Pentagon Papers*, 3:280, 284; Westmoreland, *A Soldier Reports*, p. 120; two military interviews.

29. *Pentagon Papers*, 3:284–286, 318–320, 342ff, 4:1–4; three military interviews.

30. John B. Henry, "February, 1968," *Foreign Policy* 4 (Fall 1971): 8, 16-17, 202; Townsend Hoopes, *The Limits of Intervention* (New York: McKay, 1969); Don Oberdorfer, *Tet!* (Garden City: Doubleday, 1971), pp. 257–316; Kalb and Abel, *Roots of Involvement*, pp. 205–217; Hedrick Smith and William Beecher, "The Vietnam Policy Reversal of 1968," in D. M. Fox, ed., *The Politics of U.S. Foreign Policy Making* (Pacific Palisades: Goodyear, 1971); Westmoreland, *A Soldier Reports*, pp. 310–334, 350–362. One military interview and three civilian interviews.

31. On the Cambodia decision: Stewart Alsop, "On the President's Yellow Pad," *Newsweek*, 1 June 1970, p. 106; Rowland Evans and Robert Novak, *Nixon in the White House* (New York: Random House, 1971), p. 245ff.; Kalb and Abel, *Roots of Involvement*, pp. 294–299; David R. Maxey, "How Nixon Decided to Invade Cambodia," *Look* 34, no. 16 (11 July 1970); Hedrick Smith, "Nixon's Decision to Invade Cambodia," in Fox, ed., *Politics of U.S. Foreign Policy Making;* William Safire, *Before the Fall* (New York: Belmont Tower, 1975), pp. 181–201. In contrast to the time constraint imposed by withdrawal deadlines is the situation where lack of time prevents intervention. Examples of this problem were the Iraq coup in 1958 and the seizure of the U.S.S. *Pueblo* in 1968 when the ship was forced into Wonsan harbor before U.S. aircraft arrived. On Vietnamization: three military interviews; Thomas B. Ross, "Laird Reported Blunting Kissinger's Influence," *Boston Globe*, 12 July 1974; Halperin, *Bureaucratic Politics*, pp. 185–187.

32. Henry Brandon, *The Retreat of American Power* (Garden City: Doubleday, 1973), p. 336; Tad Szulc, "Behind the Vietnam Cease-Fire

Agreement," *Foreign Policy* 15 (Summer 1974): 38–40, 49–50, 58; Admiral Elmo Zumwalt, USN (Ret.), *On Watch* (New York: Putnam, 1976), p. 384; four military interviews; Jack Anderson, "Vietnam Peace Progress Disrupted by Joint Chiefs," *Boston Globe*, 5 January 1973; Safire, *Before the Fall*, pp. 667–668; Keyes Beech, "American Officer Hits Senate Action: U.S. Arms Aid Cut Called Crushing Blow to Saigon," *Washington Post*, 23 August 1974, p. A-20.

3. Professionalism, Position, and Power: The Background of Influence

1. Samuel Huntington, *The Soldier and the State* (Cambridge: Harvard Universiy Press, 1957), pp. 84–85, 71–72. The classic exposition of traditional administration theory is Woodrow Wilson, "The Study of Administration," *Political Science Quarterly* 2, no. 2 (June 1887). "Wilson's conception of 'policy' had a hidden corollary... He was rigid in forbidding military interference with policy... he could not read in a newspaper that the army was planning possible campaigns against Germany without feeling outraged. He ordered such activities stopped. But he thought it equally clear that... neither should policy-makers meddle in military affairs." Ernest R. May, "Wilson," in Ernest May, ed., *The Ultimate Decision* (New York: Braziller, 1960), p. 113.

2. For example: Richard Neustadt, *Presidential Power* (New York: Wiley, 1960); Harold Seidman, *Politics, Position, and Power* (New York: Oxford University Press, 1970); Graham T. Allison, *Essence of Decision* (Boston: Little, Brown, 1971); I. M. Destler, *Presidents, Bureaucrats, and Foreign Policy* (Princeton: Princeton University Press, 1972); Morton Halperin, with the assistance of Priscilla Clapp and Arnold Kanter, *Bureaucratic Politics and Foreign Policy* (Washington, D.C.: Brookings, 1974). The best attempt to bridge traditional administration theory and the insights of bureaucratic revisionism is Don K. Price, *The Scientific Estate* (Cambridge: Harvard University Press, 1965).

3. The ideal types of traditional administrative theory and objective control embody several values: the pattern of organization is a pyramidal hierarchy; administrative priorities include efficiency, economy, and professionalism of subordinates; the administrative process is one of command and obedience; and the politicization of the bureaucracy is minimal. In the ideal types of bureaucratic revisionism and subjective control, the organizational principles emphasize functional redundancy and flexibility in the chain of command; priorities are political control and detailed civilian control of operations; the administrative process is marked by negotiation and accommodation; and the bureaucracy is highly politicized.

4. On defense management and executive recruitment under Eisenhower: Warner R. Schilling, Paul Hammond, and Glenn H. Snyder, *Strategy, Politics, and Defense Budgets* (New York: Columbia University Press, 1962); Samuel P. Huntington, *The Common Defense* (New York:

Columbia University Press, 1961); Marver H. Bernstein, *The Job of the Federal Executive* (Washington, D.C.: Brookings Institution, 1958). On McNamara's management: Alain Enthoven and K. Wayne Smith, *How Much Is Enough?* (New York: Harper & Row, 1971); Charles Hitch, *Decision-Making for Defense* (Berkeley: University of California Press, 1965); William W. Kaufmann, *The McNamara Strategy* (New York: Harper & Row, 1964); J. A. Stockfish, *Plowshares into Swords* (New York: Mason & Lipscomb, 1973).

5. The directive is quoted in General Maxwell D. Taylor, USA, "Military Advice: Its Uses in Government," *Vital Speeches* 30, no. 11 (15 March 1964): 339; see also General Maxwell D. Taylor, USA (Ret.), *Swords and Plowshares* (New York: Norton, 1972), pp. 189, 198, 255. Wheeler speech quoted in Roger Hilsman, *To Move a Nation* (Garden City: Doubleday, 1967), p. 426. Eisenhower's first secretary of defense, Charles Wilson, had also instructed the Joint Chiefs to incorporate non-military considerations in their advice, but he used less pressure than McNamara did. Huntington, *Soldier and State*, p. 395.

6. Huntington, *Common Defense*, p. 22. Morris Janowitz, *The Professional Soldier*, 2d ed. (New York: Free Press, 1971), pp. 420–421; two military interviews.

7. Military interview. One famous soldier known for his acerbic irony once confided to his journal, "The term 'diplomat' to the average American evokes a vision of an immaculately dressed being—pin-stripe pants, spats, cutaway, and topper—and a coldly severe and superior manner which masks the lightning-like play of the intellect that guides the Ship of State, moves the pieces on the board, and invariably turns up in Washington without his shirt. Or rather our shirt... It is common knowledge that an Army officer has a one-track mind, that he is personally interested in stirring up wars so that he can get promoted and be decorated and that he has an extremely limited education, with no appreciation of the finer things in life." Lieutenant General Joseph W. Stilwell, USA, *The Stilwell Papers*, ed. Theodore White (New York: Sloane, 1948), pp. 256–257.

8. Walter Millis, ed., with the collaboration of E. S. Duffield, *The Forrestal Diaries* (New York: Viking, 1951), pp. 312, 315–316. Army representatives opposed State Department consideration of altering the Italo-Yugoslav border line in 1947, fearing that such an attempt would lead to fighting and U.S. involvement.

9. Huntington, *Soldier and State*, pp. 380–382, and *Common Defense*, pp. 36–37. On the decline of the State Department and the ascendancy of the military in the early 1940s, see Huntington, *Soldier and State*, chap. 12; Hanson W. Baldwin, "The Military Move In," *Harper's* 195 (December 1947): 481–489; George F. Kennan, *Memoirs: 1925–1950* (Boston: Atlantic-Little, Brown, 1967), pp. 143ff, 173, 370–372; Richard J. Barnet, *Roots of War* (New York: Atheneum, 1972), pp. 24–29. The view that civilians became more militarized than the military after

World War II is also held by some radical critics, among them Richard J. Barnet, *The Economy of Death* (New York: Atheneum, 1969), pp. 83–84.

10. Civilian letter.

11. Charles Stevenson, *The End of Nowhere: American Policy Toward Laos Since 1954* (Boston: Beacon Press, 1972), pp. 143, 151; Walt W. Rostow, *The Diffusion of Power* (New York: Macmillan, 1972), pp. 664–665n, 269. Rostow described the meeting as "extraordinarily disheveled." Army Chief Decker said there was "no good place to fight" in the region and that the United States "cannot win a conventional war in Southeast Asia; if we go in, we should go in to win, and that means bombing Hanoi, China, and maybe even using nuclear bombs." Memo of conversation (by LeMay), 28 April 1961, U.S., Department of Defense, *United States-Vietnam Relations, 1945–1967* (Washington, D.C.: Government Printing Office, 1971), 11:63–64. Corroborating accounts of this meeting in six military interviews; two civilian interviews; Stewart Alsop, *The Center* (New York: Harper & Row, 1968), pp. 146–147; Hilsman, *To Move a Nation*, pp. 128–129, 144; David Halberstam, *The Best and the Brightest* (New York: Random House, 1972), p. 89. Some naval officers favored a landing at Vinh in North Vietnam and a move overland through "the source of the trouble." Military interview.

12. Commission on Organization of the Executive Branch of the Government, Task Force on Personnel and Civil Service, *Report on Personnel and Civil Service* (Washington, D.C.: Government Printing Office, February 1955), p. 8.

13. Dean E. Mann, "The Selection of Federal Political Executives," *American Political Science Review 58*, no. 1 (March 1964): 90. The tendency to fill high posts with experienced political appointees rather than careerists is even more pronounced in Defense than in State. It is quite common for foreign service officers to serve as assistant secretaries of state. Active military officers never serve in positions higher than deputy assistant secretary of defense, and rarely in those.

14. The apparent paradox that Stephen Krasner cites in his critique of bureaucratic politics theory, where a militaristic secretary of state opposed a more pacific secretary of defense in the Cuban missile crisis, amends bureaucratic revisionism more than it discredits it. "Are Bureaucracies Important? or Allison Wonderland," *Foreign Policy* 7 (Summer 1972):165.

15. Attributed to Rufus Miles by Seidman, *Politics, Position, and Power*, p. 20. Allison attributes the axiom to Don K. Price; *Essence of Decision*, p. 316n.

16. Janowitz, *Professional Soldier*, p. 368.

17. Eugene Zuckert, "The Service Secretary: Has He a Useful Role?" *Foreign Affairs* 44, no. 3 (April 1966); Gene M. Lyons, "The New Civil-Military Relations," *American Political Science Review* 55, no. 1 (March 1961):55, 59. Lyons mitigates the negative implications for revisionists by noting the "professionalization of civilian leadership."

18. James C. Thomson, Jr., "How Could Vietnam Happen? An Autopsy," *The Atlantic* 221, no. 4 (April 1968):49.

19. Average tenure on the JCS has been 3.5 years for the chairman, 2.6 for the army chief of staff, 2.8 for the chief of naval operations, 3.4 for the air force chief of staff, and 3.9 for the commandant of the marine corps. Median tenure has been four, two, two, four, and four years, respectively. Calculations are based on all chiefs and chairmen since 1945 and marine commandants since 1951 (when they gained JCS representation) but exclude those still sitting in February 1977.

20. Max Weber, "Parliament and Government in a Reconstructed Germany," in *Economy and Society* (New York: Bedminster Press, 1968), 3:1406.

21. Huntington, *Common Defense*, pp. 64–87, 135–165, and *Soldier and State*, pp. 415–416.

22. Samuel Huntington, "Power, Expertise, and the Military Profession," *Daedalus* 92 no. 4 (Fall 1963):796. House report quoted in Congressional Quarterly, *Congress and the Nation* (Washington, D.C.: Congressional Quarterly, 1969), 2:841.

23. Colonel Laurence J. Legere, USA (Ret.), "Defense Spending (2): A Presidential Perspective," *Foreign Policy* 6 (Spring 1972):86–88; Tom Wicker, *JFK and LBJ* (New York: Morrow, 1968), p. 197. Hickenlooper quoted in Colonel William R. Smith (USAF), "The Military Role in Arms Control Policy Development," *Public Policy* 16 (1967): 221–222. On legislators' injunctions to report disagreements, see, for example, U.S., Congress, Senate, Committee on Armed Services, *Hearing, Nomination of Lt. Gen. Harold K. Johnson to be Chief of Staff, Army*, 88th Cong., 2d sess., 1964, pp. 4–5.

24. Congressional Quarterly, *Congress and the Nation*, vol. 1:*1945–1946* (Washington, D.C.: Congressional Quarterly, 1965), pp. 299–300.

25. General J. Lawton Collins, USA (Ret.), *War in Peacetime* (Boston: Houghton Mifflin, 1969), p. 381; Theodore Sorensen, *Kennedy* (New York: Harper & Row, 1965), pp. 607–608; U.S., Congress, House, Committee on Armed Services, *Hearing, Subcommittee No. 3 Consideration of H.R. 6600, to Amend Title 10, United States Code, with Respect to the Appointment of the Members of the Joint Chiefs of Staff*, 88th Cong., 2d sess., 1963, pp. 6194, 6202, 6214, 6233–37, 6247–48, 6255–59, 6264–65; *Congress and Nation*, 1:325–326. Ironically the administration also opposed the nonrenewable four-year term, which was already the legal requirement for the commandant of the marine corps, because it prevented the desired reappointment of Kennedy's favorite service chief, David M. Shoup. Congressional Quarterly, *Weekly Reports* 25, no. 22, 2 June 1967, p. 922.

26. Chalmers Roberts, "The Day We Didn't Go to War," *The Reporter* 11, no. 14, 14 September 1954; Robert Kennedy, *Thirteen Days* (New York: Norton, 1969), pp. 53–54; Sorensen, *Kennedy*, p. 702. When Chief of Naval Operations Arleigh Burke presented his case for intervention in Laos to a congressional group in 1961, none supported him vocally,

although he knew that Senator Styles Bridges agreed with him. Later when he asked Bridges why he had not spoken up, the senator told Burke that he was naive and had fallen into a political trap. Congressmen like to be consulted but will rarely propose strategy of their own. The senator did not want to have to answer for "the Bridges strategy" if anything went wrong. Military interview.

27. U.S., Congress, Senate, Committees on Armed Services and Foreign Relations, *Hearings, Military Situation in the Far East*, 82d Cong., 1st sess., 1951; U.S., Congress, Senate, Committee on Foreign Relations, *Hearings, Supplemental Foreign Assistance Fiscal Year 1966—Vietnam*, 89th Cong., 2d sess., 1966; U.S., Congress, Senate, Committee on Armed Services, Preparedness Investigating Subcommittee, *Hearings, Air War Against North Vietnam*, 90th Cong., 1st sess., 1967. On opinion regarding Vietnam: John E. Mueller, *War, Presidents and Public Opinion* (New York: Wiley, 1973), pp. 55, 266; Milton J. Rosenberg, Sidney Verba, and Philip E. Converse, *Vietnam and the Silent Majority* (New York: Harper & Row, 1970), pp. 33, 37, 49.

28. Huntington, *Soldier and State*, pp. 163, 177, 191. Of course disagreements do not always pit Congress as an entity against the executive. Views of members of an Armed Services Committee sometimes differ from those of the House or Senate as a whole.

29. Destler, in *Presidents, Bureaucrats, and Foreign Policy*, and Allison, in *Essence of Decision*, scarcely mention Congress; Seidman, in *Politics, Position, and Power*, portrays it basically as obstructive and incompetent. Slightly greater consideration of Congress's role can be found in the post-Watergate third edition of Neustadt's *Presidential Power* (1976), pp. 65–69, and Neustadt and Allison's afterword to the second edition of Robert Kennedy's *Thirteen Days* (1971), pp. 140ff.

30. Lavelle's insubordination was never definitively established. The Defense Department charged him with unilaterally ordering the bombings and falsifying the action reports, which led Air Force Chief of Staff John Ryan to relieve him and to demote him to lieutenant general (and later to major general). Lavelle was exonerated, however, by Senator Stennis and the House Armed Services Committee; see U.S., Congress, House, Committee on Armed Services, Investigating Subcommittee, *Report, Unauthorized Bombing of Military Targets in North Vietnam*, 92d Cong., 2d sess., 1972, and "House Committee Says Unauthorized Raids Were Justified," *Boston Globe*, 19 December 1972. The air force also dropped the court-martial charges against Lavelle and refused to provide more than a summary of the Rules of Engagement (the official rules of permissible tactics in combat situations) to the House subcommittee. Lavelle claimed that his superiors knew of the raids and gave more than tacit approval, citing a secret wire from Moorer in April 1971 that "encouraged us in very specific terms to use the protective reaction authority to make future strikes." Quoted in "Excerpts from General Lavelle's Letter to Senator Stennis," *New York Times*, 6 October 1972, p. 14. Seymour Hersh also cited testimony by numerous

pilots that "briefings on planned 'protective reaction' bombing missions were routinely provided to Adm. John S. McCain" (the commander in chief, Pacific) in 1970 and 1971. See his series in the *New York Times:* "Unauthorized Bombing Is Laid to Relaxation of Nixon Control," 19 June 1972, p. 2; "Lavelle Testifies Superiors Gave Permission for Raids," 13 September 1972, pp. 1, 13; "Raids Approved, Lavelle Insists," 16 September 1972, pp. 1, 4; "A Question of Command in the Lavelle Hearings," 18 September 1972, p. 12; "Ex-Airmen Tell of 20 Planned Raids a Month in '70–'71," 16 October 1972, p. 3. After the revelations the inspector general system was overhauled, and, when bombing was renewed in 1972, targets had to be approved by Laird, the Washington Special Action Group, or the President. William Beecher, "Pentagon Official Hints Laird Was Cool to Resuming Bombing in the Hanoi Area," *New York Times*, 18 March 1972, p. 19. Some believe that Kissinger knew about Lavelle's raids and wanted to use them to coerce the North Vietnamese negotiators. Circumstantial evidence cited for this view came out in the Watergate investigations when John Ehrlichman charged that Secretary Laird had no knowledge of crucial secret bombings in 1971, with the President giving orders directly to the military. JCS Chairman Moorer denied this allegation. Laurence Stern, "Ehrlichman Disputed on '71 Bombing," *Washington Post*, 22 June 1974, pp. A-1, A-12.

31. Samuel Finer, *The Man on Horseback* (New York: Praeger, 1962), pp. 25–26.

32. Quoted in Richard Rovere and Arthur Schlesinger, Jr., *The General and the President* (New York: Farrar, Straus, & Young, 1951), p. 315.

33. Reprinted in General Matthew B. Ridgway, USA (Ret.), with Harold Martin, *Soldier* (New York: Harper, 1954), p. 207.

34. Lawrence J. Korb, *The Joint Chiefs of Staff: The First Twenty-five Years* (Bloomington: Indiana University Press, 1976), p. 177. See also Morris Janowitz, "Toward a Redefinition of Military Strategy in International Relations," *World Politics* 26, no. 4 (July 1974):495.

4. CHOOSING AND USING THE CHIEFS: STRUCTURING INFLUENCE

1. Taft quoted in General Matthew B. Ridgway, USA (Ret.), with Harold Martin, *Soldier* (New York: Harper, 1954), p 330. See John Wiltz, "The MacArthur Inquiry, 1951," in Arthur Schlesinger, Jr., *Congress Investigates: A Documented History, 1792–1974* (New York: Chelsea House, 1975), vol. 5.

2. General Maxwell D. Taylor, USA (Ret.), *The Uncertain Trumpet* (New York: Harper, 1959), pp. 19–20, and *Swords and Plowshares* (New York: Norton, 1972), p. 157.

3. Taylor, *Swords and Plowshares*, pp 196–200; Hanson W. Baldwin, *Strategy for Tomorrow* (New York: Harper & Row, 1970), p. 13.

4. For some additional data on selection of the Joint Chiefs, see

Lawrence J. Korb, *The Joint Chiefs of Staff: The First Twenty-five Years* (Bloomington: Indiana University Press, 1976).

5. Admiral Arleigh A. Burke, USN (Ret.), U.S. Naval Institute interview, on deposit in Columbia University library. The air force purposely placed its best candidates in the position of vice-chief. One who could not seriously be considered for succession was LeMay's vice-chief, Bozo McKee, who was not a pilot. Before LeMay's term was completed, successor John McConnell was moved into McKee's job. General Curtis E. LeMay, USAF (Ret.), with Mackinlay Kantor, *Mission with LeMay* (Garden City: Doubleday, 1965), p. 510.

6. Morris Janowitz, *The Professional Soldier*, 2d ed. (New York: Free Press, 1971), pp. 165–171. Taylor, who speaks seven languages, was spirited into Rome in 1943 before the Allies reached the city to negotiate surrender of the city. Lemnitzer landed secretly in North Africa to contact French officials before the 1942 Allied landings, and in 1945 he negotiated with German representatives in Switzerland over surrender of their army in Italy. Ridgway performed several diplomatic functions in Latin America. Thomas White, one of the few air force exceptions to the traditional command route, studied Chinese in Peking in the 1920s and was fluent in Italian, Greek, Spanish, Portuguese, and Russian. He was an air attaché in Moscow and Rome in the 1930s and held staff jobs during World War II until its last year.

7. While MacArthur was chief of staff in the early 1930s, Marshall was exiled to national guard training in Illinois. In 1936 Secretary of War George Dern was looking for officers for higher command, and General Frank McCoy, a friend of Pershing's, arranged a dinner in Chicago for Dern to meet Marshall. Janowitz, *Professional Soldier*, pp. 296–299.

8. Ridgway, *Soldier*, pp. 35, 41–42, 45, 49–50, 81; military interview; K. Bruce Galloway and Robert B. Johnson, *West Point* (New York: Simon and Schuster, 1973), p. 164; Ernest Furgurson, *Westmoreland: The Inevitable General* (Boston: Little, Brown, 1968), pp. 124–125. There is also a negative network. The most notorious case of high-level discrimination against an officer was Marshall's persistent striking of Colonel James Van Fleet from the World War II promotion list. This occurred because Marshall confused him with someone with a similar sounding name who had met Marshall and badly impressed him in previous years. When this mistake was pointed out after the Normandy invasion, Van Fleet's career blossomed quickly.

9. One military interview and three civilian interviews; Nitze quoted in Captain John N. Horrocks, Jr., USN, "The Art, Science and Innocence Involved in Becoming Chief of Naval Operations," *U.S. Naval Institute Proceedings* 96, no. 1 (January 1970):31.

10. Military interview. Westmoreland was a prime example. In World War II he became chief of staff of a division although he was only a thirty-year old colonel. In Korea he commanded the 187th Regimental Combat Team, the only airborne unit in the war. Service leaders considered attendance at the command and general staff college—the usual

preparation for high command—superfluous for Westmoreland, and he was thus exempted. He became a brigadier general at the very young age of thirty-eight and secretary of the general staff under Taylor. As the youngest major general in the army, he commanded the 101st Airborne, was superintendent of West Point, and commander of an airborne corps in 1963 when he was selected to replace Paul Harkins as commander, U.S. military assistance command, Vietnam.

11. An example of the first type of process was when Navy Secretary Sullivan asked Marine Commandant Vandegrift for the files of eight generals he deemed eligible to succeed him. Sullivan narrowed the field to Cates and Shepherd, who were then called to the White House. Truman selected Cates because he was older and slightly senior in grade, telling Shepherd he would have his chance later, which he did. General A. A. Vandegrift, USMC (Ret.), with Robert B. Asprey, *Once a Marine: The Memoirs of General A. A. Vandegrift* (New York: Norton, 1964), p. 327. This process operated differently in the various services. In the army every three- and four-star general was asked to list ten names, excluding himself, in order of merit. Military interview. On Anderson and Brown: military interview; "Head of Joint Chiefs of Staff: George Scratchley Brown," *New York Times*, 6 June 1974, p. 3; Michael Getler, "Gen. Brown to Head Joint Chiefs," *Washington Post*, 15 May 1974, p. A-1. Pentagon civilians' preferences may be overridden by professional and public pressure. This occurred when Truman appointed Chester Nimitz chief of naval operations after World War II against the wishes of Secretary of the Navy Forrestal. E. B. Potter, *Nimitz* (Annapolis: Naval Institute Press, 1976), chap. 24.

12. Burke chose vice-chiefs as devil's advocates rather than as apprentices. Asked to recommend his replacement, he refused, on grounds that his choice would be leaked and that if the recommendation were rejected, the officer would be in a poorer position than if he had never been recommended. When pressed, Burke listed six alternatives verbally, including Anderson. Burke, U.S. Naval Institute interview. McDonald and Zumwalt both recommended their successors. Horrocks, "Art, Science, Innocence," p. 31; "Choice for Chief of Naval Operations: James Lemuel Holloway 3d," *New York Times*, 29 March 1974, p. 14. Marine Commandant Cushman's choice for replacement, Earl Anderson, was turned down in favor of Louis Wilson, in part because of a controversy over charges that Anderson had used his position as assistant commandant to find out what names were recommended by marine generals who were polled. J. Y. Smith, "26th Commandant Takes Over: New Head Marine Says 'Get in Step,'" *Washington Post*, 1 July 1975, p. A-3; John W. Finney, "Marines' New Leader: Louis Hugh Wilson," *New York Times*, 1 July 1975, p. 14. A new chief is also rarely named without the unofficial concurrence of the other Chiefs since they will have to work with him. Military interview.

13. One military interview and three civilian interviews. The Taft clearances were given explicitly in a meeting. Glenn H. Snyder, "The

'New Look' of 1953," in Warner P. Schilling, Paul Hammond, and Glenn H. Snyder, *Strategy, Politics, and Defense Budgets* (New York: Columbia University Press, 1962), pp. 411–412. For a good example of the perfunctory confirmation process, see U.S., Congress, Senate, Committee on Armed Services, *Hearing, Gen. John P. McConnell to be Chief of Staff of Air Force*, 89th Cong., 1st sess., 1965.

14. One civilian executive high in the Pentagon was convinced that if President Eisenhower had picked his own chiefs, he would not have wound up with many of the ones he appointed, judging from his acerbic comments about many of them in private. He never turned down a name that had come through the system to his desk. Civilian interview. If Eisenhower did exercise more discretion, it was probably only in his army appointments.

15. Eisenhower quoted in Horrocks, "Art, Science, Innocence," p. 30. Military interview and civilian interview.

16. Military interview and civilian interview.

17. On Lemnitzer: John S. D. Eisenhower, *Strictly Personal* (Garden City: Doubleday, 1974), pp. 191–192. On Wheeler: Henry F. Graff, *The Tuesday Cabinet* (Englewood Cliffs: Prentice-Hall, 1970), p. 132; Lloyd Norman, "The Chiefs, Part I," *Army* 20, no. 4 (April 1970):23. Kennedy's instructions quoted in Major General Chester V. Clifton, USA, "Hail to the Chief," *Army* 14, no. 6 (January 1964):31. On promotion board changes: ibid.; Ward Just, *Military Men* (New York: Knopf, 1970), pp. 114–115; U.S., Congress, Senate, Committee on Armed Services, Subcommittee on Officer Grade Limitations, *Hearing, Army General Officer Promotion Policy*, 88th Cong., 1st sess., 1963.

18. David Halberstam, *The Best and the Brightest* (New York: Random House, 1972), p. 559; civilian interview; George C. Wilson, "Creighton Abrams: From Agawam to Chief of Staff," *Washington Post*, 5 September 1974, p. D-4. On General Johnson's selection: Vincent Davis, *The Admirals Lobby* (Chapel Hill: University of North Carolina Press, 1967), p. 237. Johnson was deputy chief of staff for operations under Wheeler, who was also influential in securing his succession.

19. Four military interviews.

20. "The New Brass," *Time*, 25 May 1953, p. 21; "Armed Forces: Man behind the Power," *Time*, 25 February 1957, p. 21; Wilson quoted in Edgar Kemler, "No. 1 Strong Man: The Asia First Admiral," *The Nation*, 17 July 1954, p. 47.

21. Taylor, *Swords and Plowshares*, pp. 180, 195.

22. There was opposition within the military to naming Haig allied commander in Europe on grounds that politicians should not be generals and that Haig did not have suitable command experience. The counter-arguments were that the post is really a political and diplomatic one and that neither Eisenhower, Lucius Clay, nor Laurus Norstad, in the same position, had any significant previous command experience. Andrew Goodpaster, whom Haig replaced, had risen militarily through a White

House position. Drew Middleton, "Reports on NATO Post for Haig Stir a Lively Army Controversy," *New York Times*, 15 September 1974, p. 54; Stuart H. Loory, "Gen. Haig's Credentials Seem to Be in Order," *New York Times*, 22 September 1974, p. E-3.

23. Taylor, *Uncertain Trumpet*, p. 21.

24. Ibid., pp. 107–108; military interview.

25. Three military interviews. Wallace Greene feared that an unconscious filtering process occurred, whereby the man who carried recommendations from the Joint Chiefs to the President watered them down. Greene wanted Taylor to bring the Chiefs with him to the White House more often. This feeling was reminiscent of Ridgway's objection to having Radford represent the army's views to the National Security Council when Ridgway could do so himself. Two military interviews. All the Chiefs under Taylor except Wheeler also opposed the creation of the post of assistant to the chairman, which was finally approved only after extended debate in Congress (and after being denounced in the press as another step on the road to the Prussian general staff system). See U.S., Congress, Senate, Committee on Armed Services, *Hearing, Nomination of Maj. Gen. A. J. Goodpaster and Miscellaneous Bills*, 88th Cong., 1st sess., 1963, pp. 1–13, and John G. Norris, "New Call for Joint Defense Staff Stirs Fear of 'Man on Horseback,'" *Washington Post*, 3 February 1965, p. A-4.

26. Military interview; Halberstam, *Best and Brightest*, p. 600.

27. Hanson W. Baldwin, "Changes in the Joint Chiefs," *New York Times*, 1 June 1955, p. 16; civilian interview and military interview. Ridgway writes that he had decided before accepting his initial appointment that he would not serve more than two years. *Soldier*, p. 260.

28. Hugh Sidey, *John F. Kennedy, President* (New York: Atheneum, 1963), p. 202.

29. Civilian interview.

30. Taylor, *Swords and Plowshares*, p. 174.

31. Military interview and civilian interview.

32. Horrocks, "Art, Science, Innocence," pp. 30–31.

33. Dwight D. Eisenhower, *Mandate for Change: 1953–1956* (Garden City: Doubleday, 1963), pp. 6, 12.

34. According to General Lucius Clay, Ridgway was appointed because the State Department wanted him out of Tokyo (where he was commander in chief, Far East, and military governor of Japan) when the Japanese peace treaty was ratified; politicians had told Truman not to appoint Gruenther because of his close ties to Eisenhower (he had even helped Eisenhower draft his announcement of presidential candidacy at NATO headquarters); and Bradley's supporters, who wanted the job for him but knew he could not get it, wanted someone who was not so closely identified with Eisenhower. Cited by C. L. Sulzberger, *A Long Row of Candles* (New York: Macmillan, 1969), p. 748.

35. Taylor, *Swords and Plowshares*, p. 251.

5. The Range of Necessity: Policy and Strategy

1. The debate on fundamental policy occurred soon after World War II and consensus emerged in mid-1946. The debate reopened only fleetingly in 1952 when liberation was considered as an alternative to containment. Continuity marked most of the postwar period as the perceived bipolar division of the world between free and totalitarian camps allowed Wilsonian liberalism and conservative realpolitik to converge and destroy isolationism. Traditionalists date the cold war from 1947, revisionist historians do so from 1945. My analysis, though close to that of traditionalists, follows the synthesis of this debate exemplified in Arthur Schlesinger, Jr., "The Origins of the Cold War," *Foreign Affairs* 46, no. 1 (October 1967), and John Lewis Gaddis, *The United States and the Origins of the Cold War* (New York: Columbia University Press, 1972). General Marshall, ironically, became a target for both right wing and left wing revisionists, characterized by the former as a dupe or traitor instrumental in surrendering Western advantages to the communists at Yalta and in China and portrayed by the latter as an architect of provocation and American imperialism.

2. Alfred Vagts, *Defense and Diplomacy* (New York: King's Crown Press, 1956), pp. 329–335; Harry S Truman, *Years of Trial and Hope* (Garden City: Doubleday, 1958), p. 383; Samuel P. Huntington, "To Choose War or Peace," *U.S. Naval Institute Proceedings* 83, no. 4 (April 1957); Curtis LeMay with Mackinlay Kantor, *Mission with LeMay* (Garden City: Doubleday, 1965), pp. 481–482, 560–561 (LeMay implied the desirability of preventive war against China as late as 1965); Major Perry M. Smith, USAF, *The Air Force Plans for Peace: 1943–1945* (Baltimore: Johns Hopkins University Press, 1970), pp. 39, 44, 49; George Quester, *Nuclear Diplomacy: The First Twenty-Five Years* (Cambridge: Dunellen, 1970), pp. 67–69; Bernard Brodie, *Strategy in the Missile Age* (Princeton: Princeton University Press, 1965), p. 229ff.

3. Ernest R. May, "The Nature of Foreign Policy: The Calculated vs. the Axiomatic," *Daedalus* 91, no. 4 (Fall 1962):656ff; May, "The Development of Political-Military Consultation in the United States," in Aaron Wildavsky, ed., *The Presidency* (Boston: Little, Brown, 1969), p. 666; Theodore White, ed., *The Stilwell Papers* (New York: Sloane, 1948), p. 256; General of the Army Omar N. Bradley, *A Soldier's Story* (New York: Holt, 1951), p. 5; George F. Kennan, *Memoirs: 1925–1950* (Boston: Atlantic-Little, Brown, 1967), p. 257; Jean Edward Smith, *The Defense of Berlin* (Baltimore: Johns Hopkins University Press, 1963), pp. 59–60; U.S., Department of State, *Foreign Relations of the United States, Diplomatic Papers: The Conferences at Malta and Yalta, 1945* (Washington, D.C.: Government Printing Office, 1955); Charles Bohlen, *Witness to History: 1929–1969* (New York: Norton, 1973), p. 164. Samuel Huntington, *The Soldier and the State* (Cambridge: Harvard University Press, 1957), pp. 316–317, 326–328.

4. See Fleet Admiral William D. Leahy, *I Was There* (New York:

Whittlesey House, 1950); C. L. Sulzberger, *The Last of the Giants* (New York: MacMillan, 1970), pp. 124–215; General Albert C. Wedemeyer, USA (Ret.), *Wedemeyer Reports!* (New York: Holt, 1958), pp. 3, 10, 152–153, 169–170, 186, 248–249, 416–417.

5. Harry S Truman, *Year of Decisions* (Garden City: Doubleday, 1955), pp. 211–213; Winston Churchill, *Triumph and Tragedy* (Boston: Houghton Mifflin, 1953), pp. 457–468. See also Stephen Ambrose, *Eisenhower and Berlin, 1945* (New York: Norton, 1967); Forrest C. Pogue, "The Decision to Halt on the Elbe (1945)," in Kent Roberts Greenfield, ed., *Command Decisions* (New York: Harcourt, Brace, 1959); Forrest C. Pogue, *The Supreme Command* (Washington, D.C.: Department of the Army, 1954), pp. 441–474; Smith, *Defense of Berlin*, pp. 34–53; General of the Army Dwight D. Eisenhower, *Crusade in Europe* (Garden City: Doubleday, 1948); General Walter Bedell Smith, USA (Ret.), *Eisenhower's Six Great Decisions* (New York: Longmans, Green, 1956), pp. 185–186; John Ehrman, *Grand Strategy* (London: Her Majesty's Stationery Office, 1956), 6:131–151. Bradley, *A Soldier's Story*, p. 535.

6. Dwight D. Eisenhower, "My Views on Berlin," *Saturday Evening Post*, 9 December 1961, p. 20. Patton quoted in John Toland, *The Last 100 Days* (New York: Pocket Books, 1969), p. 371.

7. Major General John R. Deane, USA, *The Strange Alliance* (New York: Viking, 1947), pp. 262–266; Bohlen, *Witness to History*, p. 195; Truman, *Year of Decisions*, p. 411; U.S., Department of Defense, *The Entry of the Soviet Union into the War Against Japan: Military Plans, 1941–1945* (Washington, D.C.: Government Printing Office, 1955); Louis Morton, "Soviet Intervention in the War with Japan," *Foreign Affairs* 40, no. 4 (July 1962); Ernest R. May, "The United States, the Soviet Union, and the Far Eastern War, 1941–1945," *Pacific Historical Review* 24 (May 1955); Walter Millis, ed., *The Forrestal Diaries* (New York: Viking, 1950), p. 31; General of the Army Douglas MacArthur, *Reminiscences* (New York: McGraw-Hill, 1964), pp. 244–245, 261; Louis Morton, "The Decision to Use the Atomic Bomb (1945)," in Greenfield, ed., *Command Decisions*, pp. 396–397; Gaddis, *Origins of Cold War*, p. 214.

8. Eisenhower quoted in Peter Lyon, *Eisenhower: Portrait of the Hero* (Boston: Little, Brown, 1974), p. 365. His wartime naval aide recalls similar optimism by Eisenhower; Captain Harry C. Butcher, USNR, *My Three Years with Eisenhower* (New York: Simon & Schuster, 1946), p. 855. Patton was an exception, voicing virulent reactionary and anticommunist sentiments in mid-1945. Martin Blumenson, ed., *The Patton Papers* (Boston: Houghton Mifflin, 1974), 2, chap. 8.

9. Chennault was nominally subordinate to Stilwell but had independent leverage. First, he was chief of staff of the Chinese air force and intimate with Chiang Kai-shek; second, his aide Captain Joseph Alsop was a cousin of Franklin Roosevelt and undercut Stilwell with direct personal letters to friends in the White House. Marshall and Stimson tried, through Harry Hopkins, to defend Stilwell against these sallies.

Marshall and Stilwell objected to Chennault's strategy, arguing that as soon as an air campaign began to be effective, the Japanese would move against the airfields on the ground. Roosevelt chose the Chennault plan, the Japanese launched a ground offensive just as Marshall and Stilwell had predicted, and the Chinese front broke and nearly crumbled at the end of 1944. Charles Romanus and Riley Sunderland, *Stilwell's Mission to China* (Washington, D.C.: Department of the Army, 1955), pp. 23–24, 415–416; Wedemeyer, *Wedemeyer Reports!* pp. 201, 203, 269; Tang Tsou, *America's Failure in China* (Chicago: University of Chicago Press, 1963), pp. 78–80, 95, 109, 111; Leahy, *I Was There*, p. 158; Charles Romanus and Riley Sunderland, *Time Runs Out in CBI* (Washington, D.C.: Department of the Army, 1958), pp. 3–8; Barbara Tuchman, *Stilwell and the American Experience in China* (New York: Macmillan, 1971), pp. 310–311; John Morton Blum, ed., *The Price of Vision: The Diary of Henry A. Wallace, 1942–1946* (Boston: Houghton Mifflin, 1973), pp. 354, 387. See also Major General Claire Chennault, USAAF (Ret.), *Way of a Fighter* (New York: Putnam, 1949), and Tyler Abell, ed., *Drew Pearson Diaries: 1949–1959* (New York: Holt, Rinehart and Winston, 1974), p. 60.

10. Wedemeyer, *Wedemeyer Reports!* pp. 363, 348, 452–453; Herbert Feis, *The China Tangle* (Princeton: Princeton University Press, 1953), p. 374; General A. A. Vandegrift, with Robert B. Asprey, *Once a Marine: The Memoirs of General A. A. Vandegrift* (New York, Norton, 1964), pp. 309–312; U.S., Congress, Senate, Committees on Armed Services and Foreign Relations, *Hearings, Military Situation in the Far East*, 82d Cong., 1st sess., 1951, pp. 382–383.

11. See the summary of 1954 testimony before the Senate Judiciary Committee in Congressional Quarterly, *Congress and the Nation* (Washington, D.C.: Congressional Quarterly, 1965), 1:1727–28. On Shoup and Thurmond: Tristram Coffin, *The Armed Society* (Baltimore: Penguin, 1968), pp. 139–144; Colonel Robert D. Heinl, Jr., USMC, *Soldiers of the Sea* (Annapolis: U.S. Naval Institute, 1962), pp. 599–600.

12. On attitudes: Richard Christie, cited by Adam Yarmolinsky, *The Military Establishment* (New York: Harper & Row, 1971), p. 401; E. P. Hollander, "Authoritarianism and Leadership Choice in a Military Setting," *Journal of Personality* 24 (1955):365–370; Kurt Lang, "Military Organization," in James G. March, ed., *Handbook of Organizations* (Chicago: Rand McNally, 1965), pp. 850–852; Bernard Mennis, *American Foreign Policy Officials* (Columbus: Ohio State University Press, 1971), pp. 116–121, 136–137, 141–142, 168. On Laos: Charles Stevenson, *The End of Nowhere* (Boston: Beacon Press, 1972), p. 27. In November 1954 the Chiefs had opposed any support of the Lao army. Arthur Dommen, *Conflict in Laos*, 3d ed. (New York: Praeger, 1971), pp. 98–99; Bernard Fall, *Anatomy of a Crisis* (Garden City: Doubleday, 1969), p. 163.

13. Morris Janowitz, *The Professional Soldier*, 2d ed. (New York: Free Press, 1971), pp. 236–243. Huntington, *Soldier and State*, pp. 89–94, 315–344.

14. Maurice Matloff and Edwin Snell, *Strategic Planning for Coalition Warfare: 1941–1942* (Washington, D.C.: Department of the Army, 1953); William R. Emerson, "FDR," in Ernest May, ed., *The Ultimate Decision* (New York: Braziller, 1960), p. 157; Louis Morton, "The Decision to Withdraw to Bataan (1941)," in Greenfield, ed., *Command Decisions;* John Jacob Beck, *MacArthur and Wainwright: Sacrifice of the Philippines* (Albuquerque: University of New Mexico Press, 1974). MacArthur's crony Charles Willoughby claimed that the general did not know of the Europe First decision. MacArthur was aware, however, that war plans assumed probable conquest of the Philippines before a U.S. counteroffensive. D. Clayton James, *The Years of MacArthur* (Boston: Houghton Mifflin, 1975), 2:85–86.

15. MacArthur, *Reminiscences,* pp. 32, 121–133, 183, 341, 370–376; Wedemeyer, *Wedemeyer Reports!* chaps. 8–11,

16. Glenn D. Paige, *The Korean Decision* (New York: Free Press, 1968), p. 147; General J. Lawton Collins, USA (Ret.), *War in Peacetime* (Boston: Houghton Mifflin, 1969), pp. 197–198.

17. Senate Armed Services and Foreign Relations Committees, *Far East Hearings,* pp. 76, 80, 101, 119–120; MacArthur, *Reminiscences,* pp. 337, 390–391.

18. Robert Donovan, *Eisenhower: The Inside Story* (New York: Harper, 1956), pp. 18–19; Richard Rovere, *Affairs of State: The Eisenhower Years* (New York: Farrar, Strauss, and Cudahy, 1956), p. 249. Eisenhower placed his former chief of staff, Europeanist General Walter Bedell Smith, in the important position of under secretary of state. The bureaucratic changes designed to accomplish the administration tilt to Asia were also sometimes cosmetic. For instance, the Europe-oriented army chief of psychological warfare, Major General Robert A. McClure, was replaced by Brigadier General William C. Bullock, identified with the Asia group, but the change was only symbolic because the psychological warfare division immediately declined in importance, and its functions were substantially taken over by the Central Intelligence Agency. Janowitz, *Professional Soldier,* p. 332.

19. Janowitz, *Professional Soldier,* pp. 264–278, 303–320.

20. Dulles quoted in Carl Solberg, *Riding High: America in the Cold War* (New York: Mason & Lipscomb, 1973), p. 228. Clay quoted in Sulzberger, *Long Row of Candles,* p. 767. On Solarium: General Andrew Goodpaster, USA, Eisenhower Project oral history interview, on deposit in Columbia University library; Lyon, *Eisenhower,* pp. 520, 529n; Robert Cutler, *No Time for Rest* (Boston: Atlantic-Little, Brown, 1966), pp. 307–310.

21. According to one report, Radford thought "that Red China would have to be destroyed even at the cost of a fifty-year war on the Asian mainland." Edgar Kemler, "No. 1 Strong Man," *The Nation,* 17 July 1954, p. 45. Radford was often accused of advocating preventive war against China. If he did so, he did it infrequently or elliptically. One of his chief antagonists on the Joint Chiefs of Staff does not recall his ever

making such a recommendation. Military interview. In a memo to the secretary of defense at the time Dienbienphu fell, though, Radford said the only way to prevent the fall of the rest of Asia would be through a Korea-type static defense (which he opposed) or by an offensive attack on "the source of Communist military power." He recommended that if the Chinese intervened in Indochina, nuclear weapons should be used "whenever advantageous," air operations should be unleashed against selected targets inside China, Hainan should be seized, the Chinese coast blockaded, and Nationalist troops sent to the mainland. U.S., Department of Defense, *The Senator Gravel Edition: The Pentagon Papers* (Boston: Beacon Press, 1971), 1:509–511.

22. U.S., Department of Defense, *United States-Vietnam Relations, 1945–1967* (Washington, D.C.: Government Printing Office, 1971), 10: 710–713; General Matthew B. Ridgway, USA (Ret.), with Harold Martin, *Soldier* (New York: Harper, 1956), p. 279; Lieutenant General James Gavin, USA (Ret.), with Arthur T. Hadley, *Crisis Now* (New York: Random House, 1968), p. 45.

23. Military interview. On monism and pluralism, see Samuel P. Huntington, "Radicalism and Conservatism in National Defense Policy," *Journal of International Affairs* 8, no. 2 (1954).

24. Radford quoted in "Armed Forces: Man Behind the Power," *Time*, 25 February 1957, p. 27. On Taiwan Straits: Chalmers Roberts, "Battle on 'the Rim of Hell': President vs. War Hawks," *The Reporter* 11, no. 11 (16 September 1954); Chalmers Roberts, *First Rough Draft* (New York: Praeger, 1973), p. 123; Cutler, *No Time for Rest*, p. 323; Donovan, *Eisenhower*, pp. 301–302; Townsend Hoopes, *The Devil and John Foster Dulles* (Boston: Atlantic-Little, Brown, 1973), p. 236.

25. Goodpaster, Eisenhower Project oral history interview.

26. Dwight D. Eisenhower, *Waging Peace: 1956–1961* (Garden City: Doubleday, 1965), p. 299n.

27. Admiral Arleigh A. Burke, USN (Ret.), John Foster Dulles Oral History Project interview, on deposit in Princeton University library.

28. Hoopes, *Devil and John Foster Dulles*, p. 26; Admiral Arleigh A. Burke, USN (Ret.), U.S. Naval Institute interview, on deposit in Columbia University library.

29. Jerome Slater, *Intervention and Negotiation* (New York: Harper & Row, 1970), pp. 113–115. Slater says all evidence indicates the military incursions were not planned to coerce the constitutionalists. The U.S. commander, General Bruce Palmer, complained that political decisions were made "without taking into account important military considerations." Abraham Lowenthal, *The Dominican Intervention* (Cambridge: Harvard University Press, 1972), pp. 105, 107, 123, 127–128.

30. General Mark W. Clark, USA (Ret.), *From the Danube to the Yalu* (New York: Harper, 1954), p. 316; Taylor, *Swords and Plowshares*, p. 137; military letter.

31. Willoughby and Bradley cited in Sulzberger, *Long Row of Candles*, pp. 571, 639. Admiral Arthur W. Radford, USN (Ret.), foreword to Forrest Davis and Robert Hunter, *The Red China Lobby* (New York:

Fleet, 1963), pp. ix–x, and "We Give Military Advice Only," *U.S. News and World Report,* 25 February 1955, p. 44. Barr testimony in Senate Committees on Armed Services and Foreign Affairs, *Far East Hearings,* p. 2959.

32. Truman, *Years of Trial and Hope,* pp. 124–216; Robert Murphy, *Diplomat Among Warriors* (Garden City: Doubleday, 1964), p. 316; Smith, *Defense of Berlin,* pp. 107–111, 286–287; Bohlen, *Witness to History,* p. 216; W. Phillips Davison, *The Berlin Blockade* (Princeton: Princeton University Press, 1958), pp. 150–151; U.S., Department of State, *Foreign Relations of the United States: 1948* (Washington, D.C.: Government Printing Office, 1973), 2:994; U.S., Department of State, *Foreign Relations of the United States: 1949* (Washington, D.C.: Government Printing Office, 1974), 3:821–826.

33. Eisenhower, *Waging Peace,* pp. 331, 340–341. Dulles and the allies were more cautious. JCS Chairman Twining feared that the diplomats' timidity might force the United States into a spot where it made a move to challenge a Soviet obstacle, went halfway, and then quit. He believed the country should be ready to risk general war. John S. D. Eisenhower, *Strictly Personal* (Garden City: Doubleday, 1974), pp. 219–220.

34. Military interview. Morton Halperin and Tang Tsou, "United States Policy Toward the Offshore Islands," *Public Policy* 15 (1966): 124–216. On the 1958 misgivings, see Brigadier General Thomas R. Phillips, USA (Ret.), "The Military Worth of Quemoy," *The Reporter* 19, no. 5 (2 October 1958):14–15. Some of the soldiers feared Chiang Kai-shek was luring U.S. diplomats toward war. Since 1955 the Nationalists had built up their forces on Quemoy and Matsu with U.S. aid, drawing the U.S. incrementally into heavier commitment. The Joint Chiefs wanted Chiang to reduce this garrison, which he eventually did. Military letter.

35. Yarnell quoted in Theodore Sorensen, *Kennedy* (New York: Harper & Row, 1965), p. 204.

36. Burke, U.S. Naval Institute interview. Stump and Felt testimony in Commander Jonathan Trumbull Howe, USN, *Multicrises: Sea Power and Global Politics in the Missile Age* (Cambridge: M.I.T. Press, 1971), pp. 172, 173n.

37. Eisenhower, *Mandate for Change,* p. 463; Ridgway, *Soldier,* p. 278. Since Nixon's trip to China in 1971, the idea of these tiny islands leading the United States to the brink of war seems archaic. When asked in 1974 what present policy toward the offshore islands was, "a State Department spokesman said he didn't know but suspected there wasn't any." *New York Times,* 25 August 1974, p. 31. The last three U.S. military advisers were withdrawn from the islands in June 1976.

6. The Range of Possibility: Capabilities and Choices

1. William R. Emerson, "FDR," in Ernest May, ed., *The Ultimate Decision* (New York: Braziller, 1960), pp. 140–147; Fred Greene, "The Military View of American National Policy," *American Historical*

Review 66, no 2 (January 1961):370–376; Herbert Feis, *The Road to Pearl Harbor* (New York: Atheneum, 1962), pp. 231–232, 240–242.

2. General J. Lawton Collins, USA (Ret.), *War in Peacetime* (Boston: Houghton Mifflin), p. 248.

3. Dwight D. Eisenhower, *Waging Peace: 1956–1961* (Garden City: Doubleday, 1965), p. 366.

4. Samuel P. Huntington, *The Common Defense* (New York: Columbia University Press, 1961), pp. 42, 218–233, 369–425; General Maxwell D. Taylor, USA (Ret.), *Swords and Plowshares* (New York: Norton, 1972), p. 170; Ernest May, "Eisenhower and After," in May, ed., *Ultimate Decision*, p. 216. In practice McNamara's ceiling-free budgeting system did not work as rhetoric implied is should; unofficial limits were in fact imposed. J. P. Crecine, "Making Defense Budgets," in Commission on the Organization of the Government for the Conduct of Foreign Policy (Murphy Commission), *Appendices* (Washington, D.C.: Government Printing Office, June 1975), 4:99, 100n.

5. Morton Halperin, "The Decision to Deploy the ABM," *World Politics* 25, no. 1 (October 1972):77–78; Robert J. Art, "Restructuring the Military-Industrial Complex," *Public Policy* 22, no. 4 (Fall 1974): 433–434, 434n.

6. Not all professional soldiers are as eager to increase the defense budget as might be assumed. One survey found that 15 percent of advanced naval officers polled, 55 percent of army respondents, and 50 percent of air force officers believed defense expenditures should be lower. Only 38 percent, 15 percent, and 40 precent respectively, believed they should be higher (the rest agreed with current levels). Thomas L. Brewer, "Military Officers' Attitudes Toward Arms Control" (paper presented at the International Studies Association Convention, March 1973), table 4.

7. Huntington, *Common Defense*, pp. 33–37, 46–47; U.S., Department of State, *Foreign Relations of the United States: 1948* (Washington, D.C.: Government Printing Office, 1974), 4:95; Walter Millis, ed., with the collaboration of E. S. Duffield, *The Forrestal Diaries* (New York: Viking, 1951), pp. 373–378; military interview; Collins, *War in Peacetime*, pp. 45–69, 77–78.

8. Peter Braestrup, "Limited Wars and the Lessons of Lebanon," *The Reporter* 20 no. 9 (30 April 1959): 27; Jack Raymond, "U.S. Pacific Chief Said to Question Policy on Quemoy," *New York Times*, 11 September 1958, p. 2. See also Burke's testimony, U.S. Congress, Senate, Committee on Foreign Relations, *Hearings, Disarmament and Foreign Policy*, 86th Cong., 1st sess., 1959, pp. 106–109.

9. Jack M. Schick, *The Berlin Crisis: 1958–1962* (Philadelphia: University of Pennsylvania Press, 1971), pp. 46–49. Jack Raymond, "President Holds Special Council on Berlin Crisis," *New York Times*, 6 March 1959, p. 1; Eisenhower quoted in Stephen E. Ambrose, "The Military Impact on Foreign Policy," in Ambrose and Commander James Alden Barber, USN, eds., *The Military and American Society* (New York: Free Press, 1972), pp. 132–133.

10. On Berlin: Ambrose, "Military Impact," p. 133; Theodore Sorensen, *Kennedy* (New York: Harper & Row, 1965), pp. 587–588; military interview; Lieutenant Colonel Edward L. King, USA (Ret.), *The Death of the Army* (New York: Saturday Review Press, 1972), pp. 138–139. On *Pueblo* and Jordan: military interview; Admiral Elmo Zumwalt, USN (Ret.), *On Watch* (New York: Putnam, 1976), pp. 279, 294–297.

11. General Mark W. Clark, USA (Ret.), *From the Danube to the Yalu* (New York: Harper, 1954), p. 3; Adam Yarmolinsky, *The Military Establishment* (New York: Harper & Row, 1971), p. 127.

12. Morton Halperin, "Clever Briefers, Crazy Leaders and Myopic Analysts," *Washington Monthly* 6, no. 7 (September 1974): 43–44. In an analysis that suggests the reasons that U.S. army leaders were less vocal in their doubts about intervention in Vietnam in 1965 than they had been a decade earlier, Halperin writes: "In arguing for the acquisition of new weapons systems, the services frequently find themselves in a position in which the logic of the debate forces them to overstate the likely performance characteristics ... having promised certain performance ... they ... find it difficult to come back later and argue that the systems cannot perform in that way during a particular crisis or war situation. Thus, if asked to carry out a mission, they may feel obliged to agree to it, while having their own doubts about whether it can be successfully accomplished ... the Japanese navy, prior to World War II, pressed for certain naval forces. When they were given these forces, Japanese admirals found it difficult to argue that the Japanese navy was not prepared for war with the United States, since they had justified those forces as necessary for engaging in combat with the United States." "War Termination as a Problem in Civil-Military Relations," *The Annals* 392 (November 1970): 92. Stewart Alsop, applying this logic, wrote that "Kennedy decided not to intervene in Laos because he couldn't and Johnson decided to intervene in Vietnam because he could." *The Center* (New York: Harper & Row, 1968), p. 149.

13. Even now, however, severe limitation of U.S. conventional capabilities—such as McGovern's campaign proposal for massive budget cuts in 1972 (Sen. George McGovern [D-SD], "Towards a More Secure America—An Alternative National Defense Posture," *Congressional Record*, 19 January 1972, pp. E 147–161)—is rational only if the premise is that the United States will not intervene conventionally anywhere outside western Europe where significant military opposition may be encountered. One complication in the premise is that few advocates of such a policy agree that the desirability of "No More Vietnams" means that the United States could accept "No More Israel." For instance, the example Graham Allison used to illustrate capability-as-temptation was the fast deployment logistic ship, which was never built. "Military Capabilities and American Foreign Policy," *The Annals* 406 (March 1973). The C-5 jumbo transport plane, however, fulfills a similar function, and it was the C-5 that was attacked by liberal critics of the defense budget (though principally on grounds of program mismanagement) but was instrumental in military resupply of the Israeli war machine in

October 1973. If the U.S. transport capability had remained unchanged since the 1958 Lebanon operation, it is questionable whether the Israeli army would have been able to sustain intense forward operations by the third week of the war.

14. Kenneth M. Glazier, Jr., "The Decision to Use Atomic Weapons against Hiroshima and Nagasaki," *Public Policy* 18, no. 4 (Summer 1970): 464, 472, 474, 499–500; Louis Morton, "The Decision to Use the Atomic Bomb (1945)," in Kent Roberts Greenfield, ed., *Command Decisions* (New York: Harcourt Brace, 1959), pp. 391, 393; Charles L. Mee, Jr., *Meeting at Potsdam* (New York: Evans, 1975), pp. 78–79; Gar Alperovitz, *Atomic Diplomacy* (New York: Simon & Schuster, 1965), p. 14. To one of Roosevelt's principal military advisers "the use of this barbarous weapon was of no material assistance in our war with Japan." Fleet Admiral William H. Leahy, *I Was There* (New York: Whittlesey House, 1950), p. 441.

15. Millis, ed., *Forrestal Diaries*, pp. 487–488; David E. Lilienthal, *The Journals of David E. Lilienthal* (New York: Harper & Row, 1964), 2: 406; Charles Bohlen, *Witness to History: 1929–1969* (New York: Norton, 1973), p. 278; George Quester, *Nuclear Diplomacy* (Cambridge: Dunellen, 1970), pp. 1–6; Theodore Taylor cited by John McPhee, *The Curve of Binding Energy* (New York: Ballantine, 1975), pp. 63–64.

16. Harry S Truman, *Years of Trial and Hope* (Garden City: Doubleday, 1958), pp. 395–396; General Thomas S. Power USAF (Ret.), with Albert A. Arnhym, *Design for Survival* (New York: Coward McCann, 1965), p. 232; Lieutenant General James M. Gavin, USA (Ret.), *War and Peace in the Space Age* (New York: Harper, 1958), p. 116; Taylor, *Swords and Plowshares*, p. 134.

17. Collins, *War in Peacetime*, p. 83; military interview; military letter; U.S., Congress, Senate Committee on Armed Services and Foreign Relations, *Hearings, Military Situation in the Far East*, 82d Cong., 1st sess., 1951, p. 3074; K. Bruce Galloway and Robert B. Johnson, *West Point*, (New York: Simon & Schuster, 1973), p. 177. Ridgway believed use of nuclear weapons to relieve stalemate would have been "the ultimate in immorality." General Matthew B. Ridgway, USA (Ret.), *The Korean War* (Garden City: Doubleday, 1967), p. 76.

18. General of the Army Douglas MacArthur, *Reminiscences* (New York: McGraw-Hill, 1964), pp. 409–411; Dwight D. Eisenhower, *Mandate for Change: 1953–1956* (Garden City: Doubleday, 1963), pp. 180–181; David Rees, *Korea: The Limited War* (New York: St. Martin's, 1964), pp. 402–420; Robert Cutler, *No Time for Rest* (Boston: Atlantic-Little Brown, 1966), p. 305; Roscoe Drummond and Gaston Coblentz, *Duel at the Brink* (Garden City: Doubleday, 1960), p. 112; two military interviews; military letter.

19. Taylor, *Swords and Plowshares*, pp. 164–165.

20. U.S., Department of Defense, *United States-Vietnam Relations, 1945–1967* (Washington, D.C.: Government Printing Office, 1971), 9: 705–706.

21. Drummond and Coblentz, *Duel at the Brink*, p. 26; military interview; Colonel Raymond Brohon to General d'armée Henri Navarre, quoted in Jules Roy, *The Battle of Dienbienphu*, trans. Robert Baldick (New York: Pyramid, 1965), pp. 245, 251, 262. For Radford's quasi-denials see his John Foster Dulles Oral History Project interview, on deposit in Princeton University library; interview cited in Melvin Gurtov, *The First Indochina Crisis* (New York: Columbia University Press, 1967), p. 191n; and letter quoted in Robert McClintock, *The Meaning of Limited War* (Boston: Houghton Mifflin, 1967), p. 168n.

22. General Nathan Twining, USAF (Ret.), John Foster Dulles Oral History Project interview, on deposit in Princeton University library; Carl Solberg, *Riding High: America in the Cold War* (New York: Mason & Lipscomb, 1973), p. 230. LeMay quoted in McClintock, *Meaning of Limited War*, p. 167. Some military advisers believed the proximity of the defenders and attackers made use of nuclear weapons nonsensical: military letter; "Random Notes from Washington: Air Aid to Dienbienphu Opposed," *New York Times*, 26 April 1954, p. 4.

23. Morton Halperin and Tang Tsou, "United States Policy toward the Offshore Islands," *Public Policy* 15 (1966): 137; Eisenhower, *Mandate for Change*, p. 476; Eisenhower, *Waging Peace*, p. 295; Jack Raymond, "U.S. Pacific Chief Said to Question Policy on Quemoy," *New York Times*, 11 September 1958, p. 2; Commander Jonathan Trumbull Howe, USN, *Multicrises* (Cambridge: MIT Press, 1971), p. 239; Brigadier General Thomas Phillips, USA (Ret.), "The Military Worth of Quemoy," *The Reporter* 19, no. 5, 2 October 1958, p. 14; General William C. Westmoreland, USA (Ret.), *A Soldier Reports* (Garden City: Doubleday, 1976), p. 338; civilian interview.

24. The common view of Norstad as a proponent of using nuclear weapons in the crisis is based on Arthur Schlesinger, Jr., *A Thousand Days* (Boston: Houghton Mifflin, 1965), p. 852. Actual Norstad views cited in three civilian interviews; two military interviews; one civilian letter; *Department of State Bulletin* 36 (18 February 1957): 251–255; C. L. Sulzberger, *The Last of the Giants* (New York: Macmillan, 1970), pp. 588–589; Morris Janowitz, *The Professional Soldier*, 2d ed. (New York: Free Press, 1971), p. 317. Confusion may have arisen because Norstad favored a tough declaratory policy (along with DeGaulle and Acheson) but a more cautious action policy.

25. General Curtis E. LeMay, USAF (Ret.), with Major General Dale O. Smith, USAF (Ret.), *America Is in Danger* (New York: Funk & Wagnalls, 1968), p. 127.

26. Radford quoted in U.S. Department of Defense, *Statements by Secretaries and Chiefs of Staff before Congressional Committees, 1955* (Washington, D.C.: Government Printing Office, n.d.), p. 37. LeMay quoted in Rowland Evans and Robert Novak, *Lyndon B. Johnson: The Exercise of Power* (New York: New American Library, 1966), p. 538. C. L. Sulzberger recalls a story told by Averell Harriman: "When Lemay [*sic*] was air force chief of staff, he was planning to visit Chiang Kai-

shek and called on Harriman in his office first. Harriman told him to warn Chiang not to expect help in landing in China. 'I agree,' Lemay said to Harriman, chomping a huge cigar. 'That's not the way to do it. We must take out China's industry.' Harriman asked if he meant China's nuclear installations—something he, too, was prepared to consider. 'Nope, all her industry.' Harriman asked how many people this would kill. 'Oh, a few million. They've got plenty.' And what would happen when they rebuilt their industry? 'Hit 'em again,' said Lemay." *An Age of Mediocrity* (New York: Macmillan, 1973), p. 463.

27. Taylor, *Swords and Plowshares*, p. 280.

28. Colonel William Y. Smith, USAF, "The Military Role in Arms Control Policy Development," *Public Policy* 16 (1967): 224.

29. U.S., Congress, Senate, Committee on Armed Services, *Hearings, Study of Airpower*, 84th Cong., 2d sess., 1956, p. 220; Power, *Design for Survival*, pp. 136–137; General Curtis E. LeMay, USAF (Ret.), with MacKinlay Kantor, *Mission with LeMay* (Garden City: Doubleday, 1965), pp. 561–562. LeMay, who refused to endorse racial segregation, was persuaded to accept the vice-presidential nomination for George Wallace's American Independent party in 1968 only when Wallace agreed to support the general's opposition to strategic parity. Lewis Chester et al., *An American Melodrama: The Presidential Campaign of 1968* (New York: Dell, 1969), pp. 778–781; Walter Rugaber, "Gen. LeMay Joins Wallace Ticket as Running Mate," *New York Times*, 4 October 1968, pp. 1, 50.

30. Morton Halperin, with the assistance of Priscilla Clapp and Arnold Kanter, *Bureaucratic Politics and Foreign Policy* (Washington, D.C.: Brookings, 1974), pp. 27, 35, 100, 102, 297, 303–309. Wheeler quoted in Smith, "Military Role in Arms Control," p. 221.

31. Philip W. Dyer, "Will Tactical Nuclear Weapons Ever Be Used?" *Political Science Quarterly* 88, no. 2 (Summer 1973): 216–218.

32. Military interview; Lieutenant General James M. Gavin, USA (Ret.), *War and Peace in the Space Age* (New York: Harper, 1958), pp. 235–236, 265.

33. Edward Weintal and Charles Bartlett, *Facing the Brink* (New York: Scribner's, 1967), p. 4; Braestrup, "Lessons of Lebanon," p. 27; Eisenhower, *Waging Peace*, p. 286n.

34. David Halberstam, *The Best and the Brightest* (New York: Random House, 1972), p. 470.

35. Two military interviews; General Maxwell D. Taylor, USA (Ret.), "The Legitimate Claims of National Security," *Foreign Affairs* 52, no. 3 (April 1974): 588–589; General James H. Polk, USA (Ret.), "The Realities of Tactical Nuclear Warfare," *Orbis* 17, no. 2 (Summer 1973): 444–447. General Andrew Goodpaster, USA, quoted in Dyer, "Will Tactical Nuclear Weapons Ever Be Used?" p. 220n. See also ibid., pp. 224–229.

36. "Adm. Arthur Radford, 77, Ex-Joint Chiefs Head, Dies," *New York Times*, 18 August 1973, p. 24; Robert R. Bowie cited by Chalmers

Roberts, *First Rough Draft* (New York: Praeger, 1973), p. 164; Janowitz, *Professional Soldier*, p. 315.

37. Millis, ed., *Forrestal Diaries*, pp. 458, 460ff., 490; Lewis L. Strauss cited by Halperin, *Bureaucratic Politics and Foreign Policy*, p. 122.

38. Duncan L. Clarke, "Role of Military Officers in the US Arms Control and Disarmament Agency," *Military Review* 54, no. 2 (December 1974): 48; Smith, "Military Role in Arms Control," pp. 209, 215.

39. Clarke, "Role of Military Officers," pp. 48–52. Clarke notes that there was a dual loyalty problem at one time. For a while in the early 1960s, "two of ACDA's assistant directors, one of whom was a military officer, were not on speaking terms. It also meant that military input into agency decisionmaking would be minimal." When Vice-Admiral John Lee became the head of the Weapons Evaluation and Control Bureau, though, he had "such a unique enthusiasm for arms control that 'loyalty' virtually ceased being an issue." The 1973 reorganization also integrated the military more into the policy areas of the agency, as opposed to the previous situation where officers were primarily in support functions. Ibid., pp. 51–52.

40. Sorensen, *Kennedy*, 739; Schlesinger, *A Thousand Days*, p. 911; civilian interview, military interview; Ronald J. Terchek, *The Making of the Test Ban Treaty* (The Hague: Martinus Nijhof, 1970), pp. 42–43, 152. See U.S. Congress, Senate, Committee on Armed Services, Preparedness Subcommittee, *Hearings, Military Aspects and Implications of Nuclear Test Ban Proposals and Related Matters*, 88th Cong., 1st sess., 1963.

41. Ibid., p. 733; Terchek, *Making of Test Ban*, pp. 45–46, 152; Schlesinger, *A Thousand Days*, p. 456; Smith, "Military Role in Arms Control," pp. 217–220; Le May, *Mission with LeMay*, p. 544. The conditions were maintenance of readiness to resume atmospheric tests if the Soviets broke the agreement; continued underground testing; improvement of U.S. capabilities for detection of Soviet violations; and aggressive research and development programs.

42. John Newhouse, *Cold Dawn: The Story of SALT* (New York: Holt, Rinehart and Winston, 1973), pp. 124, 125, 127–129; Brewer, "Military Officers' Attitudes Towards Arms Control," 13. Brewer lists 100 percent of naval officers sampled, 90 percent of army, and 70 percent of air force men favoring multilateral reductions, and even 15 percent, 25 percent, and 10 percent, respectively, favoring unilateral reductions.

7. Organizational Doctrines and Incentives

1. Samuel P. Huntington, *The Common Defense* (New York: Columbia University Press, 1961), pp. 157, 378; Gene M. Lyons, "The New Civil-Military Relations," *American Political Science Review* 55, no. 1 (March 1961): 53; Michael Howard, "Civil-Military Relations in Great Britain and the United States, 1945–58," *Political Science Quarterly* 75, no. 1 (March 1960): 41. Civilian executives' impatience with service parochialism was aggravated by the unification debates of the late 1940s.

Disputes were so intense that in the 1948 Key West agreement that allocated missions to the services, the Joint Chiefs were reduced to semantic warfare; they specified that all wording in the agreement would be interpreted according to definitions in Webster's *New International Dictionary* (Unabridged). "Armed Forces: Charlie's Hurricane," *Time,* 4 June 1956, p. 20n.

2. Doctrinal "radicalism" is the tendency to focus on a single novel element of force (in this case airpower) as the decisive factor in war, downgrading the importance of other forces. Doctrinal "conservatism," conversely, stresses the need for diverse forces and options. Radicalism embraces confrontation because of high confidence in capabilities; conservatism shrinks from confrontation because it stresses the limitations of capabilities. See Samuel Huntington, "Radicalism and Conservatism in National Defense Policy," *Journal of International Affairs* 8, no. 2 (1954).

3. Major Perry M. Smith, USAF, *The Air Force Plans for Peace: 1943–1945* (Baltimore: Johns Hopkins University Press, 1970), pp. 8–9, 14–28, 33, 49.

4. On the EC-121: military interview and civilian interview; On *Mayaguez:* James McCartney, "Kissinger Urged B52 Raid on Cambodia," *Boston Globe,* 29 May 1975; "Mayaguez—US Rush to Judgment, Battle," *Boston Globe,* 23 May 1975; Joseph Kraft, "Significant Lessons Emerge from US Gamble in Rescuing the Mayaguez," *Boston Globe,* 19 May 1975.

5. Donald Robinson, "What Military Officers Think of Today's Vital Issues," *Parade,* 2 June 1974, p. 9.

6. Walter Millis, ed., with the collaboration of E. S. Duffield, *The Forrestal Diaries* (New York: Viking, 1951), pp. 224–225; Arthur O. Sulzberger, "The Joint Chiefs of Staff, 1941–1954" (Washington, D.C.: U.S. Marine Corps Institute, 1954), pp. 75–81; Congressional Quarterly, *Congress and the Nation* (Washington, D.C.: Congressional Quarterly, 1965), 1: 272; amendment to the National Security Act of 1947, title II, sec. 211(c).

7. Colonel James A. Donovan, USMC (Ret.), *The United States Marine Corps* (New York: Praeger, 1967), pp. 140–141; Lloyd Norman, "The Chiefs: Part I," *Army* 20, no. 4 (April 1970): 29; General David M. Shoup, USMC (Ret.), Eisenhower Project oral history interview, on deposit in Columbia University library; military interview. See Philip Selznick, *Leadership in Administration* (New York: Harper & Row, 1957), pp. 18–19, on the marines' exploitation of mystique to preserve institutional status.

8. Marine officers serve on the Joint Staff, as part of the naval complement, but the corps itself has no organic planning component. Related to this is the fact that a marine officer with a position on a central policymaking staff may have a greater role in decisions than does the commandant. For instance, in 1963 Major General Victor Krulak, the principal military representative on the Special Group for Counterinsurgency,

was in the center of Vietnam decision making while Commandant Shoup remained on the periphery. The marines have also clung to one unique asset that differentiates them from the army: an organic air arm that makes the corps the only integrated air-ground combat team. The Key West agreement had forbidden the army to develop its own tactical air support. In Vietnam, despite the compensating development of army helicopter gunships, army units continued to rely on the air force for close support.

9. "Charlie's Hurricane," 21–22; David Halberstam, *The Best and the Brightest* (New York: Random House, 1972), pp. 473–477; General Maxwell D. Taylor, USA (Ret.), *The Uncertain Trumpet* (New York: Harper, 1959), pp. 39–42.

10. General Matthew B. Ridgway, USA (Ret.), with Harold Martin, *Soldier* (New York: Harper, 1956), p. 276.

11. General William C. Westmoreland, USA (Ret.), *A Soldier Reports* (Garden City: Doubleday, 1976), pp. 159–160. The JCS also cited the failure to mobilize the reserves as a reason for not meeting the deployment schedule desired by the civilian leaders. U.S., Department of Defense, *The Senator Gravel Edition: The Pentagon Papers* (Boston: Beacon Press, 1971), 4: 279–280, 318–319, 346–348.

12. Millis, ed., *Forrestal Diaries*, pp. 374–376; Halberstam, *Best and Brightest*, p. 89; two military interviews; John B. Henry II, "February, 1968," *Foreign Policy* 4 (Fall 1971): 10–11, 16–20; Henry Brandon, "Were We Masterful," *Foreign Policy* 10 (Spring 1973): 173; David Schoenbaum, "Or Lucky?" in ibid., p. 173; Henry Brandon, *The Retreat of American Power* (Garden City: Doubleday, 1973), p. 139; William Beecher, "Foreign Policy: Pentagon Rebuffs as White House Expands Role," *New York Times*, 21 January 1971, p. 12.

13. Halberstam, *Best and Brightest*, pp. 66–67; military interview.

14. Vincent Davis, *The Admirals Lobby* (Chapel Hill: University of North Carolina Press, 1967), p. 209.

15. U.S., Congress, Senate, Committee on Appropriations, Subcommittee on Defense, *Hearings, Department of Defense Appropriations, 1959*, 85th Cong., 2d Sess., 1958, p. 143; Commander Jonathan Trumbull Howe, USN, *Multicrises* (Cambridge: MIT Press, 1971), pp. 163–164; Huntington, *Common Defense*, p. 347; Hanson W. Baldwin, "Burke's View on Defense," *New York Tmes*, 6 March 1959, p. 4; Admiral Arleigh A. Burke, USN (Ret.), "Power and Peace," *Orbis* 6, no. 2 (Summer 1962): 199.

16. Military interview; General Maxwell D. Taylor, USA (Ret.), *Swords and Plowshares* (New York: Norton, 1972), pp. 267–269. Army Chief Wheeler's position on invasion in the missile crisis is not publicly documented.

17. In the first days of the North Korean attack in 1950 Chief of Naval Operations Sherman and Air Force Chief of Staff Vandenberg believed that air and naval action alone could repel the invaders. This prospect appealed to many of the civilians who considered air power a safer and

more controllable form of intervention than ground combat. Army leaders Collins and Bradley asserted from the outset, however, that air action could not obviate the need for troops. Harry S Truman, *Years of Trial and Hope* (Garden City: Doubleday, 1956), p. 335; Glenn D. Paige, *The Korean Decision* (New York: Free Press, 1968), pp. 136, 167.

18. Robert Tucker, "Oil: The Issue of American Intervention," *Commentary* 59, no. 1 (January 1975).

19. Hanson W. Baldwin, "4 Army 'Groupings' Noted," *New York Times*, 9 May 1951, p. 22.

20. Selznick, *Leadership in Administration*, p. 71.

21. Bomber doctrine emphasized the ability to inflict crippling damage on the enemy economy and society at a cost bearable to the offensive force. Fighter doctrine emphasized the ability of defensive pursuit aircraft to damage attacking bomber forces and limit their effectiveness. "Bombardment and autonomy were natural partners, but fighters were antithetical to both," according to Perry Smith's analysis; air corps planners "developed a force structure that ignored every air lesson of World War II save the need for long-range escort." *Air Force Plans for Peace*, pp. 22–26, 31, 33–34.

22. Morris Janowitz, *The Professional Soldier*, 2d ed. (New York: Free Press, 1971), pp. 305–306.

23. Ibid., pp. 316, 318; Huntington, *Common Defense*, pp. 309–312; Admiral Arleigh A. Burke, USN (Ret.), U.S. Naval Institute interview, on deposit in Columbia University library; Paul Hammond, "NSC-68," in Warner Schilling, Paul Hammond, and Glenn Snyder, *Strategy, Politics, and Defense Budgets* (New York: Columbia University Press, 1962), p. 365; Morton Halperin, with assistance of Priscilla Clapp and Arnold Kanter, *Bureaucratic Politics and Foreign Policy* (Washington, D.C.: Brookings, 1974), pp. 28–29; "Armed Forces: Man Behind the Power," *Time*, 25 February 1957, p. 22; "Soviet Military Hints at Dissent on Arms Issue," *New York Times*, 2 December 1974, p. 2.

24. George Ball, "In Defense of the Military," *Newsweek*, 5 July 1971, p. 48.

25. Michael T. Klare, *War Without End* (New York: Knopf, 1972), p. 58; Seymour Deitchman, *Limited War and American Defense Policy* (Cambridge: MIT Press, 1964), p. 253; Arthur Schlesinger, Jr., *A Thousand Days* (Boston: Houghton Mifflin, 1965), p. 341.

26. Three military interviews; Deitchman, *Limited War*, p. 234. The President personally ordered that all army colonels eligible for promotion to brigadier general rotate through Vietnam on short tours and required that they show evidence of specific training or experience in counterinsurgency before being promoted. Taylor, *Swords and Plowshares*, p. 202.

27. Three military interviews; Janowitz, *Professional Soldier*, p. xxxvii; Schlesinger, *A Thousand Days*, pp. 340–341. Lemnitzer quoted in Roger Hilsman, *To Move a Nation* (Garden City: Doubleday, 1967), pp. 415–416.

28. Military interview.

29. Military interview; Townsend Hoopes, *The Limits of Intervention* (New York: McKay, 1969), pp. 66–67; *Pentagon Papers*, 2: 132, 142; Hilsman, *To Move a Nation*, p. 426.

30. Military interview; Halberstam, *Best and Brightest*, p. 185.

31. *Pentagon Papers*, 2: 517; David G. Marr, "The Rise and Fall of 'Counterinsurgency': 1961–1964," in Noam Chomsky and Howard Zinn, eds., *The Pentagon Papers, Volume 5* (Boston: Beacon Press, 1972), pp. 203–204.

32. General Lewis W. Walt, USMC (Ret.), *Strange War, Strange Strategy* (New York: Award Books, 1970). The subordination of politico-military theory to traditional military practice was exemplified by the marines' abbreviation of the official counterinsurgency mission of "winning hearts and minds" to the acronym "WHAM." Marr, "Rise and Fall of 'Counterinsurgency,' " p. 205.

33. Military interview; *Pentagon Papers*, 2: 1–2, 37; Major General Edward G. Lansdale, USAF (Ret.), *In the Midst of Wars: An American's Mission to Southeast Asia* (New York: Harper & Row, 1971), p. 378; Halberstam, *Best and Brightest*, pp. 128, 164; Taylor, *Swords and Plowshares*, pp. 201–203.

34. Military interview.

35. Lieutenant Colonel Anthony Herbert, USA (Ret.), with James T. Wooten, *Soldier* (New York: Holt, Rinehart and Winston, 1973), pp. 92ff.

36. *Pentagon Papers*, 2: 128–129, 139–143, 420, 434.

37. The 82d division suffered over 50 percent casualties in Normandy; officer casualties were much higher. The 101st division lost a third of its combat strength in each of its three major campaigns. Ridgway, *Soldier*, pp. 7–10, 69–73; Taylor, *Swords and Plowshares*, pp. 52, 79–83; Lieutenant General James M. Gavin, USA (Ret.), *War and Peace in the Space Age* (New York: Harper, 1958), pp. 55–68, 80.

38. Charles B. MacDonald, "The Decision to Launch Operation MARKET-GARDEN (1944)," in Kent Roberts Greenfield, ed., *Command Decisions* (New York: Harcourt, Brace, 1959), pp. 334–335, 340–341; Forrest Pogue, *The Supreme Command* (Washington, D.C.: Department of the Army, 1954), pp. 281–282; Cornelius Ryan, *A Bridge Too Far* (New York: Simon and Schuster, 1974); Ridgway, *Soldier*, p. 111; Taylor, *Swords and Plowshares*, pp. 91, 96.

39. Taylor, *Swords and Plowshares*, pp. 44–45; Lieutenant Colonel Roy E. Appleman, USAR, *South to the Naktong, North to the Yalu: (June–November 1950)* (Washington, D.C.: Department of the Army, 1961), pp. 655–658.

40. William Cockerham, "Selective Socialization: Airborne Training as Status Passage," *Journal of Political and Military Sociology* 1, no. 2 (Fall 1973): 215–229; Taylor, *Swords and Plowshares*, p. 105; Melford S. Weiss, "Rebirth in the Airborne," *Trans-action* 4: no. 6 (May 1967): 23–26; Edward L. Katzenbach, "The Horse Cavalry in the Twentieth

Century: A Study on Policy Response," *Public Policy* 8 (1958): 136, 139–140.

41. Ibid., p. 126; Ward Just, *Military Men* (New York: Knopf, 1970), p. 131; Major General James M. Gavin, USA, *Airborne Warfare* (Washington, D.C.: Infantry Journal Press, 1947); Gavin, "Cavalry, and I Don't Mean Horses," *Harper's* 208 (April 1954): 54–60; Gavin, *War and Peace in the Space Age*, pp. 271–272.

42. Lieutenant Colonel John R. Galvin, USA, *Air Assault: The Development of Airmobile Warfare* (New York: Hawthorn, 1969), pp. 276–279, 281; General Hamilton Howze, USA (Ret.), "Howze Board, I," *Army* 24, no. 2 (February 1974), "Howze Board, II: Airmobility Becomes More Than a Theory," *Army* 24, no. 3, (March 1974), and "Howze Board, III: Winding up a 'Great Show,'" *Army* 24, no. 4 (April 1974); Alain Enthoven and K. Wayne Smith, *How Much Is Enough?* (New York: Harper & Row, 1971), pp. 100ff.

43. Galvin, *Air Assault*, p. 287.

44. Ibid., pp. 274–275, 279; Howze "Howze Board, I," p. 19, and "Howze Board, II," pp. 19–20, 24.

45. Brigadier Sir Robert Thompson, RA (Ret.), *No Exit from Vietnam* (New York: McKay, 1969), p. 136.

46. Marr, "Rise and Fall of 'Counterinsurgency,'" p. 205.

47. "The Helicopter War," *Forbes* 115, no. 9 (1 May 1975): 15–16.

8. Positions, Preparations, and Prejudices

1. Peter Karsten, *The Naval Aristocracy* (New York: Free Press, 1973), chap. four; Marvin Lichterman, "To the Yalu and Back," in Harold Stein, ed., *American Civil-Military Decisions* (Birmingham; University of Alabama Press, 1963), p. 583; Stephen Ambrose, *Eisenhower and Berlin, 1945* (New York: Norton, 1967), p. 50; Colonel William R. Kintner, USA (Ret.), "The Politicalization of Strategy," in David M. Abshire and Richard V. Allen, eds., *National Security: Political and Economic Strategies in the Decade Ahead* (New York: Praeger, for the Hoover Institution, 1963), p. 389.

2. General J. Lawton Collins, USA (Ret.), *War in Peacetime* (Boston: Houghton Mifflin, 1969), pp. 120–217, 141–142, 160–161, 211; Morton Halperin, "War Termination as a Problem in Civil-Military Relations," *The Annals* 390 (November 1970): 93; Richard Neustadt, *Presidential Power* (New York: Wiley, 1960), pp. 141–146.

3. Alain Enthoven and K. Wayne Smith, *How Much is Enough?* (New York: Harper & Row, 1971), p. 299; David Halberstam, *The Best and the Brightest* (New York: Random House, 1972), p. 595; military interview.

4. Walter Millis, ed., with the collaboration of E. S. Duffield, *The Forrestal Diaries* (New York: Viking, 1951), pp. 382ff; George F. Kennan, *Memoirs: 1925–1950* (Boston: Atlantic-Little, Brown, 1967), p. 400; General Lucius D. Clay, USA (Ret.), *Decision in Germany* (Garden

City: Doubleday, 1950), pp. 359, 366, 376; Jean Edward Smith, ed., *The Papers of General Lucius D. Clay: Germany 1945–1949* (Bloomington: Indiana University Press, 1974), 2:734–737; Jean Edward Smith, *The Defense of Berlin* (Baltimore: Johns Hopkins University Press, 1963), p. 107. In contrast to the prevalent patterns, there is historical precedent for aggressive Presidents overruling cautious field commanders, as in 1898: "Thus when General Shafter recommended acceptance of General Toral's first offer of conditional surrender at Santiago, McKinley telegraphed to him: 'What you went to Santiago for was the Spanish army. If you allow it to evacuate with its arms you must meet it somewhere else. This is not war. If the Spanish commander desires to leave the city ... let him surrender and we will then discuss the question as to what shall be done with them.' " Leonard D. White, with the assistance of Jean Schneider, *The Republican Era* (New York: Macmillan, 1958), p. 147.

5. General Matthew B. Ridgway, USA (Ret.), with Harold Martin, *Soldier* (New York: Harper, 1954), p. 219, and Ridgway, *The Korean War* (Garden City: Doubleday, 1967), pp. 191, 236; Collins, *War in Peacetime* pp. 152, 306, 311, 322, 298–330, 231–232, 255; Merle Miller, ed., *Plain Speaking* (New York: Berkley/Putnam, 1974), p. 295. Roberts quoted in Glenn D. Paige, *The Korean Decision* (New York: The Free Press, 1968), p. 130.

6. Charles Stevenson, *The End of Nowhere* (Boston: Beacon Press, 1972), pp. 81–82; U.S., Department of Defense, *The Senator Gravel Edition: The Pentagon Papers* (Boston: Beacon Press, 1971), 1:410, 2:12, 3:203, 470; Halberstam, *Best and Brightest*, p. 490; John B. Henry II, "February, 1968," *Foreign Policy* 4 (Fall 1971): 15: Wheeler said, "I guess I was influenced by those newspapers I read."

7. General Mark W. Clark, USA (Ret.), *From the Danube to the Yalu* (New York: Harper, 1954), pp. 6, 76; Enthoven and Smith, *How Much Is Enough?* p. 299; John P. Leacacos, "Kissinger's Apparat," *Foreign Policy* 5 (Winter 1971–72): 22; Halberstam, *Best and Brightest*, p. 186. For a remarkable and devastating compilation of Westmoreland's statements, see Arthur Schlesinger, Jr., *The Crisis of Confidence* (Boston: Houghton Mifflin, 1969), pp. 173–174n.

8. Smith, *Defense of Berlin*, pp. 300, 318; Hugh Sidey, *John F. Kennedy, President* (New York: Atheneum, 1963), pp. 234n, 238, 240; Bernard Brodie, *War and Politics* (New York: Macmillan, 1973), p. 402n.

9. Two military interviews; Charles Bohlen, *Witness to History: 1929–1969* (New York: Norton, 1973), p. 484; General Maxwell D. Taylor, USA (Ret.), *Swords and Plowshares* (New York: Norton, 1972), pp. 211–212; Eleanor Lansing Dulles, *The Wall: A Tragedy in Three Acts* (Columbia, S.C.: University of South Carolina Institute of International Studies, 1972), p. 82.

10. Military interview.

11. Dulles, *The Wall*, pp. 83–84; Smith, *Defense of Berlin*, pp. 315, 319–320, 322–324, 328–332.

12. Rear Admiral Daniel V. Gallery, USN (Ret.), *The Pueblo Incident* (Garden City: Doubleday, 1970), pp. 16–21, 56–57.

13. Alfred Vagts, *The Military Attache* (Princeton: Princeton University Press, 1967); Jack Shulimson, "Marines in Lebanon 1958" (Washington, D.C.: Historical Branch, G-3, U.S. Marine Corps, 1966), p. 12; Colonel H. A. Hadd, USMC, "Orders Firm but Flexible," *U.S. Naval Institute Proceedings* 88, no. 10 (October 1962): 84.

14. Theodore Draper, *The Dominican Revolt* (New York: Commentary Report, 1968), pp. 7–8, 73, 76, 110; Abraham Lowenthal, *The Dominican Intervention,* (Cambridge: Harvard University Press, 1972), pp. 69–73, 79–85, 87–90, 99, 102; Lyndon B. Johnson, *The Vantage Point* (New York: Holt, Rinehart and Winston, 1971), p. 194; civilian interview; Adam Yarmolinsky, *The Military Establishment* (New York: Harper & Row, 1971), p. 115.

15. Kenneth P. O'Donnell et al., *"Johnny, We Hardly Knew Ye"* (Boston: Little, Brown, 1972), p. 272. The marine colonel was probably the pseudonymous Colonel Haskins described in E. Howard Hunt's memoir of the operation, *Give Us This Day* (New Rochelle: Arlington House, 1973), p. 68.

16. Haynes Johnson et al., *The Bay of Pigs: The Leaders' Story of Brigade 2506* (New York: Dell, 1964), pp. 70–74, 79, 83.

17. Robert McClintock, *The Meaning of Limited War* (Boston: Houghton Mifflin, 1967), pp. 108–109.

18. Ibid., pp. 108–110; Hadd, "Orders Firm But Flexible," p. ; Camille Chamoun, *Crise au moyen orient* (Paris: Gallimard, 1963), pp. 426–427.

19. McClintock, *Meaning of Limited War,* pp. 110–11. Disputes over tactical determinism were the only bases of civilian-military conflict in the Lebanon operation. Eisenhower noted that he refused authorization to occupy more than the airfield and capital, against some military recommendations. Dwight D. Eisenhower, *Waging Peace: 1956–1961* (Garden City: Doubleday, 1965), p. 275n. Military influence on the intervention decision itself was negligible. Three military interviews; Robert Cutler, *No Time for Rest* (Boston: Atlantic-Little, Brown, 1966), pp. 363–364; Shulimson, "Marines in Lebanon," p. 6; Herbert S. Parmet, *Eisenhower and the American Crusades* (New York: Macmillan, 1972), p. 532.

20. Civilian interview.

21. Clay, *Decision in Germany,* p. 57

22. Military interview; Major General Edward G. Lansdale, USAF (Ret.), *In the Midst of Wars: An American's Mission to Southeast Asia* (New York: Harper & Row, 1971), pp. 202–204, 254.

23. Stevenson, *End of Nowhere,* p. 86; John P. Leacacos, *Fires in the In-Basket* (Cleveland: World, 1968), pp. 300–301; John C. Ausland and Colonel Hugh F. Richardson, "Crisis Management: Berlin, Cyprus, Laos," *Foreign Affairs* 44, no. 2 (January 1966): 295; W. Wendell Blancké, *The Foreign Service of the United States* (New York: Praeger, 1969), p. 155. John Kenneth Galbraith, *Ambassador's Journal* (Boston: Houghton Mif-

flin, 1969), pp. 465–466 describes another controversy over separate military communication channels.

24. Stevenson, *End of Nowhere*, pp. 85–86.

25. Jerry Brown, a former air force captain, cited by Seymour Hersh, "How We Ran the Secret Air War in Laos," *New York Times Magazine*, 29 October 1972, pp. 97–99. See also Fred Branfman, "CIA: The President's Secret Army" (unpublished manuscript), pp. 15–16, 31, 73, 76–78, 81, 82, and the accounts thinly veiled as fiction in Lieutenant Colonel John Clark Pratt, USAF, *The Laotian Fragments* (New York: Viking, 1974). Though a novel, Pratt's manuscript was classified so sensitively before publication that at one time the author himself was not allowed to see it.

26. Colonel L. Fletcher Prouty, USAF (Ret.), *The Secret Team* (Englewood Cliffs: Prentice-Hall, 1973), pp. 257–259. The National Security Act specifies that when a military officer serves in a high Central Intelligence Agency post, his connection with his military service is severed completely during his tenure. Lyman B. Kirkpatrick, *The Real CIA* (New York: Macmillan, 1968), p. 76.

27. Draper, *Dominican Revolt*, pp. 77–78; military interview.

28. Eugene Windchy, *Tonkin Gulf* (Garden City: Doubleday, 1971), pp. 2–3.

29. Prouty, *Secret Team*, pp. 6, 82–85, 88–89.

30. Roger Hilsman, *To Move a Nation* (Garden City: Doubleday, 1967), pp. 492–493; Halberstam, *Best and Brightest*, pp. 270–272.

31. Barbara Tuchman, *The Guns of August* (New York: Dell, 1962), 298–300, and *Stilwell and the American Experience in China* (New York: Macmillan, 1971), p. 44.

32. Glenn D. Paige, *The Korean Decision* (New York: Free Press, 1969), pp. 68–69, 98, 98n, 109, 128, 166, 181, 223.

33. Civilian interview; Colonel James A. Donovan, USMC (Ret.), *Militarism, USA* (New York: Scribner's, 1970), pp. 76–77; Lloyd Norman, "The Chiefs" (Part I) *Army* 20, no. 4 (April 1970): 28; General Maxwell D. Taylor, USA (Ret.), *The Uncertain Trumpet* (New York: Harper, 1959), p. 90; Richard J. Barnet, *The Roots of War* (New York: Atheneum, 1972), pp. 79–80; Lewis J. Edinger, "Military Leaders and Foreign Policy Making," *American Political Science Review* 57, no. 2 (June 1963): 398; Ole R. Holsti, *Crisis Escalation War* (Montreal: McGill-Queens University Press, 1972), p. 216.

34. Raymond Aron, *Peace and War*, trans. Richard Howard and Annette Baker Fox (Garden City: Doubleday, 1966), p. 301; Tuchman, *Guns of August*, pp. 98–100.

35. Graham T. Allison, *Essence of Decision* (Boston: Little, Brown, 1971), p. 125.

36. Ibid., p. 205; Elie Abel, *The Missile Crisis* (Philadelphia: Lippincott, 1966), pp. 100–101; Robert F. Kennedy, *Thirteen Days* (New York: Norton, 1969), p. 34; Theodore Sorensen, *Kennedy* (New York: Harper & Row, 1965), p. 684.

37. Allison, *Essence of Decision*, p. 126; Abel, *Missile Crisis*, p. 101. Allison claims the 10 percent uncertainty estimate was arrived at from the mistaken belief that the missiles were mobile. Even if this is true, the estimate was reasonable, considering the poor accuracy of bombardment against fixed targets in North Vietnam in subsequent years.

38. Adam Yarmolinsky, "Bureaucratic Structures and Political Outcomes," *Journal of International Affairs* 23, no. 2 (1969): 229ff; Lloyd Norman, "The Chiefs: Partisanship Goes Out When 'Purple Suits' Go On" (Part II), *Army* 20, no. 5 (May 1970): 38; two military interviews; Yarmolinsky, *Military Establishment*, p. 132.

39. Four military interviews; Admiral Arleigh A. Burke, USN (Ret.), U.S. Naval Institute interview, on deposit in Columbia University library; Taylor, *Swords and Plowshares*, pp. 186–187.

40. Three military interviews; Burke, U.S. Naval Institute interview; Schlesinger, *A Thousand Days*, p. 243; Kirkpatrick, *Real CIA*, p. 195; Stuart Loory, *Defeated* (New York: Random House, 1973), p. 102; Prouty, *Secret Team*, pp. 30, 38; Taylor, *Swords and Plowshares*, pp. 187–189.

41. Schlesinger, *A Thousand Days*, pp. 235, 238, 250; civilian interview; three military interviews.

42. Four military interviews; Burke, U.S. Naval Institute interview. Taylor, who carried out the post mortem on the operation for the President, told an aide that he concluded the Chiefs had erred by omission rather than commission. Military interview. Kennedy later told his military assistant that he had not known enough about JCS procedures and norms to ask the right questions before the operation was approved. Military interview.

43. Ausland and Richardson, "Crisis Management," pp. 299, 302; civilian letter.

44. James G. March and Herbert Simon, *Organizations* (New York: Wiley, 1957), pp. 185, 198, 214–220, 233–234; Kennan, *Memoirs*, p. 467; Zbigniew Brzezinski, "Purpose and Planning in Foreign Policy," *Public Interest* 14 (Winter 1969): 56; Yarmolinsky, "Bureaucratic Structures," 231–232; Allison, *Essence of Decision*, p. 92; Hilsman, *To Move a Nation*, pp. 565–568; Richard E. Neustadt, "Staffing the Presidency," in Senator Henry M. Jackson, ed., *The National Security Council* (New York: Praeger, 1965), p. 283.

45. Hanson W. Baldwin, "Joint Chiefs—Fulcrum of the 'Islands' Debate," *New York Times*, 10 April 1955, p. E-3, and Baldwin, "Scope of Command," *New York Times*, 5 February 1959, p. 12; Keith Clarke and Laurence Legere, eds., *The President and the Management of National Security* (New York: Praeger, 1969), p. 201; John Franklin Campbell, *The Foreign Affairs Fudge Factory* (New York: Basic Books, 1970), pp. 199–200; John G. Norris, "New Call for Joint Defense Staff Stirs Fear of 'Man on Horseback,'" *Washington Post*, 3 February 1965, p. A-4; William Beecher, "Laird Said to Tighten Reins on the Joint Chiefs of Staff," *New York Times*, 14 June 1970, p. 18.

46. Contrary to the model of soldiers as worst-case pessimists, there is an argument that military psychology in practice differs from prudence in principle. Game theory simulations and experimental risk-taking studies suggest that military personnel "select more high pay-off, low-probability solution than comparable civilian groups" and that there is "a lower tolerance for ambiguity in military thinking." Janowitz, *Professional Soldier*, p. 276.

47. In one case organizational interest helped generate optimistic strategic plans. In 1945 air corps planners did not identify the Soviet Union as a short-term enemy, despite the suspicions engendered in air officers by personal confrontations with the Russians over basing, aid, and other issues in World War II, because strategic bombing doctrine did not seem applicable to the USSR. Soviet industry and agriculture were dispersed and less vulnerable to destruction by air than were resources in densely populated Germany and Japan. The service planners projected resurgence in the Axis countries as the most likely postwar threat. Major Perry M. Smith, USAF, *The Air Force Plans for Peace: 1943–1945* (Baltimore: Johns Hopkins University Press, 1970), pp. 51–53. The navy at the time also dismissed the Soviet Union as a potential adversary because it had no appreciable fleet. Vincent J. Davis, *Postwar Defense Policy and the U.S. Navy, 1943–1946* (Chapel Hill: University of North Carolina Press, 1966), p. 18.

48. Kennedy, *Thirteen Days*, p. 36.

49. *Pentagon Papers*, 3:172, 179.

50. Halberstam, *Best and Brightest*, pp. 527–528.

9. Precedents and Personalities

1. General J. Lawton Collins, USA (Ret.), *War in Peacetime* (Boston: Houghton Mifflin, 1969), p. 17; Robert Sawyer, *Military Advisors in Korea* (Washington, D.C.: Department of the Army, 1962); Major General Edward G. Lansdale, USAF (Ret.), *In the Midst of Wars* (New York: Harper & Row, 1971), pp. 337–338. On "grooved thinking" see John Steinbruner, *The Cybernetic Theory of Decision* (Princeton: Princeton University Press, 1974), pp. 125–128. On mistaken applications of experience see Ernest R. May, *"Lessons" of the Past* (New York: Oxford University Press, 1973).

2. High Sidey, *John F. Kennedy, President* (New York: Atheneum, 1963), p. 228; Theodore Sorensen, *Kennedy* (New York: Harper & Row, 1965), p. 644.

3. Civilian interview.

4. Roger Hilsman, *To Move a Nation* (Garden City: Doubleday, 1967), p. 129.

5. Richard M. Bissell, Eisenhower Project oral history interview, on deposit in Columbia University library.

6. Theodore Draper, *The Dominican Revolt* (New York: Commentary Report, 1968), pp. 8–11.

7. Robert McClintock, "The American Landing in Lebanon," *U.S. Naval Institute Proceedings* 88, no. 10 (October 1962):75; Edward Weintal and Charles Bartlett, *Facing the Brink* (New York: Scribner's, 1967), p. 4.

8. General Mark W. Clark, USA (Ret.), *From the Danube to the Yalu* (New York: Harper, 1954), p. 328.

9. Five military interviews. These five former army leaders, when interviewed, rejected the designation of the Never Again Club, which was thrust on them by journalists in the 1950s and 1960s, but under questioning four revealed the same views popularly associated with that designation.

10. U.S., Department of Defense, *The Senator Gravel Edition: The Pentagon Papers* (Boston: Beacon Press, 1971), 3:272.

11. Joseph Kraft, *Profiles in Power* (New York: New American Library, 1966), p. 145.

12. Daniel Ellsberg, "The Quagmire Myth and the Stalemate Machine," *Public Policy* 19, no. 2 (Spring 1971):250–252.

13. General Albert C. Wedemeyer, USA (Ret.), *Wedemeyer Reports!* (New York: Holt, 1958), pp. 400–401; U.S., Congress, Senate, Committees on Armed Services and Foreign Relations, *Hearings, Military Situation in the Far East*, 82d Cong., 1st sess., 1951, pp. 465, 902–903; Glenn D. Paige, *The Korean Decision* (New York: Free Press, 1968), pp. 140–141.

14. Walter Millis, ed., with the collaboration of E. S. Duffield, *The Forrestal Diaries* (New York: Viking, 1951), pp. 175–176.

15. Senate Armed Services and Foreign Relations Committees, *Far East Hearings*, pp. 32, 106–108.

16. Morris Janowitz, *The Professional Soldier*, 2d ed. (New York: Free Press, 1971), p, xli.

17. "Vietnam Called 'Straitjacket' for Army," *Boston Globe*, 13 October 1971; George C. Wilson, "Marine Chief Faults 'Search and Attack' Strategy: Vietnam War Seen Fought in Vain," *Washington Post*, 22 August 1975, p. A-3; James Salter, "An Army Mule Named Sid Berry Takes Command at the Point," *People* 2, no. 10 (2 September 1974):48–49; "Ex-General Backs Bombing of North," *New York Times*, 14 March 1975, p. 10; General William C. Westmoreland, USA (Ret.), "The Demise of South Vietnam," *New York Times*, 17 May 1975, p. 27. See also Sam C. Sarkesian, "Vietnam and the Professional Military," *Orbis* 18, no. 1 (Spring 1974):263–264.

18. Ernest May, "The Development of Political-Military Consultation in the United States," in Aaron Wildavsky, ed., *The Presidency* (Boston: Little, Brown, 1969), p. 668.

19. Military interview.

20. Civilian interview and military interview.

21. Principals in the policy-making process, looking down from the top, usually dismiss the import of organizational determinants, while middle-level functionaries, looking up from below, or scholars, looking in from the side, more often emphasize them. Members of the Joint

Chiefs of Staff and cabinet-level civilians interviewed for this study minimized the influence of organizational affiliations and emphasized the differences in personal judgment. Officials at lower levels reversed this emphasis. Glenn H. Stassen agrees that "roles are especially determinative for lower-level decision-makers and for routine decisions." "Research Note: Individual Preference versus Role Constraint in Policy-Making: Senatorial Response to Secretaries Acheson and Dulles," *World Politics* 25, no. 1 (October 1972):118.

22. Commander Thomas J. Bigley, USN, "The Office of International Security Affairs," *U.S. Naval Institute Proceedings* 92, no. 4 (April 1966):70.

23. Wilber W. Hoare, Jr., "Truman (1945–1953)," in Ernest May, ed., *The Ultimate Decision* (New York: Braziller, 1960), p. 199.

24. David Rees, *Korea: The Limited War* (New York: St. Martin's, 1964), p. 214.

25. Lansdale, *Midst of Wars*, pp. ix–x, 32–124, 220ff, 316–319, 344; military interview.

26. Lansdale, *Midst of Wars*, pp. 19, 24ff, 70, 105, 202–204, 252–254; military interview.

27. See U.S., Congress, Senate, Select Committee to Study Governmental Operations with Respect to Intelligence Activities, *Interim Report, Alleged Assassination Plots Involving Foreign Leaders*, 94th Cong., 1st sess., 1975. After Kennedy's death, Vice-President Humphrey became a conduit to President Johnson for Lansdale's political approach to Vietnam, in opposition to Taylor's military approach. Hubert H. Humphrey, *The Education of a Public Man: My Life in Politics* (Garden City: Doubleday, 1976), pp. 316–317. Lansdale returned to Vietnam in late 1965 to work on pacification. His disapproval of large-scale operations isolated him from the rest of the U.S. mission, and he was gradually cut off from substantive work; "he would become an American counterpart to the elusive Vietnamese 'Third Force,' a hero to idealistic young American officials who saw the failure of American policy as a failure of tactics." Frances Fitzgerald, *Fire in the Lake* (Boston: Atlantic-Little, Brown, 1972), p. 269.

28. Dean Acheson, *Present at the Creation* (New York: Norton, 1969), pp. 140–142; Wedemeyer, *Wedemeyer Reports!* p. 122; military interview.

29. General of the Army Douglas MacArthur, *Reminiscences* (New York: McGraw-Hill, 1964), pp. 346–349, 353; Collins, *War in Peacetime*, pp. 157–158, 217; Taylor, *Swords and Plowshares*, p. 134; General Matthew B. Ridgway, USA (Ret.), *The Korean War* (Garden City: Doubleday, 1967), pp. 36, 42; Lieutenant Colonel Roy E. Appleman, USAR, *South to the Naktong, North to the Yalu: (June–November 1950)* (Washington, D.C.: Department of the Army, 1961), pp. 492–497. David Rees writes that Inchon succeeded as much by luck as by design. Navy and marine specialists maintained later that risks were taken that might have resulted in disaster. The landing "only beat a Communist

mine-laying effort in Inchon by a photo-finish," and security was almost lost. "In Japan, where the landing was known as 'Operation Common Knowledge,' a Communist spy ring had obtained full details a week before D-Day, but was unable to get through to Pyongyang ... Inchon, then, could not have happened under any other commander but Mac-Arthur. It sprang from his overwhelming personality and his self-confidence, and his plan was supported by no one else for it looked back to an age of warfare unencumbered by specialist objections and peripatetic Joint Chiefs. It remains an astonishing achievement precisely because it was a triumph not of military logic and science, but of imagination and intuition. It was justified on no other grounds, but the most overwhelming, most simple; it succeeded." *Korea*, p. 96.

30. C. L. Sulzberger, *A Long Row of Candles* (New York: Macmillan, 1969), p. 610.

31. Collins, *War in Peacetime*, p. 81.

32. Samuel Huntington, *The Soldier and the State* (Cambridge: Harvard University Press, 1957), p. 370.

33. The first instances of insubordination were at West Point, for example, when MacArthur refused a direct order to testify in an official inquiry because he would not tattle on classmates. He was not expelled, and resolved "never again was I to be in doubt about doing what I thought to be right." MacArthur graduated first in his class at the academy. In World War I he rocketed to fame and became a division commander at an exceptionally young age, despite violating the chain of command, making decisions without consulting proper authorities, and demonstrating unorthodox deportment at the front. His unique career had been fostered by family background (his father was a legendary officer), and early access to the pinnacle of power. He was the aide de campe to President Theodore Roosevelt just a few years after leaving West Point and became military assistant to Secretary of War Baker, which brought him into direct contact with President Wilson at the outbreak of World War I although he was only a Major. MacArthur, *Reminiscences*, pp. 6, 25–26, 30, 35, 44–47; Janowitz, *Professional Soldier*, pp. 155–156.

34. Ridgway, *Korean War*, p. 142.

35. Harry S Truman, *Years of Trial and Hope* (Garden City: Doubleday, 1958), pp. 443–450; Merle Miller, ed., *Plain Speaking* (New York: Berkley/Putnam, 1974), chap. 24; Acheson, *Present at the Creation*, pp. 521–528; Collins, *War in Peacetime*, pp. 283, 288–289; Tyler Abel, ed., *Drew Pearson Diaries: 1949–1959* (New York: Holt, Rinehart and Winston, 1974), pp. 159–163; Senate Armed Services and Foreign Relations Committees, *Far East Hearings*, pp. 347, 421, 517–518. See also John Spanier, *The Truman-MacArthur Controversy and the Korean War*, 2d ed. (New York: Norton, 1965), and Trumbull Higgins, *Korea and the Fall of MacArthur* (New York: Oxford University Press, 1960). In early December 1950 Deputy Chief of Staff Ridgway had been exasperated with the passive attitude and timidity of the Joint Chiefs toward the

field commander's provocative disobedience. Ridgway recalled the reaction of General Vandenberg to his suggestion that MacArthur could be relieved: "His lips parted and he looked at me with an expression both puzzled and amazed." Ridgway, *Korean War*, pp. 61–62.

36. Kenneth P. O'Donnell et al., *"Johnny, We Hardly Knew Ye"* (Boston: Little, Brown, 1972), p. 14; Sidey, *Kennedy, President*, p. 212.

37. Civilian interview. Knebel cited by Gore Vidal, "West Point and the Third Loyalty," *New York Review of Books* 20, no. 16 (18 October 1973):24.

38. Admiral Arleigh A. Burke, USN (Ret.), John Foster Dulles Oral History Project interview, on deposit in Princeton University library; Dwight D. Eisenhower, *Mandate for Change: 1953–1956* (Garden City: Doubleday, 1963), p. 459.

39. Civilian interview.

40. Arthur Schlesinger, Jr., *A Thousand Days* (Boston: Houghton Mifflin, 1965), pp. 200–201.

41. Civilian interview; Robert F. Kennedy, *Thirteen Days* (New York: Norton, 1969); Hugh Sidey, *A Very Personal Presidency* (New York: Atheneum, 1968), p. 268.

42. Military interview.

43. Military interview.

44. David Halberstam, *The Best and the Brightest* (New York: Random House, 1972), pp. 490, 564; General William C. Westmoreland, USA (Ret.), *A Soldier Reports* (Garden City: Doubelday, 1976), p. 125.

45. General Matthew B. Ridgway, USA (Ret.), with Harold Martin, *Soldier* (New York: Harper, 1956), pp. 82–83, 278; General Matthew B. Ridgway, USA, Memorandum for the Record, 17 May 1954, on deposit with Ridgway papers, Army War College, Carlisle, Pennsylvania (copy supplied by General Ridgway).

46. General David M. Shoup, USMC (Ret.), Eisenhower Project oral history interview, on deposit in Columbia University library: two military interviews; civilian interview. If Kennedy had not been statutorily prevented from appointing Shoup to another term on the JCS, decision making on Vietnam might have evolved differently. Shoup would have been more difficult for Lyndon Johnson to discount than was George Ball. Shoup's postretirement identification with the antiwar movement angered some military men. Others, such as his successors, denied that he was really a dove while in uniform. Two military interviews.

47. Hanson W. Baldwin, "Taylor and Vietnam," *New York Times*, 25 June 1964, p. 2.

48. Civilian interview; Admiral Arthur W. Radford, USN (Ret.), John Foster Dulles Oral History Project interview, on deposit in Princeton University library.

49. Halberstam, *Best and Brightest*, pp. 475–477.

50. Jack Raymond, *Power at the Pentagon* (New York: Harper & Row, 1964), pp. 102–103; Abel, ed., *Drew Pearson Diaries*, pp. 299, 316; Emmett John Hughes, *The Ordeal of Power* (New York: Dell, 1960),

pp. 36, 63, 144; military interview; John Kenneth Galbraith, *Ambassador's Journal* (Boston: Houghton Mifflin, 1969), pp. 544, 549, 562.

51. Barbara Tuchman, *Stilwell and the American Experience in China* (New York: Macmillan, 1971), pp. 57, 520; Herbert Feis, *The China Tangle* (Princeton: Princeton University Press, 1953), p. 297.

10. Careerism, Intelligence, and Misperception

1. I. M. Destler, *Presidents, Bureaucrats, and Foreign Policy* (Princeton: Princeton University Press, 1972), p. 79.

2. Variants of the quagmire theory include Arthur Schlesinger, Jr., *The Bitter Heritage* (Boston: Hougton Mifflin, 1966), and "Eyeless in Indochina," *New York Review or Book* 17, no. 6 (21 October 1971); David Halberstam, *The Best and the Brightest* (New York: Random House, 1972); James C. Thomson, Jr., "How Could Vietnam Happen: An Autopsy," *The Atlantic* (April 1968); Adam Yarmolinsky, "American Foreign Policy and the Decision to Intervene," *Journal of International Affairs* 22, no. 2 (1968). For Daniel Ellsberg's critique see "The Quagmire Myth and the Stalemate Machine," *Public Policy* 19, no. 2 (Spring 1971). For the middle view and the best general explanation, see Leslie Gelb, "Vietnam: The System Worked," *Foreign Policy* 3 (Summer 1971).

3. "In democratic armies all the soldiers may become officers, and that fact makes desire for promotion general ... each promotion has immense importance in his eyes, because his standing in society almost always depends on his rank in the army ... Something which was only a secondary consideration in an aristocratic army has become ... the essence of existence ... promotion in times of peace must be slower in democratic armies than in any other armies ... Therefore all the ambitious minds in a democratic army ardently long for war, because war makes vacancies available and allows violation of the rule of seniority ... We thus arrive at the strange conclusion that of all armies those which long for war most ardently are the democratic ones, but that of all peoples those most deeply attached to peace are the democratic nations." Alexis de Tocqueville, *Democracy in America,* ed. and trans. George Lawrence and J. P. Mayer (Garden City: Doubleday, 1969), p. 647.

4. The post-Vietnam cutbacks in military manpower, ironically, are not likely to reinvigorate professionalism vis-à-vis careerism, because the cuts have not coincided with the deflation of opportunities that followed previous wars. In contrast to earlier instances, grade inflation (the high number of high-ranking officers) has been only moderately curtailed. In 1975 there were still more generals in the army than at the end of World War II when the service was six times as large. Regular officers were not demoted after Vietnam, as they were after previous wars (though a few were forced into early retirement). Military compensation has also risen because of the volunteer army program to the point that it exceeds that for comparable civilian employment. In earlier times officers served at

financial disadvantage. Professional commitment then depended more on commitment to military ideals and spartan life-style. Pervasive preoccupation with retirement and a second career also increased after World War II and weakened professional commitment. None of these developments does anything to weaken the trend from selfless service to cash-nexus careerism. See Morris Janowitz, *The Professional Soldier*, 2d ed. (New York: Free Press, 1971), pp. 104–123, 181–187; Adam Yarmolinsky, *The Military Establishment* (New York: Harper & Row, 1971), p. 72; Lieutenant Colonel William L. Hauser, USA, *America's Army in Crisis* (Baltimore: Johns Hopkins University Press, 1973), pp. 169–186; Colonel Martin Binkin, USAF (Ret.), *The Military Pay Muddle* (Washington, D.C.: Brookings, 1975).

5. Bernard Brodie, *War and Politics* (New York: Macmillan, 1973), p. 484; Luigi Einaudi in Richard Pfeffer, ed., *No More Vietnams?* (New York: Harper & Row, 1968), p. 101. Service leaders feared that giving a smaller percentage of officers an advantage in promotion would demoralize too many others and believed giving a large number experience in the war zone would produce higher service effectiveness in the long term. Morton Halperin, with the assistance of Priscilla Clapp and Arnold Kanter, *Bureaucratic Politics and Foreign Policy* (Washington, D.C.: Brookings, 1974), p. 56. On moves to reform the incentive structure since Vietnam, see Hauser, *Army in Crisis*, p. 184.

6. Halberstam, *Best and Brightest*, p. 249.

7. Barbara Tuchman, *The Guns of August* (New York: Dell, 1962), pp. 463–464.

8. Richard Holbrooke, "The Smartest Men in the Room," *Harper's* 250 (June 1975):5.

9. A classic example of probity was Brigadier General Lawrence Kuter, assistant chief of plans for the air staff in 1943. The staff issued an estimate that despite the Allied bombing campaign, German aircraft production was increasing. Air Corps Chief Arnold asked him to change the estimate. Kuter replied in a memo: "The paper in question is Staff advice to the Commanders. I cannot subscribe to putting in that paper any advice that cannot be supported. Consequently, this particular paper will not be rewritten in the manner in which you expect. It is very clearly the prerogative of the Commander to throw the advice away and place any figure he may choose in a command paper." Quoted in Major Perry M. Smith, USAF, *The Air Force Plans for Peace: 1943–1945* (Baltimore: Johns Hopkins University Press, 1970), p. 108.

10. Lacy Wright, "John Paul Vann: Portrait of an Activist," *Foreign Service Journal* 50, no. 3 (March 1973):15–16, 30–32; Halberstam, *Best and Brightest*, pp. 201–204, 561. Vann was killed in 1972.

11. Halberstam, *Best and Brightest*, pp. 278–280; U.S., Department of Defense, *The Senator Gravel Edition: The Pentagon Papers* (Boston: Beacon Press, 1971), 3:7.

12. Quoted in Ellsberg, "Quagmire Myth and Stalemate Machine," p. 263.

13. Frances Fitzgerald, *Fire in the Lake* (Boston: Atlantic-Little, Brown, 1972), pp. 364–366.

14. James Markham, "Communists in '75 Vietnam Offensive Showing a New Flexibility," *New York Times*, 25 March 1975, p. 9.

15. Quoted in Thomas H. Karas, "Organizational Process and Foreign Policy Failure: The United States in Vietnam" (Ph.D. diss., Harvard University, 1971), p. 228.

16. Quoted in James P. Sterba, "Ex-Advisers Link Saigon's Defeats to the Defects of Vietnamization," *New York Times*, 13 March 1975, p. 18. See also Lieutenant Colonel William L. Corson, USMC (Ret.), *The Betrayal* (New York: Norton, 1968), pp. 243–261; Joseph B. Treaster, "Paper Army: The Fraud of Vietnamization," *Harper's* 251 (July 1975); and Patrick J. McGarvey, *CIA: The Myth and the Madness* (New York: Saturday Review Press, 1972), pp. 133–137.

17. Lieutenant Colonel Monroe T. Smith, USAF, "Reporting Inaccuracies—A Rose by Another Name," *Air University Review* 25, no. 2 (January–February 1974): 83–88.

18. Morris Blachman (formerly captain, USAF), "The Stupidity of Intelligence," in Charles Peters and Timothy J. Adams, eds., *Inside the System* (New York: Praeger, 1970), pp. 275–276; Patrick J. McGarvey, "DIA: Intelligence to Please," in Morton Halperin and Arnold Kanter, eds., *Readings in American Foreign Policy: A Bureaucratic Perspective* (Boston: Little, Brown, 1973), pp. 324–325.

19. Ward Just, *Military Men* (New York: Knopf, 1970), p. 201.

20. *Pentagon Papers*, 2:152–153.

21. Barbara Tuchman, *Stilwell and the American Experience in China* (New York: Macmillan, 1971), pp. 513, 526; Tang Tsou, *America's Failure in China: 1941–50* (Chicago: University of Chicago Press, 1963), pp. 143–145, 201–203; Joseph Esherick, ed., *Lost Chance in China: The World War II Dispatches of John S. Service* (New York: Random House, 1974).

22. Halberstam, *Best and Brightest*, pp. 257–258, 379–392; Paul P. Brocchini, " 'Pipeline' Postscript," *New York Times*, 23 April 1975, p. 39; William A. Bell, "The Costs of Cowardice: Silence in the Foreign Service," in Peters and Adams, eds., *Inside the System*; Chris Argyris, "Some Causes of Organizational Ineffectiveness within the Department of State" (Washington, D.C.: Department of State, January 1967).

23. Harvey Meyerson, *Vinh Long* (Boston: Houghton Mifflin, 1970), pp. 151–152; James W. Markham, "U.S. Envoy Runs Tight Saigon Ship: Curbs News, Strongly Backs Thieu," *New York Times*, 17 January 1972, p. 2.

24. George F. Kennan, *Memoirs: 1925–1950* (Boston: Atlantic-Little, Brown, 1967), chap. 11; *Pentagon Papers*, 1:226.

25. U.S., Department of Defense, *United States-Vietnam Relations: 1945–1967* (Washington, D.C.: Government Printing Office, 1971), 12: 447–454; military interview; General Maxwell D. Taylor, USA (Ret.), *Swords and Plowshares* (New York: Norton, 1972), pp. 338, 341, 347.

26. Military interview; C. L. Sulzberger, *A Long Row of Candles* (New York: Macmillan, 1969), p. 639.

27. Morton Halperin, "War Termination as a Problem in Civil-Military Relations," *The Annals* 392 (November 1970): 94; McGarvey, "Intelligence to Please," pp. 320, 322; John Leacacos, "Kissinger's Apparat," *Foreign Policy* 5 (Winter 1971–72): 21.

28. General Matthew B. Ridgway, USA (Ret.), *The Korean War* (Garden City: Doubleday, 1967), pp. 59–60; Alan Whiting, *China Crosses the Yalu* (Santa Monica: RAND Corporation, 1960); Lieutenant Colonel Roy E. Appleman, USAR, *South to the Naktong, North to the Yalu: (June-November 1950)* (Washington, D.C.: Department of the Army, 1961).

29. Stephen Ambrose, *Eisenhower and Berlin, 1945* (New York: Norton, 1967, pp. 73–79; Rodney G. Minott, *The Fortress That Never Was* (New York: Holt, Rinehart and Winston, 1964).

30. Michael Handel, *Perception, Deception and Surprise: The Case of the Yom Kippur War*, Jerusalem Papers on Peace Problems No. 19 (Jerusalem: Leonard Davis Institute of International Relations, 1976); Avi Shlaim, "Failures in National Intelligence Estimates: The Case of the Yom Kippur War," and Abraham Ben-Zvi, "Hindsight and Foresight: A Conceptual Framework for the Analysis of Surprise Attacks," *World Politics* 28, no. 3 (April 1976); U.S. Congress, House, Select Committee on Intelligence, *Hearings, U.S. Intelligence Agencies and Activities: The Performance of the Intelligence Community*, 94th Cong., 1st sess., 1975, pp. 636–660; Leslie Gelb, "U.S. Intelligence Sees Hanoi Push," *New York Times*, 14 January 1974.

31. *Pentagon Papers*, 3:7, 32–35; Chester Cooper, "The CIA and Decision-Making," *Foreign Affairs* 50, no. 2 (January 1972).

32. Henry Brandon, *The Retreat of American Power* (Garden City: Doubleday, 1973), p. 103; Don Oberdorfer, *Tet!* (Garden City: Doubleday, 1971), p. 120. The running battle between CIA's intelligence analysts and military analysts led to despair in some quarters of CIA, military victory in most of the bureaucratic battles, and eventual modification of CIA's analysis procedures in the direction of military perspectives. There was also disagreement within the analytical branch of CIA: by 1967, most of the analysts were pessimistic, but George Carver, at the top, was not, and it was he who reported to Rostow. Halberstam, *Best and Brightest*, p. 638. According to Victor Marchetti and John Marks, McCone resigned as director of central intelligence in 1965 in part because he "could not cope with the Pentagon juggernaut," which was aggrandizing control of intelligence collection, and because President Johnson did not appreciate the Office of National Estimates' judgments. Successor Helms was so demoralized by the rise of the Pentagon within the intelligence community that he gave up trying to manage the community. Helms's successor Colby, in turn, abolished the one organ that had provided arguments against the military agencies: the Office of National Estimates. He replaced it, in what some saw as a surrender to the military, under pressure

from Kissinger's National Security Council staff, with national intelligence officers, who then concentrated on more short-term estimates. *The CIA and the Cult of Intelligence* (New York: Knopf, 1974), pp. 67–70, 94–99; David Binder, "C.I.A., Bruised by Vietnam and Watergate, Undergoes Quiet Changes Under Colby," *New York Times*, 7 June 1974, p. 8. Perhaps the most shocking description of this process of bureaucratic corruption is CIA analyst Sam Adams's memoir, "Vietnam Cover-Up: Playing War with Numbers," *Harper's* 251 (June 1975): 41–44, 62–66. Adams asserts that he proved by careful documentary research that command headquarters in Vietnam was purposely deflating statistics on the Vietcong order of battle. The Defense Intelligence Agency tried to suppress Adams's research and objected to his higher estimates in the annual meeting of the Board of National Estimates and at a conference in Saigon in September 1967. "Every time I'd argue one category [of enemy strength] up," Adams recounts, "the military would drop another category down ... As we were driving back from the conference that day, an Army officer in the car with us explained what the real trouble was: 'You know, our basic problem is that we've been told to keep our numbers under 300,000.' " When Westmoreland returned to Washington in November, he said in a press conference, "The enemy is running out of men," basing the statement on the military's numbers. Only when Tet discredited the old numbers did the White House stop using the military numbers and turn to the CIA figures. Other officials dispute Adams's story; see letters by Vice Admiral Rufus L. Taylor, USN (Ret.), and James C. Graham, *Harper's* 251 (July 1975): 14, 16.

33. *Pentagon Papers*, 1:89–90, 392, 392n, 399, 399n, 433.

34. John Newhouse, *Cold Dawn* (New York: Holt, Rinehart and Winston, 1973), p. 75; Leslie Gelb, "Schlesinger for Defense, Defense for Détente," *New York Times Magazine*, 4 August 1974, p. 10; U.S., Congress, Senate, Select Committee to Study Governmental Operations with Respect to Intelligence Activities, *Final Report, Foreign and Military Intelligence*, book I, 94th Cong., 2d sess., 1976, pp. 76–77, 270–271.

35. Marchetti and Marks, *Cult of Intelligence*, p. 206.

36. Hanson W. Baldwin, "Army Intelligence—I: Grow's Diary Incident Brings to Light Misassignments of Military Attaches," *New York Times*, 13 April 1952, p. 12, and "Army Intelligence—II: Army Policy Shortcomings Held Factor in G-2 Miscasting of Officers Like Grow," *New York Times*, 14 April 1952, p. 4. The traditional low repute of the intelligence function in the army is reflected in the size of the General Staff Military Intelligence Section at the beginning of World War II: two officers and two clerks. General Peyton C. March, USA (Ret.), *The Nation at War* (New York: Doubleday, Doran, 1932), p. 226.

37. Major Marc B. Powe, USA, "Which Way for Tactical Intelligence After Vietnam?" *Military Review* 54, no. 9 (September 1974): 49ff, 52; Halberstam, *Best and Brightest*, p. 186; De Poix testimony in U.S., Congress, House, Committee on Appropriations, *Hearings, Department of Defense Appropriations for 1974*, 93d Cong., 1st sess., 1973, pp. 417–424.

38. *Pentagon Papers*, 2: 164, 167–168, 183–184, 189, 3: 24–25; Halberstam, *Best and Brightest*, pp. 275–277. The prejudice of operational authorities against intelligence specialists is analyzed in Harold Wilensky, *Organizational Intelligence* (New York: Basic Books, 1967).

39. Colonel L. Fletcher Prouty, USAF (Ret.), *The Secret Team* (Englewood Cliffs: Prentice-Hall, 1973), pp. 205–206; Lyman B. Kirkpatrick, *The Real CIA* (New York: Macmillan, 1968), p. 17; Samuel Huntington, *The Soldier and the State* (Cambridge: Harvard University Press, 1957), p. 434; R. Harris Smith, *OSS: The Secret History of America's First Central Intelligence Agency* (Berkeley: University of California Press, 1972), pp. 361–367; Corey Ford, *Donovan of OSS* (Boston: Little, Brown, 1970), pp. 315–324. For the most balanced and authoritative CIA history, see Anne Karalekas, "History of the Central Intelligence Agency," in Senate Intelligence Committee, *Foreign and Military Intelligence Report*, book 4. On the Bay of Pigs: Roger Hilsman, *To Move a Nation* (Garden City: Doubleday, 1967), p. 31; Lyman Kirkpatrick, "Paramilitary Case Study: The Bay of Pigs," *U.S. Naval War College Review* 25, no. 2 (November–December 1972): 40.

40. Senate Intelligence Committee, *Foreign and Military Intelligence Report*, pp. 349–354; Arthur Schlesinger, Jr., *A Thousand Days* (Boston: Houghton Mifflin, 1965), p. 428; two civilian interviews; Kirkpatrick, *Real CIA*, pp. 225–227; Wilensky, *Organizational Intelligence*, pp. 41–60; Gilbert W. Fitzhugh et al., *Report to the President and the Secretary of Defense on the Department of Defense by the Blue Ribbon Defense Panel* (Washington, D.C.: Government Printing Office, 1970), pp. 45–46. Implying one rationale behind the services' tenacious resistance to intelligence centralization, an army assistant G-2 once said in congressional testimony, "A lap . . . is better than a gap." Quoted in Harry Howe Ransom, *The Intelligence Establishment* (Cambridge: Harvard University Press, 1969), p. 116.

41. Noise is the high volume of indicators that prevents distinguishing relevant signals from irrelevant data. See Roberta Wohlstetter, *Pearl Harbor: Warning and Decision* (Stanford: Stanford University Press, 1962).

42. *Pentagon Papers*, 2:99. See Alexander George, "The Case for Multiple Advocacy in Making Foreign Policy," *American Political Science Review* 66, no. 3 (September 1972). On the theory that decision makers assimilate contradictory data without changing their premises, as long as the contradictions accrue piecemeal, but will question the premises if the contradictions appear massively at one time, see Robert Jervis, "Hypotheses on Misperception," *World Politics* 20, no. 2 (April 1968). The Tet offensive performed the latter function.

43. Halberstam, *Best and Brightest*, pp. 497, 638. An officer close to Rostow disputes the view that his selection of data was biased; military interview.

44. Confirmed in conversations with numerous infantry platoon leaders and company commanders.

45. McGarvey, "Intelligence to Please," pp. 322–323; Blachman, "Stupidity of Intelligence," pp. 272–276; Seymour Hersh, "Raids' Impact Overstated, Ex-Air Force Men Say," *New York Times*, 21 July 1972, p. 14.

46. Fitzgerald, *Fire in the Lake*, p. 364. See also Captain Robert L. Sansom, USAF, *The Economics of Insurgency in the Mekong Delta of Vietnam* (Cambridge: MIT Press, 1970), pp. xiv–xv.

47. Tocqueville, *Democracy in America*, p. 653; James Gould Cozzens, *Guard of Honor* (New York: Harcourt, Brace, 1948), pp. 370–371. On "the overcommitted middle" see Samuel Huntington's comments in Richard M. Pfeffer, ed., *No More Vietnams?* (New York: Harper & Row, 1968), p. 111.

48. Five military interviews; civilian interview; "Interview With General Nathan Twining," *U.S. News and World Report*, 25 December 1953, p. 42; John A. Lauder, "Lessons of the Strategic Bombing Survey for Contemporary Defense Policy," *Orbis* 18, no. 3 (Fall 1974): 772–773. The complete survey consists of nearly a hundred volumes of detailed reports on particular campaigns. The distillation appears in U.S. Strategic Bombing Survey (USSBS), *Summary Report (European War)* (Washington, D.C.: Government Printing Office, September 1945), and *Summary Report (Pacific War)* (Washington, D.C.: Government Printing Office, July 1946).

49. Ibid.; USSBS, *Summary (European)*, pp. 7–12, 15–16; civilian interview; Anthony Verrier, *The Bomber Offensive* (New York: Macmillan, 1968), pp. 7, 18.

50. U.S., Congress, Senate, Armed Services and Foreign Relations Committees, *Hearings, Military Situation in the Far East*, 82d Cong., 1st sess., 1951, pp. 19, 42–44; Collins, *War in Peacetime*, p. 215; Lieutenant General James M. Gavin, USA (Ret.), with Arthur T. Hadley, *Crisis Now* (New York: Random House, 1968), p. 43; Lieutenant General James M. Gavin, USA (Ret.), *War and Peace in the Space Age* (New York: Harper, 1958), pp. 96–100, 102–104; Ridgway, *Korean War*, p. 244; David Rees, *Korea: The Limited War* (New York: St. Martin's, 1964), pp. 370–378; M. W. Cagle and F. Manson, *The Sea War in Korea* (Annapolis: U.S. Naval Institute, 1957), chap. 8; Bernard Brodie, *War and Politics* (New York: Macmillan, 1973), p. 179; Gregory A. Carter, "Some Historical Notes on Air Interdiction in Korea" (Santa Monica: RAND Corporation P-3452, September 1966), pp. 15–19.

51. Gurtov, *First Indochina Crisis*, p. 199n; Robert Guillain, "Sauver l'armée française," *Le monde*, 29 April 1954, pp. 1–2; Townsend Hoopes, *The Limits of Intervention* (New York: McKay, 1969), p. 88; Seymour Hersh, "How We Ran the Secret Air War in Laos," *New York Time Magazine*, 29 October 1972, pp. 100–102; Halberstam, *Best and Brightest*, p. 359. Bombing did save Khe Sanh in 1968 but only by conducting it on an unprecedented scale. See Bernard C. Nolty, *Air Power and the Fight for Khe Sanh* (Washington, D.C.: Office of Air Force History, 1973), chap. 7.

52. Blair Clark, "Westmoreland Appraised," *Harper's* 241 (November 1970): 99–100; Westmoreland, *A Soldier Reports*, pp. 105, 112; *Pentagon Papers*, 4:24–25; Halberstam, *Best and Brightest*, pp. 356–358, 485; George Ball, "Top Secret: The Prophecy the President Rejected," *The Atlantic* (July 1972): 39.

53. *Pentagon Papers*, 3:6, 4:204–205; Department of Defense, *United States-Vietnam Relations*, 4:IV-C-3 64, 135–140; U.S., Senate, Committee on Armed Services, Preparedness Subcommittee, *Hearings, Air War Against North Vietnam*, 90th Cong., 1st sess., 1967, pp. 275ff, 303–307, 313, 515; Harry McPherson, *A Political Education* (Boston: Atlantic-Little, Brown, 1970), pp. 430–431; Hoopes, *Limits of Intervention*, pp. 83ff; military interview; George Christian, *The President Steps Down* (New York: Macmillan, 1970), pp. 54, 84, 88, 269; Henry F. Graff, *The Tuesday Cabinet* (Englewood Cliffs: Prentice-Hall, 1970), pp. 163–164; Halberstam, *Best and Brightest*, p. 539.

54. Robert F. Futrell, Brigadier General Lawton F. Moseley, USAF, and Albert F. Simpson, *The United States Air Force in Korea 1950–1953* (New York: Duell, Sloan, and Pearce, 1961), pp. 184–187, 623–629, 653–658; Brodie, *War and Politics*, p. 180; Hoopes, *Limits of Intervention*, pp. 80ff; three military interviews.

55. *Pentagon Papers*, 3:6, 4:115–120, 217ff, 222–228; military interview; Admiral Ulysses S. Grant Sharp, USN (Ret.), "Airpower *Could* have Won in Vietnam," *Air Force* 54, no. 9 (September 1971):83. Rostow quoted in Graff, *Tuesday Cabinet*, p. 142. On NSSM-1: "Excerpts from 1969 National Security Study of Vietnam War Requested by Nixon," *New York Times*, 26 April 1972, p. 16; Henry Brandon, *The Retreat of American Power* (Garden City: Doubleday, 1973), pp. 52–60.

56. Four military interviews; Hanson W. Baldwin, *Strategy for Tomorrow* (New York: Harper & Row, 1970), p. 32; Sharp, "Airpower *Could* Have Won," pp. 82–83; Senate Armed Services Preparedness Subcommittee, *Air War Hearings*, pp. 4–194, 211–212, 225–226; General George J. Eade, USAF, "Reflections on Airpower in the Vietnam War," *Air University Review* 25, no. 1 (November–December 1973):2–9. Air force history also blames restrictions—in this case imposed by the Joint Chiefs—for disappointing results from bombing in Korea. Futrell, Moseley, and Simpson, *Air Force in Korea*, pp. 183, 401–402.

Sources

LIST OF INTERVIEWS

Anderson, Admiral George W., USN (Ret.)
   (Chief of naval operations)
   26 June 1974
Bonesteel, General Charles H., III, USA (Ret.)
   (Defense member, National Security Council Planning Board;
   assistant to chairman, JCS; commander in chief, United Nations
   command, Korea)
   28 June 1974
Bowie, Robert R.
   (Director, Policy Planning Staff, Department of State;
   counselor, Department of State)
   3 March 1975
Bundy, McGeorge
   (Special assistant to the President for national security affairs)
   9 October 1974
Burke, Admiral Arleigh A., USN (Ret.)
   (Chief of naval operations)
   1 July 1974
Chapman, General Leonard F., Jr., USMC (Ret.)
   (Commandant, marine corps)
   4 September 1974
Clifford, Clark M.
   (Naval aide to President Truman; member and chairman, President's
   Foreign Intelligence Advisory Board; secretary of defense)
   23 August 1974
Clifton, Major General Chester V., USA (Ret.)
   (Military assistant to President Kennedy)
   7 October 1974
Collins, General J. Lawton, USA (Ret.)
   (Chief of staff, army; Presidential envoy to South Vietnam)
   5 September 1974

Decker, General George H., USA (Ret.)
  (Chief of staff, army)
  7 October 1974
Gates, Thomas S.
  (Under secretary of the navy; secretary of the Navy; secretary of
  defense)
  11 October 1974
Gavin, Lieutenant General James M., USA (Ret.)
  (Chief of army plans, research, and development)
  7 August 1974
Gilpatric, Roswell L.
  (Deputy secretary of defense)
  8 October 1974
Ginsburgh, Major General Robert N., USAF
  (Member, Policy Planning Council, State Department; senior staff
  member, National Security Council, and Rostow liaison with
  Joint Chiefs of Staff; deputy director, Joint Staff)
  25 June 1974
Greene, General Wallace M., USMC (Ret.)
  (Military representative, National Security Council Planning Board;
  commandant, marine corps)
  11 October 1974
Lansdale, Major General Edward G., USAF (Ret.)
  (Covert operations officer, Philippines and Indochina;
  assistant to the secretary of defense for special operations)
  27 June 1974
Legere, Colonel Laurence J., USA (Ret.)
  (Assistant to the military representative of the President;
  senior staff member, National Security Council)
  25 June 1974
Lemnitzer, General Lyman L., USA (Ret.)
  (Chief of staff, army; chairman, Joint Chiefs of Staff;
  supreme allied commander in Europe)
  27 June 1974
McConnell, General John P., USAF (Ret.)
  (Chief of staff, air force)
  20 August 1974
Moorer, Admiral Thomas H., USN (Ret.)
  (Chief of naval operations; chairman, Joint Chiefs of Staff)
  11 October 1974
Nitze, Paul H.
  (Vice-chairman, U.S. Strategic Bombing Survey; director, Policy
  Planning Staff, Department of State; assistant secretary of defense for
  international security affairs; secretary of the navy; deputy secretary
  of defense; member, U.S. SALT delegation)
  15 October 1974

Ridgway, General Matthew B., USA (Ret.)
  (Commander in chief, United Nations command, Korea;
  supreme allied commander in Europe; chief of staff, army)
  15 October 1974
Shoup, General David M., USMC (Ret.)
  (Commandant, marine corps)
  26 June 1974
Taylor, General Maxwell D., USA (Ret.)
  (Commander in chief, United Nations command, Korea;
  chief of staff, army; military representative of the President;
  chairman, Joint Chiefs of Staff; ambassador to South Vietnam)
  24 June 1974
Vance, Cyrus R.
  (Secretary of the army; deputy secretary of defense)
  31 January 1975
Yarmolinsky, Adam
  (Chief of U.S. emergency relief mission to the Dominican Republic;
  principal deputy assistant secretary of defense for international
  security affairs)
  1 October 1974
Several officers still on active duty were interviewed but most requested
that their names not be cited.

LETTERS TO THE AUTHOR

Carney, Admiral Robert B., USN (Ret.)
  (Chief of naval operations)
  Undated; received 31 October 1974
Clark, General Mark W., USA (Ret.)
  (Commander in chief, United Nations command, Korea)
  4 November 1974
Lemnitzer, General Lyman L., USA (Ret.)
  25 November 1974
McDonald, Admiral David L., USN (Ret.)
  (Chief of naval operations)
  28 October 1974
Shepherd, General Lemuel C., USMC (Ret.)
  (Commandant, marine corps)
  4 December 1974
Stanley, Timothy W.
  (Member, Berlin task force)
  3 December 1974
Taylor, General Maxwell D., USA (Ret.)
  22 September 1974

Index

ABM, *see* Antiballistic missile
Abrams, Creighton, 59, 60, 65–66, 72
Absolutist school of conflict, 84–87,
110
ACDA, *see* Arms Control and Disarmament Agency
Acheson, Dean: Cuban missile crisis
and, 4, 156; Korea and, 17, 18, 92;
and Vietnam, 29, 124; at MacArthur
hearings, 54; and State Department,
172
Administration, political: and military
autonomy, 8–12, 49–51, 99, 138,
228*n*16, 234*n*1, 238*n*30; subjective
control of, 32–33, 38, 40, 49, 100;
objective control of, 32, 38, 40–41,
49, 99–100, 234*n*1; objective vs. subjective, 33–34, 38, 40–42, 48–49,
234*n*3; executive vs. professional
and, 40–42, 225*nn*1,2, 232*n*23, 237*n*19
Air Assault Division, 136
Air Force (US), 116–118
Alienation of military, 7–11, 12
Allison, Graham, 155–156
Almond, General, 80, 143
Anderson, George, 44, 46, 72; and
Kennedy administration, 10, 69, 70,
71; route to JCS, 60, 62, 241*n*12
Anderson, Robert, 119
Antiballistic missile (ABM), 108
Anticommunism, and military con-
servatism, 76–81
Appointments of JCS, 2, 56, 58–67, 74,
210, 243*n*34; routine-professional,
58–63, 73–74, 240*n*5, 241*nn*11, 12,
242*n*14; professional-political, 58,
63–66, 74; exceptional-political, 58,
66–67, 74; method of choice for,
73–74
Arms Control and Disarmament
Agency (ACDA), 44, 112, 255*n*39
Army Air Corps, *see* Air Force
(US)
Army (US), 119–122

Army War Plans Division, 97
Asia Firsters, 81–83, 84, 93, 247*n*18
Atomic Energy Commission, 112
Authority, fragmentation of, 149–151
Autonomy, military, 8–12, 49–51, 99,
138, 228*n*16, 234*n*1, 238*n*30

Ball, George, 24, 129, 162, 201, 203
Barr, David G., 92
Basic National Security Policy
(BNSP), 157
Bay of Pigs (Cuba) crisis, 9, 35, 129,
148–149, 158, 159, 198
Bennett, W. Tapley, 147–148
Berlin, 10, 92–93, 94, 101–102; capture
of, 77–78, 193; and Kennedy, 92,
145, 101–102; and Clay, 93, 141, 142,
145–146, 150, 260*n*4; and nuclear
weapons, 105, 107, 110
Berry, Sidney, 170
Bidault, Georges, 106
Bien Hoa, 25
Bissell, Richard, 165
Blachman, Morris, 189
BNSP, *see* Basic National Security
Policy
Bohlen, Charles, 145
Bombing, aerial, 104–105, 116–117,
203–208
Bosch, Juan, 147
Bradley, Omar, 29, 105, 141; Korea
and, 17, 19, 20, 257*n*17; protégés of,
60; on officer views, 77; on Berlin,
78; on Taiwan, 92; as organization
man, 181; and MacArthur, 192; and
JCS appointment, 243*n*34
Brant, Kirby, 7, 227*n*8
Brereton, Lewis, 135
Brown, Ambassador, 150
Brown, George, 35, 62, 117
Budget, military, 99, 250*n*6
Bundy, McGeorge, 25, 142, 162, 177
Bundy, William, 23
Bunker, Ellsworth, 91, 132

283